THE BEST
AMERICAN
MAGAZINE
WRITING
2001

THE BEST AMERICAN MAGAZINE WRITING 2001

Edited by

Harold Evans

PUBLICAFFAIRS NEW YORK

BOOK DESIGN BY JENNY DOSSIN.

The Best American Magazine Writing 2001
ISBN 1–58648–088–X

First Edition
10 9 8 7 6 5 4 3 2 1

DEDICATED TO

MARLENE KAHAN,

TIRELESS EXECUTIVE DIRECTOR

OF THE

AMERICAN SOCIETY

OF MAGAZINE EDITORS,

WITH GRATITUDE

FOR HER 25 YEARS

OF LOYAL SERVICE TO ASME

AND ITS PARENT ORGANIZATION,

THE MAGAZINE PUBLISHERS

OF AMERICA.

The American Society of Magazine Editors (ASME) is the professional organization for editors of U.S. consumer magazines and business publications, as well as editors of online magazines.

ASME's mission is to:

- Acquaint the general public with the work of magazine editors and the special character of magazines as a medium of communication.

- Speak out on public policy issues, particularly those pertaining to the First Amendment.

- Uphold editorial integrity.

- Encourage and reward outstanding and innovative achievement in the creation of magazines.

- Disseminate useful information on magazine editing to magazine staff members and others.

- Bring magazine editors together for networking.

- Attract talented young people to magazine editorial work.

ASME was founded in 1963 and currently has more than 900 members nationwide.

Contents

xiii *Introduction by Harold Evans*

xix *Acknowledgments*

xxi *Contributors*

2 "The Endless Hunt"

by Gretel Ehrlich

PUBLISHED IN
National Geographic Adventure
FINALIST—Feature Writing
EDITOR-IN-CHIEF, John Rasmus

24 "The Maria Problem"

by Anthony Lane
PUBLISHED IN *The New Yorker*
WINNER—Reviews and Criticism
EDITOR, David Remnick

36 "Skating Home Backward"

by Bill Vaughn
PUBLISHED IN *Outside*
FINALIST—Essays
EDITOR, Hal Espen

50   "In the Jungle"

by Rian Malan
PUBLISHED IN *Rolling Stone*
FINALIST—Reporting
EDITOR AND PUBLISHER,
Jann Wenner

84   "My Favorite Teacher"

by Robert Kurson
PUBLISHED IN *Esquire*
FINALIST—Feature Writing
EDITOR-IN-CHIEF, David Granger

106   "The Weasel, Twelve Monkeys and the Shrub"
by David Foster Wallace
PUBLISHED IN *Rolling Stone*
WINNER—Feature Writing
EDITOR AND PUBLISHER,
Jann Wenner

154   "The Perfect Fire"

by Sean Flynn
PUBLISHED IN *Esquire*
WINNER—Reporting
EDITOR-IN-CHIEF, David Granger

202   "The Pitchman"

by Malcolm Gladwell
PUBLISHED IN *The New Yorker*
WINNER—Profiles
EDITOR, David Remnick

228   "Mail"

>   by Anne Fadiman
>   PUBLISHED IN *The American Scholar*
>   FINALIST—Essays
>   EDITOR, Anne Fadiman

242   "The Million-Dollar Nose"

>   by William Langewiesche
>   PUBLISHED IN *The Atlantic Monthly*
>   FINALIST—Profiles
>   EDITOR, Michael Kelly

294   "The Ghost"

>   by Elizabeth Gilbert
>   PUBLISHED IN *GQ*
>   FINALIST—Profiles
>   EDITOR-IN-CHIEF, *Art Cooper*

320   "Fair Warning"

>   by Robert Olen Butler
>   PUBLISHED IN *Zoetrope: All-Story*
>   WINNER—Fiction
>   FOUNDING EDITOR, Francis Ford Coppola
>   EDITOR-IN-CHIEF, Adrienne Brodeur

350   "Big Money & Politics: How the Little Guy Gets Crunched"
378   "Soaked by Congress"
400   "Throwing the Game"

>   by Donald L. Barlett
>   and James B. Steele
>   PUBLISHED IN *Time*
>   WINNER—Public Interest
>   MANAGING EDITOR,
>   Walter Isaacson (emeritus)

414   "Paris on the Hudson"

by Jonathan Gold
PUBLISHED IN *Gourmet*
FINALIST—Reviews and Criticism
EDITOR-IN-CHIEF, Ruth Reichl

420   "Stupor Mundi"

by Lewis H. Lapham
PUBLISHED IN *Harper's* Magazine
FINALIST—Reviews and Criticism
EDITOR, Lewis H. Lapham

431   "The Glory of J.F. Powers"

by Donna Tartt
PUBLISHED IN *Harper's* Magazine
FINALIST—Reviews and Criticism
EDITOR, Lewis H. Lapham

446   "Forever Young"

by James Wolcott
PUBLISHED IN *Vanity Fair*
FINALIST—Reviews and Criticism
EDITOR, Graydon Carter

463   *Permissions*
465   *National Magazine Award Winners and Finalists*

Introduction

Here's a first-class ticket for adventure, for romance, for comedy, for inspiration, for excitement. All in one book! You're not going to spend $25 for this amazing compendium, for hours and hours of entertainment and enlightenment. Not $24. Not $23, not $22, not even $20. I'm giving it to you for $17. No, let's make that $15—$15 measly dollars!

My pitch to you is plagiarized. I bowdlerized Ron Popeil. You will know him as the mesmerizer who induced you to acquire kitchen gadgets you didn't know you needed: your Veg-O-Matic, your Dial-O-Matic, your Ronco Showtime Rotisserie and BBQ, and your Ronco Electric Food Dehydrator. If you don't have any of these nifty machines, you will surely join the millions who do, the moment you find yourself watching Ron pitch his wares on QVC.

I am unabashed in poaching a little Popeil to launch the publication of this collection of magazine articles, selected from submissions to the judges in the annual competition organized by the American Society of Magazine Editors. Ron is a character in the book—the subject of a rollicking but uncondescending profile by Malcolm Gladwell—and there is a commonality in what we say about our products. We just know they're the best. As a culinary inventor, Ron is apt to lie awake at night thinking of still newer ways to chop an onion so that the only tears choppers shed are tears of joy. As an editor, I lie awake thinking what a joy it would be to gather all the writers represented in this book within the covers of a single magazine. It's an impossible and vainglorious dream for reasons of copyright and space and markets and contracts, but it is also a redundant one since here they all are up to their best tricks and in good readable type with no jumps and no perfume to rouse distracting thoughts.

They are an agreeable definition of literary eclecticism. In style and substance, in range and ambition, they also display the marvelous range and perspective possible in the malleable format of a contemporary magazine. The common denominator of the stories here—about sailors, Zulus, songwriters, chefs, bears, firemen, novelists, epistolographists, murderers, skaters, Eskimos, lobbyists, witch doctors, actors, vintners, and a rock and roll star long dead at thirty-seven but much mourned—is good writing.

Sean Flynn evokes a scene so well, we are not reading about a lethal fire in Worcester; we are trapped in the dark furnace of a 200 degree warehouse gasping our air tank's last wisps of oxygen. Jonathan Gold writes so well about food, I'd rather read him than eat it. It's fun to sit in a honky-tonk dive in downtown Nashville and soak in the idiom of country music as Elizabeth Gilbert introduces us to a "six-foot-two-inch, 144-pound, twangy-voiced, heavily tattooed, longhaired skeleton" by the name of Hank-3. He's the ghost of Hank Williams, his grandfather, and as she demurely remarks, a little hard to miss: "It would be like if Elvis Presley had a dead-ringer grandson who someday tried to walk around Memphis without getting any attention."

Good writers breathe a kiss of life into old dead facts. I covered the presidential election and read and heard so much about John McCain's privations as a prisoner of war in Vietnam, it was torture to read any more. Been there, done that. Then I read David Foster Wallace's idiomatic narration of the same events, prose with the frost off, and for the first time my reaction was visceral. Wow! None of the other perfectly respectable writing, not even McCain's own, had broken through the skin to make me feel the pain inflicted on him, gasp at the cruelties of his captors, appreciate the moral courage, gutsiness, and downright nobility of his self-sacrifice in refusing to abandon his fellow prisoners for a cushy passage home. "The Weasel, Twelve Monkeys and the Shrub" ought to be forced on everyone who says politicians are all alike.

My interest in pop music is at the other end of the scale to my interest in politics. But again, I didn't want to miss a beat in Rian Malan's epic of musical detection: how the megahit "The Lion Sleeps Tonight," a haunting melody of fifteen notes, made fortunes for American music legends but too little, too late for its true creator, a Zulu herdsman by the name of Solomon Linda. He died a pauper. Did you know about the musical genius Paul Campbell, who never existed except as an alias to claim ownership royalties on uncopyrighted songs like "The Lion" reworked from the public domain? Solomon Linda's chant, as Malan writes, "was just out there, like a wild horse or a tract of virgin land on an unconquered continent." He has a neat way with simile and metaphor. You know just how it was when he says that one of the Tin Pan Alley fat cats "retreated into the labyrinth of his voice-mail system." The article has deft characterization, wit, analytical power, and subtle rhythms of its own, but it is also ingenious in its laconic advocacy. Because we are not hectored, we fill in the gaps with our own mounting sense of injustice, like the mob provoked by Mark Antony's funeral oration.

Good writing is a term that accommodates as many styles as good architecture or good anything else. There is always something to learn about how the bricks are laid. Lewis Lapham is an editor and writer of long experience, but in his review of Patrick O'Brian he acknowledges "copying out one or another of O'Brian's paragraphs (for the pleasure of the rhythms as well as for the lesson in rhetoric) and sometimes I made short lists . . . of words unknown that fell graciously on my ear." David Foster Wallace writes long, loose sentences studded with knuckle-dusting vulgarities. He seizes you by the lapels. The short story writer Robert Olen Butler paints in pastels. The critic Anthony Lane comes upon you by stealth. A civil discourse on Proustian memory is interspersed with sentences that unwind in a giggle. In a review of *The Sound of Music,* he writes of Hitler's invasion of Austria: "Even now, no historian has been able to ascertain if this was a genuine bid for power or the only possible means whereby the Führer could eradicate the threat of close-harmony singing." He touches on the architectural properties of a cinema that has nobly resisted the urge to smarten up. "The stalls, flouting a rule of theatrical design which has obtained since the fifth century B.C., appear to slope downward toward the back, so that customers in the rear seats can enjoy an uncluttered view of their own knees." James Wolcott's cultural references are gems. Bobby Darin "couldn't brood in song the way Sinatra did, as if the night would never end, or croon a mellow tune with tonsils dipped in molasses, like Dean Martin or Perry Como." Bob Dylan was "off fishing the cosmic stream." Kevin Spacey's smile is "a small click-device." His pay-off line is a killer: "Death was just another door he slammed behind him." Anne Fadiman and Bill Vaughn, on the other hand, write sweetly on apparently dull subjects, yet keep our attention by the piquancy of their humor and manifest goodwill. You have finished their pieces before you realize it. Gretel Ehrlich is brilliant in changing pace. When the Eskimos she is traveling with corner a polar bear whose cub has been mangled by the dogs, the denouement comes in staccato sentences to echo the action:

> The bear's fur is pale yellow, and the ice wall is blue. The sun is hot. Time melts. What I know about life and death, cold and hunger, seems irrelevant. There are three gunshots. A paw goes up in agony and scratches the ice wall. She rolls on her back and is dead.

About the only style you won't find in this collection, in fact, is the mandarin style characterized by complex sentences with many dependent clauses, the subjunctive and the conditional, allusions, conceits, and Latin terminology. Its cardinal assumption, as Cyril Connolly wrote, is that neither the writer nor the reader is in a hurry, both being in possession of a classical education and a private income. The writers here all nurse neuroses about the restlessness of the besieged reader. The first requirement of journalism, as of sex, is the arousal of interest, so their opening remarks are beguiling. This is a somewhat more subtle matter than putting the news in the first paragraph, as news reporters are taught to do, a rule that provoked James Thurber to rebel: "Dead. That's what the man was when he was picked up." All the articles in this collection come with a health warning: if you inhale, you will be hooked for the duration.

Rian Malan intrigues us at once: "This is an African yarn, but it begins with an unlikely friendship between an aristocratic British imperialist and a world-famous American Negro." Robert Kurson opens: "One night twenty years ago, my biology teacher picked up a seventeen-year-old hitchhiker named Jefferson Wesley," tempting us to say, "So what?"—when we linger for the answer we are taken on a terrifying and poignant journey. William Langewiesche, writing a profile of Robert Parker, knows that before we set out with the pair of them into the vineyards of Bordeaux, he has to appease our panic about how little qualified we are for the journey. It is satisfying to read that Robert Parker "is not a snob or an obvious aesthete, as one might imagine, but an ordinary American, a burly, awkward, hardworking guy from the backcountry of northern Maryland, about half a step removed from the farm. . . . In his baggy shirts and summer shorts, with his heavy arms hanging wide, he looks as if he could wrestle down a cow. He couldn't, because at age fifty three, he has a bad back."

Of course, the longer articles could not sustain our interest without careful construction, without accelerations and surprises. Sean Flynn has the tricky task of filling us in on the lives of the firemen while the fire roars on. Malcolm Gladwell wisely resists opening with the most dramatic bit of his yarn about the Popeil family. You're on cruise control three-quarters of the way through when he murmurs: "In 1974, S.J.'s second wife, Eloise, decided to have him killed, so she hired two hit men—one of whom, aptly, went by the name of Mr. Peeler. . . . Eleven months later, after Eloise got out of prison, S.J. married her again."

What, Popeil again? Why not? Even the master wordsmith Wolcott has to doff his hat. In one of his similes for Darin, he writes: "He danced like a Veg-O-Matic, slicing, dicing and chopping, one of the few white men capable of executing the James Brown slide step without looking dorky."

Who'll give me the first $15?

HAROLD EVANS

Acknowledgments

Thanks, first of all, to the writers and editors of the nineteen articles reproduced in this book, the second annual compilation of *The Best American Magazine Writing*. These pieces are an exemplary sample of the 1,586 print and online magazine entries received for this year's National Magazine Awards (NMA), the Oscars of our industry, which are sponsored by the American Society of Magazine Editors (ASME) in association with the Columbia University Graduate School of Journalism. Some two hundred editors spent several long days poring over every word to come up with the finalists and winners, a process that can be grueling but is always exhilarating—an annual reminder of why we all love what we do.

If you read the dedication to this book, you'll get a sense of the supreme role of Marlene Kahan, executive director of ASME, and her able staff, Andrew Rhodes and Stephanie Bukovac. We are grateful to Columbia "J. School" dean Tom Goldstein and associate dean Evan Cornog for their support, and could not begin to imagine the process without Columbia's NMA director Robin Blackburn, who does the heavy lifting in more ways than one. Applause to her right-hand man, Barnet Shindlman, and to the students who help her coordinate the massive screening and judging operation.

We are indebted to our publishers, Peter Osnos and Lisa

Kaufman of PublicAffairs, and our agent, David McCormick, of IMG Literary, for giving these stories the longer shelf-life they deserve. And finally, a tip of the blue pencil to the editor of this volume, the great Harry Evans, who faced the unenviable task of winnowing down so many strong nominees to this sparkling few.

CYNDI STIVERS
President, American Society of Magazine Editors

Contributors

DONALD L. BARLETT is an editor-at-large for Time Inc. He and his reporting partner, James B. Steele, are the longest running and one of the best known investigative reporting teams in American journalism. Recipients of virtually every major national journalism award, including two National Magazine Awards and two Pulitzer Prizes, Barlett and Steele have examined the IRS, the oil industry, foreign aid, nuclear waste, private tax breaks enacted secretly by members of Congress for favored constituents and friends, and the dismantling of America's middle class, and corporate welfare. Barlett has co-authored six books with Steele: *Empire: The Life, Legend and Madness of Howard Hughes* (1979); *Forevermore: Nuclear Waste in America* (1985); *America: What Went Wrong?* (1992); *America: Who Really Pays the Taxes?* (1994); *America: Who Stole the Dream?* (1996); and *The Great American Tax Dodge* (2000).

ROBERT OLEN BUTLER is the Francis Eppes Professor holding the Michael Shaara Chair in Creative Writing at Florida State University in Tallahassee. He has published eleven books since 1981, nine novels—*The Alleys of Eden, Sun Dogs, Countrymen of Bones, On Distant Ground, Wabash, The Deuce, They Whisper, The Deep Green Sea,* and *Mr. Spaceman*—and two volumes of short fiction—*Tabloid Dreams* and *A Good Scent from a Strange Mountain,* which won the 1993 Pulitzer Prize for Fiction. His stories have appeared widely in such publications as *The New Yorker, Esquire, The Paris Review, Harper's* Magazine, *GQ, Zoetrope,* and *The Sewanee Review.* Butler is a recipient of both a Guggenheim Fellowship in fiction and a National Endowment for the Arts grant. He also was a finalist for the PEN/Faulkner Award. Since 1995 Butler has written feature-length screenplays for numerous studios and two teleplays for HBO.

GRETEL EHRLICH is the author of many works of nonfiction, fiction, and poetry, including *A Match to the Heart, The Solace of Open Spaces, Heart Mountain,* and *Islands, the Universe, Home.* She is the recipient of an NEA Fellowship, a Guggenheim fellowship, a Bellagio fellowship, the Whiting Award, and the Harold V. Purcell Award from the American Academy of Arts and Letters. Ehrlich's next book, *This Cold Heaven: Seven Seasons in Greenland,* will be published by Pantheon in October 2001. She divides her time between California and Wyoming.

ANNE FADIMAN is the editor of *The American Scholar.* She is the author of *The Spirit Catches You and You Fall Down,* which won a National Book Critics Circle Award, and *Ex Libris: Confessions of a Common Reader.* Fadiman lives in western Massachusetts and teaches writing at Smith College.

SEAN FLYNN started his journalism career in 1986, after graduating from Ohio University. Flynn went to work for the *Marietta* (Ohio) *Times,* followed by the *Boston Phoenix,* and *Boston Magazine* before moving to the *Boston Herald,* where he covered crime. From 1996 to 2000, he worked as a senior editor at *Boston Magazine.* Flynn's journalism has been awarded a silver medal for "Writer of the Year" from the City and Regional Magazine Association in 1999 and several Associated Press and New England Press Association prizes (including one for coverage of religious and ethnic issues). Flynn wrote his first feature for *Esquire* in 1998.

ELIZABETH GILBERT is a writer-at-large at *GQ*. In 1999, her story, *The Last Real American Man* was nominated for a National Magazine Award in the Feature Writing category. Her stories have been published in *Esquire, Story, Ploughshares, Mississippi Review, The London Sunday Telegraph*, and *The Paris Review*. *Pilgrims: Stories*, her first book, was published by Houghton Mifflin in September 1997. Her first novel, *Stern Men*, was published in 2000.

MALCOLM GLADWELL joined *The New Yorker* as a staff writer in June 1996. His articles include reports on the inventor of the birth control pill, retail anthropology, race and sports, and physical genius. In July 1996, Gladwell obtained the first interview with the family of a woman viciously beaten in New York's Central Park. His 1997 article on the 1918 influenza pandemic was turned into a television movie. His 1996 *New Yorker* article "The Tipping Point" was expanded into a book, *The Tipping Point: How Little Things Can Make a Big Difference*. Gladwell came to *The New Yorker* from *The Washington Post*, where he began as a staff writer in 1987, first in the business section and later as a science reporter, and in 1993 was named the newspaper's New York City bureau chief. In 1995, Gladwell was a National Magazine Award finalist for an article on mammography published in *The New Republic*.

JONATHAN GOLD is the New York restaurant critic for *Gourmet*. He was a restaurant columnist for *California, Los Angeles* magazine, *L.A. Weekly*, and the *Los Angeles Times*, and has written for *Spin, Rolling Stone*, and *Details*. He is the author of *Counter Intelligence: Eating in the Real Los Angeles*.

ROBERT KURSON is a senior editor at *Chicago* magazine. He has written for *The New York Times Magazine*, the *Chicago Sun-Times*, and *Rolling Stone*. In 2001, he was named "Writer of the Year" by the City and Regional Magazine Association. Kurson's story, "My

Favorite Teacher," was his first for *Esquire*, for which he writes frequently.

ANTHONY LANE has been a film critic for *The New Yorker* since January of 1993. He began writing book reviews for *The Independent* of London at the time of its launch, in October 1986. As a freelance writer, Lane contributed to other English newspapers, including the *Spectator* and the *Sunday Telegraph*. He became deputy literary editor of *The Independent* in 1989, and one year later was appointed film critic for the new *Independent on Sunday*.

WILLIAM LANGEWIESCHE is a correspondent for *The Atlantic Monthly*. His November 1991 *Atlantic* cover story, "The World in Its Extreme," was his first article to appear in a general-interest magazine. Since that article, from which his book *Sahara Unveiled: A Journey Across the Desert* (1996) grew, Langewiesche has reported on a diversity of subjects for *The Atlantic*: Sahara Desert Travel, the Sudanese Islamic government, and the U.S.-Mexican border—the last a two-part story that led to his first book, *Cutting for Sign* (1995). His recent writing on flight for *The Atlantic* appears in his book *Inside the Sky: A Meditation on Flight*. Langewiesche has been nominated twice for a National Magazine Award.

LEWIS H. LAPHAM is the editor of *Harper's* Magazine, where he writes a monthly essay called "Notebook." He won a 1995 National Magazine Award for a group of these essays. A collection of Lapham's essays was published in 1980 under the title *Fortune's Child*. Other books include *Imperial Masquerade* (1990); *Hotel America: Scenes in the Lobby of the Fin-de-Siècle* (1995); *Waiting for the Barbarians* (1997); *The Agony of Mammon: The Imperial Global Economy Explains Itself to the Membership in Davos, Switzerland* (1998); and *Lapham's Rules of Influence: A Careerist's Guide to Success, Status, and Self-Congratulation* (1999). Lapham has also written for *Life, The*

National Review, Elle, Fortune, Forbes, The American Spectator, Vanity Fair, The London Observer, The New York Times, and *The Wall Street Journal,* among others. He has also hosted a number of programs on public television.

RIAN MALAN is an eighth-generation Afrikaner. He freelanced for eight years in the United States before moving back to Johannesburg, where he now lives. Malan is the author of *My Traitor's Heart: A South African Exile Returns to Face His Country, His Tribe and His Conscience* (Grove).

JAMES B. STEELE is an editor-at-large for Time Inc. He and his reporting partner, Donald L. Barlett, are the longest running and one of the best known investigative reporting teams in American journalism. Recipients of virtually every major national journalism award, including two National Magazine Awards and two Pulitzer Prizes, Barlett and Steele have examined the IRS, the oil industry, foreign aid, nuclear waste, private tax breaks enacted secretly by members of Congress for favored constituents and friends, the dismantling of America's middle class, and corporate welfare. Steele has co-authored six books with Barlett: *Empire: The Life, Legend and Madness of Howard Hughes* (1979); *Forevermore: Nuclear Waste in America* (1985); *America: What Went Wrong?* (1992); *America: Who Really Pays the Taxes?* (1994); *America: Who Stole the Dream?* (1996); and *The Great American Tax Dodge* (2000).

DONNA TARTT was born in Greenwood, in the Mississippi Delta, and was educated at the University of Mississippi and Bennington College. She is the author of a best-selling novel, *The Secret History,* with another novel to be published by Knopf in the fall of 2002. She has also published short stories, poetry, essays, and literary criticism in a variety of magazines.

Bill Vaughn is a contributing editor at *Outside*. He writes an internet column about *Survivor*, the CBS reality television program, and is the author of a memoir, *Down On All Fours*.

David Foster Wallace is the author of *Infinite Jest*, *The Broom of the System*, and *Girl With Curious Hair*. His essays and stories have appeared in *Harper's* Magazine, *The New Yorker*, *Playboy*, *The Paris Review*, *Conjunctions*, *Premiere*, *Tennis*, *The Missouri Review*, and *The Review of Contemporary Fiction*. Wallace has received the Whiting Award, the Lannan Award for Fiction, the Paris Review Prize for humor, the QPB Joe Savago New Voices Award, and an O. Henry Award.

James Wolcott is currently a contributing editor and columnist for *Vanity Fair*. Since covering television and punk rock for *The Village Voice*, Wolcott has written for *Esquire*, *Harper's* Magazine, *Texas Monthly*, *The New Criterion*, *The New Republic*, and *The New Yorker*. He is the author of the novel *The Catsitters*.

THE BEST AMERICAN MAGAZINE WRITING

2001

National Geographic Adventure

FINALIST, FEATURE WRITING

The Endless Hunt

Even in this day and age, there are those who live in the wild and survive on what they kill each day. The author joins a tribe on a subsistence hunt in remote Greenland, and finds out what it means to live by harpoon, gun, and sled. Her story is a raw yet humane evocation of a way of life that is all but gone.

Gretel Ehrlich

The Endless Hunt

In northwest Greenland's frigid spring, Inuit hunters head across the ice in pursuit of walrus, seal, and polar bear.

A young Inuit friend asked if I had come to Greenland from California by dogsled. He had never traveled any other way and didn't realize that the entire world wasn't covered by ice. At age seven, he had never seen a car or a highway or been in an airplane, and he assumed the world was flat. He is part of a group of Polar Eskimos in northwest Greenland who still share in an ice-age culture that began more than 4,000 years ago, when nomadic boreal hunters began walking from Ellesmere Island across the ice to Greenland. Many of their ancient practices—hunting with harpoons, wearing skins, and traveling by dogsled—have survived despite modernizing influences that began at the turn of the century, when the explorer Robert Peary gave them rifles. The Arctic cold and ice have kept these hardy and efficient people isolated even today.

I began going to Greenland in 1993 to get above tree line. I was still recovering from being struck by lightning, which had affected my heart and made it impossible to go to altitude, where I feel most at home. In Greenland, I experienced tree line as a product of latitude, not just altitude. I had already read the ten volumes of expedition notes of Arctic explorer and national hero Knud Rasmussen, and when I met the Greenlandic people, my summer idyll turned into seven years of Arctic peregrinations that may never end.

This latest journey is taking place in April; I am traveling to Qaanaaq, the northernmost town in the world, where I will join two Inuit subsistence hunters—Jens Danielsen and Mikile Kristiansen, friends with whom I have been traveling since I first came to Greenland—on their spring trip up the coast to hunt seal, walrus, small birds called dovekies, and polar bear.

Despite their Danish names (Greenland, once a Danish colony, is now largely self-governing), Jens and Mikile are Eskimos, descendants of hunters who walked the Bering Land Bridge from Siberia to Alaska, across the Canadian Arctic, and, finally, to Greenland, following the tracks of polar bears, the migration of caribou and birds, the breathing holes of seals, the cracks in the ice where walrus and whales were found.

Greenland is 1,500 miles long and is crowned by a 700,000-square-mile sheet of ice whose summit is 11,000 feet high. The habitable fringe of land that peeks out from this icy mass is mostly rock, to which houses are bolted. No roads connect villages; transportation is by dogsled or boat, or the occasional helicopter taxi that can be summoned at a formidable price, weather permitting. The closest town to the south would take one and a half months to reach by dogsled from Qaanaaq.

The ice came in October and now paves the entire polar north—rivers, oceans, and fjords are all solid white. Like old skin, it is pinched, pocked, and nicked, pressed up into towering hummocks and bejeweled by stranded calf ice sticking up here and there like hunks of beveled glass.

.   .   .

The arrival of a helicopter is still an event in any Arctic village. Snow flies as we land, and families and friends press forward to greet their loved ones. Qaanaaq, a town of 650 people and 2,000 dogs in the northwestern corner of Greenland, is built on a hill facing a fjord. Down on the ice, there is always activity: Sleds are lined up, dogs are being fed or harnessed, hunters are coming home from a day's or month's journey or are just taking off. It's said that the Polar Eskimo begins and ends life with traveling. Even at home, they are always preparing for the next journey.

Jens Danielsen comes for me in the morning. Tall and rotund, he has a deep, gentle voice and a belly laugh that can make the ice shake. He wears sweatpants and tennis shoes despite biting cold. Almost 40, he's already beginning to gray at the temples. Jens estimates that he travels more than 3,500 miles a year by dogsled while hunting for food for his family. When not on the ice, he is a politician, heading up the Avanersuaq hunting council, a job that requires him to go below the Arctic Circle to Nuuk, Greenland's capital city. There, he testifies in front of Parliament in an effort to preserve the traditional lifestyle of northern hunters. So far, they've been able to restrict the use of snowmobiles (in Qaanaaq, one is owned by the hospital for emergencies), limit the number of motorized boats in the summer so as not to disrupt the hunting of narwhals using kayaks, and dictate the means by which animals are to be killed. Rifles are used to hunt seals and polar bears. Harpoons are used on narwhals and walrus.

A northern hunter's year could be said to begin when the new ice comes in late September or early October. They hunt walrus by dogsled in the fall. After the sun goes below the horizon on October 24, the dark months last until February. By moonlight, seals are hunted with nets set under the ice. Spring means bearded and ringed seals, polar bears, narwhals, rabbits, and foxes, and when the dovekie migration begins around May 10, hunters climb talus slopes and catch the birds with nets. In summer, narwhals are harpooned from kayaks.

To say that Jens, Mikile, and the other villagers are subsistence hunters is perhaps stretching the truth. A couple times a year, in late summer when it can make it through the ice, a supply boat comes and delivers goods from Denmark: wood, building supplies, paint, heating oil, and other necessities. It is also possible to buy small quantities of imported Danish foods—brought in by helicopter—at the tiny, sparsely stocked grocery store, but most villagers can't afford to live on Danish lamb and chicken, and, furthermore, prefer not to. During bouts of bad weather, no supplies come at all. These are hunters who, at the end of the 20th century, have chosen to stay put and live by the harpoon, gun, and sled.

At the last minute, Jens's wife, Ilaitsuk, a strong, handsome woman a few years older than her husband, decides to come with us. "*Issi*," she says, rubbing her arms. Cold. Before getting on the sled, she and I change into *annuraat ammit*—skins. We pull on *nannuk*, polar bear pants; *kapatak*, fox-skin anoraks; *kamikpak*, polar bear boots lined with *ukaleq*, arctic hare; and *aiqqatit*, sealskin mittens. Then we prepare to head north in search of animals whose meat we will live on and whose skins Jens, Mikile, and their families will wear.

Mikile has joined the hunting trip because he needs a new pair of polar bear pants. He has already packed his sled and has begun harnessing his dogs. In his mid-30s, Mikile is small and wiry, with a gentle demeanor and face. He is traveling light and carries only one passenger, photographer Chris Anderson.

Thule-style sleds are 12 to 14 feet long, with upturned front runners and a bed lashed onto the frame. Jens lays our duffels on a tarp, and Ilaitsuk places caribou hides on top. The load is tied down, and a rifle is shoved under the lash-rope. The Danielsens' five-year-old grandson, Merseqaq, who is going with us, lies on the skins with a big smile. The dogs, which are chained on long lines when not being used, are anxious to get to work. Jens bends at the waist to untangle the trace lines—something he will do hundreds of times during our journey. As soon as the dogs feel the lines being hooked to the sled, they charge off out of sheer excitement—there is no way to stop them—and the wild ride begins.

We careen down narrow paths through the village. Bystanders, children, and dogs jump out of the way. Jens leaps off as we approach the rough ice at the shoreline. Walking in front of the team, he whistles so they will follow him as Ilaitsuk steadies the sled from behind. We tip, tilt, and bump. The dogs are not harnessed two by two as they are in Alaska but fan out on lines of varying lengths. This way, they can position themselves however they want, rest when they need to, or align themselves with a friend. Ilaitsuk and Jens run hard and jump on the sled. I've been holding the little boy. Soon, we bump down onto smooth ice. Jens snaps the *iparautaq* (whip) over the dogs' heads as they trot across the frozen sea.

We head west, then straight north past a long line of stranded icebergs that, in summer, when there is open water, will eventually be taken south by the Labrador current from Baffin Bay to Davis Strait, then into the North Atlantic. In winter, the icebergs are frozen in place. They stand like small cities with glinting towers, natural arches that bridge gaping portholes through which more icebergs can be seen.

Jens snaps the whip above the dogs' backs. *"Ai, ai, ai, ai . . . ,"* he sings out in a high falsetto, urging them to go faster. Snow-covered ice rolls beneath us, and the coastline, a walled fortress, slides by. On a dogsled, there is no physical control—no rudder, no brakes, no reins. Only voice commands and the sound of the whip and the promise of food if the hunt is good, which is perhaps why these half-wild, half-starved dogs obey. A dogtrot—the speed at which we move up Greenland's northwest coast—is about four miles an hour. Dog farts float by, and the sound of panting is the one rhythm that seems to keep our minds from flying away.

Half an hour north of Qaanaaq, the snow deepens, and the dogs slow down. They are already pulling 700 pounds. We follow the track of a sled that is carrying a coffin. Earlier this week, a young hunter died in an accident on the ice in front of Qaanaaq where schoolchildren were playing. Now his body is being taken home to Siorapaluk, a subsistence hunting village of a few dozen people up the coast from here. Some say the hunter was suicidal. "There are troubles everywhere. Even here," Jens says, clasping his tiny grandson on his lap at the front of the sled. "*Harru, harru!*" (go left), he yells to the dogs. "*Atsuk, atsuk!*" (Go right.) When his grandson mimics the commands, Jens turns and smiles.

We stop twice to make tea. The old Primus stove is lit and placed inside a wooden box to shelter the flame from the wind. Hunks of ice are chipped off an iceberg, stuffed into the pot, and melted for water. Danish cookies are passed. A whole frozen halibut, brought from home, is stuck headfirst into the snow. Mikile, Ilaitsuk, and Jens begin hacking at its side and eating chunks of "frozen sushi." The dogs roll in the snow to cool themselves, while we stand and shiver.

The closer we get to Siorapaluk, the colder it gets. Jens unties a dog, which had become lame, from the front of the sled, and throws him back into the pack. Appearances count: It wouldn't look right to arrive in a village with an injured dog. We slide around a bend, and Robertson Fjord opens up. Three glaciers lap at the frozen fjord, and the ice cap rises pale and still behind snowy mountains. Where one begins and the other ends is hard to tell. On the far, east-facing side of the fjord, the village comes into view. It has taken us eight hours to get here.

We make camp out on the ice in front of the village, pushing the two sleds together to serve as our *igliq* (sleeping platform) and raising a crude, bloodstained canvas tent over them. When I look up, something catches my eye: The funeral procession is winding up the snowy path above the houses. Six men are carrying the hunter's coffin. We hear faint singing—hymns—then the mourners gather in a knot as the wooden casket is laid down on the snow, blessed, and stored in a shed, where it will stay until the ground thaws enough for burial.

When the sun slips behind the mountains, the temperature plummets to 18 degrees below zero. All six of us crowd into the tent. Shoulder to shoulder, leg to leg, we are bodies seeking other bodies for warmth. With our feet on the ice floor, we sip tea and eat cookies and go to bed with no dinner. When we live on the ice, we eat what we hunt—in the spring, that means ringed seals, walrus, or polar bears. But we did not hunt today.

. . .

The sound of 300 dogs crooning and howling wakes me. I look across the row of bodies stuffed into sleeping bags. Jens is holding his grandson against his barrel chest. They open their eyes: two moon faces smiling at the canine chorus. There are gunshots. Mikile sticks his head out of the tent, then falls back on the igliq, grunting. "They shot at something but missed," he says. "At what?" I ask. "*Nanoq, immaqa*" (a polar bear, maybe), he says, smiling mischievously.

Bright sun, frigid breeze. It must be midday. We sit in silence, watching ice melt for tea water. "Issi," Ilaitsuk says again. Cold. My companions speak very little English, and my Greenlandic is, well, rudimentary. Some days we talk hardly at all. Other times we pool our dictionaries and enjoy a feast of words. I try to memorize such useful phrases as: "*nauk tupilaghuunnguaju*," which means "you fool"; and "*taquliktooq*"—"dark-colored dog with a white blaze over its eye." But often, I fail, which just makes for more merriment.

Today, we break camp quietly. The pace of the preparations is deceptive: It looks laid-back because Inuit hunters don't waste energy with theatrics or melodrama. Instead, they work quietly, steadily, and quickly. Before I know it, Jens is hooking the trace lines to the sled. I grab the little boy and make a flying leap as Ilaitsuk and Jens jump aboard the already fast-moving sled. Jens laughs at his grandson for not being ready, and the boy cries, which makes Jens laugh harder. This is the Eskimo way of teaching children to have a sense of humor and to pay attention and act with precision—lessons that will later preserve their lives.

Snow begins pelting us. "The weather and the hunter are not such good friends," Jens says. "If a hunter waits for good weather, well, he may starve. He may starve anyway. But if he goes out when conditions are bad, he may fall through the ice and never be seen again. That's how it is here."

Snow deepens, and the dogtrot slows to a walk. On our right, brown cliffs rise in sheer folds striped with avalanche chutes crisscrossed by the tracks of arctic hares. "Ukaleq, ukaleq," Ilaitsuk cries out. Jens whistles the dogs to a stop. Ilaitsuk points excitedly. The rabbits' hides provide liners for *kamiks* (boots), and their flesh is eaten. We look: They are white against a white slope and bounce behind outcrops of boulders. No luck. On the ice, there are no seals. What will the six of us plus 30 dogs eat tonight?

As we round a bend and a rocky knob, a large bay opens up. We travel slowly across its wide mouth. Looking inward, I see a field of talcum powder, then a cliff of ice: the snout of an enormous glacier made of turquoise, light, and rock, carrying streambed debris like rooftop ornaments. My eyes move from the ice cap above to the frozen fjord below. Bands of color reveal the rhythm of ablation and accumulation for what it is: the noise and silence of time—Arctic time—which is all light or all dark and has no hours or days. When you're on a dogsled, the 24-hour day turns into something elastic, and our human habits move all the way around the clock; we find ourselves eating dinner at breakfast time, sleeping in the all-day light, and traveling in the all-light night. What we care about is not a schedule but warmth and food and good weather as we push far north of the last village and see ahead only cold and snow and a growing hunger that makes us ache.

.   .   .

We change course. The going has been torturously slow. Instead of following the coastline straight north, we now veer out onto the frozen ocean; we follow a lead in the ice, looking for seals. The snow comes on harder. The cowl of a storm approaches, crossing Ellesmere Island, pulling over the hundred-mile-wide face of Humboldt glacier. Wind whips the storm's dark edge; it fibrillates like a raven's wing feathers, and as it pulls over, the great dome light of inland ice goes dark.

There are breathing holes all along the crack, but no *uuttuq*—seals that have hauled themselves out on ice—which are usually common in the spring. We keep going in a westward direction, away from the historic camping sites of Neqi, where we will sleep tonight, and Etah.

All afternoon and evening, we travel in a storm. I remember a hunter once telling me about getting vertigo. "Sometimes when we are on our dogsleds and there is bad fog or snow, we feel lost. We can't tell where the sky is, where the ice. It feels like we are moving upside down." But today we aren't lost. "We can tell by wind direction," the same hunter told me, "and if we keep traveling at the same angle to the drifting snow, we're OK."

All is white. We stop for tea, pulling the two sleds close together and lashing a tarp between for a windbreak. We scrounge through our duffels for food. Chris finds a jar of peanut butter. I'm dismayed to see the words "reduced fat" on the label. Never mind. We spread it on crackers, then drink tea and share a bittersweet chocolate bar. Bittersweet is what I am feeling right now: happy to be in Greenland among old friends but getting hungrier with each bite I take.

It's easy to see how episodes of famine have frequently swept through the Arctic, how quickly hunting can go bad, how hunger dominates. Before stores and helicopters, pan-Arctic cannibalism was common. After people ate their dogs and boiled sealskins, they ate human flesh—almost always the bodies of those who had already died. It was the key to survival, repellent as it was. Peter Freuchen, a Danish explorer who traveled with Knud Rasmussen for 14 years, wrote of the practice: "At Pingerqaling I met a remarkable woman, Atakutaluk. I had heard of her before as being the foremost lady of Fury and Hecla Strait—she was important because she had once eaten her husband and three of her children."

Freuchen went on to describe the ordeal. Atakutaluk's tribe had been traveling across Baffin Island when a warm spell hit and it became impossible to use a sled. There were no animals in the area. When they ran out of food, they ate their dogs, then the weaker people in their hunting party. When Freuchen met Atakutaluk, she said, "Look here, Pita. Don't let your face be narrow for this. I got a new husband, and I got with him three new children. They are all named for the dead ones that only served to keep me alive so they could be reborn."

We head north again, crossing back over a large piece of frozen ocean. Rabbit tracks crisscross in front of us, but we see no animals. The edge of the storm frays, letting light flood through. Snow, ice, and air glisten. Ilaitsuk and I tip our faces up to the sun. Its warmth is a blessing, and for a few moments, we close our eyes and doze.

There's a yell. Ilaitsuk scrambles to her knees and looks around. It is Mikile far ahead of us. He's up on his knees on his fast-moving sled: "Nanoq! Nanoq!" he yells, pointing, and then we see: A polar bear is trotting across the head of a wide fjord.

Jens's dogs take off in that direction. Mikile has already cut two of his dogs loose, and they chase the bear. He releases two more. "*Pequoq, pequoq,*" Jens yells, urging his dogs to go faster. It is then that we see that there is a cub, struggling in deep snow to keep up. The mother stops, wheels around, and runs back. Mikile's loose dogs catch up and hold the bear at bay. Because she has a young one, she will not be killed; an abandoned cub would never survive.

Now we are between the cub and the she-bear. Repeatedly, she stops, stands, and whirls around to go back to her cub. The dogs close in: She paws, snarls, and runs again. Then something goes terribly wrong: One of the dogs spies the cub. Before we can get there, the dog is on the cub and goes for his jugular. We rush to the young bear's rescue, but the distances are so great and the going is so slow that by the time we make it, the dog is shaking the cub by his neck and has been joined by other dogs. Mikile and Jens leap off their sleds and beat the dogs away with their whip handles, but it is too late. The cub is badly hurt.

We stay with the cub while Mikile catches up with the mother. The cub is alive but weak. A large flap of skin and flesh hangs down. Even though he's dazed and unsteady, he's still feisty. He snarls and paws at us as we approach. Jens throws a soft loop around his leg and pulls him behind the sled to keep him out of the fray; then we let him rest. Maybe he will recover enough for us to send him back to his mother.

Far ahead, the mother bear starts to get away, but the loose dogs catch up and slow her progress. Near the far side of the fjord, the bear darts west, taking refuge behind a broken, stranded iceberg. Mikile cuts more dogs loose when the first ones begin to tire. The bear stands in her icy enclosure, coming out to charge the dogs as they approach. She doesn't look for her cub; she is fighting for her own life.

The sun is out, and the bear is hot. She scoops up a pawful of snow and eats it. The slab of ice against which she rests is blue and shaped in a wide V, like an open book whose sides are melting in the spring sun. The dogs surround her in a semicircle, jumping forward to snap at her, testing their own courage, but leaping back when she charges them.

Five hundred yards behind Mikile, we watch over the cub. If we get too close, he snaps. Sometimes he stands, but he's weak. He begins panting. His eyes roll back; he staggers and is dead.

Jens ties a loop around his neck, and we pull the cub like a toy behind the sled. Mikile turns as we approach. "Is the cub dead?" he asks. Jens says that he is. The decision is made: Mikile will shoot the mother. I ask if killing her is necessary—after all, she is a young bear that can have more cubs—but my Greenlandic is unintelligible. I plead for her life using English verbs and Greenlandic nouns. Jens says, "It is up to Mikile."

Mikile, whose polar bear pants are worn almost all the way through, listens, then quietly loads his rifle. We are standing close to the bear, close enough for her to attack us, but she has eyes only for the dogs. Standing on her toes, she lays her elbow on top of the berg and looks out.

Silently, I root for her: Go, go. These are the last moments of her life, and I'm watching them tick by. Does she know she is doomed? Once again I plead for her life, but I get only questioning looks from the hunters. I feel sick. Peeking over the top of the ice, the bear slumps back halfheartedly. She is tired, her cub is gone, and there is no escape.

Ilaitsuk covers Merseqaq's ears as Mikile raises his rifle. The boy is frightened. He has seen the cub die, and he doesn't want to see any more.

The bear's nose, eyes, and claws are black dots in a world of white, a world that, for her, holds no clues about human ambivalence. She gives me the same hard stare she would give a seal—after all, I'm just part of the food chain. It is the same stare Mikile gives her now, not hard from lack of feeling but from the necessity to survive. I understand how important it is for a hunter to get a polar bear. She will be the source of food, and her skin will be used for much-needed winter clothing. It is solely because of the polar bear pants and boots that we don't freeze to death. Nevertheless, I feel that I am a witness to an execution.

The bear's fur is pale yellow, and the ice wall is blue. The sun is hot. Time melts. What I know about life and death, cold and hunger, seems irrelevant. There are three gunshots. A paw goes up in agony and scratches the ice wall. She rolls on her back and is dead.

I kneel down by her. The fur is thick between her claws. There is the sound of gurgling. It's too early in the year for running water. Then I see that it is her blood pouring from the gunshot wound that killed her.

Mikile ties his dogs back in with the others. Knives are sharpened. Tea water is put on to boil. We roll up our sleeves in the late afternoon sun. Ilaitsuk glasses the ice for other animals; Merseqaq is on the snow beside the bear and puts his tiny hand on her large paw.

The bear is laid out on her back. Jens puts the tip of his knife on her umbilicus and makes an upward cut to her neck. The fine tip travels up under her chin and through her black lip as if to keep her from talking.

Soon enough she is disrobed. The skin is laid out on the snow, and, after the blood is wiped off, it is folded in quarters and laid carefully in a gunnysack on the sled. Then her body is dismembered, and the pieces are also stowed under the tarp, so when we put away our teacups and start northwest toward Neqi, she is beneath us in pieces and we are riding her, this bear that, according to Inuit legends, can hear and understand everything human beings say. We travel the rest of the day in silence.

.   .   .

We cross the wide mouth of the fjord and continue on to Neqi, a camp used by Inuit hunters and European explorers for hundreds of years. There is no village, only a cabin, low and wide, set at the tip of a long thumb of land sticking out from between two glaciers. The cabin looks down on the frozen Smith Sound. The word "Neqi" means "meat," and this was a place where meat caches were laid in for hunters and explorers on their way to the far north of Greenland or to the North Pole. We push our sleds up through the hummocks to the cabin. The meat racks are crowded with walrus flippers, dead dogs, and bits of hacked-up seals. Half sanctuary, half charnel ground.

We stand on the ice terrace in front of the cabin. Looking out at the wide expanse of frozen ocean, we salute the rarely seen sun. Its warmth drives into us, and for the first time, we relax. A hidden beer emerges from Jens's duffel bag and is passed around.

The strangled cry of a fox floats out over the frozen bay where we shot the bear. Now a band of fog rises from that place, a blindfold covering the labanotations—the script of the bear's death dance: where she stopped, wheeled around, attacked, and kept running; the hieroglyphics of blood and tracks; and the hollows in the snow where the dogs rested after the chase. I'm glad I can't see.

A Primus is lit, and water is put on to boil. Then the backstrap of the polar bear—the most tender part—is thrown in the pot. It's so warm, we take off our anoraks and hats. Jens passes paper plates. "Nanoq. Nanoq," he says in a low voice. "The polar bear is king. We have to eat her in a special way. We boil her like the seal, but we pay special respects to her so her soul shall not have too much difficulty getting home."

After 20 minutes, chunks of meat are doled out. They steam on our plates. "*Qujanaq,*" I say, thanking Mikile, Jens, and, most of all, the bear. The meat is tender and good, almost like buffalo.

Later, we get into our sleeping bags and lie on the igliq. It is still warm, and no one can sleep. Jens and Ilaitsuk hold their grandson between them as Jens begins a story: "A long time ago, when shamans still flew underwater and animals could talk, there was a woman named Anoritoq who lived on that point of land north of Etah. The name Anoritoq means 'windswept one.' This woman had no husband, and her only son was killed by a hunter out of jealousy, because the young boy had no father but was becoming a great hunter anyway. After her son died, a hunter brought the woman a polar bear cub, which she raised just like a son. The bear learned the language of the Eskimo and played with the other children. When he grew up, he hunted seals and was very successful. But she worried about him. She was afraid a hunter might kill him, because he was, after all, a bear, and his skin was needed for clothing. She tried covering him with soot to make him dark, but one day, when some of his white fur was showing, a hunter killed him. She was so sad, she stopped eating and went outside and stayed there all the time and looked at the sea. Then, she changed into a stone. Now when we go bear hunting in that area, we put a piece of seal fat on the rock and pray for a good hunt."

. . .

Morning. We follow the coast north to Pitoravik. It's not a long trip. From there, we will determine our route to Etah—either up and over part of the inland ice or following the coast if there is no open water or pressure ice. A wind begins to blow as Jens and Mikile take off to investigate the trail over the glacier. They are gone several hours, and when they come back, they shake their heads. "The drifts are too deep and the crevasses too wide, and the snow hides them," Jens says. "Down below, the ice is badly broken with open water. Too dangerous. We'll wait until morning. If the weather is good, we'll try to go over the top. If not, then we'll go to the ice edge out there, toward Canada, and hunt walrus and narwhal."

In the morning, the weather is no better. A continuous, mesmerizing snow falls. "I think the hunting will be better out there," Jens says, using our vantage point to look out over Smith Sound. Beyond, Ellesmere Island is a blue line of mountains with a ruffle of white clouds. We descend and go in a southwesterly direction toward the island of Kiatak.

For three or four days, we travel in weather that keeps closing down on us. When we stop to rest the dogs, Ilaitsuk, Merseqaq, and I play tag on the ice to keep warm. The child never complains. When his feet get cold, he merely points to his toes, and Ilaitsuk puts on the over-boots she sewed together when we were in the cabin at Neqi. Then he sits at the front of the sled, wind blasted and happy, echoing his grandfather's commands, snapping the long whip, already becoming a man.

Patience and strength of mind are the hunter's virtues. Also, flexibility and humor. Jens shoots at a seal and misses. Another one catches his scent and dives down into its hole. He returns to the sled, laughing at his failures, explaining to Mikile exactly what he did wrong. Later, he reverts to winter-style seal hunting called *agluhiutuq*, hunting at the *agluq* (breathing hole). But even this fails.

We continue on. "*Hikup hinaa*," Jens says. The ice edge. That's what we are now looking for. There we will find plentiful seal, walrus, and narwhal. My stomach growls, and I think of the legend of the Great Famine, when winters followed one after the other, with no spring, summer, or fall in between. Jens says that this last winter and spring have been the coldest in his memory. Ironically, colder weather in the Arctic may be a side effect of global warming. As pieces of the ice cap melt and calve into the ocean, the water temperature in parts of the far north cools, as, in turn, does the air. Maybe global warming will cancel itself out, I say. Jens doesn't understand my "Greenenglish." "Issi," he says, rubbing his arms. Cold. "Maybe we will have to eat each other like they did in the old days," he says, smiling sweetly.

.   .   .

For the Eskimo, solitude is a sign of sheer unhappiness. It is thought to be a perversion and absolutely undesirable. Packed tightly together on the sled, we are fur-wrapped, rendered motionless by cold. It's good to be pressed between human bodies. We scan the ice for animals. Shadows made by standing bits of ice look like seals.

Then we do see one, a black comma lying on the alabaster extravagance.

Jens and Mikile stop their dogs. Jens mounts his rifle on a movable blind—a small stand with a white sailcloth to hide his face. The snow is shin-deep, but the wind is right. He creeps forward, then lies down on his belly, sighting in his rifle. All 30 dogs sit at attention, with ears pricked. When they stop panting, the world goes silent. As soon as they hear the muffled crack of the gun, off they go, running toward Jens as they have been trained to do.

We stand in a semicircle around a pool of blood, backs to the wind. Quickly and quietly, Jens flenses the seal. He cuts out the liver, warm and steaming, holds it on the end of his knife, and offers it to us. This is an Inuit delicacy. Eating the steaming liver has helped to save starving hunters. In gratitude, we all have a bite. Our mouths and chins drip with blood. There is a slightly salty taste to the lukewarm meat.

Ilaitsuk folds the sealskin and lays it under the tarp alongside the polar bear skin. Jens cuts a notch through the back flipper for a handhold and drags the pink body, looking ever more diminutive, over the front of the sled. Lash lines are pulled tight, and we take off as snow swirls.

We are still traveling at 10:30 in the evening when the storm breaks. We watch the dark edge pull past, moving faster than the sled. Under clear skies, the temperature plummets to somewhere near 20 degrees below zero.

One seal for 30 dogs and six humans isn't very much meat. We stop at an iceberg and hack out slabs of ice, then make camp. As Ilaitsuk and I unload the sleds, Jens and Mikile cut up seal meat. The dogs line up in rows, avidly waiting for food. It has been two days since they've eaten fresh meat. A chunk is flung through the air, then another and another. Jens's and Mikile's aims are so perfect, every dog gets its share, and the faster they eat, the more they get.

Jens cuts up the remaining seal for our dinner. Inside the tent, we watch as lumps of meat churn in brown water. As the hut warms up, we strip down. Merseqaq's tiny red T-shirt reads: "I love elephants," though he has never seen one and probably never will.

We eat in silence, using our pocketknives and fingers. A loaf of bread is passed. We each have a slice, then drink tea and share a handful of cookies. After, Ilaitsuk sets a piece of plywood in a plastic bucket and stretches the sealskin over the top edge. With her *ulu*—a curved knife with a wooden handle—she scrapes the blubber from the skin in strong, downward thrusts. When the hide is clean, she turns to her *kiliutaq*—a small, square knife used to scrape the brownish pink oil out of a fur.

Ilaitsuk lets me have a try at scraping. I'm so afraid I'll cut through and ruin the skin, I barely scratch the surface.

Later, lying in my sleeping bag, I listen to wind. Jens tells stories about the woman who adopted a bear, the hunter who married a fox, and the origin of fog. His voice goes soft, and the words drone, putting us into a sweet trance of sleep so pleasurable that I don't know if I'll ever be able to sleep again without those stories.

.　　.　　.

In the next days, we search for the ice edge, camping on the ice wherever we find ourselves at the end of the night. We travel straight west from the tip of Kiatak Island out onto the frozen ocean between Greenland and Ellesmere Island. On the way, Jens teaches his grandson voice commands and how to use the whip without touching the backs of the animals. "Will Merseqaq be a hunter, too?" I ask. Jens says, "I am teaching him what he needs to know. Then the decision will be up to him. He has to love this more than anything."

When we reach a line of icebergs, Jens and Mikile clamber to the top and glass the entire expanse of ice to the west. It feels like we're already halfway across Smith Sound. Jens comes back shaking his head. "There is no open water," he says incredulously. "It is ice all the way to Canada." This has never happened before in any spring in memory. It is May 8.

We turn south to an area where sea currents churn at the ice. Maybe there will be an ice edge there. Down the coast at Kap Parry, we meet two hunters who are coming from the other direction. As usual, there is a long silence, then a casual question about open water. They shake their heads. No ice edge this way, either.

That night, I lie in my sleeping bag, squeezed tightly between Mikile and Ilaitsuk. "I feel as if we are stuck in winter," Mikile said earlier, looking frustrated. He has a big family to feed. Along with Jens, he is considered one of the best hunters in Qaanaaq, but even he can't kill enough game if spring never comes. We lie awake listening to wind.

At midday, we climb an iceberg that is shaped like the Sydney

Opera House, to see if the ice edge has appeared. Jens shakes his head no. As we climb down, Mikile yells and points: "Nanoq." Far out, a polar bear dances across the silvered horizon, blessedly too distant for us to hunt. A mirage takes him instead of a bullet, a band of mirrored light floating up from the ice floor. It takes his dancing legs and turns them into waves of spring heat still trying to make its way past the frigid tail end of winter.

.   .   .

Finally we head for home, traveling along the east side of Kiatak. Walls of red rock rise in amphitheaters; arctic hares race across snow-dappled turf and grass. A raven swoops by, and a fox floats its gray tail along the steep sidehill. Near the bottom of the cliff, icicles hang at odd angles from beds of rock. We pass over a floor of broken platelets that look as if they'd been held up like mirrors, then tossed down and broken, making the sled tip this way and that. Some pieces of ice are so exquisite that I ask Jens to stop so I can stare at them: a finely etched surface overlaid with another layer of ice punctured by what look like stars.

The dogs bring me back. They fight and fart and snarl and pant. One of them, Pappi, is in heat, and the other dogs can think of nothing except getting to her. Pappi slinks behind the others, clamping her tail down and refusing to pull. Then the males fall back, too, fighting one another, and the sled eventually comes to a stop. Jens unties Pappi and fastens her behind the sled, but this doesn't work, either. She falls and is dragged and can't get up.

Finally Jens cuts Pappi loose. There's a moment of relief, as if she had been freed from a tight world of ice and cold and discipline. Ilaitsuk looks at me and smiles. Her face is strong in the late evening sun. The boy is ensconced in his grandfather's lap, wearing dark glasses. We have failed to bring home much meat, but Jens shrugs it off, reminding me that worrying has no place in the

Arctic. He and all those before him have survived day by day for 4,000 years, and one bad hunting trip won't set him back. There is always tomorrow.

Now Pappi is running free and happy. Jens urges her to go on ahead. The snow is hard and icy, and the sled careens as the dogs give chase. Sometimes when we are airborne, flying over moguls, little Merseqaq gets on his hands and knees and squeals with delight. The cold and hunger and terrible hunting conditions are behind us now, and as we near Qaanaaq, the dogs, ever optimistic, run very fast.

The New Yorker

WINNER, REVIEWS AND
CRITICISM

The Maria Problem

Anthony Lane is a rare critic who is unafraid to express, and even instill, delight. His reviews are laugh-out-loud funny, but also insightful and evocative. His stylish prose and pin-point perceptions make him one of the most elegant writers of our time.

Anthony Lane

The Maria Problem

Going wild for "The Sound of Music"— with subtitles.

L et's start at the very beginning. (It's a very good place to start.) Maria Augusta Kutschera was born in 1905. As a young woman, she became a postulant at the Nonnberg Abbey, in Salzburg, Austria, but suffered from ill health. It was deemed beneficial that she should venture outside and adopt the post of governess in the home of a naval captain. She married him in 1927, which put an end to any postulating. The captain already had seven children; Maria bore him three more and formed a family musical group, whose success was cut short when Hitler invaded his native land. Even now, no historian has been able to ascertain if this was a genuine bid for power or the only possible means whereby the Führer could eradicate the threat of close-harmony singing.

Maria and her family fled to Italy, England, and, finally, the United States. The captain died in 1947; two years later, Maria published "The Story of the Trapp Family Singers." In 1956, the book was turned into a hit German movie; theatrical producers began to sniff around, and in November, 1959, "The Sound of Music," with original songs by Rodgers and Hammerstein, opened on Broadway. Twentieth Century Fox soon acquired the movie rights, but the film proved hard to bring to birth. After nearly five years of wrangles and pangs, "The Sound of Music," directed by Robert Wise and starring Julie Andrews, had its New York première, on March 2, 1965. To date, the picture has earned a hundred and sixty million dollars. It remains the most popular musical film in history. One woman in Wales has seen it almost a thousand times. In Hong Kong, it is entitled "Fairy Music Blow Fragrant Place, Place Hear."

All of which is how I came to be standing on a sidewalk on a dark December evening, waving a foam nun.

.   .   .

The Prince Charles Cinema sits in central London, a hundred yards east of Piccadilly, between the Notre Dame dance hall and a row of Chinese restaurants. When it opened, in 1991, the idea was that you could catch new and recent pictures for less than two dollars—a fraction of what they cost around the corner, in the plush movie theatres of Leicester Square. Even now, the Prince Charles has nobly resisted the urge to smarten up; the furnishings are a touching tribute to wartime brown, and the stalls, flouting a rule of theatrical design which has obtained since the fifth century B.C., appear to slope downward toward the back, so that customers in the rear seats can enjoy an uncluttered view of their own knees. The cinema shows three or four films a day; come the weekend, everything explodes. Since August, every Friday evening and Sunday afternoon the program has been the same: "Singalong-a-Sound-of-Music."

The idea is simple. You watch the film—uncut, as nature intended, in a scuzzy print, with alarming color shifts as the reels change. The only difference is the added subtitles, which come alive, like the hills, during every song. These enable viewers to join in, which they do with undisguised lustiness. The titling of "The Sound of Music" was prepared by Martin Wagner, for London's

National Film Theatre, and it struck me as the one work of unquestionable genius that I encountered last year. I tend to be embarrassed by subtitles; their audacious efforts to snatch at foreign vernaculars end up stressing, rather than allaying, the alien qualities of the setting. With "The Sound of Music," however, they bring home just how tightly, even soothingly, we are wrapped in this unignorable film. In a sense, Wagner had a head start; what was required was not translation from another tongue but the simple transcription, for karaoke purposes, of words that most of us know pretty well. (I was appalled to discover that, after a thirty-year break, I was close to word perfect.) This, however, is where Wagner shows his hand; who else would have thought to include the *Latin chant* that rises from the abbey as we pan down from Julie Andrews on a hillside and get ready for "(How Do You Solve a Problem Like) Maria?" I had never noticed it before—no audience is meant to notice filler, the blah that keeps a soundtrack ticking along—but suddenly there it was at the bottom of the screen (*"In saecula saeculorum"*). Things get even better halfway through the picture, as the children gather at the foot of the stairs to bid the party guests good night. Friedrich sings, and the titles follow him closely:

> So long, farewell, auf Wiedersehen, adieu,
> Adieu, adieu, to yieu and yieu and yieu.

That was it for me. For thirty years, I have wondered about this torturing little rhyme. It should have been easy to avoid; if you want "Adieu" to chime with "you," don't pronounce it in French—simply opt for the Anglicized version, "Adyoo," and take it from there. But no: "The Sound of Music" made a tragic move to sound classy, and it paid the price. As for the yodelling in the puppet scene, it inspires Wagner to his finest work—a cluster bomb of meaningless vowels. For anyone who believes that "The Sound of

Music" shows Hollywood at its most hopelessly square, what could be more bracing than to see it reborn as a Dadaist art happening?

All nonsense is a pleasure, of course, from Lewis Carroll down to Alexander Haig, but what lends particular spice to "The Sound of Music" is that it is known nonsense, remembered and revered. And that is why the Prince Charles has become a place of pilgrimage. It occasionally screens "The Rocky Horror Show," too, to a gathering of addicts. But that film is already armored by a sense of camp; nothing you can throw at it will dent its knowingness, whereas "The Sound of Music," the most unwitting of cults, is blissfully up for grabs.

When I arrived on a Friday night, an hour before the start, the area around the cinema was packed. To be specific, it was packed with nuns. Many of them bore guitars. I was one of the few pathetic creatures who had not made the effort to come in costume. There were Nazis, naturally, as in every major city, plus a load of people who looked like giant parcels. I didn't get it. "Who are they?" I said to a nun who was having a quick cigarette before the film. She looked at me with celestial pity and blew smoke. "Brown Paper Packages Tied Up with Strings," she replied. I am relieved, on the whole, that I missed the rugby team who piled into one screening as Girls in White Dresses with Blue Satin Sashes; on the other hand, it is a source of infinite sadness to me that I wasn't at the Prince Charles when a guy turned up in a skintight, all-over body costume in bright yellow; asked which character he was intended to represent, he explained that he was Ray, a Drop of Golden Sun. I have hung around the entrance a couple of times as showtime approached, just in case this heroic gentleman returns as Warm Woollen Mittens—or, more challenging still, as Tea, a Drink with Jam and Bread—but no luck so far.

The impressive thing about all this is the apostolic level of dedication. I sat in a whole row of nuns—nurses from a private hospital, as it happened, having a cheap night out. (One had lovingly constructed her wimple from black cloth and a rolled-up pair of white knickers.) During the screening, they drank beer in almost Austrian quantities; one of them kept jumping up and hurrying to the exit. "What's the matter with that nun?" I asked the beefy sister beside me. "Pregnant," she said.

Nominally a reserved people, the British like to bottle up their exhibitionist tendencies and then, at opportune moments, let them flood out in a rush; this is the basis of pantomime, for instance, with its flagrant worship of cross-dressing. Even now, there is almost certainly a quiet soul who is preparing to attend "The Sound of Music" as Schnitzel with Noodles. To brush yourself with egg and roll around in bread crumbs for a while requires a nerveless ingenuity; but to walk to the nearest tube trailing ribbons of buttered pasta, and to sit on the train with a dignified expression, in the thick of the Friday rush hour, argues a fortitude bordering on the superhuman. I couldn't do it, but somebody will, and I think I know who that somebody will be. "Singalong-a-Sound-of-Music" is currently starting a British national tour, and then, in April, it will hit America, where bottling is less of an issue. Twentieth Century Fox will not yet name the lucky cinemas where it will screen, but I can safely reveal that New York and San Francisco, among others, should be girding their loins for Schnitzel Time.

It goes without saying that "Singalong-a-Sound-of-Music" is now a compulsory fixture on the gay calendar; it began life, indeed, as a one-off special for the London Lesbian and Gay Film Festival. Every screening gets its own m.c., who oversees a Best Costume competition during the intermission. (One week, just to confuse the issue, the winner was a real nun. What did she think the other nuns were?) At my screening, there was Rhona Cameron, a cheery Scottish lesbian who hosts a gay show on British TV. Rhona checked that there were no children in the audience, and then issued instructions: "Don't worry if you can't sing; the gay men in the audience will carry you." Fragrant music blow fairy place, place go wild.

I usually loathe any hint of live entertainment at the movies, preferring to hibernate in peace and quiet; but "Singalong-a-Sound-of-Music" launches so frontal an assault on reticence that everyone caves in. It is a stout rebuke to the couch culture of "home cinema"—a contradiction in terms, if ever I heard one. The bloodless interaction promised by DVD technology, for instance, in which the lone viewer can pause "The Matrix" to command a reverse view of Keanu Reeves's butt, cannot hold a candle to the sight of two hundred people whistling at Christopher Plummer when he enters with a riding crop, and waving their lighters above their heads, like a rock crowd, during his rendition of "Edelweiss." For an extra five dollars, ticket-holders at the Prince Charles can buy a helpful gift pack that includes a fake edelweiss, a packet of cough drops for sore throats, a head scarf, and, yes, a small foam-rubber nun, in which you are urged to "stick your fingers" and "sway along."

The repartee at "Singalong-a-Sound-of-Music" is of the very highest order. "Free the nuns!" was the cry as the sisters clustered behind an iron grille during Maria's wedding. Some of the backchat involves a dexterous cross-reference to other works; when Maria, having been ticked off by the Baroness (Eleanor Parker), packs her bag to leave, someone shouted, "Don't forget the hat stand!"—reminding us of a similar scene in "Mary Poppins." And, as the Mother Abbess lingered in the shadows in preparation for "Climb Ev'ry Mountain," she was told in no uncertain terms, "Do not go into the light!"—the tag line from "Poltergeist," if you please. The instructions issued to Rolf as he danced with Liesl in the gazebo came from somewhere behind my shoulder; they were explicit, and they were repeated with such urgency that, after a while, they acquired the pathos of a plea—as if it were in some way unsportsmanlike, even unromantic, for a seventeen-year-old Nazi not to deflower a motherless sixteen-year-old while he had the chance. "You need someone older and wiser telling you what to do," crooned Rolf, and we sniggered at his nerve.

The joke is, of course, that Charmian Carr, who plays Liesl, was already twenty-one when the film was made (she kept quiet at the audition), and thus in no need of tutelage from a mere boy; the deeper joke is that, in the history of blockbusting movies, nothing can touch "The Sound of Music" for sheer, blank indifference to the reproductive act. No wonder Heather Menzies, who played Louisa, answered the call to strip for *Playboy* in the nineteen-seventies; the pressure of untouchability must have felt like prison. Captain Von Trapp has seven children, but the enigma of his fertility remains as unplumbed as his willingness, as a serving naval officer, to play the guitar in public. The Baroness, with her glinting coiffure and cinched suits, could be taken, in a certain light, for a woman of the world; yet the Captain throws her over for the sake of a certifiable virgin with a boy's haircut. "For here you are, standing there, loving me," he and Maria sing to one another; love, in so immaculate a world, is pure abstraction, unruffled by the physical. In the intermission at the Prince Charles, Rhona Cameron asked one nun what she liked best about the film. Without hesitation, the nun replied, "The sex."

.   .   .

"The Sound of Music" is not a good film. It is blithe, efficient, and constructed with care; the songs are carolled con brio; but it is not a good film. Famously, it received some of the most noxious notices of its era. Steeped in the flow of the counterculture, American critics should have been ready for the sight of small children

dressed in flowery curtains, but somehow the psychedelic properties of the film eluded them. In the *Herald Tribune,* Judith Crist
called it "icky sticky," as if she'd needed to rinse her hands afterward. In *McCall's,* Pauline Kael continued the candy motif, trash-
ing the movie as a "sugar-coated lie that people seem to want to
eat"; her review so affronted readers that she was fired from her
post and landed shortly afterward at this magazine. Here she
reigned supreme for the next quarter of a century, thus proving
that "The Sound of Music" is so saintly that it confers a happy ending on all who touch its hem, even those of little faith. The film did
more than any other, perhaps, to widen the split between critics
and public from crack to chasm; it encouraged producers, like
political hopefuls, to reach out over the heads of professional
carpers and appeal directly to popular taste. (That it collared the
Academy Award for Best Picture in 1966 merely sealed the deal.)
The way to solve a problem like Maria is to love her for what she
is, with or without wimple, and the movie begs the same indul-
gence; by ignoring the mean of spirit, it wishes them away.

All of which serves only to confirm the Kael line, and to
demonstrate that you can fool all of the people all of the time. The
lies perpetuated by Wise's film range from the personal—the real
Maria Von Trapp, for instance, looked nothing like Julie Andrews
and an awful lot like Nice Guy Eddie from "Reservoir Dogs"—to
the broadly historical. If the Nazis' worst crime had indeed been to
hang swastikas over people's doorways, the twentieth century
would have been somewhat easier to bear. I was a sucker for such
untruths; my family even travelled to Salzburg in order to haunt
the byways where Julie Andrews had made so ringingly clear what
the first three notes just happened to be. Being below critical age,
I did not yet grasp the criteria by which a film could be adjudged
good or bad, much less the procedures by which it arrived
onscreen. If you had explained that the screenplay for "The Sound
of Music" came from the pen of one Ernest Lehman, who had

written "North by Northwest" and "Sweet Smell of Success," this bewildering detail would have been lost on me.

To be fair, even some of his friends had trouble taking it in. When Burt Lancaster ran into Lehman at the Fox commissary and learned what he was working on, he said, "Jesus, you must need the money." That story comes from Julia Antopol Hirsch's "The Sound of Music: The Making of America's Favorite Movie," a loving compendium of arcana. Here we learn, for instance, that both Walter Matthau and Sean (Edelweish) Connery were considered for the role of the captain. A more damning fact is that some of the Osmond boys turned up to audition, thus demonstrating that, however much "The Sound of Music" makes your flesh crawl, it could have been so much worse.

You could argue that the triumphal saga of the Von Trapp family was so sweetly outlandish that any dramatic representation of it was doomed to rot the teeth. But consider another family, the Smiths of Missouri—equally close, no less pure of heart, and, like the Von Trapps, given to bursting into song at the slightest provocation. So why does "Meet Me in St. Louis" maintain the status of a nimble masterpiece, while "The Sound of Music" limps along behind? Then again, how come Vincente Minnelli's picture of 1944 was reckoned merely a success, while Robert Wise's picture, made twenty years later, is a gold-plated phenomenon? The answer to both questions is the same: because Minnelli showed happiness to be the most fragile of possessions, whereas Wise backed it as a sure thing. For all the highs and lows of its melodrama, "The Sound of Music" never dreams that there is any way but up, whether you are ascending a scale or an alp; and that, today and forever, is what moviegoers want to hear. "From now on, our troubles will be out of sight," Judy Garland sings near the end of "Meet Me in St. Louis," but the throb and catch in her voice give the lie to such game hope, and, by the penultimate line of the number, the message is decidedly mixed: "We'll have to muddle through somehow." Julie Andrews, by comparison, is a muddle-free zone: "I have confidence in confidence alone; Besides which, you see, I have confidence in me!"

Garland was singing during the Second World War, of course, when a certain lyrical worry was inevitable. Andrews hit her stride in the midst of the Cold War; the whole of "The Sound of Music" can perhaps be read as the artistic equivalent of antifreeze. It offered one of the last breaths of innocence in American cinema—after all, the same year saw female nudity in "The Pawnbroker," and "Bonnie and Clyde" was only two years away. That is why we go back to Wise's film; we all know better now, but most of us secretly wish that we didn't. The atmosphere at the Prince Charles, during "Singalong-a-Sound-of-Music," was strangely unmock-ing, even in its coarsest moments. We assume that deconstruction is a heartless business, in which the vengeful ironist strips the decorous past to its underclothes; but the hoarse crowd that streamed out into Leicester Square seemed to have drawn strength from a communal act of fond consolidation. When they cried at "Edelweiss," it was not because the song is, in itself, anything more than slush; it was because they had cried at it in 1965.

Film, in other words, has revivified the Proustian principle that memory is not ours to command; that, for all our searchings and suppressings, the past comes unbidden or not at all. If, for millions of people, that past consists of a lonely goatherd on strings, so be it. Proust himself was more fortunate; for him, a typical throw-back consisted of tripping over a paving stone and suddenly recalling a similar stumble in Venice. Few of us can rely on such tasteful apparitions. It is generally agreed, for example, that the last Golden Age of cinema occurred in the mid-seventies—the epoch of "The Godfather," "Chinatown," and "McCabe and Mrs. Miller." I feel privileged to have been there; unfortunately, I spent my pocket money on tickets for "Zeppelin," "Earthquake," and "Rollercoaster" (in Sensurround). I now realize that "Chinatown" is a great picture and that "The Towering Inferno" is dreck; but the sight of a weary, begrimed Steve McQueen emerging from the tower is burned into my mind with a fierceness that Jack Nicholson, with his nicked nostril, can never match. I missed the Golden Age; catching up later was an education, but nothing I can do will bring it back.

What we feel about a movie—or, indeed, about any work of art, high or low—matters less than the rise and fall of our feelings over time. The "King Lear" that we see as sons and daughters (of Cordelia's age, say) can never be the same play that we attend as parents; the sound of paternal fury, and of the mortal fears that echo beyond it, will knock ever more insistently at our hearts. Weekly critics cannot do justice to that process; when we are asked to nominate favorite films, all we can say is "Well, just now I quite like 'Citizen Kane' or 'Police Academy 4,' but ask me again next year." By then we will have grown, by a small but significant slippage, into someone else, and we have yet to know who that person will be, or what friable convictions he or she will hold. The revellers at the Prince Charles Cinema were all in their thirties and forties; no one younger than us would have had the remotest clue what we were doing there, or why we were having such fun. Even our younger selves, of ten years ago, would probably have been mystified, if not humiliated, by the air of semi-delirium that prevailed; how could consenting adults join forces to declare their love for a bad film? Time, as ever, has played its comic trick, and all I can do is adapt the words of Captain Von Trapp and his lovely governess: somewhere in our youth or childhood, we must have seen something good.

Outside

FINALIST, ESSAYS

Skating Home Backward

At first, all writer Bill Vaughn wants to do is clean a badly polluted pond in his backyard. The essay begins casually, as if it were a tossed-off personal reflection; by the end, it's an unguarded revelation of the author's obsessive personality. But Vaughn retains his piquant humor to the last, when he unveils the clear, smooth, ice pond on which he and his family can skate backward in the moonlight, attempting to reverse the flow of time.

Bill Vaughn

Skating Home Backward

How one man transformed a vile, polluted, dank little swamp into the perfect glassy ice pond. A wetland restoration comedy.

While other men spend their power decades harvesting money for their golden years, I've devoted the prime of my life to a swamp. And not even a real swamp, not some righteous nightmare of cottonmouths and feral pigs, but a mere back water, a slough, really, that meanders through our place in western Montana, rising and falling with the Clark Fork River nearby. In the summer the main channel of this marsh oozes sweet and fragrant between its walls of red dogwood and offers an array of refreshing temperatures as you plunge deeper to flee horseflies and the heat. Around Halloween it freezes. Then, with the vigilance of a patriarch whose family business is on the verge of going public, I stand guard over this ice till it melts in April, plowing off the snow, sealing the cracks, polishing its surface in the quest for a kind of perfection that's just not possible anywhere else, at least not for me. And when it *is* perfect and my skates sigh across its water-colored sheen, I can almost convince myself that everything's going to be all right.

When my wife Kitty and I moved into Dark Acres, our slough lay concealed under a midden of agricultural squalor. The ranch family that sold us a slice of its empire, huddled in the shadows of Black Mountain, had used this wetland for three generations as its own private dump. When you looked at its main channel you expected water; what you saw was junk and decay. But since we had the river to play in and didn't need no redneck swimmin' pool, we figured to bury this eyesore with fill. Maybe even install a nice tennis court on top.

But one morning during our first spring, I was drawn from the house by the hysterical barking of Radish, our red heeler. I supposed the racket was about an insubordinate magpie or a treed cat. But the thing making the dog insane turned out to be a western painted turtle. The size of *Atlas Shrugged*, she'd withdrawn into her shell to wait for all the gnashing to go away. Behind her in a sandy depression glistened four leathery white eggs. The turtle must have wandered away from the river, I guessed, or one of our mosquito havens, and lost her bearings. After a while four clawed feet emerged from the shell, then an ancient head in yellow and green and red. Radish growled and the hair on the ridge of his spine stood up like a mohawk. I put my arm around him. *There and so and well,* I said, reciting the mantra that always calms him down. The turtle waddled down the bank of the slough, out onto a rotten railroad tie through an obstacle course of brambles and beer cans, and, to my surprise, vanished with a wet slap, proving that this water was still alive. I pulled sand over her eggs with the toe of my boot.

It took me three years to clean the slough. I went after the lightest stuff first, standing on the banks to wrestle things from the tangle with a rake. Then, surrendering to the inevitable, I waded chest-deep across an uncertain bed to extract what I couldn't reach from shore. What refused to come to hand I fished out with a chain hooked to my old pickup. Each month more water opened to the sun. This progress, satisfying in ways I wouldn't understand until later, had no immediate reward beyond the fact that it was progress.

When this first stage was finished, I took inventory: 289 tires, a tractor, two riding plows, a ton of farm implement parts and horse tack and barbed wire and rotten hay, a heap of dolls, a medley of overstuffed furniture, the carcass of a Hereford, the skeleton of a beaver, and much festive plastic jetsam. Then there were endless chunks of timber washed from the forest floor into the slough when the river flooded once a decade. As it dried I reduced it with a chainsaw and stacked it into pyres. The night the Blue Jays beat the Phillies in the World Series I went around with a can of gasoline. The neighbors must have thought I was some kind of Canuck. The fires were still smoldering three days later.

Soon, some of the slough's former tenants began to return. A mated pair of mallards came first, winging around till they finally landed in the skinny stretch of water I'd opened. Then came a school of tiny black fish, a spotted frog, and a muskrat, only his nose breaking the surface to leave a hallucinogenic wake. Once I surprised a great blue heron standing on a log, one leg tucked as it eyeballed the place for snacks. It issued an indignant squawk so loud it made my heart flutter.

I was close to being finished with the restoration. Only a half-dozen cottonwood trunks were still floating around in the slough, and they were so massive the pickup couldn't pull them ashore. Standing in the water, working like a tug, I maneuvered these hundred-foot behemoths against the banks and anchored them to the brush with yellow rope while Radish took rides on their backs.

The next day I rose from bed creaking as if I'd been gang-tackled by the Oakland Raiders and made my way down to the slough with coffee and a lawn chair. For the first time since I'd discovered it, I intended to sit by this water without feeling the neurotic obsession to make it better. And, in fact, it could no longer be made better. There wasn't even a stray leaf to mar its seamless length. The hideous reek of rotten hay that had greeted us when we moved in had been replaced with a perfume of pennyroyal and wild roses. I counted 29 turtles that had climbed onto my cotton-wood trunks to take the morning sun.

Since the act of cleaning the swamp had also restored its health, I named it the Mabel, after my mother's mother. When she worked as a public health nurse in the fifties, one of Mabel's stops was a squatter's camp on Hill 57 above the outskirts of Great Falls, Montana, my hometown. Her patients were Blackfeet and Cree who weren't welcome on the reservations or wouldn't live there. Sometimes when I drift around in my rowboat or sit in the broadgrass to absorb the Mabel's serenity, I'm reminded of my grandmother. I remember the photographs she loved to take, hanging on the walls of the house my grandfather built. Most of these pictures, which won blue ribbons at the state fair, were portraits of the denizens of Hill 57. One was of a woman so old she could recount scenes from the Indian wars. I used to get mesmerized by that face, by the depth of the wrinkles and their number, an infinite criss-crossing of lines that mimicked the pattern of game paths after a rain. And next to this picture was one of a landscape that captured a creek in a cold snap radiating mist as it cut its way through fresh snow. It was the purity of this scene that appealed to me then—and that still appeals to me, a summation of my earliest Montana memories, a place sweetly indifferent to the camera, innocent and absent of malice.

.　　.　　.

On a frozen Sunday when I was ten, I stood in my pj's decorated with rearing stallions and glared with contempt at the church clothes I'd flung on my bed. Here were wool slacks, a starched white shirt, a bow tie, a checkered sport coat, a pair of oxfords, and a ludicrous black fedora.

"Jesus fucking Christ!" my old man suddenly bellowed. When I opened my bedroom door and looked around the house, I discovered it was empty. Dad had disappeared, and so had my six-year-old sister, Laura. The back door had been thrown open, admitting a wall of frigid air, so I went there to see what I could see. And what I saw left me utterly bewildered. There was the old man, butt-naked, his breath rising in angry clouds, charging down the snowy slope behind the house to Sand Coulee Creek, a ribbon of wind-polished ice winding through the shabby rural sprawl we called Rat Flats. I wrapped my arms around my bony self and stared.

When he got to the creek he fell to his knees and skittered across it like a fugitive in a prison flick. Had he caught on fire like those people you read about who suddenly burst into flames? Was he drunk?

Then I saw the hole, a devious blue crease. Suddenly uncoiling, he plunged his arm into it, his 225 pounds of muscle and sinew straining as he groped for something within. The air stunk of smoke from the coal furnaces everyone used. Danny, our Labrador, was out on the ice too, barking at the crease the same way he did when he trapped prairie rattlers against the chicken coop.

Dad lunged twice and brought forth a steaming thing in a fleecy blue snowsuit. Although I had begun to sense the importance of what was taking place, I had only one reference for what I was seeing: the breech birth of a neighbor's horse I witnessed that ended well when the man reached into the mare and yanked her astounded foal into the world. What Dad was now rushing back to the house wasn't a foal, of course. It was Laura. As he strode by, the sodden little doofus yowling in his arms, one of her skates trailing a lace, I saw that his face was lathered with shaving cream. Laura had disobeyed the rule about skating alone and was saved only because the old man happened to glance through the bathroom window as she crashed through the ice.

The next day I lay beside the crease and studied its architecture, fascinated by the fact that the ice had become as dangerous as it was fun. In the summer, the Sand Coulee was a simple, good-natured yokel whose water was clean enough to drink and harbored sunfish, crawdads, and even the occasional trout. We dropped into it every day from a tire swing roped to a box elder and poled around in it on our rafts and constructed elaborate mud cities on its shores.

In the winter, the creek became a different sort of sanctuary. It was a snap to skate the 300 yards from our place to the lagoon where the Missouri accepted the stream, but what I yearned to do was skate to the creek's headwaters, where I would live in tree houses and steal chickens from ranches. It wasn't just the easy pleasure of forward motion that seduced me when I took to the ice, but also the chance to escape all the unpredictable emotional weather back at the house. Yet I never got farther upstream than three miles. When I was old enough to mount a serious quest, it was too late. The creek began running the color of old blood, poisoned by acids and heavy metals leached from the coal mines. The frogs and the fish disappeared first, and finally the turtles. And then it dried up.

.   .   .

Instant snow removal is the key to perfect ice. This is a fact of winter in western Montana that I learned the hard way. I'd been spoiled as a boy by wind that whistled across the Sand Coulee so incessantly snow just didn't have the chance to pile up. But here on the Pacific side of the Continental Divide, wet, balmy fronts slug it out all winter with arctic air pushing south from Canada. Midnight rain can give way to two feet of morning powder the afternoon sun reduces to slush, which freezes by midnight. After hissy, pathetic gusts announce a front moving in, all this weather usually happens in a dead calm.

There is even the odd season when most ice doesn't thicken enough to skate on. That's never the case, however, with the Mabel. Its bed is insulated by the brush that surrounds it, like a beer cooler, so once it freezes it seems to absorb more cold and freeze even deeper. Snow left to melt on the surface of the slough will eventually freeze as well, causing leprous disfigurements—welts and pits and hedgerows, or the crumbly, porous stuff we call Crackers, or even the bulbous, lumpy outrage called Casserole. The object of snow management is Glaze, that flawless, diaphanous glass that can only be laid down when rain or thaw is followed by a hard freeze. Or when I can summon the energy to flood the ice from a hole I've chopped.

Of course, I knew none of this the day the restored Mabel was finally frozen and ready for business. I thought I was ready too. It had been three decades, but I was convinced that skating was as indelible a muscle memory as riding a horse. For a week the weather had been clear and sharp, with subfreezing lows and small melts in the afternoons. I put on knee pads and went down to the Mabel with a pair of old hockey skates bandaged with duct tape. I laid the skates on my lawn chair and walked onto the ice in my rubber pig-farmer boots with the sort of mincing steps you'd employ on a ledge. Radish cocked his head like a bird and pawed at the hard thing his swimming hole had become. As usual, he started barking. After I'd gone a few steps there was a groan as the Mabel adjusted to my weight and a rumbling crack that echoed back from the Bitterroot Range on the other side of the river. But after this scare I walked the length of my ice without incident, and then back, looking for devious blue creases. What I did find was Glaze nine inches thick. My pulse was racing. There was no longer any excuse to put it off.

I laced my skates and stepped forth with ankles wobbling and feet that felt bound. From the start there was forward motion, halting at first, no faster than a runaway Rascal in a nursing home hallway, but velocity that increased as I gained confidence. Then it all came back: the angle of the stroke, the bent knees and stooped posture, the gliding rhythm. A neighbor doing breakfast dishes in her trailer looked up, startled to see someone in the backyard. Or maybe what alarmed her was the sight of a middle-aged man on skates. Her husband was off sleepwalking through a 12-hour shift at the paper mill. I waved, happy to be here instead of there.

I tried some backward skating, which I had begun to learn as a kid because not knowing how put you at a disadvantage in hockey. But when my feet nearly went out from under me, I decided I wasn't ready yet for anything in reverse. Plowing ahead, I skated six laps, about three miles, and then stumbled over to my chair, winded. My ankles would no longer support me. Sweat rolled down my spine. I whispered to my thudding heart, *Whoa, there, big fella.*

I woke up the next morning to discover that a foot of wet snow had fallen overnight, with a ton more still coming down. In the Jungle, a four-acre briar patch between the Mabel and the river, the fireberry hawthorns were bent double under the weight. I didn't worry about the effect of the blizzard on the Mabel because I didn't know enough yet to worry. And besides, my feet were too sore to skate anyway. But when I walked down that afternoon to admire my fine green Glaze again, I was horrified to discover that not only had the snow not been blown away as it always was on the Sand Coulee, but the weight of it had fractured the ice and flooded the snow. That night the temperature dropped to zero. Next morning my Mabel was ridged and pocked and zitted, worthless to anyone except the whitetails that crossed it to get from the forest to our haystack. But by the end of the week a warm rain smoothed the Mabel's skin, and when the temperatures dropped again my beautiful Glaze was back.

.　　.　　.

The next time it snowed I was all over the Mabel at once with a shovel. I soon gave up the notion that I could clean off a quarter-mile of ice by hand, but after a couple of hours I had opened enough to skate laps. Then the shovel broke. Kitty came down once to watch me sweat and steam in the sun.

"I'm training for the Elfstedentocht," I gasped.

"Say again?"

"The skating race in Holland. You know, from city to city."

At dinner I looked up from my corn bread to find her staring at me. "What."

"So you're going to waste all morning every time it snows?"

"Waste?" I said, patting my belly. "Yuppie scum pay good money for this kind of workout."

"Then why don't you shovel the driveway?"

Of course, fitness had nothing to do with it. But I couldn't explain the emancipation I felt when I skated on the Mabel, because I didn't understand it myself. I hoped its source was something profound, and not just a cliché: I was taking up juvenile sports in order to ward off the implications of my approaching 50th birthday and its promise of the desiccation to come; or I just wanted to feel again the breathless ardor a child feels as the game begins; or I was bored with the unfinished man I'd become and had fallen in love with the happy boy I now believed I had been. I figured it wouldn't take much of a shrink to identify the disenchantment with adult life underlying my affair with the Mabel and my reawakened love of skating, but where would that get me?

I'd still have to clear off the ice. The solution, I realized, was way more cost-effective than therapy: Sears.

I found the snowblowers lined up like an armada of fighter planes. They ranged from a bantamweight with 3.8 horsepower to a ten horsepower gangster.

"What is it, sir, you are having to blow?"

I knew this voice instantly. When I turned around there he was, my favorite Bengali salesman. The birdsong of his accent wasn't any more Americanized than it had been when he'd sold me a clothes dryer a year earlier. ("You cannot go wrong, sir, with the Wrinkle Guard feature," he had promised.)

"Well, there's a patio," I said.

The salesman patted the baby bear model. "Very adequate for such a task."

"And a driveway. A long one."

He pointed to the mama bear version. "Five horsepower and many choices of blowing angles."

"And a quarter-mile of ice."

"Oh, my."

"For skating."

His eyebrows lifted and a smile of good fortune spread over his face as he slid the edge of one hand across the palm of the other.

In the end, of course, I went home with the papa bear model and two attachments. I knew Kitty would hit the roof, so I picked up a bribe. When she lifted the white figure skates from their box I saw that she'd been expecting something made of silk instead.

"What did you really buy?"

"A snow thing."

"You mean another shovel?"

"Not exactly."

I led her out to the pickup and my glowering new machine.

"If it keeps snowing like this we're going to need something to dig us out," I reasoned. I could see that this shot connected. In fact, we'd already been trapped once that winter and had had to hire a neighbor to plow the driveway.

When she asked the price, my answer was only 20 percent false. Her mouth fell open.

"Hey, I'll do the road right now," I offered. The snow was beginning to fall again.

The papa bear sucked up the six inches of dry powder on our driveway like a crackhead in a coke factory and then sprayed it contemptuously into a pasture. An hour later a raisin-colored overcast moved in, and the snow turned wet. I abandoned the driveway and hurried down to the Mabel to set loose the beast before my newest layer of Glaze was compromised. Things went like clockwork at first, but as the afternoon grew warmer the threads that stripped the snow from the ice and hurled it through the blower got clogged with slush. I cleaned them as best I could with a stick. Finally, blubbering and whining, the papa bear— triumph of American technology—just gave up. The ice I couldn't liberate began to sink under the weight of what would be a record snowfall.

By noon I was able to clear a path along the driveway for the pickup. Even in four-wheel-drive I barely made it out. When I pushed the papa bear through the doors at Sears, my salesman saw me and hurried over, stricken. Snowblowers just don't seem to work very well against wet snow, I told him, though they are dynamite with powder. His eyes were liquid and sorrowful but totally uncomprehending. Then I felt a force at my back and turned around. Sears had fallen silent and dreamy and, except for one section of floor space, completely dark. And in that space, glowing with menace, was a column of riding mowers fitted with snow plows.

Look away, I told myself.

.　　.　　.

The following spring a black bear moved into the Jungle, attracted by its maze of hiding places and its wild raspberries. We saw him from time to time when he made his way from the vineries to drink from the Mabel. The horses would bolt in their pens, wide-eyed and snorting, but they soon grew used to bear-smell, and peace returned. I built a dock and spent the first hot afternoon of May throwing pebbles into the water for Radish to chase, an easy way to scour off the beggar's-lice he had gotten into. Then I jumped in myself for the helpless flailing I call swimming.

The Mabel froze early that fall. I fell twice trying to get down my strokes for skating backward, and my knee swelled up like a bag of microwave popcorn. After it healed I picked dead leaves off the ice every morning before they could absorb the sun and melt holes in the shape of themselves. Near Thanksgiving the heavens opened and a foot of perfect powder fell down. I thought: Snow, you bastard. I am no longer your slave.

Pheasants exploded into the air and dogs howled when I revved up my 15.5-horsepower Sears Craftsman riding mower with its automatic transmission and its Kohler Command engine and its four-foot snowplow. After I made quick work of the driveway, which pleased Kitty, I rumbled down the bank and onto the Mabel, the chains on the weighted back tires clattering ominously. In a half hour I was done. The Mabel sparkled.

The next day we had a hockey game. A dance professor accidentally smacked a crime reporter in the face with her stick and broke his nose. Radish rushed to lick the blood from the ice, rolling his eyes in pleasure.

During the holidays a horde of in-laws forgathered at Dark Acres to play cards and gossip about horses. On Christmas Eve, under a bone moon, we lit a bonfire and took to the ice for an hour of sport before our nightly games of pitch and boo-ray. Kitty looked dreamy as she sailed across the ice in her new skates. The kids sped around, hissing at the adults and pulling at Kitty's mother, whose knee pads and elbow pads and Carhartt coveralls made her look like the Michelin Man's wife.

When everyone else tired I decided to take one last spin alone. It was time. I glided to the far end of the Mabel, Radish at my side. Then, as the moon cast my shadow before me, I skated home backward.

Rolling Stone

FINALIST, REPORTING

In the Jungle

In this extraordinary story, Rian Malan "follows the money" to the origin of one of America's classic pop songs, "The Lion Sleeps Tonight." The trail, from the corridors of the American music industry to the ghettos of Johannesburg, leads to an obscure Zulu singer who earned almost nothing from a song that might have brought him an estimated $15 million in royalties. In the end, Malan's reporting helps rectify the wrong, as royalties finally begin to flow to the late songwriter's destitute family.

Rian Malan

In the Jungle

It is one of the great musical mysteries of all time: how American music legends made millions off the work of a Zulu tribesman who died a pauper. After six decades, the truth is finally told.

Once upon a time, a long time ago, a small miracle took place in the brain of a man named Solomon Linda. It was 1939, and he was standing in front of a microphone in the only recording studio in black Africa when it happened. He hadn't composed the melody or written it down or anything. He just opened his mouth and out it came, a haunting skein of fifteen notes that flowed down the wires and into a trembling stylus that cut tiny grooves into a spinning block of beeswax, which was taken to England and turned into a record that became a very big hit in that part of Africa.

Later, the song took flight and landed in America, where it mutated into a truly immortal pop epiphany that soared to the top of the charts here and then everywhere, again and again, return-ing every decade or so under different names and guises. Navajo Indians sing it at powwows. The French favor a version sung in Congolese. Phish perform it live. It has been recorded by artists as diverse as R.E.M. and Glen Campbell, Brian Eno and Chet Atkins, the Nylons and Muzak schlockmeister Bert Kaempfert. The New Zealand army band turned it into a march. England's 1986 World Cup soccer squad turned it into a joke. Hollywood put it in *Ace Ventura: Pet Detective*. It has logged nearly three centuries' worth of continuous radio airplay in the U.S. alone. It is the most famous melody ever to emerge from Africa, a tune that has penetrated so deep into the human consciousness over so many generations that one can truly say, here is a song the whole world knows.

Its epic transcultural saga is also, in a way, the story of popular music, which limped, pale-skinned and anemic, into the twenti-eth century but danced out the other side vastly invigorated by transfusions of ragtime and rap, jazz, blues and soul, all of whose bloodlines run back to Africa via slave ships and plantations and ghettos. It was in the nature of this transaction that black men gave more than they got and often ended up with nothing.

This one's for Solomon Linda, then, a Zulu who wrote a melody that earned untold millions for white men but died so poor that his widow couldn't afford a stone for his grave. Let's take it from the top, as they say in the trade.

PART I:
A story about music

This is an African yarn, but it begins with an unlikely friendship between an aristocratic British imperialist and a world-famous American Negro. Sir Henry Brougham Loch is a rising star of the British Colonial Office. Orpheus McAdoo is leader of the celebrated Virginia Jubilee Singers, a combo that specializes in syncopated spirituals. They meet during McAdoo's triumphant tour of Australia in the 1880s, and when Sir Henry becomes governor of the Cape Colony a few years later, it occurs to him that Orpheus might find it interesting to visit. Next thing, McAdoo and his troupe are on the road in South Africa, playing to slack-jawed crowds in dusty villages and mining towns.

This American music is a revelation to "civilized natives," hitherto forced to wear starched collars and sing horrible dirges under the direction of dour white missionaries. Mr. McAdoo is a stern old Bible thumper, to be sure, but there's a subversively rhythmic intensity in his music, a primordial stirring of funk and soul. The African brothers have never heard such a thing. The tour turns into a five-year epic. Wherever Orpheus goes, "jubilee" music outfits spring up in his wake; eventually, they penetrate even the loneliest outposts of civilization.

One such place is Gordon Memorial School, perched on the rim of a wild valley called Msinga, which lies in the Zulu heartland, about 300 miles southeast of Johannesburg. Among the half-naked herd boys who drift through the mission is a rangy kid named Solomon Linda, born 1909, who gets into the Orpheus-inspired syncopation thing and works bits of it into the Zulu songs he and his friends sing at weddings and feasts.

In the mid-thirties they shake off the dust and cow shit and take the train to Johannesburg, city of gold, where they move into the slums and become kitchen boys and factory hands. Life is initially very perplexing. Solly keeps his eyes open and transmutes what he sees into songs that he and his homeboys perform a cappella on weekends. He has songs about work, songs about crime, songs about how banks rob you by giving you paper in exchange for real money, songs about how rudely the whites treat you when you go to get your pass stamped. People like the music. Solly and his friends develop a following. Within two years they turn themselves into a very cool urban act that wears pinstriped suits, bowler hats and dandy, two-tone shoes. They become Solomon Linda and the Evening Birds, inventors of a music that will later become known as *isicathamiya*, arising from the warning cry *"Cothoza, bafana"*—"Tread carefully, boys."

These were Zulus, you see, and their traditional dancing was punctuated by mighty foot stompings that, when done in unison, quite literally made the earth tremble. This was fine in the bush, but if you stomped the same way in town, you smashed wooden floors, cracked cement and sometimes broke your feet, so the whole dance had to be restrained and moderated. Cognoscenti will recall Ladysmith Black Mambazo's feline and curiously fastidious movements onstage. That's treading carefully.

In any event, there were legions of careful treaders in South Africa's cities, usually Zulu migrants whose Saturday nights were devoted to epic, beer-fueled bacchanalias known as "tea meetings." These were part fashion show and part heroic contest between rival a cappella gladiators, often with a stray white man pulled off the street to act as judge and a cow or goat as first prize. The local black bourgeoisie was mortified by these antics. Careful treaders were an embarrassment, widely decried for their "primitive" bawling and backward lyrics, which dwelled on such things as witchcraft, crime and using love potions to get girls. The groups had names like the Naughty Boys or the Boiling Waters, and when World War II broke out, some started calling themselves " 'mbombers," after the divebombing Stukas they'd seen on newsreels. 'Mbombers were by far the coolest and most dangerous black thing of their time.

Yes! Dangerous! Skeptics are referred to "Ngazula Emagumeni" (on Rounder CD 5025), an early Evening Birds track whose brain-rattling intensity thoroughly guts anyone who thinks of a cappella songs as smooth tunes for mellow people. The wild, rocking sound came from doubling the bass voices and pumping up their volume, an innovation that was largely Solomon's, along with the high style and the new dance moves. He was the Elvis Presley of his time and place, a shy, gangly thirty-year-old, so tall that he had to stoop as he passed through doorways. It's odd to imagine him singing soprano, but that was usually his gig in the group: He was the leader, the "controller," singing what Zulus called *fasi pathi*, a blood-curdling falsetto that a white man might render as first part.

The Evening Birds were spotted by a talent scout in 1938 and taken to an office building in downtown Jo'burg. There they saw the first recording studio in sub-Saharan Africa, shipped over from England by Eric Gallo, a jovial Italian who started in the music business by selling American hillbilly records to working-class Boers. Before long he bought his own recording machine and started churning out those Dust Bowl ditties in local languages, first Afrikaans, then Zulu, Xhosa and what have you. His ally in this experiment was Griffith Motsieloa, the country's first black producer, a slightly stiff and formal chap whose true interests were classical music and eisteddfods, in which polished African gentlemen entertained one another with speeches in highfalutin king's English. Motsieloa was appalled by the boss's cultural slumming, but what could he do? Gallo was determined to sell records to blacks. When Afro-hillbilly failed to catch on, they decided to take a chance on some *isicathamiya*.

Solomon Linda and the Evening Birds cut several songs under Motsieloa's direction, but the one we're interested in was called "Mbube," Zulu for "the lion," recorded at their second session, in 1939. It was a simple three-chord ditty with lyrics something along the lines of "Lion! Ha! You're a lion!" inspired by an incident in the Birds' collective Zulu boyhood when they chased lions that were stalking their fathers' cattle. The first take was a dud, as was the second. Exasperated, Motsieloa looked into the corridor, dragooned a pianist, guitarist and banjo player, and tried again.

The third take almost collapsed at the outset as the unrehearsed musicians dithered and fished for the key, but once they started cooking, the song was glory bound. "Mbube" wasn't the most remarkable tune, but there was something terribly compelling about the underlying chant, a dense meshing of low male voices above which Solomon howled and scatted for two exhilarating minutes, occasionally making it up as he went along. The third take was the great one, but it achieved immortality only in its dying seconds, when Solly took a deep breath, opened his mouth and improvised the melody that the world now associates with the words:

In the jungle, the mighty jungle, the lion sleeps tonight.

Griffith Motsieloa must have realized he'd captured something special, because that chunk of beeswax was shipped all the way to England and shipped back in the form of ten-inch 78-rpm records, which went on sale just as Hitler invaded Poland. Marketing was tricky, because there was hardly any black radio in 1939, but the song went out on "the re-diffusion," a land line that pumped music, news and "native affairs" propaganda into black neighborhoods, and people began trickling into stores to ask for it. The trickle grew into a steady stream that just rolled on for years and years, necessitating so many re-pressings that the master disintegrated. By 1948, "Mbube" had sold in the region of 100,000 copies, and Solomon Linda was the undefeated and undefeatable champion of hostel singing competitions and a superstar in the world of Zulu migrants.

.   .   .

Pete Seeger, on the other hand, was in a rather bad way. He was a banjo player living in a cold-water flat on MacDougal Street, in Greenwich Village, with a wife, two young children and no money. Scion of wealthy New York radicals, he'd dropped out of Harvard ten years earlier and hit the road with his banjo on his back, learning hard-times songs for people in the Hoovervilles, lumber camps and coal mines of Depression America. In New York he joined a band with Woody Guthrie. They wore work shirts and jeans, and wrote folk songs that championed the downtrodden common man in his struggle against capitalist bloodsuckers. Woody had a slogan written on his guitar that read, "This machine kills fascists." Pete's banjo had a kinder, gentler variation: "This machine surrounds hate and forces it to surrender." He was a proto-hippie, save that he didn't smoke reefer or even drink beer.

He was also a pacifist, at least until Hitler invaded Russia. Scenting a capitalist plot to destroy the brave Soviet socialist experiment, Pete and Woody turned gung-ho overnight and started writing anti-Nazi war songs, an episode that made them briefly famous. After that, it was into uniform and off to the front for Pete, where he played the banjo for bored GIs. Discharged in '45, he returned to New York and got a gig of sorts in the public-school system, teaching toddlers to warble the half-forgotten folk songs of their American heritage. It wasn't particularly glorious, the money was rotten, and on top of that, he was sick in bed with a bad cold.

There came a knock on the door, and, lo, there stood his friend Alan Lomax, later to be hailed as the father of world music. Alan and his dad, John, were already famous for their song-collecting forays into the parallel universe of rural black America, where they'd discovered giants like Muddy Waters and Lead Belly. Alan was working for Decca, where he'd just rescued a package of 78s sent from Africa by a local record company in the vain hope that someone might want to release them in America. They were about to be thrown away when Lomax intervened, thinking, "God, Pete's the man for these."

And here they were: ten shellac 78s, one of which said "Mbube" on its label. Pete put it on his old Victrola and sat back. He was fascinated—there was a catchy chant and that wild, skirling falsetto was amazing.

"Golly," he said, "I can sing that." So he got out pen and paper and started transcribing the song, but he couldn't catch the words through all the hissing on the disc. The Zulus were chanting, *"Uyimbube, uyimbube,"* but to Pete it sounded like *awimboowee,* or maybe *awimoweh,* so that's how he wrote it down. Later he taught "Wimoweh" to the rest of his band, the Weavers, and it became, he says, "just about my favorite song to sing for the next forty years."

This was no great achievement, given that the Weavers' late-Forties repertoire was full of dreck like "On Top of Old Smoky" and "Greensleeves." Old Pete won't admit it, but one senses that he was growing tired of cold-water flats and work shirts, and wanted a proper career, as befitting a thirtysomething father of two. He landed a job in TV, but someone fingered him as a dangerous radical, and he lost it before it even started. After that, according to his biographer David King Dunaway, he fell into a funk that ended only when his band landed a gig at the Village Vanguard. Apparently determined to make the best possible impression, Pete allowed his wife to outfit the Weavers in matching blue corduroy jackets—a hitherto unimaginable concession to showbiz.

The pay was $200 a week, plus free hamburgers, and the booking was for two weeks only, but something unexpected happened: Crowds started coming. The gig was extended for a month, and then another. The Weavers' appeal was inexplicable to folk purists, who noted that most of their songs had been around forever, in obscure versions by blacks and rednecks who never had hits anywhere. What these critics failed to grasp was that Seeger and his comrades had managed to filter the stench of poverty and pig shit out of the proletarian music and make it wholesome and fun for Eisenhower-era squares. Six months passed, and the Weavers were still at the Vanguard, drawing sellout crowds, even the odd refugee from the swell supper clubs of Times Square.

One such figure was Gordon Jenkins, a sallow jazz cat with a gigolo's mustache and a matinee idol's greased-back hairstyle. Jenkins started out by arranging for Benny Goodman before scoring a hit in his own right with an appalling piece of crap, "I'm Forever Blowing Bubbles." Now he was arranging for Frank Sinatra and was also musical director at Decca Records. Jenkins loved the Weavers, returning night after night, sometimes sitting through two consecutive shows. He wanted to sign them up, but his bosses were dubious. It was only when Jenkins offered to pay for the recording sessions himself that Decca capitulated and gave the folkies a deal.

Their first recording came out in June 1950. It was "Goodnight Irene," an old love song they'd learned from their friend Lead Belly, and it was an immediate click, in the parlance of the day. The flip side was an Israeli hora called "Tzena, Tzena, Tzena," and it clicked too. So did "The Roving Kind," a nineteenth-century folk ditty they released that November, and even "On Top of Old Smoky," which hit Number Three the following spring. The Weavers leapt from amateur hootenannies to the stages of America's poshest nightspots and casinos. They wore suits and ties, Brylcreamed their hair, appeared on TV and pulled down two grand a week. Chagrined and envious, their former comrades on the left started sniping at them in magazines. "Can an all-white group sing songs from Negro culture?" asked one.

The answer, of course, lay in the song that Seeger called "Wimoweh." His version was faithful to the Zulu original in almost all respects save for his finger-popping rhythm, which was arguably a bit white for some tastes but not entirely offensive. The true test was in the singing, and here Seeger passed with flying colors, bawling and howling his heart out, tearing up his vocal cords so badly that by the time he reached age seventy-five, he was almost mute. "Wimoweh" was by far the edgiest song in the Weavers' set, which is perhaps why they waited a year after their big breakthrough before recording it.

Like their earlier recordings, it took place with Gordon Jenkins presiding and an orchestra in attendance. Prior to this, Jenkins had been very subdued in his instrumental approach, adding just the occasional sting and the odd swirl of strings to the Weavers' cheery singalongs. Maybe he was growing bored, because his arrangement of "Wimoweh" was a great Vegas-y explosion of big-band raunch that almost equaled the barbaric splendor of the Zulu original. Trombones blared. Trumpets screamed. Strings swooped and soared through Solomon's miracle melody. And then Pete cut loose with all that hollering and screaming. It was a revolutionary departure from everything else the Weavers had ever done, but *Billboard* loved it, anointing it a Pick of the Week. *Cash Box* said, "May easily break." *Variety* said, "Terrific!"

But around this time *Variety* also said, FIVE MORE H'WOODITES NAMED REDS AND CHAPLIN BEING INVESTIGATED. It was January 1952, and America was engaged in a frenzied hunt for Reds under beds. The House Un-American Affairs Committee was probing Hollywood. *Red Channels* had just published the names of artists with commie connections. And in Washington, D.C., one Harvey Matusow was talking to federal investigators.

Matusow was a weaselly little man who had once worked alongside Pete Seeger in People's Songs, a reddish organization that dispatched folk singers to entertain on picket lines and in union halls. He had undergone a change of heart and decided to tell all about his secret life in the communist underground. On February 6th, 1952, just as "Wimoweh" made its chart debut, he stepped up to a mike before HUAC and told one of the looniest tales of the entire McCarthy era. Evil reds, he said, were "preying on the sexual weakness of American youth" to lure recruits into their dreaded movement. What's more, he was willing to name names of Communist Party members, among them three Weavers—including Pete Seeger.

The yellow press went apeshit. Reporters called the Ohio club where the Weavers were scheduled to play that night, demanding to know why the Yankee Inn was providing succor to the enemy. The show was called off, and it was all downhill from there. Radio stations banned their records. TV appearances were canceled. "Wimoweh" plummeted from Number Six into oblivion. Nightclub owners wouldn't even talk to the Weavers' agents, and then Decca dropped them too. By the end of the year they'd packed it in, and Pete Seeger was back where he'd started, teaching folk songs to kids for a pittance.

.   .   .

So the Weavers were dead, but "Wimoweh" lived on, bewitching jazz ace Jimmy Dorsey, who covered it in 1952, and the sultry Yma Sumac, whose cocktail-lounge version caused a minor stir a few years later. Toward the end of the decade, it was included on *Live From the Hungry I*, a monstrously popular LP by the Kingston Trio that stayed on the charts for more than three years (178 weeks), peaking at Number Two. By now, almost everyone in America knew the basic refrain, so it should've come as no particular surprise to find four nice Jewish teenagers popping their fingers and going *ah-weem-oh-way, ah-weem-oh-way* in the summer of 1961.

The Tokens were clean-cut Brooklyn boys who had grown up listening to DJs Alan Freed and Murray the K, and the dreamy teen stylings of Dion and the Belmonts and the Everly Brothers. Hank Medress and Jay Siegel met at Lincoln High, where they sang in a doo-wop quartet that briefly featured Neil Sedaka. Phil Margo was a budding drummer and piano player, also from Lincoln High, and Mitch Margo was his kid brother, age fourteen. One presumes that girls were already casting eyes in their direction, because the Tokens had recently been on TV's *American Bandstand*, decked out in double-breasted mohair suits with white shirts and purple ties, singing their surprise Top Twenty hit, "Tonight I Fell in Love."

And now they were moving toward even greater things. Barely

out of high school, they landed a three-record deal with RCA Victor, with a $10,000 advance and a crack at working with Hugo Peretti and Luigi Creatore, ace producers for Sam Cooke, Frankie Lymon and many, many others. These guys worked with Elvis Presley, for God's sake. "This was big for us," says Phil Margo "Very big."

The Tokens knew "Wimoweh" through their lead singer, Jay, who'd learned it from an old Weavers album. It was one of the songs they'd sung when they auditioned for "Huge" and "Luge," as Peretti and Creatore were known in the trade. The producers said, "Yeah, well, there's something there, but what's it about?" "Eating lions," said the Tokens. That's what some joker at the South African consulate had told them, at any rate.

The producers presumably rolled their eyes. None of this got anyone anywhere in the era of "shooby doo" and so on. They wanted to revamp the song, give it some intelligible lyrics and a contemporary feel. They sent for one George David Weiss, a suave young dude in a navy-blue blazer, then making a big name for himself in grown-up music, writing orchestrations for Doris Day, Peggy Lee and others. The Tokens took him for a hopeless square until they discovered that he'd co-written "Can't Help Falling in Love With You" for Elvis Presley. That changed everything.

So George Weiss took "Wimoweh" home with him and gave it a careful listen. A civilized chap with a Juilliard degree, he didn't much like the primitive wailing, but the chant was OK, and parts of the melody were very catchy. So he dismantled the song, excised all the hollering and screaming, and put the rest back together in a new way. The chant remained unchanged, but the melody— Solomon Linda's miracle melody—moved to center stage, becoming the tune itself, to which the new words were sung: "In the jungle, the mighty jungle. . . ."

In years to come, Weiss was always a bit diffident about his revisions, describing them as "gimmicks," as if ashamed to be associated with so frothy a bit of pop nonsense. Token Phil Margo says that's because Weiss wrote nothing save thirty-three words of doggerel, but that's another lawsuit entirely. What concerns us here is the song's bloodline, and everyone agrees on that: "The Lion Sleeps Tonight" was a reworking of "Wimoweh," which was a copy of "Mbube." Solomon Linda was buried under several layers of pop-rock stylings, but you could still see him beneath the new song's slick surface, like a mastodon entombed in a block of clear ice.

The song was recorded live in RCA's Manhattan studios on July 21st, 1961, with an orchestra in attendance and some session players on guitar, drums and bass. The percussionist muted his timpani, seeking that authentic "jungle drum" sound. A moonlighting opera singer named Anita Darian practiced her scales. Conductor Sammy Lowe tapped his baton and off they went, three Tokens doing the wimowehs, while Jay Siegel took the lead with his pure falsetto and Darian swooped and dived in the high heavens, singing the haunting countermelodies that were one of the song's great glories. Three takes (again), a bit of overdubbing, and that was more or less that. Everyone went home, entirely blind as to what they'd accomplished. The Tokens had been mortified by the new lyrics, which struck them as un-teen and uncool. Hugo and Luigi were so casual that they did the final mix over the telephone, and RCA topped them all by issuing the song as the B side of a humdrum tune called "Tina," which sank like lead.

Weird, no? We're talking about a pop song so powerful that Brian Wilson had to pull off the road when he first heard it, totally overcome; a song that Carole King instantly pronounced "a motherfucker." But it might never have reached their ears if an obscure DJ named Dick Smith in Worcester, Massachusetts, hadn't flipped the Tokens' new turkey and given the B side a listen. Smith said, "Holy shit, this is great," or words to that effect, and so his station, WORC, put "The Lion Sleeps Tonight" on heavy rotation. The song broke out regionally, hit the national charts in November and reached Number One in four giant strides.

Within a month, a cover by someone named Karl Denver reached Number One in England, too. By April 1962 it was topping the charts almost everywhere and heading for immortality. Miriam Makeba sang her version at JFK's last birthday party, moments before Marilyn Monroe famously lisped, "Happy birthday, Mr. President." Apollo astronauts listened to it on the launchpads at Cape Canaveral, Florida. It was covered by the Springfields, the Spinners, the Tremeloes and Glen Campbell. In 1972 it returned to the charts, at Number Three, in a version by Robert John. Brian Eno recorded it a few years later.

In 1982 it was back at Number One in the U.K., this time performed by Tight Fit. R.E.M. did it, as did the Nylons and They Might Be Giants. Manu Dibango did a twist version. Some Germans turned it into heavy metal. A sample cropped up on a rap epic titled "Mash Up da Nation." Disney used the song in *The Lion King,* and then it got into the smash-hit theatrical production of the same title, currently playing to packed houses around the world. It's on the original Broadway cast recording, on dozens of kiddie CDs with cuddly lions on their covers and on an infinite variety of nostalgia compilations. It's more than sixty years old, and still it's everywhere.

What might all this represent in songwriter royalties and associated revenues? I put the question to lawyers in several countries, and they scratched their heads. Around 160 recordings of three versions? Fourteen movies? A half-dozen TV commercials and a hit play? Number Seven on Val Pak's semi-authoritative ranking of the most-beloved golden oldies, and ceaseless radio airplay in every corner of the planet? It was impossible to accurately calculate, to be sure, but no one blanched at $15 million. Some said $10 million, some said $20 million, but most felt that $15 million was in the ballpark.

Which raises an even more interesting question: What happened to all that loot?

PART II:
A story about money

"It was a wonderful experience," said Larry Richmond, hereditary president of the Richmond Organization. He was talking about his company's "wonderful efforts" to make sure that justice was done to Solomon Linda. Larry was in Manhattan, and I was in Johannesburg, where it was 2 A.M., so I said, "Hold it right there. I'll come see you." I hung up, started packing, and a few days later, I walked into TRO's HQ, a strangely quiet suite of offices on West Nineteenth Street.

The dusty old guitar in the waiting room was a relic of a long-gone era. Back in the Forties, when TRO was young, eager songwriters streamed in here to audition their wares for Larry's dad, Howie Richmond, the firm's founder. If he liked the songs, he'd sign 'em up, transcribe 'em and secure a copyright. Then he'd send song pluggers out to place the tunes with stars whose recordings would generate income for the composer and the publisher, too. At the same time, salesmen would be flogging the sheet music, while bean counters in the back office collected royalties and kept an eye out for unauthorized versions.

In its heyday, TRO was a music-publishing empire that spanned the globe, but it was forced into decline by the Seventies advent of savvy rock & roll accountants who advised clients to publish themselves, which was fairly easy and doubled their songwriting income, given that old-style publishers generally claimed fifty percent of royalties for their services. By 1999, TRO was little more than a crypt for fabulously valuable old copyrights, manned by a skeleton crew that licensed old songs for TV commercials and movies.

Larry Richmond was an amiable bloke in an open-necked shirt and beige slacks. We drank coffee and talked for an hour or two, mostly about social justice and TRO's commitment to the same. There were stories about Woody Guthrie and Pete Seeger, the famous radical troubadours in TRO's stable. There was a story about the hospital in India to which the Richmonds made generous donations. And finally, there were some elliptical remarks about Solomon Linda and TRO's noble attempts to make sure that he received his due. I was hoping Larry would give me a formal interview on the subject, but first I had to get some sleep. That was a mistake. By the time I'd recovered, he had retreated into the labyrinth of his voice-mail system, from which he would not emerge.

So there I was in New York, with no one to talk to. I called music lawyers and record companies, angling for appointments that failed to materialize. I wandered into *Billboard* magazine, where a veteran journalist warned that I was wasting my time trying to find out what any song had ever earned and where the money had gone. But I'd come a long way, so I kept looking and, eventually, figured some of it out.

The story begins in 1939, when Solomon Linda was visited by angels in black Africa's only recording studio. At the time, Jo'burg was a hick mining town where music deals were concluded according to trading principles as old as Moses: Record companies bought recordings for whatever they thought the music might be worth in the marketplace; stars generally got several guineas for a session, unknowns got almost nothing. No one got royalties, and copyright was unknown. Solomon Linda didn't even get a contract. He walked out of that session with about one pound cash in his pocket, and the music thereafter belonged to the record company, which had no further obligations to anyone. When "Mbube" became a local hit, the loot went to Eric Gallo, the playboy who owned the company. All Solomon Linda got was a menial job at the boss's packing plant, where he worked for the rest of his days.

When "Mbube" took flight and turned into the Weavers' hit "Wimoweh," Gallo could have made a fortune if he had played his cards right. Instead, he struck a deal with Howie Richmond, trading "Mbube" to TRO in return for the dubious privilege of administering "Wimoweh" in such bush territories as South Africa and Rhodesia. Control of Solomon Linda's destiny thus passed into the hands of Howie and his faithful sidekick, one Al Brackman.

Howie and Al shared an apartment in the Thirties, when they were ambitious young go-getters on Tin Pan Alley. Howie was tall and handsome, Al was short and fat, but otherwise, they were blood brothers with a passion for night life and big-band jazz. Following World War II, Howie worked as a song promoter before deciding to become a publisher in his own right. He says he found a catchy old music-hall number, had a pal write new lyrics and placed the song with Guy Lombardo, who took it to Number Ten as "Hop Scotch Polka." Howie was on his way. Al joined up in 1949, and together they put a whole slew of novelty songs on the hit parade. Then they moved into the burgeoning folk-music sector, where big opportunities were opening up for sharp guys with a shrewd understanding of copyright.

After all, what was a folk song? Who owned it? It was just out there, like a wild horse or a tract of virgin land on an unconquered continent. Fortune awaited the man bold enough to fill out the necessary forms and name himself as the composer of a new interpretation of some ancient tune like, say, "Greensleeves." A certain Jessie Cavanaugh did exactly that in the early Fifties, only it wasn't really Jessie at all—it was Howie Richmond under an alias. This was a common practice on Tin Pan Alley at the time, and it wasn't illegal or anything. The object was to claim writer's royalties on new versions of old songs that belonged to no one. The aliases may have been a way to avoid potential embarrassment, just in case word got out that Howard S. Richmond was presenting himself as the author of a madrigal from Shakespeare's day.

Much the same happened with "Frankie and Johnny," the hoary, old murder ballad, and "The Roving Kind." There's no way Al Brackman could really have written such songs, so when he filed royalty claims with the performing-rights society BMI, he attributed the compositions to Albert Stanton, a fictitious tune-smith who often worked closely with the imaginary Mr. Cavanaugh, penning such standards as "John Henry" and "Michael Row the Boat Ashore." Cavanaugh even claimed credit for a version of "Battle Hymn of the Republic," a feat eclipsed only by a certain Harold Leventhal, who copyrighted an obscure what-not later taken as India's national anthem.

Leventhal started out as a gofer for Irving Berlin and wound up promoting concerts for Bob Dylan, but in between, he developed a serious crush on the Weavers. In 1949, he showed up at the Village Vanguard with an old friend in tow—Pete Kameron, a suave charmer who was scouting around for an entree into showbiz. Leventhal performed some introductions, and Kameron became the Weavers' manager. Since all these men knew one another, it was natural that they should combine to take charge of the band's business affairs. Leventhal advised; Kameron handled bookings and tried to fend off the redbaiters. Howie and Al took on the publishing, arranging it so that Kameron owned a fifty percent stake. The Weavers sang the songs and cut the records, and together they sold around 4 million platters in eighteen months or so.

Toward the end of 1951, these men found themselves contemplating the fateful 78-rpm record from Africa and wondering exactly what manner of beast it could be. The label read "MBUBE," BY SOLOMON LINDA'S ORIGINAL EVENING BIRDS, but it had never been copyrighted. Anything not copyrighted was a wild horse, strictly speaking, and wild horses in the Weavers' repertoire were usually attributed to one Paul Campbell. The Weavers' version of "Hush Little Baby" was a Paul Campbell composition, for instance. The same was true of "Rock Island Line" and "Kisses Sweeter Than Wine," tunes the folkies had learned from Lead Belly at Village hoots and rewritten in their own style.

On the surface of things, Paul Campbell was thus one of the most successful songwriters of the era, but of course the name was just another alias used to claim royalties on reworked songs from the public domain. "Mbube" wasn't public domain at all, but it was the next best thing—an uncopyrighted song owned by an obscure foreign record label that had shown absolutely no interest in protecting Solomon Linda's rights as a writer. So the Zulu's song was tossed in among the Weavers' wild horses and released as "Wimoweh," by Paul Campbell.

As the song found its fans, money started rolling in. Every record sale triggered a mechanical royalty, every radio play counted as a performance—which also required payment—and there was always the hope that someone might take out a "sync license" to use the tune in a movie or a TV ad. Al, Howie and Kameron divided the standard publisher's fifty percent among themselves and distributed the other half to the writers—or in this case, the adapters: Pete Seeger and the Weavers. Solomon Linda was entitled to nothing.

This didn't sit well with Seeger, who openly acknowledged Solomon as the true author of "Wimoweh" and felt he should get the money. Indeed, Seeger had been hassling his publishers for months to find a way of paying the Zulu.

"Originally they were going to send the royalties to Gallo," Seeger recalled. "I said, 'Don't do that, because Linda won't get a penny.'" Anti-apartheid activists put Seeger in touch with a Johannesburg lawyer, who set forth into the forbidden townships to find Solomon Linda. Once contact was established, Seeger sent the Zulu a $1,000 check and instructed his publisher to do the same with all future payments.

He was still bragging about it fifty years later. "I never got author's royalties on 'Wimoweh,'" Seeger said. "Right from '51 or '52, I understood that the money was going to Linda. I assumed they were keeping the publisher's fifty percent and sending the rest."

Unfortunately, Solomon's family maintains that the money only arrived years later, and even then, it was nothing like the full writer's share Seeger was hoping to bestow. We'll revisit this conundrum in short order, but first, let's follow the further adventures of "Wimoweh," which fell into the hands of RCA producers Hugo and Luigi, by way of the Tokens, in the summer of 1961. In addition to being ace producers and buddies of Presley's, these men were wild-horse breakers of the very first rank. They'd put their brand on a whole herd of them—"Pop Goes the Weasel," "First Noel," you name it. They even had "Grand March From Aida," a smash hit for Giuseppe Verdi in the 1870s.

As seasoned pros, these guys would have checked out the "Wimoweh" composer of record, Paul Campbell, and discovered that the name was an alias and that his *oeuvre* consisted largely of folk songs from previous centuries. They seemingly leapt to the obvious conclusion: "Wimoweh" was based on an old African folk song that didn't belong to anyone. As such, it was fair game, so they summoned George Weiss, turned "Wimoweh" into "The Lion Sleeps Tonight" and sent it out into the world as a Weiss/Peretti/Creatore composition. They did exactly the same thing four months later with "The Click Song," a Xhosa tune popularized in America by Miriam Makeba: Weiss cooked up some more doggerel about jungle drums and lovelorn maidens, the Tokens sang it, and it landed in record stores as "B'wanina," another "composition" by the same trio.

But they had made a mistake. "The Click Song" was indeed a

wild horse that had been roaming Africa for centuries, but "Mbube" was an original: the subject of a U.S. copyright taken out by Gallo in '52 and subsequently traded to TRO in the "Wimoweh" deal. When "The Lion Sleeps Tonight" began playing on America's radios, Howie Richmond instantly recognized its bloodline and howled with outrage. He set his lawyers on the Tokens and their allies, and what could they say? It must have been deeply embarrassing, but what the heck—Howie was on first-name terms with Hugo and Luigi, and was deeply respectful of Weiss' lyrical talents. He would be willing to forget the whole thing—provided the publishing rights to "Lion" came back to him.

Within a week there was a letter on Howie's desk acknowledging infringement, and urgent settlement talks were underway. Why urgent? Because "The Lion Sleeps Tonight" was soaring up the charts, and the Weiss/Peretti/Creatore cabal would have been desperate to avoid a dispute that might abort its trajectory. This put Richmond and Brackman in a position to dictate almost any terms they pleased. They didn't have a contract with Solomon Linda, but there was nothing to prevent them from making demands on his behalf. They could even have forced Luigi, Hugo and Weiss to settle for a smaller adapters' cut and allocated everything else to the Zulu, but this probably would have soured an important business relationship. They weren't legally obliged to Solomon, and so they allowed the three men they were later to describe as "plagiarists" to walk away with 100 percent of the writer's royalties on a song that originated in Solomon Linda's brain.

And why not? It was no skin off their noses. TRO received the full fifty-percent publisher's cut. Huge and Luge and Weiss were happy. The only person who lost out was Solomon, who wasn't even mentioned in any document: The new copyright described "Lion" as "based on a song by Paul Campbell."

The paperwork was finalized on December 18th, 1961, just as

the song commenced its conquest of the world's hit parades. "The Lion Sleeps Tonight" was Number One in the States on Christmas Day and reached South Africa two months later, just in time to bring a wan smile to the face of a dying Solomon Linda. He'd been ailing since 1959, when he lost control of his bowels and collapsed onstage. Doctors diagnosed kidney disease, but his family suspected witchcraft.

If true, this would make Solomon a victim of his own success. Sure, he was nothing in the world of white men, but "Mbube" made him a legend in the Zulu subculture, and to be a legend among "the people of heaven" was a pretty fine destiny, in some respects. Strangers hailed him on the streets, bought him drinks in shebeens. He was in constant demand for personal appearances and earned enough to afford some sharp suits, a second bride and a windup gramophone for the kinfolk in mud huts back in Msinga.

A thousand bucks from Pete Seeger aside, most of his money came from those uproarious all-night song contests, which remain a vital part of urban Zulu social life to this day. Most weekends, Solly and the Evening Birds would hire a car and sally forth to do battle in distant towns, and they always came back victorious. Competitors tried everything, including potions, to make their voices hoarse and high like Solomon's, but nothing worked. The aging homeboys would take the stage and work themselves into such transports of ecstasy that tears streamed down Solly's face, at which point the audience would go wild and the Evening Birds would once again walk off with first prize—sometimes a trophy, sometimes money, sometimes a cow that they slaughtered, roasted and shared with their fans as the sun came up. Blinded by the adulation, Solomon wasn't particularly perturbed when his song mutated into "The Lion Sleeps Tonight" and raced to the top of the world's charts.

"He was happy," said his daughter Fildah. "He didn't know he was supposed to get something."

Fildah is Solomon's oldest surviving child, a radiant woman who wears beads in her hair and a goatskin bangle on her right wrist, the mark of a *sangoma*, or witch doctor. Her sister Elizabeth works as a nurse in a government clinic, but she announced, giggling, that she is a *sangoma* too. A third daughter, Delphi, had just had surgery for arthritis, but she was also, under her sisters' direction, using ancestral medicine—a plant called *umhlabelo*, apparently. Elizabeth thought a water snake might be useful, too, and wondered where she could obtain such a thing. Though they live in an urban slum, they are deeply Zulu people, down to the cattle horns on the roof above the kitchen door—relics of sacrifices to the spirits of their ancestors. Only Elizabeth spoke fluent English, but even she didn't flinch at the talk of witchcraft.

Their aunt Mrs. Beauty Madiba was the one who brought it up. A sweet old lady in her Sunday best, she remembered meeting Solomon in the late Forties, when he started to court her sister Regina. The singer was at the peak of his career then and had no trouble raising the ten cattle their father was asking as the bride price. The wedding feast took place in 1949, and Regina went to live in Johannesburg. Beauty joined her a few years later and had a ringside seat when Solomon was brought down by dark forces. "People were jealous, because all the time, he won," she explained. "They said, 'We will get you.' So they bewitched him."

Elizabeth muttered something about renal failure, but she agreed there was something odd about the way her father's disease refused to respond to treatment. He grew so sick that he had to stop singing. By the time "The Lion Sleeps Tonight" was released, he had been in and out of the hospital constantly, and on October 8th, 1962, he died.

Everyone sighed. Rival a cappella groups were to blame,

growled Victor Madondo, a burly old warrior whose father had sung alto in the Evening Birds. "They were happy, because now they could go forward nicely."

But they went nowhere. Solomon was the one whose influence lived on, becoming so pervasive that all Zulu male choral singing came to be called "Mbube music." Ethnomusicologists dug up the early Birds recordings, and Solomon was posthumously elevated to godhead—"one of the great figures in black South African music," according to professor Veit Erlmann, of the University of Texas. Latter-day Mbube stars like Ladysmith Black Mambazo sent gifts to this very house when they made it big, a tribute to the spirit of a man they venerated. And then I came along, asking questions about money.

It soon became clear that the daughters had no understanding of music publishing and related arcana. All they knew was that "people did something with our father's song outside" and that monies were occasionally deposited in their joint bank account by mysterious entities they could not name. I asked to see documents, but they had none, and they were deeply confused as to the size and purpose of the payments. "Mr. Tucker is helping us," they said. "Mr. Tucker knows everything."

Raymond Tucker is a white lawyer with offices in a grand old colonial mansion on the outskirts of downtown Jo'burg. On the phone, he explained that Pete Seeger and TRO contacted him at some point in the mid-1960s, asking him to act as a conduit for payments to Solomon's widow. Tucker was honored to help out, he said. As we spoke, he flipped through his files, assuring me that the royalty payments that came in were "pretty regular, with proper accounting" and "totally and absolutely aboveboard."

Solomon's daughters didn't contest this, but they were surprised to learn that their mother had received royalties back in the Sixties. Solomon Linda's widow, Regina, was an illiterate peasant with no job and six children to feed. Her husband's death, in 1962, was a catastrophe beyond reckoning. She brewed and sold beer in a desperate attempt to make ends meet. Her girls walked to school barefoot, took notes on cracked bits of slate and went to bed hungry. Critical Zulu death rites went unperformed for years, because the family was too poor to pay a *sangoma* to officiate.

"This house, it was bare bricks," said Elizabeth. "No ceiling, no plaster, no furniture, just one stool and one coal stove." Her eldest brother left school and started working, but he was murdered by gangsters. Her second brother became the breadwinner, only to die in an accident, whereupon Delphi took a job in a factory to keep the family going. "There was suffering here at home," said Elizabeth. She thought that the money "from outside" arrived only after 1980. Her sisters agreed. That was when they erected a tombstone for their father, who had rested in a pauper's grave since 1962. That's how they knew.

I asked Tucker if I could see his files, but he balked, citing his client's confidentiality. I obtained a letter of introduction from the daughters and called to discuss it, but he slammed down the phone. I wrote a note, pointing out that the daughters were legally and morally entitled to information. In response came a series of letters reminding me that he had nothing to do with the calculations of royalties and accusing me of misrepresenting myself as a "white knight" when I was clearly just a devious muckraker intent on "writing an article for your own gain." "I have absolutely no intention of cooperating to assist in your exploration," he sniffed, saying that he would speak only to a lawyer.

Defeated on that front, I sent an e-mail to Larry Richmond, asking him to clarify the size and nature of TRO's payments to Solomon's family. "It will take some time to review your letter," he wrote back. "I hope to get back to you in due course." Months passed, but nothing happened, so I appealed to Harold Leventhal, the grandfatherly figure who had once managed the Weavers' affairs. "You're in a void," he said, sounding sympathetic. "All you can do is describe it, or you'll never finish your story." A wise man would have heeded his advice, but I plodded onward until someone took pity and provided some key documents to me. Ambiguities remained, but at least I found out why the Americans were so coy about making disclosures: It looked as if Solomon's family had been receiving just 12.5 percent of the writer's royalties on "Wimoweh," along with a tiny fraction of those from "The Lion Sleeps Tonight."

The payments on "Lion" were coming out of "performance royalties," jargon for the bucks generated when a song is broadcast. The sums in question averaged around $275 a quarter in the early Nineties, but who are we to raise eyebrows? Solomon's family was desperate and grateful for the smallest blessing. The money "from outside" enabled his widow to feed her children and educate the two youngest, Elizabeth and Adelaide. After Regina's death in 1990, Raymond Tucker set up a joint bank account for the daughters in which small sums of money continued to materialize from time to time. It was never very much, but it was enough to build a tin shack in their back yard and rent it out for extra money, even enough to start a little shop at the front gate. In American terms, their poverty remains appalling, but in their own estimation, this was a happy ending—until I showed up, and told them what might have been.

**PART III:
The annals
of a curious lawsuit**

It's November 1991 in a bland conference room in the American Arbitration Association's New York headquarters. At the head of a long table sit three veteran copyright lawyers who will act as judges in these proceedings. Ranged before them are the warring parties: the entire cast of the 1961 "Lion Sleeps Tonight" plagiarism contretemps, either themselves or their legal representatives.

Hugo Peretti died a few years back, but fortune has smiled on the rest of the guys since last we saw them. Howie Richmond published the Rolling Stones and Pink Floyd for a while and is now rich beyond wild imaginings. His sidekick Al Brackman (who got ten percent of all Howie's deals) is rich too, and putters around in boats on weekends and winters at his second home near San Diego. Luigi Creatore has retired to Florida on the proceeds of his many hit records, and George Weiss is a successful composer of movie scores and musicals.

So why are they spending time cooped up here, flanked by lawyers? It's another long story.

In the fall of 1989, just as the initial copyright on "The Lion Sleeps Tonight" was about to expire, Howie and Al were notified by George Weiss that he and his fellow writers would dispense with TRO's publishing services in the renewal term unless they were paid a handsome bonus. Failing this, they would renew the "Lion" copyright in their own names and thereafter publish the song themselves, thus cutting Howie and Al out entirely and pocketing their fifty-percent share. The publishers were incensed, pointing out that "Lion" would never have existed if they hadn't allowed Weiss and Co. to "plagiarize" the underlying music, "Mbube" and "Wimoweh." To which the "Lion" team responded, in effect, how can you accuse us of stealing something you gave us in 1961? The fight went to court in 1990 and wound up in this arbitration months later—a band of rich white Americans squabbling over ownership of the most famous melody ever to emerge from Africa.

The music industry is riveted, because these men are pillars of the showbiz establishment. Al sits on the board of the Music Publishers' Association. Howie founded the Songwriters Hall of Fame. George Weiss is president of the Songwriters Guild of

America and a tireless champion of downtrodden tunesmiths. As such, he can't possibly state that "The Lion Sleeps Tonight" infringes on the work of a fellow composer, and so he doesn't. Sure, he says at the hearing, the Tokens "threw the music together" using a "few themes they knew from this Weavers' record," but so what? Weiss said he'd been told that "Wimoweh" was just Pete Seeger's interpretation of "an old thing from Africa," so they hadn't really plagiarized anyone. To prove his point, Weiss produces the liner notes of an old Miriam Makeba record in which "Mbube" is described as "a familiar Zulu song about a lion hunt."

TRO counters by presenting a yellowing affidavit in which the Zulu swears that "Mbube" was wholly original. At this juncture Weiss backs down, saying, in essence, "Gee, sorry, all this is news to me," and the hearing moves on to the real issue, which is the validity of the 1961 contract between TRO and the "Lion" trio. Drawn up in a spirit of incestuous back-scratching, the contract allows the Weiss parties free use of "Wimoweh" and "Mbube" in "The Lion Sleeps Tonight," with no royalty provisions for the author of the underlying songs. Some observers now find it a bit curious that TRO should start shouting, "Hold on! Our own contract's inaccurate! The underlying music never belonged to them! They can't just take it!"

Apparently worried that they might not be taken seriously, the men from TRO now depict themselves as the righteous defenders of Solomon Linda's heirs, openly accusing their rivals of "greed." "The defendants seek to deprive Mr. Linda's family of royalties," declares Larry Richmond, directing the brunt of his attack at George Weiss. The president of the Songwriters Guild should be "protecting the poor families of songwriters," he says, not robbing them. In the face of these accusations, the Weiss parties say that if they win the case, they'll give a share to Solomon's estate. The publishers then raise the ante, declaring that the family is rightfully entitled to up to a half of the enormous "Lion" spoils.

Amazing, no? If TRO had enforced such a distribution in 1961, Solomon's daughters might be millionaires, but nobody informed them that this dispute was taking place, so there was no one to laugh (or cry) on their behalf.

The arbitrators weren't very impressed, either—they awarded "The Lion Sleeps Tonight" to Weiss and Co., with the agreed proviso that they send "ten percent of writers' performance royalties" to the family. The order came into effect on January 1st, 1992, just as the song set forth on a new cycle of popularity. That year, a new recording of the song hit the Japanese charts. Pow Wow's version made Number One in France, in 1993. Then someone at Disney wrote a cute little scene in which a cartoon wart hog and meerkat pranced together, singing, "In the jungle, the mighty jungle. . . ." The song had been used in at least nine earlier movies, but *The Lion King* turned into a supernova. Every kid on the planet had to have the video and the vast array of nursery CDs that went with it. The Tokens' recording bounced back onto the U.S. charts, and Disney vocal arranger Lebo M's version (on *The Lion King: Rhythm of the Pridelands*) was the centerpiece of an album that went gold.

George Weiss could barely contain his glee. "The song leads a magical life," he told reporters. "It's been a hit eight or nine times but never like this. It's going wild!" The great composer came across as a diffident fellow, somewhat bemused by his enormous good fortune. "The way all this happened was destiny," he said. "It was mysterious, it was beautiful. I have to say God smiled at me."

I was hoping to talk to Weiss about God and Solomon Linda, but his lawyer said he was out of town and unavailable. On the other hand, he was visible in the *New York Times'* Sunday magazine last August, which ran a spread on his awesome retreat in rural New Jersey. I drove out to Oldwick and found the place—an eighteenth-century farmhouse in a deer-filled glade, with a pool and a recording studio in the outbuildings—but Weiss wasn't there. Maybe he was in Santa Fe, where he maintains a hacienda of sorts. Maybe he was in Cabo San Lucas, Mexico, where he and his wife were building a house on a bluff overlooking the sea. I gave up, returned to my hotel and wrote him a letter. Weiss faxed back almost immediately, saying he was "distressed" to hear that Solomon had been shabbily treated in the past. "As you can see," he continued, "none of that was our doing. While we had no legal obligation to Mr. Linda whatsoever, when we gained control of our song, we did what we thought was correct and equitable so that his family would share in the profits."

A nice gesture, to be sure, but what did "Lion" earn in the Nineties? A million dollars? Two? Three? Ten? And what trickled down to Soweto? Judging from the tattered scraps of paper in the daughters' possession, ten percent of the writer's performance royalties amounts to about $20,000 over the decade. Handwritten and unsigned, the notes appeared to be royalty statements, but there was no detailed breakdown of the song's overall earnings, and Weiss' business people declined to provide one, despite several requests.

Twenty grand was nice money in Soweto terms, but split several ways it changed little or nothing. Solomon Linda's house still had no ceiling, and it was like an oven under the African summer sun. Plaster flaked off the walls outside; toddlers squalled underfoot; three radios blared simultaneously. Fourteen people were living there, sleeping on floors for the most part, washing at an outdoor tap. Only Elizabeth was working, and when she moved out, most of the furniture went with her. Last time I visited, in January, the kitchen was barren save for six pots and a lone Formica table. Solomon's youngest daughter, Adelaide, lay swooning under greasy bedclothes, gravely ill from an infection she was too poor to have properly treated. A distant relative wandered around in an alcoholic stupor, waving a pair of garden shears and singing snatches of "Mbube." Elizabeth put her hands to her temples and said, "Really, we are not coping."

All the sisters were there: Fildah, with her *sangoma*'s headdress swathed in a bright red scarf; Elizabeth and Delphi in their best clothes; Adelaide, swaying back and forth on a chair, dazed, sweat pouring down her gaunt cheekbones. I'd come to report back to them on my adventures in the mysterious overseas, bringing a pile of legal papers that I did my best to explain. I told them about Paul Campbell, the fictitious entity who seemed to have collected big money that might otherwise have come their way, and about Larry Richmond, who wept crocodile tears on their behalf in a legal proceeding that might have changed their destiny, if only they'd been aware of it. And, finally, I showed them the letter in which George Weiss assured me that the amounts his underlings were depositing into the bank account of their mother, "Mrs. Linda" (who had been dead and buried for a decade), were a "correct and equitable" share.

The daughters had never heard of any of these foreigners, but they had a shrewd idea of why all this had happened. "It's because our father didn't attend school," Elizabeth said. "He was just signing everything they said he must sign. Maybe he was signing many papers." Everyone sighed, and that was that.

PART IV:
In which a moral is considered

Once upon a time, a long time ago, a Zulu man stepped up to a microphone and improvised a melody that earned many millions. That Solomon Linda got almost none of it was probably inevitable. He was a black man in white-ruled South Africa, but his American peers fared little better. Robert Johnson's contribution to the blues went largely unrewarded. Lead Belly lost half of his publishing to his white "patrons." DJ Alan Freed refused to play Chuck Berry's "Maybellene" until he was given a songwriter's cut. Led Zeppelin's "Whole Lotta Love" was lifted from Willie Dixon. All musicians were minnows in the pop-music food chain, but blacks were most vulnerable, and Solomon Linda, an illiterate tribesman from a wild valley where lions roamed, was totally defenseless against sophisticated predators.

Which is not to say that he was cheated. On the contrary, all the deals were perfectly legal, drawn up by respectable men. No one forced him to sell "Mbube" to Eric Gallo for ten shillings, and if Gallo turned around and traded it at a profit, so what? It belonged to him. The good old boys of TRO were perfectly entitled to rename the song, adapt it as they pleased and allocate the royalties to nonexistent entities. After all, they were its sole and uncontested owners. Solomon was legally entitled to nothing. The fact that he got anything at all seemed to show that the bosses were not without conscience or pity.

So I sat down and wrote long letters to George Weiss and Larry Richmond, distancing myself from pious moralists who might see them as sharks and even suggesting a line of reasoning they might take. "The only thing worse than exploitation," I mused, "is not being exploited at all." And then I enumerated all the good things old Solomon gained from making up the most famous melody that ever emerged from Africa: one pound cash, a big reputation, adulation and lionization; several cool suits, a windup gramophone, a check from Pete Seeger and a trickle of royalties that had spared his daughters from absolute penury. "All told," I concluded, "there is a case to be made against the idea that Solomon Linda was a victim of injustice."

I sat back and waited for someone to make it. I waited in vain. Months passed. Seasons changed. This article was completed and edited and about to go to press, but I was haunted by the thought that I'd missed something, so I sent a final appeal to the publishing honchos in America. And, lo, Howie Richmond got back to me, saying that he wanted to accept responsibility for some "gross errors." The blame for this "tragic situation," he continued, lay with a long-dead Gallo executive, who had never provided written proof that "Mbube" was Solomon's creation.

Beyond that, Howie insisted that TRO had paid "semiannual royalties" to Solomon "since the first commercial success of 'Wimoweh'" in 1951. But a document he provided to back his claim indicated that regular payments (aside from at least one, Pete Seeger's check, in the 1950s) commenced at least eleven years later. He said Pete Seeger never profited from his adaptation, then said that Seeger had indeed received a cut, but that it "may have been paid to nonprofit institutions" and/or passed on to Solomon's widow.

But what the hell, Howie's heart seemed to be in the right place. He wanted to fly me to California to work out a grand scheme of atonement. Then I received a call one morning from Solomon Linda's daughter Elizabeth, who said thugs had barged into her new house a few nights earlier, terrorized her family at gunpoint and looted her possessions. Her front door was still hanging off its hinges, and so she couldn't leave to check out a rumor she had heard from her bank. I investigated on her behalf and called back an hour later. "Money is pouring into your account from America," I said. "Nearly $15,000 in the last ten days." This was a fortune in local terms, an awesome mountain of cash. Elizabeth said nothing for a long time. I couldn't be sure, but I thought she was crying.

The windfall arose from use of "Wimoweh" in a U.S. TV commercial for a hotel. A big chunk of money had gone at first to Pete Seeger, who'd turned it back. It seemed he'd been receiving royalties on the song all along.

"I just found out," he tells me on the phone. "I didn't know."

Esquire

FINALIST, FEATURE WRITING

My Favorite Teacher

"My Favorite Teacher" is an unforgettable story of trust, betrayal, and the complexity of the criminal mind. The story's driving force is the author's need to reconcile two visions of the same man—a teacher who had a profoundly good influence on his life but was also a serial sex offender who molested and murdered a teenage hitchhiker. This narrative is riveting from beginning to end.

Robert Kurson

My Favorite Teacher

Sometimes, role models do bad things. Very bad things.

One night twenty years ago, my biology teacher picked up a seventeen-year-old hitchhiker named Jefferson Wesley.

Hitchhikers were rare on Chicago's exclusive North Shore, where kids owned Camaros and carried plenty of taxi cash. Even rarer were high school teachers who picked them up. It was midnight. Mr. Lindwall pulled over his yellow Toyota Land Cruiser and told Wesley to hop in.

Down the road, Mr. Lindwall stopped the Land Cruiser and asked Wesley to wait a second, the spare tire was rattling in back. Wesley said cool.

Mr. Lindwall shut off the headlights, exited the vehicle, and popped open the back hatch. Among a pile of tools, he found his hunting knife, which he unsheathed and poked at Wesley's back. He ordered the boy to bend over and locate the hangman's noose by his feet. Wesley found it and tightened it around his neck in the way Mr. Lindwall instructed.

My teacher climbed back into the driver's seat and explained: The seat belts in this jeep don't unfasten. Put your head between your legs. I'm going to tape your hands behind your back. This noose is attached to a series of pulleys. If you struggle, I can pull tight from here and control you.

Wesley now had good reason to believe he'd be killed. The son of a Chicago cop, he'd heard his share of stories, and in those stories kids wearing nooses didn't live.

2

Recently, I wrote a letter to Mr. Lindwall. It's been twenty years since we've seen each other, I said, but I remember you. I'd like to visit, to catch up and talk about our lives.

What I didn't tell Mr. Lindwall was that I'd never stopped thinking about him. While his name had become a sick punch line to anyone who had known him, I still admired him. And I needed to figure out why.

3

Northbrook, Illinois, happens to a person when life is good. The average home costs $340,000; 97 percent of the kids go to college; and when you buy groceries at Sunset Foods, crimson-vested valets scurry to load your car. Northbrook offers gazebos to its picnickers and electronic scoreboards to its Little Leaguers. Seniors who stroll the downtown's winding lanes enjoy handsome discounts on hand-dipped ice cream.

My family moved to Northbrook when I was fourteen. Fashionable welcome ladies helped me pronounce the name of my new street—Michelline Lane—and instructed me to celebrate my lucky transplant into Glenbrook North High School, the crown jewel in this gilded community and one of the top high schools in the country. My personal high school guidance counselor raved about Glenbrook North's high SAT scores and swimming-pool wing and plans for the multimillion-dollar Center for the Performing Arts. Kids who attend GBN, he said, turn out to be doctors, lawyers, CEOs; in short, adults worthy of living in Northbrook.

You've seen Glenbrook North before. Perhaps not in person but in near-documentary form in *The Breakfast Club, Sixteen Candles*, and *Ferris Bueller's Day Off*, the films based on the high school by director and Northbrook favorite son John Hughes (Glenbrook North, '68). Show up at Glenbrook North with the wrong folder, the wrong parents, the wrong nose, and you didn't just amuse students, you sickened them.

Feeling like an alien in high school of course did not make me unique, but it felt so at the time. Looking back, it seems like Glenbrook North decided up front to hate me. My Afro was fucked. My voice was fucked. My clothes were fucked. Even my name—Rob, the most innocuous name on the planet—somehow was fucked. In class, on the bus, in Sunset Foods with my mom on Saturday, just the sight of me offended important students—and at Glenbrook North they were all important. They took to blurting "Rob!" into the air whenever I was around, turning the word into the latest euphemism for *asshole.* "You're such a Rob!" one girl squealed to another in the participation-counts algebra class I was flunking for fear of making a peep.

I would have given my life to become invisible at Glenbrook North, but at six three, with my gangly limbs and towering Dr. J. Afro sprawling in all directions, that was impossible.

And soon enough, I came around to Glenbrook North's way of thinking. At home, I'd pound the crap out of my little brother because he still thought my hair looked cool or because he continued to dub himself "the Kurs Jr.," in honor of my nickname from the days in the old neighborhood, where people had liked me. I told my mom to go to hell in front of frail relatives when she remarked at a family wedding that I looked handsome, because who can deal with a parent who's too stupid to see what a hundred rich kids can see so clearly every day in school—that I was as ugly as they came?

Against this backdrop appeared Mr. Lindwall, perhaps the only individual at Glenbrook North more out of place than I was. A giant, bearded bear of a man, Mr. Lindwall lived in a trailer, adored the outdoors, and walked apologetically, with shoulders hunched in, as I did. His potbelly was proof that he didn't belong to any of the many area health clubs, and his baggy pants made him look like a kid whose mom shopped outlet and never knew enough to iron. By all rights, GBN students should have eaten this science teacher alive, sent him and his rusty jeep and corny sweater-vests whimpering back to whatever the hell Yosemite National Redwood Sherwood Forest he crawled out from.

Instead, they embraced him, sensed something safe about him. Mr. Lindwall had an intuition about kids. Before learning names, he divined who required extra attention, who was hurting at home, who needed to call him Rick. He listened for underlying messages, and he understood that sometimes a question about amoebas was really a question about alienation.

Almost immediately, an impressed administration asked him to devote time to the school's "alternatives" program, Northbrook code for the outsider-druggie-loser program. To most teachers, it would have been a baby-sitting sentence. To Mr. Lindwall, it was a calling. In weeks, kids who had been thrown away by mom, by life, by Northbrook, were learning science for "Rick" and calling him the greatest teacher they'd ever had.

My first contact with Mr. Lindwall came in the training room during football season, where he taped athletes' ankles and worked out their aches after school. When I needed treatment, he taught me how to stretch to avoid shinsplints as if I actually fit in at Glenbrook North. And he did this despite my football teammates' obvious and noisy disdain for me—made it seem as if he didn't even hear them blurt out "Rob!" when I climbed onto the training table. Other athletes probably figured Mr. Lindwall's lack of eye contact to be his need to concentrate on their ailments. But I knew that downward stare. This was a man who ached with shame on the inside, who prayed that if he couldn't see you, you couldn't see him. That other people adored Mr. Lindwall made him my favorite teacher in the school, because if Mr. Lindwall could still be liked despite not liking himself, there was hope for me, too.

4

Able to manipulate the noose around Jefferson Wesley's neck from the driver's seat, Mr. Lindwall turned on the Land Cruiser's headlights, adjusted the AM radio, and pulled onto Route 120. His trailer home near Northbrook was just twenty miles away, but he zigzagged along side roads for more than an hour in order to disorient the boy.

Perhaps Wesley thought of his mother during this ride. He had hung up on her earlier that evening when she told him to stay where he was, not to walk home, she'd come get him. Or maybe he thought of his girlfriend, Donna, whom he'd seen that night. The couple had planned to attend her turnabout dance next week. They were in love.

The Land Cruiser pulled into the trailer park near Northbrook after 1:00 A.M., and Mr. Lindwall parked it flush against his unit's screen door. He stepped around to Wesley's side, opened the door, removed the noose, and placed a hood over his head. Using a screwdriver, he jimmied the rigged seat-belt buckle until the mechanism clicked. It took only moments to drag the boy backward, heels scraping, into the trailer home.

In the living room, Mr. Lindwall laid Wesley on his back, bound the boy's ankles with athletic tape, removed the hood, and taped his eyes shut. Then he asked Wesley questions. Do you have a girlfriend? Do you poke this girlfriend? Do you masturbate? Does it shoot out? Then Mr. Lindwall went into another room to find a screwdriver and some Vaseline.

5

During class one day in my sophomore year, Mr. Popular strutted into my face, preened for his sporto buddies, then announced in front of teachers and students that he'd received an "awesome" blow job from my sister. I punched him in the face and knocked him down. I was 210 pounds, he was no more than 130, and he was clearly beat. But I wasn't done. I kicked him in the face with my boot, not once, not twice, but maybe ten, twelve times while his hysterical friends screamed, "Uncool!" and he was bleeding and begging and microscopes were shattering. In this fog of fury and resentment, I might have killed the kid, but teachers locked on to my arms and pulled me off. Only later, in the dean's office, would I realize that I had been sobbing myself while administering this beating.

Mr. Lindwall, who had been teaching in an adjacent room, rushed over, settled a hand on my shoulder, and used his back to shield me from the jeering students; he couldn't abide them watching me cry.

"You're better than that," he said in a low voice. "You're better than them."

I was stunned. Here was an adult, a man everyone loved, whose instinct was to rush past the kid with the broken face to comfort the kid with the broken feelings. I was right about Mr. Lindwall, I thought as I was led away to the dean's office. He and I come from the same place. We recognize each other.

6

Mr. Lindwall undid Wesley's brown corduroys and pushed them to his ankles, then did the same with his own pants. He ordered Wesley to open his mouth, placed his penis inside, and told Wesley to fellate him. Wesley complied, but Mr. Lindwall could not climax; he withdrew his penis and began masturbating. Near climax, he put his penis back into Wesley's mouth and ejaculated. That done, Wesley pleaded, "That's enough, that's enough, please, no more, that's enough."

An hour passed. Mr. Lindwall tied a knot in a sock, stuffed it into Wesley's mouth, and taped the boy's lips shut. Mr. Lindwall rolled the boy onto his stomach and said, "I'm going to do anal intercourse to you now," but found that he could not maintain an erection, a disaster because Wesley might think him a neuter. Mr. Lindwall scooped out some Vaseline, smoothed it over the screwdriver handle, and dragged the tool over Wesley's buttocks, telling him, "Now I'm going to do it to you." He pushed the tip of the handle inside Wesley's anus and said, "Now I'm doing it to you." A moment later, he removed the tool and told Wesley he had changed his mind.

Mr. Lindwall pulled up the boy's pants and dragged him back into the Land Cruiser, where he fastened the seat belt and reaffixed the noose. All the while, he assured Wesley that he would be dropped off near home. Wesley trembled and shook. Mr. Lindwall put the hood over the boy's head and pulled the noose tight until Wesley's head was down between his knees. Mr. Lindwall started the Land Cruiser and zigzagged back toward Wesley's town.

Near Wesley's home, the boy began to mumble and struggle again. Mr. Lindwall pulled the noose tighter and told him to relax, they were almost there. But the mumbling continued, so Mr. Lindwall turned up the radio because the groans were disturbing him. Near Route 120, he pulled off the road to let the boy out. After removing Wesley's hood, Mr. Lindwall saw that the boy wasn't moving. He loosened the noose and heard the boy gurgle, but he knew the sounds were not words. Wesley was dead.

Mr. Lindwall executed a U-turn and drove back to his home, where he lugged Wesley's corpse to the rear bedroom, undressed and unbound it, then bent it into the fetal position before rigor mortis could set in. He bathed the body, covered it with a blanket, waited until daylight, then drove to the hardware store to buy heavy-duty garbage bags. When he returned, he stuffed the naked body into two of those bags until no skin showed, pushed the heap into the Land Cruiser, and set out for a Wisconsin campground. He dumped the body next to a tree. By Monday morning, he was back at Glenbrook North, teaching sophomores about mitosis.

7

A few weeks after Mr. Lindwall shielded me and told me that I was "better than them," he was charged with the kidnapping, sexual assault, and murder of Jefferson Wesley. He also was being investigated, newspapers said, for the kidnappings and sexual assaults of two other young men nearby. Rumors swirled about more possible victims, ten of them even, about foster children he'd molested and maybe other dead Lindwall bodies out there. "Mr. Lindwall has a toothache," teachers and administrators told students who showed up for his class the morning after his arrest. Then, eventually, they assured the dumbfounded kids that Mr.

Lindwall was not anything like what he appeared. He was nothing like us.

8

After a few days, Mr. Lindwall answered my letter:

"I'll be happy to visit with you, Bob. Send me some of your recent writings so I can get a feel for the kind of man you turned out to be. Let's get together in a week. I look forward to it very much."

I shove the letter under a pile of bills in a bottom drawer. What am I looking for from this guy? Do I want him to tell me I'm a good boy? Do I need him to tell me that I wasn't as much of an asshole as all those kids in high school said I was? If so, I need more help than Mr. Lindwall can give me.

The letter stays buried in my drawer for a few days. Then I write back. "Dear Mr. Lindwall, tell me when and where to go. I look forward to seeing you, too."

9

To visit an inmate at the Joliet Correctional Center, that inmate must add your name to an approved visitors list. The process takes a few days. I spent those days investigating Mr. Lindwall's case. After all these years, I still didn't really know what had happened, whom he had killed and whom he hadn't, what was rumor and what was fact. I called classmates and teachers, some of whom I still despised, who told me about "Rick" as teacher and colleague. I read newspaper accounts and the lengthy trial transcript, including Mr. Lindwall's detailed confession and speech to the court before sentencing. For the first time since 1979, Mr. Lindwall returned to my life in three dimensions.

10

Rick Lindwall loved being a kid. If other ten-year-olds in suburban north Chicago in 1954 tempered their play with a rich-kid demurral, Rick was balls-out rough-and-tumble, a jumping bean with permanent scrapes on his elbows and knees who capped two-hour games of cowboys and Indians with mile-long swims.

Rick Lindwall loved being a kid until he was ten, when he contracted rheumatic fever and his life changed. The disease, which affects the heart, forced the boy to bed for a summer and caused him to miss eight weeks of sixth grade. For a cowboy who had slain thousands of Indians, this wasn't too much to handle. But soon after, other parts of his body betrayed him.

At age twelve, Rick developed breasts. Not just the folds of flesh you find on a fat kid, which he wasn't, but boobs, tits, the real thing. Around the same time, his penis began to shrink and his pubic hair stopped growing, until the horrified child began to wonder if he was still a boy. Rick ached to tell his parents but said nothing; he sensed that these developments had something to do with sex, and sex was taboo in the Lindwall home.

Rick managed to agonize silently for a time, but when his shame turned to despair he had to tell his parents. His father was unapproachable, a Milquetoast of a man too timid even to select a restaurant, so he confided in his mother, a domineering pants-wearer in a June Cleaver era. He begged her for help and told her he hated himself. She declared it a "general" problem and urged as much to the family doctor, who complied by treating the boy with shots and a pat on the back. When the breasts grew larger, Mom and Doc shrugged their shoulders; sure, there were still "bumps" under his sweaters, but listen, kids grow out of things, why ever bring it up again?

Nobody knew in 1956 that Rick Lindwall likely had something called Klinefelter's syndrome. People with this condition have an extra X chromosome and a jumble of sexual characteristics and are sexually sterile. A few injections of testosterone would have made Rick feel like a boy again, might have restored his masculine appearance, at least might have helped him withstand what was to come.

At school, Rick became choice locker-room fodder for boys whose own fresh pubic hair had infused them with newfound bravado. "Where's your bra?" "You're in the wrong class," they singsonged in falsetto, pointing him to the girl's bathroom. It was in the locker room that Rick began to consider himself "God's mistake."

Through junior high and high school, Rick kept no friends and managed just a single date. Consumed by shame, he didn't dare allow anyone to know him, because you don't come across a neuter every day. He kept himself close to sports, which he loved, by becoming the high school's athletic trainer, the guy who tapes the football players. Inside the training room, he found himself captivated by physiques, and, here's the curious thing, not in a sexual way, because Rick still didn't know what sexual feelings were, didn't know they existed. He stared at the jocks to gather information about what he should have been.

At Ripon College in Wisconsin, Mr. Lindwall rushed Delta Upsilon. He hadn't made a friend since he was ten, but these guys liked him, actually wanted him. When he discovered that initiation included a Hell Week during which pledges removed their shirts, he quit. For the remainder of college and into the Air Force, peers ridiculed him mercilessly with the familiar "Where's your bra?" Had he not lucked into a medical discharge, he might have turned suicide in the Air Force. Instead, Mr. Lindwall became a teacher.

Northbrook Junior High was thrilled to get Mr. Lindwall. He was smart, knew his science, and didn't take himself too seriously. The administration believed him ideal for that toughest of junior high classes, sex education. Mr. Lindwall accepted the assignment with equanimity, then dashed to the bookstore to cram the basics. He was twenty-seven years old and had never even masturbated.

Kids at the junior high loved Mr. Lindwall, loved that he dug science the way they dug Led Zeppelin, loved the scientific but silly pictures he drew on their notebooks and arms. They told their parents about him, sometimes so fervently that mom or dad would schedule an appointment just to thank him in person. All the while, he knew little about his subject. If a kid asked a technical question, he'd chuckle and suggest, "Let's check the book for that one!" If a student used sexual slang, he'd approach another teacher after school and ask, "How would you answer a kid who wants to know if you can get VD from eating a girl out?" caring little about the VD part but desperate to know what "eating out" meant.

Mr. Lindwall spent seven years teaching sex ed and science at Northbrook Junior High before getting the call to the big leagues, Glenbrook North High School. There, he impressed the administration as he had at the junior high, and soon he was teaching the bad kids in the "alternatives" program and prompting those freaks to issue their ultimate compliment, *He's cool, but I actually learn shit.* He also settled in as GBN's athletic trainer. Coaches loved the guy because he'd give anything for the team; they called him "Lindoo Can-Do," because what better nickname could you hang on a great guy who always said yes? After victories on the road, the coaches would invite Mr. Lindwall out to Tonelli's for pizza and beer, their treat, but he always took the rain check. In the hallways at Glenbrook North, students, staff, and janitors felt good about themselves when Mr. Lindwall smiled at them. But when they invited him to parties, Mr. Lindwall declined, because who knew if it might require removing your shirt? Or discussing dating. Folks got the message. In the nearly ten years Mr. Lindwall taught in Northbrook, only three people, family included, ever visited him at home.

11

A year and three weeks after Mr. Lindwall disposed of Jefferson Wesley, he picked up another late-night hitchhiker. Kelly Smith, eighteen, needed a lift to a tavern.

Mr. Lindwall's method was consistent—rattling tire, hunting knife, noose, tape, hood. His application this time, however, was unthorough. He taped Smith's wrists loosely, allowing the young man to stretch the binds during the circuitous ride back to the trailer.

Once inside, Mr. Lindwall didn't tape Smith's ankles. He forced him down face-first on the carpet, then exited the room, saying he needed to move his Land Cruiser. Smith, believing his execution to be imminent, worked a hand free from behind his back and flung off the hood and noose. He could now make out the figure of his captor outside the front door, so he scrambled for a rear exit. When he could find none, he rushed the front door and came face-to-face with Mr. Lindwall, who ordered him to stop.

Smith hurtled past him and into the trailer park's common area, banging on doors and shrieking, "Help! Help! Police!" Moments later, a squad car arrived and took the teenager to the Glenview police station, just two miles from Glenbrook North High School.

When Smith arrived at the station, he was startled to see Mr. Lindwall parking his Land Cruiser. Officers questioned Smith in the basement and made note of his appearance—white athletic tape around one sleeve of his blue windbreaker, inflamed wrists, three punctures in the back of the jacket. Smith told police his story.

Upstairs, Mr. Lindwall told a different version. He calmly explained that after he had picked up Smith, the two had decided to hit the bars and needed to return to the trailer for money. Inside, he had observed Smith stealing various items and naturally had chased the young man away.

When officers asked if they could search the Land Cruiser and the trailer home, Mr. Lindwall said, Of course—I am a respected member of the community and a teacher at Glenbrook North and I have nothing to hide. At his trailer home, Mr. Lindwall urged the police to look around and said, I want to get to the bottom of this as much as you do and I am a good person and a foster parent who takes in wayward boys.

The two officers worked from front to back. In the bedroom, one found a roll of film marked boys, which Mr. Lindwall said had been taken during a high school camping trip, and hundreds of snapshots of boys, which Mr. Lindwall said showed the same. On a kitchen chair, one officer found a rope inside a hood. The rope is for camping, Mr. Lindwall told them. Outside, with dawn breaking, one officer spotted a noose, a knife, and three rolls of athletic tape and asked Mr. Lindwall if he'd like to tell them what really happened.

12

By the time Mr. Lindwall reached trial in the summer of 1980, he was suicidal and had done everything in his power to convince the state to execute him. His confessions were detailed, his memory sharp, and his despair complete as he informed investigators of nine to twelve hitchhikers abducted and molested over the past three years. He advised his lawyers, "Don't work too hard for me; I just want to die."

The state charged Mr. Lindwall with the murder, aggravated kidnapping, and deviate sexual assault of Jefferson Wesley, plus the aggravated kidnappings of Kelly Smith and another young man. Dozens of other charges were put on hold to make the trial manageable.

Reporters shoved for position when opening arguments began Wednesday morning, July 16. Mr. Lindwall's mother and brother had visited with him before the proceedings, visited so loudly in fact that a sheriff's deputy found Judge James M. Bailey in chambers and told him, Sad story, Judge, I just overheard that man's family ask him why he doesn't do everyone a favor and just kill himself.

Mr. Lindwall drooped into court wearing a V-neck sweater-vest, the same style he'd worn countless times to cover his breasts at Glenbrook North, even during sweltering Indian-summer days. During the weeklong trial, witnesses would continue to identify Mr. Lindwall in court by pointing to "the man over there in the tan sweater-vest." For his part, Mr. Lindwall would spend most of the trial with his head in his hands.

The state's case was cinematic and lurid. The other young man told of trick seat belts and nooses and an abduction in which he was masturbated by Mr. Lindwall four times over twelve hours, with respite only when Mr. Lindwall retired to another room to watch the Bears game on TV. Prosecutors dragged the seat from Mr. Lindwall's Land Cruiser into the courtroom, and Kelly Smith climbed in, fastened the inescapable seat belt, slipped the noose around his neck, and allowed lawyers to poke at him with a knife the way Mr. Lindwall had. Smith identified for the jury the athletic tape, the hood, the noose that still bore his gnaw marks. The state's psychiatrist swore Mr. Lindwall was sane.

The public defender called Mr. Lindwall's mother, who testified to her son's boyhood days and his loose-fitting shirts and get-out-of-gym notes. Among the character witnesses from the Glenbrook North faculty was the head of the science department, who averred his teacher's sterling character and reputation. The defense psychiatrist declared Mr. Lindwall insane.

Mr. Lindwall testified, too. He swore that he molested boys not for sexual thrills but to process what they "had," to watch their penises "get real hard and point up toward their heads" while his wouldn't, to watch theirs "spurt out" because his didn't. He claimed to abduct boys only on weekends because he didn't want to upset their weekly routine, they were in school. He insisted that he had never been homosexual and never meant to kill Jefferson Wesley. Such claims were routine and always false inside the Cook County Courthouse, but from the melancholy and self-incriminating Mr. Lindwall, they rang true. Medical witnesses agreed that Wesley's death was most likely accidental.

The jury took two hours to convict Mr. Lindwall on all counts. The next morning, headlines blared from the Chicago daily newspapers, and the city wanted blood. Sensing that the judge had been moved by Mr. Lindwall's story, his lawyer opted to have Bailey decide the sentence rather than the jury. Mr. Lindwall would be allowed to address the court first.

"I have the life of Jefferson Wesley on my conscience, and that's something that will stay there until I die. I would publicly like to apologize to his parents for the terror and grief, the suffering I've put them through. And to the other young men who have had the misfortune of crossing my path, I also apologize and hope that the scars that may remain will soon disappear.

"I am not looking for sympathy, nor am I offering excuses. I believe those of you who knew me deserve an explanation. I also believe there is something to be learned from all that has occurred."

Mr. Lindwall described his boyhood, the cruelty he endured as his body changed, and the impossibility of living as a neuter, as God's mistake. He expressed relief that he had been stopped when he had.

"In closing, if any of you have a problem which hurts you to the point of altering how you feel about yourselves, for God's sake don't keep it to yourself. Don't get trapped into believing that no one can help. If the first person you go to does not ease your concerns, then try someone else. Whatever you do, don't surrender to your problem.

"Nothing I say can bring back Jefferson Wesley, or get rid of all the pain and suffering I've caused. But, God, don't let it happen to somebody else."

While Mr. Lindwall spoke, Judge Bailey scratched these notes into his oversized notebook: "He lived a good life." "No prior criminal record." "Bizarre case." Then he announced to the courtroom, "I must say, the defendant is a very unusual one as far as this court is concerned. In ten years as a judge here and four years as a federal prosecutor, you come across very few defendants like this one. . . . Considering the factors involved here, I have no alternative but to sentence the defendant to the Illinois penitentiary on the murder charge for natural life without parole, and sixty years on the other charges, all to run concurrent. That's it."

Expressionless, Mr. Lindwall gathered his papers just as he had after biology class, waited a moment to make sure no one needed him, then disappeared into the Illinois penal system. He was thirty-six years old.

13
_____

I'm thirty-six years old. Today, I go to see Mr. Lindwall.

The mustard stone walls at the Joliet Correctional Center have stood sentry over 140 years of broken men. The prison, landscaped in pillowy bales of barbed wire, will hold Mr. Lindwall until he dies.

At the sign-in counter, a guard checks a list for my name and informs me that, whoa, the dude I'm here to see never gets any visitors. He points me to a locker for my belongings, then searches me in a no-man's holding zone to make sure I'm not stashing anything in my hair or between my toes—visitors are not allowed to bring anything, not even a pencil, into a visit. I'm moved to a waiting area that sells ice cream sandwiches and Joliet Correctional Center T-shirts, then stamped on the hand with an ultraviolet blotch and led through two sets of iron doors and into the visiting room.

I search for the bushy-bearded, 240-pound teacher, but he's not among the tattooed convicts, their weary-faced women, or yelping kids. Only one man sits alone in this room, but he's got a neatly trimmed gray beard and weighs no more than 160 pounds. He wears his prison-issue blue shirt looser than the other prisoners, and he has kind eyes. Mr. Lindwall and I shake hands.

He apologizes for not remembering me. I'm nervous and can only muster a dopey "Wow, you look great." He says he's in the best shape of his life, jogs every day and lifts weights like this, he says, hoisting two invisible dumbbells and grinning. We sit on bolted-down stools at opposite ends of a pizza-sized table. He fills me in on the incidentals of his everyday life. His day always begins with a hot chocolate, then six hours of laundry folding before working crossword puzzles, the harder the better. He resents Oprah for asking guests, "How did that make you feel?" since he's discovered that nothing "makes" you feel any way—you decide how to feel.

Mr. Lindwall is polite and gracious, but then he turns to me. Why are you interested in me? he asks. For a moment, I strain to recapture the sophisticated explanations I'd rehearsed in the car. Instead, I blurt out, "Was I wrong to like you?"

"You weren't wrong," he says after long consideration. "I was a good teacher and sometimes I was a good person. I did a lot of good things. But I led two separate lives."

"Why did you do it?" I ask.

And then he begins telling me about his crimes.

"I'm not homosexual. These weren't sex crimes. I did them to . . . satisfy my curiosity," he says. "The newspapers said that I never touched any of my foster children. Well, that's not true. And I did other . . . things . . . that didn't, let's say, come out completely. If you think someone like me starts committing crimes when he's thirty-one, you're wrong. These things go back a long, long way.

"Did you know I had already resigned from Glenbrook North before I got caught? I did that because I was going to hurt my own students. The things I was doing weren't satisfying me anymore. I knew I was going to take things to . . . another level. If I hadn't been caught, I would have turned into another Gacy. No. I was going to live as a hermit, and I would have been worse than Gacy."

Mr. Lindwall asks if I remember his trial. I tell him that I'd read the papers and, like everyone else, admired his speech to the court.

"That speech was bullshit," Mr. Lindwall says softly. "I remember believing it at the time—I'm not saying I purposely lied. But I had no feeling for my victims, nothing. It took me years in here before I felt anything for victims, mine or anyone else's.

"Remember Sporto Hall? I remember once, this very sensitive kid walked down Sporto Hall and the jocks were merciless, teasing him, and when this guy came back he was in tears. I embraced him, tried to comfort him. I felt so bad for the kid, I just wanted to ease his pain. But even then, at the very moment I was comforting him, I also wanted to hurt him."

After a while, a guard pokes me and says time's up. Mr. Lindwall apologizes for focusing so much on his crimes and says that he'd like me to come back, so perhaps we can get to know each other better. I am a little disoriented and react by trying to buy him a Mountain Dew for the road. He smiles and says, No thanks, it's not allowed. Mr. Lindwall shakes my hand as I leave. "I feel like you came here for a reason," he says. "I'm not very religious, so I don't mean this religiously. But I feel like you showed up, I mean right now, at this time, for a purpose. I don't know the purpose, but I appreciate it."

In the parking lot, I scribble out notes:

"Smart. Articulate. Soft voice. Honest."

"Was about to hurt own students."

"Says he was ready to become serial killer, worse than Gacy."

"Other crimes no one knows about."

"Remembers wanting to comfort—but also hurt—'sensitive' kid in GBN hallway."

"Still a good guy."

.　　.　　.

I'm numb as I pull onto the snowy expressway, back to North-brook, the place I despised, so of course it's where I now live, and I'm wondering what I have discovered about Mr. Lindwall. Wondering if this is finally over for me. My mind is full and racing, skimming across the surface of the experience like a smooth stone. Is it possible to reconcile fond feelings for someone who had been such a positive influence yet had turned out to be capable of such evil? It happens all the time, I suppose—adults in positions of responsibility betraying impressionable children, sometimes much worse. How is a kid supposed to process that? And I'm driv-ing and thinking about our conversation, about his laundry detail and Oprah and undiscovered crimes and crimes that had been planned and not executed, combing, combing for clues. And then suddenly, halfway between prison and home, I take my foot off the accelerator and the car drifts slowly over to the icy shoulder.

"Still a good guy."

Eighteen-wheelers blast by, sending up the snow in a dirty swirl, as I sit there staring straight ahead, engine running. I'm thinking about the sensitive student Mr. Lindwall had comforted yet wanted to hurt.

And I know that Mr. Lindwall was talking about me.

Rolling Stone

WINNER, FEATURE WRITING

The Weasel, Twelve Monkeys and the Shrub

This story is a rollicking dispatch filed after a week on the road with John McCain's presidential campaign. It updates "The Boys on the Bus" with wit, style, and fierce intelligence. The author lays bare the cynicism many citizens feel—especially the current readers of Rolling Stone—*for the American political process and passionately urges those young voters to give a damn.*

David Foster Wallace

The Weasel, Twelve Monkeys and the Shrub

Seven days in the life of the late, great John McCain

Prologue: Who Cares?

Since you're reading "Rolling Stone," the chances are you're an American between say 18 and 35, which demographically makes you a Young Voter. And no generation of Young Voters has ever cared less about politics and politicians than yours. There's hard demographic and voter-pattern data backing this up . . . assuming you give a shit about data. In fact, even if you're reading other stuff in RS, it's doubtful you're going to read much of this article—such is the enormous shuddering yawn that the Political Process evokes in us now, in this post-Watergate-post-Iran-Contra-post-White-water-post-Lewinsky era, an era when politicians' statements of principle or vision are understood as self-serving ad copy and judged not for their sincerity or ability to inspire but for their tac-tical shrewdness, their marketability. And no generation has been marketed and Spun and pitched to as ingeniously and relentlessly as today's demographic Young. So when Senator John McCain says, in Michigan or South Carolina (which is where ROLLING STONE sent the least professional pencil it could find to spend the standard media Week on the Bus with a candidate who'd never ride higher than he is right now), when McCain says. "I run for president not to Be Somebody, but to Do Something," it's hard to hear it as anything more than a marketing angle, especially when he says it as he's going around surrounded by cameras and reporters and cheering crowds . . . in other words, Being Somebody.

And when Senator John McCain also says—constantly, thumping it at the start and end of every speech and THM—that his goal as president will be "to inspire young Americans to devote themselves to causes greater than their own self-interest," it's hard not to hear it as just one more piece of the carefully scripted bullshit that presidential candidates hand us as they go about the self-interested business of trying to become the most powerful, important and talked-about human being on earth, which is of course their real "cause," to which they appear to be so deeply devoted that they can swallow and spew whole mountains of noble-sounding bullshit and convince even themselves that they mean it. Cynical as that may sound, polls show it's how most of us feel. And it's beyond not believing the bullshit; mostly we don't even hear it, dismiss it at the same deep level where we also block out billboards and Muzak.

But there's something underneath politics in the way you have to hear McCain, something riveting and unSpinnable and true. It has to do with McCain's military background and Vietnam combat and the five-plus years he spent in a North Vietnamese prison, mostly in solitary, in a box, getting tortured and starved. And the unbelievable honor and balls he showed there. It's very easy to gloss over the POW thing, partly because we've all heard so much about it and partly because it's so off-the-charts dramatic, like something in a movie instead of a man's life. But it's worth considering for a minute, because it's what makes McCain's "causes greater than self-interest" line easier to hear.

You probably already know what happened. In October of '67 McCain was himself still a Young Voter and flying his 23rd Vietnam combat mission and his A-4 Skyhawk plane got shot down over Hanoi and he had to eject, which basically means setting off an explosive charge that blows your seat out of the plane, which ejection broke both McCain's arms and one leg and gave him a concussion and he started falling out of the skies right over Hanoi. Try to imagine for a second how much this would hurt and how scared you'd be, three limbs broken and falling toward the enemy capital you just tried to bomb. His chute opened late and he landed hard in a little lake in a park right in the middle of downtown Hanoi. Imagine treading water with broken arms and trying to pull the lifevest's toggle with your teeth as a crowd of Vietnamese men swim out toward you (there's film of this, somebody had a home-movie camera, and the N.V. government released it, though it's grainy and McCain's face is hard to see). The crowd pulled him out and then just about killed him. U.S. bomber pilots were especially hated, for obvious reasons. McCain got bayoneted in the groin; a soldier broke his shoulder apart with a rifle butt. Plus by this time his right knee was bent 90° to the side with the bone sticking out. Try to imagine this. He finally got tossed on a jeep and taken five blocks to the infamous Hoa Lo prison—a.k.a. the "Hanoi Hilton," of much movie fame—where they made him beg a week for a doctor and finally set a couple of the fractures without anesthetic and let two other fractures and the groin wound (imagine: *groin wound*) stay like they were. Then they threw him in a cell. Try for a moment to feel this. All the media profiles talk about how McCain still can't lift his arms over his head to comb his hair, which is true. But try to imagine it at the time, yourself in his place, because it's important. Think about how *diametrically* opposed to your own self-interest getting knifed in the balls and having fractures set without painkiller would be, and then about getting thrown in a cell to just lie there and hurt, which is what happened. He was delirious with pain for weeks, and his weight dropped to 100 pounds, and the other POWs were sure he would die; and then after a few months like that after his bones mostly knitted and he could sort of stand up they brought him in to the prison commandant's office and offered to let him go. This is true. They said he could just leave. They had found out that McCain's father was one of the top-ranking naval officers in the U.S. Armed Forces (which is true—both his father and grandfather were admirals), and the North Vietnamese wanted the PR coup of mercifully releasing his son, the baby-killer. McCain, 100 pounds and barely able to stand, refused. The U.S. military's Code of Conduct for Prisoners of War apparently said that POWs had to be released in the order they were captured, and there were others who'd been in Hoa Lo a long time, and McCain refused to violate the Code. The commandant, not pleased, right there in the office had guards break his ribs, rebreak his arm, knock his teeth out. McCain still refused to leave without the other POWs. And so then he spent four more years in Hoa Lo like this, much of the time in solitary, in the dark, in a closet-sized box called a "punishment cell." Maybe you've heard all this before; it's been in umpteen different media profiles of McCain. But try to imagine that moment between getting offered early release and turning it down. Try to imagine it was you. Imagine how loudly your most basic, primal self-interest would have cried out to you in that moment, and all the ways you could rationalize accepting the offer. Can you hear it? If so, would you have refused to go? You simply can't know for sure. None of us can. It's hard even to imagine the pain and fear in that moment, much less know how you'd react.

But, see, we *do* know how this man reacted. That he chose to spend four more years there, in a dark box, alone, tapping code on the walls to the others, rather than violate a Code. Maybe he was nuts. But the point is that with McCain it feels like we *know*, for a proven *fact*, that he's capable of devotion to something other, more, than his own self-interest. So that when he says the line in speeches in early February you can feel like maybe it isn't just more candidate bullshit, that with this guy it's maybe the truth. Or maybe both the truth *and* bullshit: the guy does—did—want your vote, after all.

But that moment in the Hoa Lo office in '68—right before he refused, with all his basic normal human self-interest howling at him—that moment is hard to blow off. All week, all through MI and SC and all the tedium and cynicism and paradox of the campaign, that moment seems to underlie McCain's "greater than self-interest" line, moor it, give it a weird sort of reverb that's hard to ignore. The fact is that John McCain is a genuine hero of the only kind Vietnam now has to offer, a hero not because of what he did but because of what he suffered—voluntarily, for a Code. This gives him the moral authority both to utter lines about causes beyond self-interest and to expect us, even in this age of Spin and lawyerly cunning, to believe he means them. Literally: "moral authority," that old cliché, much like so many other clichés— "service," "honor," "duty," "patriotism"—that have become just mostly words now, slogans invoked by men in nice suits who want something from us. The John McCain we've seen, though—arguing for his doomed campaign-finance bill on the Senate floor in '98, calling his colleagues crooks to their faces on C-SPAN, talking openly about a bought-and-paid-for government on *Charlie Rose* in July '99, unpretentious and bright as hell in the Iowa debates and New Hampshire Town Hall Meetings—something about him made a lot of us feel the guy wanted something different from us, something more than votes or money, something old and maybe corny but with a weird achy pull to it like a whiff of a childhood smell or a name on the tip of your tongue, something that would make us think about what terms like "service" and "sacrifice" and "honor" might really *refer* to, like whether they actually *stood* for something, maybe. About whether anything past well-Spun self-interest might be real, was ever real, and if so then what happened? These, for the most part, are not lines of thinking that the culture we've grown up in has encouraged Young Voters to pursue. Why do you suppose that is?

Glossary of Relevant Campaign-Trail Vocab

(Mostly Courtesy of Jim C. and the Network-News Techs)

22.5 The press corps' shorthand for McCain's opening remarks at THMs (see **THM**), which remarks are always the same and always take exactly 22 and a half minutes.

BAGGAGE CALL The grotesquely early a.m. time when you've got to have your suitcase back in the bus's bowels and have a seat staked out and be ready to go or else you get left behind and have to try to wheedle a ride to the first THM (see **THM**) from Fox News, which is a drag in all kinds of ways.

BUNDLED MONEY A way to get around the Federal Election Commission's $1,000 limit for individual campaign contributions. A wealthy donor can give $1,000 for himself, and then can say that yet another $1,000 comes from his wife, and another $1,000 from his kid, and another from his Aunt Edna, etc. The Shrub's (see **Shrub**) favorite trick is to designate CEOs and other top corporate executives as "Pioneers," who each pledge to raise $100,000 for Bush2000—$1,000 comes from them individually, and the other 99 one-grand contributions come "voluntarily" from their employees. McCain makes a point of accepting neither bundled money nor soft money (see **soft money**).

DT Drive Time, the slots in the daily schedule set aside for caravaning from one campaign event to another.

F&F An hour or two in the afternoon when the campaign provides downtime and an F&F Room for the press corps to File and Feed (see **File and Feed**).

FILE AND FEED What print and broadcast press, respectively, have to do every day, i.e. print reporters have to finish their daily stories and file them via fax or e-mail to their papers, while the techs (see **tech**) and field producers have to find a satellite or Gunner (see **Gunner**) and feed their film, standups (see **standup**), and anything else their bosses might want to the network HQ.

GUNNER A portable satellite-uplink rig that the networks use to feed on-scene from some campaign events. Gunner is the company that makes and/or rents out these rigs, which consist of a blinding white van with a boat-trailerish thing on which is an eight-foot satellite dish angled upward 40° at the southwest sky and emblazoned in fiery blue caps GUNNER GLOBAL UPLINKS FOR NEWS, NETWORKING, ENTERTAINMENT.

HEAD Local or network TV correspondent.

ODT Optimistic Drive Time, which refers to the daily schedule's nagging habit of underestimating the amount of time it takes to get from one event to another, causing the Straight Talk Express driver to speed like a maniac and to incur the rabid dislike of the official Bullshit 1 driver, whose name is Jay.

OTS Opportunity to Smoke.

PENCIL A member of the Trail's print press.

PRESS-AVAIL (or **-AVAIL**) Brief scheduled opportunity for traveling press corps to interface as one body w/McCain or staff High Command, often deployed for Reacts (see **React**).

REACT McCain's or McCain2000 High Command's on-record response to a sudden major development in the campaign, usually some tactical move or allegation from the Shrub (see **Shrub**).

SCRUM (*n*) The moving 360° ring of techs (see **tech**) and heads around the candidate as he makes his way from the Straight Talk Express into an event or vice versa; (*v*) to gather around the candidate in such a ring.

THE SHRUB GOP presidential candidate George W. Bush.

SOFT MONEY The best-known way to finesse the FEC's limit on campaign contributions. Enormous sums are here given to a certain candidate's political party instead of to the candidate, but the party then by some strange coincidence ends up dispersing those enormous sums to exactly the candidate the donor had wanted to give to in the first place.

STANDUP A head giving a remote report from some event McCain's at.

STICK A sound tech's (see **tech**) black telescoping polymer rod (full extension = 9'7") with a boom microphone at the end, used mostly for scrums and always the most distinctive visible feature thereof because of the way a fully extended stick wobbles and boings when the sound tech (which, again, see **tech**) walks with it.

TECH A TV news camera or sound technician.

THM Town Hall Meeting, McCain2000's signature campaign event, where the 22.5 is followed by an hour-long unscreened Q&A with the audience.

THE TWELVE MONKEYS (or **12M**) The techs' private code-name for the most elite and least popular pencils in the McCain press corps, who on DTs are almost always allowed into the red-intensive salon at the very back of the Straight Talk Express to interface with McCain and political consultant Mike Murphy. The 12M are a dozen marquee journalists and political-analysis guys from the really important papers and weeklies and news services, and tend to be so totally identical in dress and demeanor as to be almost surreal—twelve immaculate and wrinkle-free navy-blue blazers, half-Windsored ties, pleated chinos, oxford-cloth shirts that even when the jackets come off stay 100% buttoned at collar and sleeves, Cole Haan loafers, and tortoiseshell specs they love to take off and nibble the arm of, plus always a uniform self-serious-ness that reminds you of every overachieving dweeb you ever wanted to kick the ass of in school. The Twelve Monkeys never smoke or drink, and always move in a pack, and always cut to the front of every scrum and Press-Avail and line for Continental Breakfast in the hotel lobby before Baggage Call, and whenever any of them are rotated however briefly back onto Bullshit 1 they always sit together identically huffy and pigeon-toed with their attaché cases in their laps and always end up discussing incredibly esoteric books on political theory and public policy in voices that are all the exact same languid honk. The techs (who all wear old jeans and surplus-store parkas and also all tend to hang in a pack) avoid and try to pretty much ignore the Twelve Monkeys, who in turn treat the techs the way someone in an executive washroom treats the attendant. As you might already have gathered, ROLLING STONE dislikes the 12M intensely, for all the above reasons, plus the fact that they're tighter than a duck's butt when it comes to sharing even very basic general-knowledge political information that might help somebody write a slightly better article, plus the issue of two separate occasions at late-night hotel check-ins when one or more of the Twelve Monkeys just out of nowhere turned and handed ROLLING STONE their suitcases to carry, as if ROLLING STONE were a bellboy or gofer instead of a hard-working journalist just like them even if he didn't have a portable Paul Stuart steamer for his blazer.

WEASEL The weird gray fuzzy thing sound techs put over their boom mikes at scrums to keep annoying wind-noise off the audio. It looks like a large floppy mouse-colored version of a certain popular kind of fuzzy bathroom slipper. (N.B.: Weasels, which are also sometimes worn by sound techs as headgear during OTS's when it's really cold, are thus sometimes also known as "tech toupees.")

Substantially Farther Behind the Scenes Than You're Apt to Want to Be

It's now precisely 1330h. On Tuesday, 8 February '00, aboard Bullshit 1, proceeding southeast on I–26 toward Charleston SC. There's so much press and staff and techs and stringers and field producers and photographers and heads and pencils and political columnists and hosts of political radio shows and local media covering John McCain and the McCain2000 phenomenon post-

New Hampshire that there's now more than one campaign bus. Here in South Carolina there are three, a veritable convoy of Straight Talk, plus Fox News's green SUV and the MTV crew's sprightly red Corvette and two much-antennae'd local-TV vans (one of which has severe muffler trouble). On DTs like this McCain's always in his personal red recliner next to political consultant Mike Murphy's red recliner in the little press salon he and Murphy have in the back of the lead bus, the well-known Straight Talk Express, which is up ahead and gaining. Bullshit 1 is the caravan's second bus, a luxury Grumman with good current and workable phone jacks, and a lot of the national pencils use it to pound out copy on their laptops and send faxes and e-mail stuff to their editors. The campaign's logistics are dizzyingly complex, and one of the things the staff has to do is rent different buses and decorate the nicest one with STRAIGHT TALK EXPRESS and MCCAIN2000.COM in each new state. The two press buses in SC are known as Bullshit 1 and Bullshit 2, names conceived as usual by the extremely cool and laid-back NBC News cameraman Jim C. and—to their credit—immediately seized on and used with great glee at every opportunity by McCain's younger Press Liaisons, who are themselves so cool and unpretentious it's tempting to suspect that they are *professionally* cool and unpretentious.

It helps to conceive a campaign week's events in terms of boxes, boxes inside other boxes, etc. The national voting audience is the great huge outer box, then the SC-electorate audience, mediated respectively by the inner layers of national and local press, just inside which lie the insulating boxes of McCain's staff's High Command, who plan and stage events and Spin stuff for the layers of press to interpret for the layers of audience, and the Press Liaisons, who shepherd the pencils and heads and mediate their access to the High Command and control which media get rotated onto the S.T. Express (which is itself a box in motion) to interface with McCain himself, a candidate whose biggest draw of course is that he's an anticandidate, someone who's open and accessible and "thinks outside the box," but is in fact the campaign's Chinese boxes' central and inscrutable core box, and whose own intracranial thoughts on all these boxes and layers and lenses and whether this new kind of enclosure is anything like Hoa Lo's dark box are pretty much anyone in the media's guess, since all he'll talk about is politics.

Bullshit 1 is also a box, of course, just as anything you can't exit till somebody tells you becomes, and right now there are 27 members of the national political media on board, halfway to Charleston, where a certain percentage of them will get rotated back off the Trail tonight and be gone tomorrow. That's what these pros call it, the Trail, the same way musicians talk about the Road. The schedule is fascist: Wake-up call and backup alarm at 0600h., Express Checkout, Baggage Call at 0700 to throw bags and techs' gear under the bus, DT to McCain's first THM at 0800, then another, then another, maybe an hour off to F&F someplace if ODTs permit, then usually two big evening events, plus hours of dead Interstate DT between functions, finally getting in to the night's Marriott or Hampton Inn at like 2300 just when Room Service closes so you're begging rides from Fox News to find a restaurant still open, then an hour at the hotel bar to try to shut your head off so you can hit the rack at 0130 and get up at 0600 and do it all again. Usually it's four to six days for the average pencil and then you go off home on a gurney and your editor rotates in fresh meat. The network techs, who are old hands at the Trail, stay on for months at a time. The McCain2000 staff has been doing this full-time since Labor Day, and even the young ones look like the walking dead. Only McCain seems to thrive. He's 63 and practically Rockette-kicks onto the Express every morning. It's either inspiring or frightening.

Here's a quick behind-the-scenes tour of everything that's happening on BS1 at 1330h. A few of the press are slumped over sleeping, open-mouthed and twitching, using their topcoats for pillows. The CBS and NBC techs are in their usual place on the couches way up front, their cameras and sticks and boom mikes and boxes of tapes and big Duracells piled around them, discussing obscure stand-up comedians of the early '70s and trading Press badges from New Hampshire and Iowa and Delaware. NBC's Jim C., who looks like a chronically sleep-deprived Elliott Gould, is also watching the Press Liaison's leather bookbag swing metronomically by its overshoulder strap as the Liaison leans against the driver's seat and secretly dozes. All the couches and padded chairs face in, perpendicular to BS1's length, instead of a regular bus's forward-facing seats, so everyone's legs are always in the aisle, but there's none of the normal social anxiety about your legs touching somebody else on a bus's leg because nobody can help it and they're too tired to care. About two-thirds of the way down the aisle is a little area that has the bus's refrigerator and the liquor cabinets (totally empty on BS1) and the bathroom with the hazardous door. There's also a little counter area piled with Krispy Kreme doughnut boxes, plus a sink whose water nobody ever uses (for what turn out to be good reasons). Krispy Kremes are sort of the Deep South equivalent of Dunkin' Donuts, ubiquitous and cheap and great in a sort of what-am-I-doing-eating-dessert-for-breakfast way, and are a cornerstone of what Jim C. calls the Campaign Diet.

Behind the buses' digestive areas is another couch-intensive section, in which right now Mrs. McCain's personal assistant on the Trail, Wendy—who has electric-blue contact lenses and very complex and rigid blond hair and designer outfits and immaculate makeup and accessories and French nails and can perhaps best be described as a very *Republican*-looking young lady indeed—is eating a large styrofoam cup of soup and using her cellphone to try to find someplace in downtown Charleston where Mrs. McCain can get her nails done. Just why Wendy is arranging for her mistress's manicure on a press bus is unclear, but Mrs. McC.'s sedulous attention to her own person's dress and grooming is already a minor legend among the press corps, and some of the techs speculate that stuff like getting her nails and hair done, together with being almost Siametically attached to Ms. Lisa Graham Keegan (who is AZ's Education Superintendent and supposedly traveling with the Senator as his "Adviser on Issues Affecting Education" but is quite obviously really along because she's Cindy McCain's friend and confidante and the only person in whose presence Mrs. McC. doesn't look like a jacklighted deer), are the only things keeping this extremely fragile person together on the Trail, where she's required to stand under hot lights next to McCain at every speech and THM and Press-Avail and stare cheerfully into the middle distance while her husband speaks to crowds and lenses—in fact some of the cable-network techs have a sort of running debate about what she's really looking at as she stands onstage being scrutinized but never getting to say anything . . . and anyway everybody understands and respects the enormous pressure Wendy's under to help Mrs. McC. keep it together, and nobody makes fun of her for things like getting more and more stressed out as it becomes obvious that there's some special Southeast-U.S. idiom for "manicure" that Wendy doesn't know, because nobody she talks to on the cellphone seems to have any idea what she means by "manicure."

If this all seems really static and dull, by the way, then understand you're getting a bona fide media-eye look at the reality of life on the Trail, 85% of which consists of wandering around killing time on Bullshit 1 while you wait for the slight significant look from the Press Liaison which means that after the next stop you're getting rotated up into the big leagues on the Express to sit squished and paralyzed on the crammed red press-couch in back and to listen to John S. McCain and his aide-de-camp Mike Murphy answer the Twelve Monkeys' questions and to look up-close and personal at McCain and the way he puts his legs way out on the salon's floor and crosses them at the ankle and sucks absently at his right bicuspid and twirls the coffee in his MCCAIN2000.COM mug and to try to penetrate the innermost box of this man's thoughts on the enormous hope and enthusiasm he's generating in press and voters alike. . . . Which you should be told upfront does not and cannot happen, this penetration, partly for the reason that when you are finally rotated up into the Straight Talk salon you discover that most of the questions the Twelve Monkeys ask back here are too vapid and obvious for McCain to waste time on, and he lets Mike Murphy handle them, and Murphy is so funny and dry and able to make such delicious sport of the 12M—

MONKEY: If, say, you win here in South Carolina, what do you do then?

MURPHY: Fly to Michigan that night.

MONKEY: And what if, hypothetically, you, say, lose here in South Carolina?

MURPHY: Fly to Michigan that night win or lose.

MONKEY: Can you perhaps talk about why?

MURPHY: 'Cause the plane's already paid for.

MONKEY: I mean can you explain why specifically Michigan?

MURPHY: It's the next primary.

MONKEY: I think what we're trying to get you to elaborate on, Mike, is: what will your goal be in Michigan?

MURPHY: To get a whole lot of votes. That's part of our secret strategy for winning the nomination.

—that it's hard even to notice McCain's there or what his face or feet are doing because it takes almost all your concentration not to start giggling like a maniac at Murphy and the way the 12M all nod somberly at him and take whatever he says down in their absolutely identical steno notebooks.

What's hazardous about Bullshit 1's lavatory door is that it opens and closes laterally, sliding with a *Star Trek*ish whoosh at the light touch of the door button just inside—i.e., you go in, lightly push DOOR to close, attend to business, lightly push DOOR again to open: simple—except that the DOOR button's placement puts it only inches away from the left shoulder of any male journalist standing over the commode attending to business, a commode without rails or handles or anything to (as it were) hold on to, and even the slightest leftward lurch or lean makes said shoulder touch said button—which remember this is a moving bus—causing the door to whoosh open while you're right there with business underway, and with the consequences of suddenly whirling to try to stab at the button to reclose the door while you're in *medias res* being too obviously horrid to detail, with the result that by 9 February the great unspoken rule among the regulars on Bullshit 1 is that when any male gets up and goes two-thirds of the way back into the lavatory anybody who's back there clears the immediate area and makes sure they're not in the door's line of sight; and the way you can tell that a journalist is a local or newly rotated onto the Trail and this is their first time on BS1 is the small strangled scream you always hear when they're in the lavatory and the door unexpectedly whooshes open, and usually the grizzled old Charleston *Post and Courier* pencil will give a small smile and call out "Welcome to national politics!" as the new guy stabs frantically at the button, and Jay at the helm will hit the horn with the heel of his hand in mirth, taking these long and mostly mindless DTs' fun where he finds it.

Who Even Cares Who Cares?

It's hard to get good answers to why Young Voters are so uninterested in politics. This is probably because it's next to impossible to get someone to think hard about why he's not interested in something. The boredom itself preempts inquiry; the fact of the feeling's enough. Surely one reason, though, is that politics is not cool. Or say rather that cool, interesting, alive people do not seem to be the ones who are drawn to the Political Process. Think back to the sort of kids in high school or college who were into running for student office: dweeby, overgroomed, obsequious to authority, ambitious in a sad way. Eager to play the Game. The kind of kids other kids would want to beat up if it didn't seem so pointless and dull. And now consider some of 2000's adult versions of these very same kids: Al Gore, best described by CNN sound tech Mark A. as "amazingly lifelike"; Steve Forbes, with his wet forehead and loony giggle; G.W. Bush's patrician smirk and mangled cant; even Clinton himself with his big red fake-friendly face and "I feel your pain." Men who aren't enough like human beings even to dislike— what one feels when they loom into view is just an overwhelming lack of interest, the sort of deep disengagement that is so often a defense against pain. Against sadness. In fact the likeliest reason why so many of us care so little about politics is that modern politicians make us sad, hurt us in ways that are hard even to name, much less to talk about. It's way easier to roll your eyes and not give a shit. You probably don't want to hear about all this, even.

One reason a lot of the media on the Trail like John McCain is simply that he's a cool guy. Nondweeby. In school, Clinton was in Student Government and Band, whereas McCain was a Varsity wrestler and a hellraiser whose talents for partying and getting laid are still spoken of with awe by former classmates. At 63, he's funny, and smart, and he'll make fun of himself and his wife and his staff and other pols and the Trail, and he'll tease the press and give them shit in a way they don't ever mind because it's the sort of shit that makes you feel like here's this very cool, important guy who's noticing you and liking you enough to give you shit. Sometimes he'll wink at you for no reason. If all this doesn't sound like that big a deal, you have to remember that most of these pro reporters have to spend a lot of time around politicians, and most politicians are painful to be around. As one political columnist told ROLLING STONE and another pencil new to the Trail, "If you saw more of how the other candidates conduct themselves, you'd be way more impressed with [McCain]. It's that he acts somewhat in the ballpark of the way a real human being would act." And the grateful press on the Trail transmit—maybe even exaggerate— McCain's humanity to their huge audience, the electorate, which electorate in turn seems so paroxysmically thankful for a presidential candidate *somewhat in the ballpark of a real human being* that it has to make you stop and think about how starved voters are for just some minimal level of genuineness in the men who want to "lead" and "inspire" them.

There are, of course, still some groups of Young Voters way, way into modern politics. There's Rowdy Ralph Reed's far-Right Christians, for one, and then way out at the other end of the spectrum there's ACT UP and the sensitive men and angry womyn of the PC Left. What's interesting is that what gives these small fringe blocs so much power is the basic failure of mainstream Young Voters to get off their ass and vote. It's like we all learned in jr. high social studies: if I vote and you don't, my vote counts double. And it's not just the fringes that benefit—the fact is that it's to some very powerful Establishments' advantage that most young people hate politics and don't vote. This, too, deserves to be thought about, if you can stand it.

There's another thing John McCain always says. He makes sure he concludes every speech and THM with it, so the buses' press hear it about 100 times this week. He always pauses a second for effect and then says: "I'm going to tell you something. I may have said some things here today that maybe you don't agree with, and I might have said some things you hopefully do agree with. But I will always. Tell you. The truth." This is McCain's closer, his last big reverb on the six-string as it were. And the frenzied standing-O it always gets from his audience is something to see. But you have to wonder: why do these crowds from Detroit to Charleston cheer so wildly at a simple promise not to lie?

Well it's obvious why. When McCain says it, the people are cheering not for him so much as for how good it feels to believe him. They're cheering the loosening of a weird sort of knot in the electoral tummy. McCain's résumé and candor, in other words, promise not empathy with voters' pain, but relief from it. Because we've been lied to and lied to, and it hurts to be lied to. It's ultimately just about that complicated: it hurts. It denies you respect for yourself, for the liar, for the world. Especially if the lies are chronic, systemic, if hard experience seems to teach that everything you're supposed to believe in's really a game based on lies. Young Voters have been taught well and thoroughly. You may not personally remember Vietnam or Watergate, but it's a good bet you remember "No new taxes" and "Out of the loop" and "No direct knowledge of any impropriety at this time" and "Did not inhale" and "Did not have sex with that woman" and etc. etc. It's depressing and painful to believe that the would-be "public servants" you're forced to choose between are all phonies whose only real concern is their own care and feeding and who will lie so outrageously with such a straight face that you just know they have to believe you're an idiot. So who wouldn't fall all over themselves for a top politician who actually seemed to talk to you like you were a person, an intelligent adult worthy of respect? A politician who all of a sudden out of nowhere comes on TV as this total longshot candidate and says that Washington is paralyzed, that everybody there's been bought off, and that the only way to really "return government to the people" the way all the other candidates claim they want to do is to outlaw huge unreported political contributions from corporations and lobbies and PACs . . . all of which are obvious truths that everybody knows but no recent politician's had the stones to say. Who wouldn't cheer, hearing stuff like this, especially from a guy we know chose to sit in a dark box for four years instead of violate a Code? Even in A.D. 2000, who among us is so cynical that he doesn't have some good old corny American hope way down deep in his heart, lying dormant like a spinster's ardor, not dead but just waiting for the Right Guy to give it to? That John S. McCain III opposed making Martin Luther King's birthday a holiday, or that he thinks clear-cut logging is good for America, or that he feels our present gun laws are not clinically insane—this stuff counts for nothing with these Town Hall crowds, all on their feet, cheering their own ability to finally really fucking cheer.

Negativity

7–13 February is pitched to ROLLING STONE as a "down week" on the GOP Trail, an interval almost breathtaking in its political unsexiness. Last week was the NH surprise; next week is the mad dash to SC's 2/19 primary, which the Twelve Monkeys all believe could now make or break both McCain and the Shrub. This week is the trenches: flesh-pressing, fundraising, traveling, poll-taking, strategizing, grinding out eight-event days in Michigan and Georgia and New York and SC. The Daily Press Schedule goes from 12-point type to 10-. Warren MI Town Hall Meeting in Ukrainian Cultural Center. Saginaw County GOP Lincoln Day Dinner. Editorial Meeting w/Detroit *News*. Press Conference at Weird Meth-Lab-Looking Internet Company in Flint. Redeye to North Savannah on Chartered 707 with Faint *Pan Am* Still Stenciled on Tail. Spartanburg SC Town Hall Meeting. Closed-Circuit TV Reception for McCain Supporters in Three States Broadcast Out of Charleston. AARP Town Forum. North Augusta THM. Live Town Hall Forum at Clemson U. with Chris Matthews of

MSNBC's *Hardball*. Goose Creek THM. Door-to-Door Campaigning with Congressmen Lindsey Graham and Mark Sanford and Senator Fred Thompson (R.-TN) and About 300 Media in Florence SC. NASCAR Tour and Test-Drive at Darlington Raceway. National Guard Armory THM in Fort Mill. Congressman Lindsey Graham Hosts Weird BBQ for a Lot of Flinty-Eyed Men in Down Vests and Trucker's Hats in Seneca SC. Taping of *Tim Russert* show for CNBC. Greer THM. Cyber-Fundraiser in Charleston. *Larry King Live* with Larry King Looking Even More Like a Giant Bug than Usual. Press-Conference in Greenville. Book Signing at Chapter 11 Books in Atlanta. On and on. Breakfast a Krispy Kreme, lunch a sandwich in Saran and store-brand chips, supper anyone's guess. Everyone but McCain is grim and stolid. "We're in maybe a little bit of a trough in terms of excitement," a Press Liaison concedes in his orientation for new pencils on Monday morning. . . .

. . . Until that very day's big tactical shift, which catches the McCain press corps unawares and gets all sorts of stuff underway for midweek's dramatic tactical climax, the Chris Duren Incident, all of which is politically sexy and exciting as hell, though not quite in the kind of way you cheer for.

The big tactical shift starts in the F&F Room of something called the Riverfront Hotel in the almost unbelievably blighted and depressing Flint MI, where all the buses' media are at 1500h. on 2/7 while McCain is huddled with the staff High Command in a suite upstairs. There is no more definitive behind-scene locale in a primary campaign than the F&F Room, which is usually some hotel's little third-string banquet- or meeting room off the lobby that McCain2000 rents (at the media's expense, precisely divided and tallied, just like each day's seat on the buses and plane and the Continental Breakfasts before Baggage Call and even the F&F Rooms' "catered lunches," which today are weird bright-red ham on Wonder Bread, Fritos, and coffee that tastes like warm water with a brown crayon in it, and the pencils all bitch about the McCain2000 food and wistfully recount rumors that the Bush2000 press lunches are supposedly hot and multi-food-group and served on actual plates by unctuous men with white towels over their arm) so that those media with PM deadlines can finish their stories and File and Feed. By 1515h., each chair is filled by a producer or pencil trying to eat and type and talk on the phone all at once, and the whole F&F Room is up and running and alive with the quaduple ding of Windows booting up, the honk and static of modem connections, the multiphase clicking of forty-plus keyboards, the needly screech of fax machines saying hello to New York and Atlanta and the murmur of people on head-set phones doing same.

Outside the Riverfront's side doors off the parking lot, where it's so cold and windy you have to smoke with mittens on, an OTS with Jim C. and his long-time friend and partner Frank C. means getting to bitch about the 12 Monkeys, and here Jim and Frank discourse with no small sympathy on the brutality of these cam-paign reporters' existence—subsisting on the Campaign Diet, which is basically sugar and caffeine (diabetes is apparently the Black Lung of political journalism), always on the road in some sort of box for weeks at a time, very alone, connected to loved ones only by cellphone and 1-800 answering service. ROLLING STONE mentions being in hotels every night, which a CBS sound guy on BS2 had said was probably the McCain media's number-one stres-sor. The Shrub apparently stays in five-star places with putting greens and spurting-nymph fountains and a speed-dial number for the in-house masseur. Not McCain2000, which favors Mar-riott, Courtyard by Marriott, Hampton Inn, Hilton, Signature Inn, Radisson, Holiday Inn, Embassy Suites, etc. ROLLING STONE, who is in no way cut out to be a road journalist, invokes the soul-killing anonymity of chain hotels, the rooms' terrible transient sameness: the ubiquitous floral design of the bedspreads, the mul-tiple low-watt lamps, the pallid artwork bolted to the wall, the whisper of ventilation, the sad shag carpet, the smell of alien cleansers, the Kleenex dispensed from the wall, the automated wakeup call, the lightproof curtains, the windows that do not open—ever. RS asks whether it could possibly be coincidence that over half of all indoor suicides take place in chain hotels. Jim and Frank say they get the idea. RS references the terrible oxymoron of "hotel *guest*." Hell could easily be a chain hotel. Is it any accident that McCain's POW prison was known as the Hanoi *Hilton*? Jim shrugs; Frank says you get used to it, that it's better not to dwell.

Monday, the first and only File and Feed in Michigan, is also the day of ROLLING STONE's introduction to the Cellular Waltz, one of the most striking natural formations of the Trail. There's a huge empty lobbylike space you have to pass through to get from the Riverfront's side doors back to the area where the F&F and bath-rooms are. It takes a long time to traverse this space, a hundred yards of nothing but flagstone walls and plaques with the sad pre-tentious names of the Riverfront's banquet halls and conference rooms—the Oak Room, the Windsor Room—but on return from the OTS now out here are also half a dozen different members of the F&F Room's press, each fifty feet away from any of the others, for privacy, and all walking in idle counterclockwise circles with a cellphone to their ear. These little orbits are the Cellular Waltz, which is probably the digital equivalent of doodling or picking at yourself as you talk on a regular landline. There's something oddly lovely about the Waltz's different circles here, which are of various diameters and stride-lengths and rates of rotation but are all iden-tically counterclockwise and telephonic. We three slow down a bit to watch; you couldn't not. From above, like if there were a mez-zanine, the Waltzes would look like the cogs of some strange, dif-fuse machine. Frank C. says he can tell by their faces something's up. Jim C. says what's interesting is that media south of the equator do the exact same Cellular Waltz but that down there all their circles are reversed.

The reason for all the lobby's Waltzing was that during the OTS word apparently started to spread in the F&F Room that Mr. Mike Murphy of the McCain2000 High Command was coming down to do a surprise impromptu -Avail regarding a fresh two-page Press Release (still slightly warm from the Xerox) which two Press Liaisons are passing out even now, and of which part of the first page is reproduced here:

BUSH CAMPAIGN CAUGHT RED-HANDED WITH NEGATIVE ADS, UNETHICAL "PUSH-POLLING"

Outraged South Carolinians Unite Against False Advertising, Universally-Condemned Negative Polling Practice, McCain Volunteer Army Waiting With Tape Recorders to Catch Bush in the Act

COLUMBIA, SC—Deceptive TV ads and negative "push polls" conducted by phone in South Carolina last night by a polling firm employed by Texas Governor George W. Bush's campaign . . .

This document is unusual not only because McCain2000's Press Releases are normally studies in bland irrelevance— "MCCAIN TO CONTINUE CAMPAIGNING IN MICHIGAN TODAY"; "MCCAIN HAS TWO HELPINGS OF POTATO SALAD AT SOUTH CAROLINA VFW PICNIC"—but because no less a personage than Mike Murphy has now indeed just come down to Spin this abrupt change of tone in the campaign's rhetoric. Murphy, who is only 37 but seems a lot older, is the McCain campaign's Senior Strategist, a professional political consultant who's already had eighteen winning Senate and gubernatorial campaigns and is as previously mentioned a constant and acerbic presence in McCain's press salon aboard the Express. Among political pros, Murphy has the reputation of being (1) smart and funny as hell and (2) a real attack-dog, working for clients like Oliver North and Michigan's own John Engler in campaigns that were absolute operas of nastiness, and known for turning out what the NY *Times* rather delicately called "some of the most rough-edged commercials in the business." He's leaning back against a wall and surrounded in a 180° arc by the Twelve Monkeys, all of whom have notebooks or tiny professional tape recorders out and keep clearing their throats and pushing their glasses up with excitement.

Murphy says he's "just swung by" to provide the press corps with "some context" on the strident Press Release and to give the corps advance notice that the McCain campaign is also preparing a special "response ad" which will start airing in South Carolina tomorrow. Murphy uses the words "response" or "response ad" nine times in two minutes, and when one of the Twelve Monkeys interrupts to ask whether it'd be fair to characterize this new ad as Negative Murphy gives him a long styptic look and spells "*r-e-s-p-o-n-s-e*" out very slowly.

He then tells the hemispheric scrum that the Press Release and new ad reflect the McCain2000 campaign's decision, after much agonizing, to respond to what he says is G.W. Bush's welching on the two candidates' public handshake-agreement in January to run a bilaterally positive campaign. For the past five days, mostly in New York and SC, the Shrub has apparently been running ads that characterize McCain's policy proposals in what Murphy terms a "willfully distorting" way. Plus there's the push-polling, a practice that's regarded as the absolute bottom-feeder of sleazy campaign tactics. But the worst, the most obviously unacceptable, Murphy emphasizes, was the Shrub standing up at a podium in SC a couple days ago with a wild-eyed and apparently notorious "fringe veteran" who publicly accused John McCain of "abandoning his fellow veterans" after returning from Vietnam, which, Murphy says, without going into McCain's well-documented personal bio and heroic legislative efforts on behalf of vets for nearly twenty years is just so clearly over the line of even minimal personal decency and honor that it pretty much necessitates some sort of response.

The Twelve Monkeys, who are old pros at this sort of exchange, keep trying to steer Murphy away from what the Shrub's done and get him to give a quotable explanation of why McCain himself has decided to run this "response ad," a transcript of which the harried Press Liaisons are now distributing from a fresh copier-box and which features, in part:

> *Audio*
> McCain: "I guess it was bound to happen.
>> Governor Bush's campaign is getting desperate with a negative ad about me.
>> The fact is, I will use the surplus money to fix Social Security, cut your taxes, and pay down the debt. . . .
>> His ad twists the truth like Clinton. We're all pretty tired of that. . . ."

—of which ad-transcript the 12M point out that in particular the "twists the truth like Clinton" part seems Negative indeed, since in '00 comparing a GOP candidate to Bill Clinton is roughly equivalent to claiming that he wears ladies' underwear under his black robes while presiding over Satanic masses.

The network techs, while checking their equipment and starting to gear up for the scrum of McCain's exit at the Riverfront's main doors, listen to ROLLING STONE's summary of the Press Release and Murphy's comments, confirm that the Shrub has indeed gone Negative (they'd heard about all this long before the

Twelve Monkeys et al., because the techs and field producers are in constant touch with their colleagues on the Shrub's buses, whereas the Monkeys' Bush2000 counterparts are as aloof and niggardly about sharing info as the 12M themselves), and kill the last of the time in the Flint F&F by quietly analyzing Bush's Negativity and McCain's response from a tactical point of view.

Leaving aside their coolness and esprit de corps, be advised that ROLLING STONE's single luckiest journalistic accident this week was his bumbling into hanging around with these camera and sound guys. This is because network-news techs—who all have worked countless campaigns, and who have neither the raging egos of journalists nor the self-interested agenda of the McCain2000 staff to muddy their perspective—turn out to be way more acute and sensible political analysts than anybody you'll read or see on TV, and their assessment of today's Negativity developments is so extraordinarily nuanced and sophisticated that only a small portion of it can be ripped off and summarized here.

Going Negative is risky. Countless polls have shown that voters find it distasteful in the extreme, and if a candidate is perceived as going Negative, it usually costs him. So the techs all agree that the first question is why Bush2000 started playing this card. One possible explanation is that the Shrub was so personally shocked and scared by McCain's win in New Hampshire that he's now lashing out like a spoiled child and trying to hurt McCain however he can. The techs reject this, though. Spoiled child or no, G.W. Bush is a creature of his campaign advisers, and these advisers are the best that $70 million and the full faith and credit of the GOP Establishment can buy, and if Bush2000 has gone Negative there must be solid political logic behind the move.

This logic turns out to be indeed solid, even brilliant, and the NBC, CBS and CNN techs flesh it out while the ABC cameraman puts several emergency sandwiches in his lens bag for tonight's flight south on a campaign plane whose provisioning is notoriously inconsistent. The Shrub's attack leaves McCain with two options. If he does not retaliate, some SC voters will credit McCain for taking the high road. But it could also come off as wimpy, might compromise McCain's image as a tough, take-no-shit guy with the balls to take on the Washington kleptocracy. So McCain pretty much has to strike back, the techs agree. But this is extremely dangerous, for by retaliating—which of course (despite all Murphy's artful dodging) means going Negative himself—McCain runs the risk of looking like just another ambitious, win-at-any-cost politician. Worse, the CBS cameraman points out, if Bush then turns around and retaliates against the retaliation, and McCain has to re-retaliate against Bush's retaliation, and so on, then the whole GOP race could quickly degenerate into the sort of boring, depressing, cynical charge- and counter-charge contest that turns voters off and keeps them away from the polls. . . . Especially Young Voters, RS and an underage local pencil from one of those weekly things that people can pick up free at Detroit supermarkets point out, both scribbling just as furiously with the techs as the 12M did with Murphy. The techs say well OK maybe but that the really important tactical point here is that John S. McCain *cannot* afford to have voters get turned off, since his whole strategy is based on exciting the people and inspiring them and pulling more voters in, especially those who'd stopped voting because they'd gotten so disgusted and bored with all the Negativity and bullshit of politics. In other words, RS and the Detroit free-weekly kid propose to the techs, it's maybe even in the Shrub's political *self-interest* to let the GOP race get ugly and Negative and have voters get so bored and cynical and disgusted with the whole thing that they don't even bother to vote. Well no shit Sherlock H., the ABC techs in essence respond, good old Frank C. then patiently explaining that, yes, if there's a low voter turnout, then the majority of the people who get off their ass and do vote will be the Diehard Republicans, meaning the Christian Right and the party faithful, and these are the groups that vote as they're told, the ones controlled by the GOP Establishment, an Establishment that's got $70 million and 100% of its own credibility invested in the Shrub. CNN's Mark A. inserts that this also explains why the amazingly lifelike Al Gore, over in the Democratic race, has been so relentlessly Negative and depressing in his attacks on Bill Bradley: since Gore, like the Shrub, has his party's Establishment behind him, with all its organization and money and the Diehards who'll fall into line and vote as they're told, it's in Big Al's (and his party's bosses') interest to draw as few voters as possible into the Democratic primaries, because the lower the overall turnout, the more the Establishment voters' ballots actually count. Which fact then in turn, the CBS cameraman says, helps explain why, even though our elected representatives are always wringing their hands and making concerned sounds about low voter-turnouts, nothing substantive ever gets done to make politics less ugly or depressing and to actually induce more people to vote: our elected representatives are incumbents, and low turnouts favor incumbents for the same reason soft money does.

Let's pause here one second for a quick ROLLING STONE PSA. If you are demographically a Young Voter, it is again worth a moment of your valuable time to consider the implications of the techs' point. If you are bored and disgusted by politics and don't bother to vote, you are in effect voting for the entrenched Establishments of the two major parties, who are not dumb and are *keenly* aware that it's in their interests to keep you disgusted and bored and cynical and to give you every possible psychological reason to stay at home doing one-hitters and watching MTV *Spring Break* on Primary Day. By all means stay home if you want, but don't bullshit yourself that you're not voting. In reality, there is *no such thing as not voting:* you either vote by voting, or you vote by staying home and tacitly doubling the value of some Diehard's vote.

But so the techs' assessment, then, is that Bush's going Negative is both tactically sound and politically near-brilliant, and that it forces McCain's own strategists to walk a very tight wire indeed in formulating a response. What McCain has to try to do, then, is retaliate without losing the inspiring high-road image that won him New Hampshire. This is why Mike Murphy took valuable huddle-with-candidate time to come down to the F&F and spoonfeed the Twelve Monkeys all this stuff about Bush's attacks being so far over the line that they have no choice but to "respond." Because the McCain2000 campaign has got to Spin today's retaliation the same way nations Spin war: McCain has to make it appear that he is not being actually aggressive himself but is merely "repelling aggression." It will require enormous discipline and cunning for McCain2000 to pull this off. And tomorrow's "response ad"—in the techs' opinion as the transcript's passed around—this is not a promising start, discipline-and-cunning-wise, especially the "twists the truth like Clinton" part that the 12M jumped on Murphy for. This line's too mean. McCain2000 could have chosen to put together a much softer and smarter ad patiently "correcting" certain "unfortunate errors" in Bush's ads and "respectfully requesting" that the push-polling cease (with everything in quotes here being Jim C.'s suggested terms) and striking just the right high-road tone. The actual ad's "twists like Clinton" does not sound high-road; it sounds pissed off, aggressive. And it will allow Bush to do a React and now say that it's *McCain* who's violated the handshake-agreement . . . which the techs say will of course be bullshit, but that it might be effective bullshit, and that it's McCain's aggressive ad that's giving the Shrub the opening to do it.

The techs' basic analysis of the motivation behind "twists the truth like Clinton" is that McCain is genuinely, personally pissed off at the Shrub, and that he has taken Murphy's leash off and let Murphy do what Murphy does best, which is gutter-fight. McCain, after all, is known for having a temper (though he's been extremely controlled in the campaign so far and never shown it in public), and Jim C. thinks that maybe the truly ingenious thing the Shrub's strategists did was to find a way to genuinely piss McCain off and make him want to go Negative even though the staff High Command had to have warned him that this was playing right into Bush's strategists' hands. This analysis suddenly reminds ROLLING STONE of the part in *The Godfather* where Sonny Corleone's fatal flaw is his temper, which Barzini and Tattaglia exploit by getting Carlo to beat up Connie and make Sonny so insanely angry that he drives off to kill Carlo and gets assassinated in Barzini's ambush at the tollbooth. Jim C., sweating heavily with forty pounds of gear on, says he supposes there are some similarities, and Randy (the taciturn but cinephilic CNN cameraman) speculates that the Shrub's brain-trust may actually have based their whole strategy on Barzini's ingenious ploy in *The Godfather,* and Frank C. observes that Bush's equivalent to slapping Connie Corleone around was probably his standing up with the wacko vet who claimed McCain dissed his Vietnam comrades, which at first looked stupid and unnecessarily nasty of Bush but from another perspective might have been sheer genius if it made McCain so angry that his desire to retaliate outweighed his political judgment.

And events of the next few days bear out the techs' analysis pretty much 100%. On Tuesday morning, on the Radisson's TV in North Savannah SC, both *Today* and *GMA* lead with "The GOP campaign takes an ugly turn" and show the part of McCain's new ad where he says "twists the truth like Clinton"; and sure enough by midday the Shrub has put out a React where he accuses John S. McCain of violating the handshake-agreement and going Negative and adds that he is "personally offended and outraged" at being compared to W.J. Clinton; and then at a Press-Avail in Hilton Head the Shrub avers that he knows less than nothing about any so-called push-polling and suggests that the whole thing might have been fabricated as a sleazy political ploy on McCain2000's part; and then on Wednesday a.m. on TV at the Embassy Suites in Charleston there's now an even *more* aggressive ad that Murphy's gotten McCain to let him run, which shows a nighttime shot of 1600 Pennsylvania Ave.'s famous façade with its palisade of blatantly ejaculatory fountains in the foreground and says "Can America afford another politician in the White House that we can't trust?," which grammatical problems aside Frank C. says that that shot of the White House is really going low with the knife and that if McCain loses South Carolina it may very well be because of this ad; and sure enough by Wednesday night focus polls are showing that South Carolina voters are finding the new ad Negative and depressing, and the next couple days' polls then have both McCain's support and the primary's projected voter-turnout falling like a rock, and the daily pencils are having to churn out piece after piece about all the endless picayune charges and counter-charges, and everyone on Bullshit 1 and 2 is starting to get severely dispirited and bored, and even the 12M's strides have lost a certain spring . . .

. . . And then out of nowhere comes the dramatic tactical climax mentioned *supra,* which hits the media like a syringe of Narcan and makes all five networks' news that night. It occurs at the Spartanburg SC THM, whose venue is a small steep theater in the Fine Arts Center of a small college nobody could ever find out the name of, and is so packed by the time the press corps gets there that even the aisles are full, so that everybody except the techs and their producers is out in the lobby.

To be honest, all the national pencils would probably be out here in the lobby even if the theater weren't full, because after a few days McCain's opening THM 22.5 becomes almost wrist-slittingly dull and repetitive. Journalists who've covered McCain since Christmas report that Mike Murphy and Co. have worked hard on him to become more "Message-Disciplined," which in political-speak means reducing everything important to brief, memory-friendly slogans—"the Iron Triangle of money, lobbyists and legislation," "I'm going to beat Al Gore like a drum"—and then punching those slogans over and over.

In fairness to McCain, he's not an orator and doesn't pretend to be. His métier is conversation, back-and-forth. This is because he's bright in a fast, flexible way that most candidates aren't. He also genuinely seems to find people and questions and arguments energizing—the latter maybe because of all his years debating in Congress—which is why he favors Town Hall Q&As and constant chats with press in his rolling salon. So, while the media marvel at his accessibility because they've been trained to equate it with vulnerability, they often don't seem to realize they're playing totally to McCain's strength when they converse with him instead of listening to his speeches. It's McCain's speeches and 22.5's that are canned and stilted, and also sometimes scary and Right-wingish, and when you listen closely to them it's as if some warm pleasant fog suddenly lifts and it strikes you that you're not at all sure it's John McCain you want choosing the head of the EPA or the at least three new Justices who'll be coming onto the Supreme Court in the next term, and you start wondering all over again what makes him so attractive.

But then the doubts again dissolve when McCain starts taking questions at THMs, which by now is what's underway in Spartanburg. The questions always run the great *vox populi* gamut, from Talmudically bearded guys asking about Chechnya and tort reform to high-school kids reading questions off printed sheets their hands shake as they hold, from moms worried about their kids' future SSI to old vets in Legion caps who call McCain "Lieutenant" and want to trade salutes, plus the obligatory walleyed fundamentalists trying to pin him down on whether Christ considered homosexuality "an abomination," and arcane questions about index-fund regulation and postal privatization, and HMO horror stories, and Internet porn, and tobacco litigation, and people who believe the Second Amendment entitles them to own grenade launchers. The questions are random and unscreened, and the candidate fields them all, and he's never better or more human than in these exchanges, especially when the questioner is angry or wrong—McCain will say "I respectfully disagree" or "We have a difference of opinion" and then detail his objections in lucid English with a gentleness that's never condescending. For a man with a temper, McCain is unbelievably patient and decent with people at THMs, especially when you consider that he's 63, in chronic pain, sleep-deprived, and under enormous pressure not to gaffe or get himself in trouble. He doesn't. No matter how stale and Message-Disciplined the 22.5 at the beginning, in the Town Hall Q&As you get an overwhelming sense that this is a decent, honorable man trying to tell the truth to people he really sees. You will not be alone in this impression.

And so but then in the Spartanburg Q&A, after two China questions and one on taxing Internet commerce, a totally demographically average thirty-something middle-class soccer mom in rust-colored slacks and big round glasses gets picked and stands up and somebody brings her the mike. It turns out her name is Donna Duren, of right here in Spartanburg SC, and she says she has a 14-year-old son named Chris, in whom Mr. and Mrs. Duren have been trying to inculcate family values and respect for authority and a non-cynical idealism about America and its duly elected leaders. They want him to find heroes he can believe in, she says. Donna Duren's whole story takes a while, but nobody's bored, and even on the monitors in the lobby you can sense a change in the theater's voltage, and the national pencils start moving in and elbowing people aside (which they're really good at) to get close to the monitors. Mrs. Duren says that Chris—clearly a sensitive kid—was "made very very upset" by the Lewinsky scandal and all the R-rated revelations and the appalling behavior of Clinton and Starr and Tripp and pretty much everybody on all sides during the impeachment thing, and Chris had a lot of very upsetting and uncomfortable questions that Mr. and Mrs. D. struggled to answer, and that basically it was a really hard time but they got through it. And then last year, at more or less a trough in terms of idealism and respect for elected authority, she says, Chris discovered John McCain and McCain2000.com, and got interested in the campaign, and his parents apparently read him some G-rated parts of *Faith of My Fathers,* and the upshot is that young Chris finally found a public hero he could believe in: John S. McCain III. It's impossible to know what McCain's face is doing during this story because the monitors are taking CNN's feed, and Randy of CNN's lens is staying hard and steady on Donna Duren, who appears so iconically prototypical and so thoroughly exudes the special quiet dignity of an average American who knows she's average and just wants a decent, non-cynical life for herself and her family that she can say things like "family values" and "hero" without anybody rolling their eyes. But then last night, Mrs. D. says, as they were all watching non-violent TV in the family room, the phone suddenly rang upstairs, and Chris went up and got it, and Mrs. D. says a little while later he came back down into the family room crying and just terribly upset and told them the phone call had been a man who started talking to him about the 2000 campaign and then asked Chris if he knew that John McCain was a liar and a cheater and that anybody who'd vote for John McCain was either stupid or unAmerican or both. That caller had been a push-poller for Bush2000, Mrs. Duren says, knuckles on her mike-hand white and voice almost breaking, and she says she just wanted Senator McCain to know about it, about what happened to Chris, and wants to know whether anything can be done to keep people like this from calling innocent young kids and plunging them into disillusionment and confusion about whether they're stupid for trying to have heroes they believe in.

At which point (0853h.) two things happen out here in the Fine Arts Center lobby. The first is that the national pencils disperse in a radial pattern, each dialing his cellphone, and the network field producers all come barreling out of the theater doors pulling their cellphone antennas out with their teeth, and everybody tries to find a little empty area to Waltz in while they call the gist of this riveting Negativity-related development in to networks and editors and try to raise their counterparts in the Bush2000 press corps to see if they can get a React from the Shrub on Mrs. Duren's story, at the end of which story the second thing happens, which is that CNN's Randy finally pans to McCain and you can see McCain's facial expression, which is pained and pale and actually looks more distraught even than Mrs. Duren's face had looked. And what McCain does, after looking silently at the floor a second, is—apologize. He doesn't lash out at Bush or at push-polling or appear to try to capitalize politically in any way. He looks sad and compassionate and regretful and says that the only reason he got into this race in the first place was to try to help inspire young Americans to feel better about devoting themselves to something, and that a story like what Mrs. Duren took the trouble to come down here to the THM this morning and tell him is just about the worst thing he could hear, and that if it's OK with Mrs. D. he'd like to call her son and apologize personally on the phone and maybe tell Chris that yes there are some bad people out there but that it's never a mistake to believe in something, that politics is still worthwhile as a Process to get involved in, and he really does look upset, McCain does, and almost as what seems like an afterthought he says that one thing Donna Duren and other concerned parents and citizens can do is call the Bush campaign and tell them to stop this push-polling, that Governor Bush is a good man with a family of his own and it's difficult to believe he'd ever endorse his campaign doing things like this if he knew about it, and that he (McCain) will be calling Bush again personally for like the umpteenth time to ask him to stop the Negativity, and McCain's eyes look . . . *wet*, as in teary, which maybe is just a trick of the techs' TV lights but is nevertheless disturbing, the whole thing is disturbing, because McCain seems upset in a way that's almost too dramatic. He takes a couple more THM questions, then stops abruptly and says he's sorry but he's just so incredibly upset about the Chris Duren thing that he's having a hard time concentrating on anything else, and he asks the THM crowd's forgiveness, and thanks them, and forgets his Message Discipline and doesn't finish with he'll always. Tell them. The truth but they applaud like mad anyway, and the lobby's monitors' feed is cut as Randy and Jim C. et al go shoulder-held to join the scrum as McCain starts to exit.

And now none of this is simple at all, especially not McCain's exaggerated-seeming distress about Chris Duren, and a small set of disturbing and possibly very cynical interconnected thoughts and questions start whirling around in the journalistic head. Like the fact that Donna Duren's story was a far more devastating indictment of the Shrub's campaign tactics than anything McCain himself could say, and is it possible that McCain, on the theater's stage, wasn't aware of this? Is it possible that some part of McCain could realize that what happened to Chris Duren is very much to John S. McCain's political advantage, and yet he's still such a decent, uncalculating guy that all he feels is horror and regret that a kid was disillusioned? Was it human compassion that made him apologize first instead of criticizing Bush2000, or is McCain just maybe shrewd enough to know that Mrs. D.'s story had already nailed Bush to the wall and that by apologizing and looking distraught McCain could help underscore the difference between his own human decency and Bush's uncaring Negativity? Is it possible that he really actually had *tears* in his eyes? And come to think of it hey, why would a push-poller even be interested in trying to push-poll somebody too young to vote? Does Chris Duren maybe have a really deep-sounding phone voice or something? But wouldn't you think a push-poller would ask somebody's age before launching into his spiel? And how come nobody asked this question, not even the jaded 12M, out in the lobby? What were they thinking?

Bullshit 1 is empty except for Jay, who's grabbing a nap on one of the couches, and through the port windows you can see all the techs and heads and talent in a king-size scrum around Mrs. Donna Duren in the gravel courtyard, and there's the additional cynical thought that doubtless some enterprising network crew is even now pulling up in front of poor Chris Duren's junior high (which unfortunately tonight on TV turns out to be just what happened). The bus idles empty for a very long time—the post-event scrums and standups last longer than the whole THM did— and then when the BS1 regulars finally do pile in they're all extremely busy trying to type and phone and file, and all the techs have to get their Sony DVS-series Digital Editors out and help their producers find and time the clip of Mrs. Duren's story and McCain's response so they can feed it to the networks right away, and the Twelve Monkeys have as more or less one body stormed the Straight Talk Express, which is just up ahead on I–85 and riding very low in the stern from all the weight in McCain's rear salon. The point is that none of the usual media pros are available to interface with and help deconstruct the Chris Duren Incident and help try to figure out what to be cynical about and what not to and which of the many disturbing questions the whole Incident provokes are paranoid or irrelevant and which ones might be journalistically valid ... such as was McCain really serious about calling Chris Duren? How was he going to get the Durens' phone number when Mrs. D. was scrummed solid the whole time he and the staff were leaving? And where were Mike Murphy and the other High Command through that whole thing, who can usually be seen Cell-Waltzing in the shadows at every THM but today were nowhere in sight? Is it just possible that McCain—maybe not even consciously—played up his reaction to Mrs. Duren's story and framed his distress to give himself a plausible, good-looking excuse to get out of the Negative spiral that's been hurting him so badly in the polls that Jim and Frank say he may well lose SC if things keep on this way? Is it too cynical even to consider such a thing?

Because at the following day's first Press-Avail, John S. McCain issues a plausible, good-looking, highly emotional statement to the whole scrummed corps. This is on a warm, pretty 2/11 morning outside the Embassy Suites (or maybe Hampton Inn) in Charleston, right after Baggage Call. McCain informs the press that the case of young Chris Duren has caused him such distress that after a great deal of late-night soul-searching he's now ordered his staff to cease all Negativity and to pull all the McCain2000 response ads in South Carolina regardless of whether the Shrub pulls his own Negative ads or not.

And of course framed as it is in the distressed context of the Chris Duren Incident, McCain's decision in no way now makes him look wimpy or appeasing, but rather like a truly decent, honorable, high-road guy who doesn't want young people's political idealism fucked with in any way if he can help it. It's a masterful statement, and a stirring and high-impact Press-Avail, and everybody in the scrum seems impressed and in some cases deeply and personally moved, and nobody (including ROLLING STONE) ventures to point out aloud that, however unfortunate the phone call was for the Durens, it turned out to be fortunate as *hell* for McCain2000 in terms of this week's tactical battle, that actually the whole thing couldn't have worked out better for McCain2000 if it had been . . . well, like, *scripted,* if like say Mrs. Donna Duren had been a trained actress or gifted amateur who'd been somehow secretly approached and rehearsed and paid and planted in that crowd of over 300 random unscreened questioners where her raised hand in that sea of average voters' hands was seen and chosen and she got to tell a moving story that made all five networks last night and damaged Bush badly and now has released McCain from this week's tactical box. Any way you look at it (and there's a long DT to think about it), yesterday's Incident and THM were an almost incredible stroke of political luck for McCain, or else a stroke of something else that no one—not ROLLING STONE, not the Twelve Monkeys or even the totally sharp and unsentimental and astute Jim C.—ever once broaches or mentions out loud, which might be understandable, since maybe even considering whether it was even *possible* would be so painful it would just break your heart and make it hard to go on, which is what the press and staff and Straight Talk caravan and McCain himself have to do all day, and the next, and the next—go on.

Suck It Up

Paradox: It is impossible to talk about the really important stuff in politics without using terms that have become such awful clichés they make your eyes glaze over and are hard to even hear. One such term is "leader," which all the big candidates use all the time—as in "providing leadership," "a proven leader," "a new leader for a new century," etc.—and have reduced to such a platitude that it's hard to try to think about what "leader" really means and whether indeed what today's Young Voters want is a leader. The weird thing is that the word "leader" itself is cliché and boring, but when you come across somebody who actually is a real leader, that person isn't cliché or boring at all; in fact he's sort of the *opposite* of cliché and boring.

Obviously, a real leader isn't just somebody who has ideas you agree with, nor is it just somebody you happen to think is a good guy. A real leader is somebody who, because of his own particular power and charisma and example, is able to inspire people, with "inspire" being used here in a serious and non-cliché way. A real leader can somehow get us to do certain things that deep down we think are good and want to be able to do but usually can't get ourselves to do on our own. It's a mysterious quality, hard to define, but we always know it when we see it, even as kids. You can probably remember seeing it in certain really great coaches, or teachers, or some extremely cool older kid you "looked up to" (interesting phrase) and wanted to be just like. Some of us remember seeing the quality as kids in a minister or rabbi, or a Scoutmaster, or a parent, or a friend's parent, or a supervisor in a summer job. And yes, all these are "authority figures," but it's a special kind of authority. If you've ever spent time in the military, you know how incredibly easy it is to tell which of your superiors are real leaders and which aren't, and how little rank has to do with it. A leader's real "authority" is a power you voluntarily give him, and you grant him this authority not with resentment or resignation but happily; it feels right. Deep down, you almost always like how a real leader makes you feel, the way you find yourself working harder and pushing yourself and thinking in ways you couldn't ever get to on your own.

Lincoln was, by all available evidence, a real leader, and Churchill, and Gandhi, and King. Teddy and Franklin Roosevelt, and de Gaulle, and certainly Marshall and maybe Eisenhower. (Of course Hitler was a real leader too, a very powerful one, so you have to watch out; all it is is a weird kind of power.)

Probably the last real leader we had as U.S. President was JFK, forty years ago. It's not that Kennedy was a better human being than the seven presidents we've had since: we know he lied about his WWII record, and had spooky Mob ties, and screwed around more in the White House than poor Clinton could ever dream of. But JFK had that weird leader-type magic, and when he said things like "Ask not what your country can do for you—ask what you can do for your country" nobody rolled their eyes or saw it as just political bullshit. Instead, a lot of them felt inspired. And the decade that followed, however fucked up it was in other ways, saw millions of Young Voters devote themselves to social and political causes that had nothing to do with getting a great job or owning nice stuff or finding the best parties; and the '60s were, by most accounts, a generally cleaner and happier time than now.

So it's worth thinking about why, when John McCain says he wants to be president in order to inspire a generation of young Americans to devote themselves to causes greater than their own self-interest (which means he's saying he wants to be a real leader), a great many of those young Americans will yawn or roll their eyes or make some ironic joke instead of feeling totally inspired the way they did with Kennedy. True, JFK's audience was more "innocent" than we are: Vietnam hadn't happened yet, or Watergate, or the Savings and Loan scandal, etc. But there's also something else. The science of sales and marketing was still in its drooling infancy in 1961 when Kennedy was saying "Ask not . . ." The young people he inspired had not been skillfully marketed to all their lives. They knew nothing of Spin. They were not totally, terribly familiar with salesmen.

Now you have to pay close attention to something that's going to seem real obvious. There is a difference between a great leader and a great salesman. Because a salesman's ultimate, overriding motivation is his own self-interest. If you buy what he's selling, the salesman profits. So even though the salesman may have a very powerful, charismatic, admirable personality, and might even persuade you that buying really is in your interest (and it really might be)—still, a little part of you always knows that what the salesman's ultimately after is something for himself. And this awareness is painful . . . although admittedly it's a tiny pain, more like a twinge, and often unconscious. But if you're subjected to enough great salesmen and salespitches and marketing concepts for long enough—like from your earliest Saturday-morning cartoons, let's say—it is only a matter of time before you start believing deep down that everything is sales and marketing, and that whenever somebody seems like they care about you or about some noble idea or cause, that person is a salesman and really ultimately doesn't give a shit about you or some cause but really just wants something for himself.

Some people believed that Ronald W. Reagan (1981–88) was our last real leader. But not many of them were young. Even in the '80s, most younger Americans, who could smell a marketer a mile away, knew that what Reagan really was was a great salesman. What he was selling, of course, was the idea of himself as a leader. And if you're under, say, 35 this is what pretty much every U.S. President you've grown up with has been: a very talented salesman, surrounded by smart, expensive political strategists and media consultants and Spinmasters who manage his "campaign" (as in "advertising campaign") and help him sell us on the idea that it's in our interests to vote for him. But the real interests that drove these guys were their own. They wanted, above all, To Be The President, wanted the mind-bending power and prominence, the historical immortality—you could smell it on them. (Young Voters tend to have an especially good sense of smell for this sort of thing.) And this is why these guys weren't real leaders: because their deepest, most elemental motives were selfish, there was no chance of them ever inspiring us to transcend our own selfishness. Instead, they helped reinforce our market-conditioned belief that everybody's ultimately out for himself and that life is about selling and profit and that words and phrases like "service" and "justice" and "community" and "patriotism" and "duty" and "Give government back to the people" and "I feel your pain" and "Compassionate Conservatism" are just the politics industry's proven sales-pitches, exactly the same way "Anti-Tartar" and "Fresher Breath" and "Four Out of Five Dentists Surveyed Recommend" are the toothpaste industry's pitches. We may vote for them, the same way we may go buy toothpaste. But we're not inspired. They're not the real thing.

Yes, this is simplistic. All politicians sell, always have. FDR and JFK and MLK and Gandhi were great salesmen. But that's not all they were. People could smell it. That weird little extra something. It had to do with "character" (which, yes, is also a cliché—suck it up).

All of this is why watching John McCain hold Town Hall Meetings and be all conspicuously honest and open and informal and idealistic and no-bullshit and say "I run for president not to Be Somebody, but to Do Something" and "We're on a national crusade to give government back to the people" in front of these cheering crowds just seems so much more goddamn *complicated* than watching old b/w clips of John Kennedy's speeches. It feels impossible, in February '00, to tell whether John McCain is a real leader or merely a very talented political salesman, just another entrepreneur who's seen a new market-niche and devised a way to fill it.

Because here's another paradox: Spring 2000—midmorning in America's hangover from the whole Lewinsky-and-impeachment thing—represents a moment of almost unprecedented cynicism and disgust with national politics, a moment when blunt, I-don't-give-a-shit-if-you-elect-me honesty becomes an incredibly attractive and salable and *electable* commodity. A moment when an anticandidate can be a real candidate. But of course if he becomes a real candidate, is he still an anticandidate? Can you sell someone's refusal to be sold?

There are a lot of elements of the McCain2000 campaign—naming and touting the bus for "Straight Talk," the timely publication of *Faith of My Fathers,* the much-hyped "openness" and "spontaneity" of the Express's media salon, the Message-Disciplined way McCain thumps "Always. Tell you. The truth"—that indicate some very shrewd, clever marketers are trying to market this candidate's rejection of shrewd, clever marketing. Is this bad? Is it hypocritical? Is it hypocritical that one of McCain's ads' lines in South Carolina is ". . . telling the truth even when it hurts him politically," which of course since it's an ad means that McCain's trying to get political benefit out of his indifference to political benefit? What's the difference between hypocrisy and paradox? Does the whole thing seem awfully confusing?

The fact of the matter is that if you are a true-blue, marketing-savvy Young Voter, the only real certainty you're going to feel about John McCain's 2000 campaign is that it produces in you a very modern and very *American* kind of confusion, a sort of interior war between your deep need to believe and your deep belief that the need to believe is bullshit, that's there's nothing left anywhere but salesmen. When your cynicism's winning, you'll find it's possible to see even McCain's most attractive qualities as just marketing angles. His famous habit of bringing up his own closet's skeletons, for example—bad grades, messy divorce, indictment as one of the Keating Five—this could be real honesty and openness, or it could just be McCain's shrewd way to preempt criticism by criticizing himself before anyone else gets the chance. The humble way he talks about his heroism as a POW—"It doesn't take much talent to get shot down"; "I wasn't a hero, but I was fortunate enough to serve my time in the company of heroes"—this could be real humility, or it could be McCain's clever way of appearing both heroic *and* humble.

The confusion you'll feel is not all your fault. There's a very real, very American tension between what John McCain's appeal is and the way that appeal must be structured and packaged in order to make him politically viable. To get you to buy. And sometimes

McCain himself seems a little too good at the packaging, as with for example recall 2/10's Chris Duren Incident in Spartanburg and McCain's enormous distress and his promise to phone and apologize personally to the disillusioned kid. So the next afternoon, at a pre-F&F Press-Avail back in North Charleston, the new unilaterally non-Negative McCain informs the corps that he's going up to his hotel room right now to call young Chris. The phone call is to be "a private one between this young man and me," McCain says. Then a Press Liaison steps in looking very serious and announces that only network techs will be allowed in the room, and while they can film the whole call, only the first ten seconds of audio will be permitted. "Ten seconds, then we kill the sound," the Liaison says, looking hard at Frank C. and the other audio guys. "This is a private call, not a media event." So why let TV cameras film McCain making it? And why only ten seconds of sound? Why not either sound or no sound?

The answer is modern and American and shrewd and right out of Marketing 101. McCain's campaign wants to publicize McCain keeping his promise and calling a traumatized kid, but also to publicize the fact that McCain is calling him "privately" and not exploiting Chris Duren for crass political purposes. There's no other possible reason for the ten-second audio cutoff, which of course will require networks that run the film to explain why there's no sound after the initial Hello, which of course will make McCain look doubly good, both caring and nonpolitical. Does the shrewd calculation of appeal here imply that McCain doesn't really care about Chris and want to buck him up and restore the kid's faith in the Political Process? Not necessarily. But what it does mean is that McCain2000 wants to have it both ways, rather like modern corporations who give to charity and then try to reap PR benefits by hyping their altruism in their ads. Does stuff like this mean the gifts and phone call aren't "good"? The answer depends on how gray-area-tolerant you are about sincerity vs. marketing, or sincerity plus marketing, or leadership plus the packaging and selling of same. Nobody else can tell you how to see it or convince you you shouldn't yawn and turn away in disgust. Maybe McCain deserves the disgust; maybe he's really just another salesman.

But if you, like poor old ROLLING STONE's nonprofessional pencil, have come to a point on the Trail where you've started fearing your own cynicism every bit as much as you fear your credulity and the salesmen who feed on it, you're apt to find your thoughts returning again and again to a certain dark box in a certain Hilton half a world and three careers away, to the torture and fear and offer of reprieve and a certain Young Voter named John McCain's refusal to violate a Code. Because there were no techs' cameras in that box, no aides or consultants, no paradoxes or gray areas; nothing to sell. There was just one guy and whatever in his character sustained him. This is a huge deal. In your mind, that Hoa Lo box becomes sort of a dressing room with a star on the door, the private place behind the stage where one imagines "the real John McCain" still lives. But the paradox here is that this box that makes McCain "real" is: impenetrable. Nobody gets in or out. That's why, however many behind-the-scenes pencils get put on the case, be apprised that a "profile" of John McCain is going to be just that: one side, exterior, split and diffracted by so many lenses there's way more than one man to see. Salesman or leader or neither or both: the final paradox—the really tiny central one, way down deep inside all the other boxes and enigmas that layer McCain—is that whether he's For Real depends now less on what's in his heart than on what might be in yours. Try to stay awake.

Esquire

WINNER, REPORTING

The Perfect Fire

With grace, care, and restraint, this article tells the haunting story of a disastrous warehouse fire in Worcester, Massachusetts, that claimed the lives of six firefighters. The author spent months gaining the trust and cooperation of the victims' families, building excruciating details into a powerful narrative. The result is a moving tale of ordinary people and their community, faced with almost unimaginable tragedy.

Sean Flynn

The Perfect Fire

It started with a candle in an abandoned warehouse. It ended with temperatures above 3,000 degrees and the men of the Worcester Fire Department in a fight for their lives.

The men who fight fires in Worcester, Massachusetts, spend a lot of time waiting. They sit around on chairs they fish out of the Dumpster behind Commonwealth Stationers, eating communal dinners they pay for by pitching in four bucks a man. They play pinochle or find a spot on an old, threadbare couch and watch some TV. On the day shift, they clean bathrooms and polish trucks and coil hoses, but even then they're just waiting for the bell to go off.

It's not so much a bell, really, as an electronic horn, short and shrill. When it goes off, firefighters freeze and listen for the sound that comes next. Usually, only words follow. "Engine 1," the dispatcher might say—or "Engine 8" or "Ladder 5," but only one truck—before reciting an address and a task. One tone signals a medical run or some minor emergency, like going out to stabilize a car-crash victim or a coronary case until an ambulance arrives, breaking a toddler out of a locked-up Taurus, or squirting water on a flaming car. Milk runs.

Sometimes, maybe every fifth time, a second tone will follow the first. Two tones is more serious, perhaps a fire alarm ringing somewhere, probably triggered by nothing more than a stray wisp of cigarette smoke or a burp of electrical current jiggling a circuit. Dispatch sends two engines and one ladder truck for those, picking whichever units are available and close.

Even rarer is three tones. Three tones means a reported structure fire, a house or a condo or a strip mall already blowing smoke into the sky. Three tones means blazing orange heat, black smoke, and poison gas; sirens and lights and steam and great torrents of water; men ripping into walls with axes and long metal spears, smashing windows and cutting shingles from roofs, teetering on ladders a hundred feet long. It doesn't always turn out that way, but three tones, at least, offers the chance of action. Firefighters love a triple.

Late autumn had been a slow stretch for the men working under Mike McNamee, the gray-haired forty-nine-year-old chief of Group II, North End District, Worcester Fire Department. They had spent their shifts cooking and cleaning and sleeping, interrupted only by sporadic milk runs and false alarms. The night of December 3, 1999, was quiet enough for McNamee to tend to his bureaucratic duties, riding shotgun in a Ford Expedition to the far-flung stations, retrieving vacation requests from the rank and file. Once his aide, George Zinkus Jr., had wheeled him to all six stations in the district, they would return to Central Station, where dinner, twenty-five pounds of beef, was roasting in the oven.

Thirteen minutes after six o'clock, McNamee's Expedition—or

Car 3, as it is officially known—was on Clark Street, in the northern reaches of the city, Zinkus steering it toward the Greendale Station, when the first tone sounded. McNamee cocked his head toward the radio. A second tone, then a third. "Striking box 1438, Franklin and Arctic, for a fire at 266 Franklin," the dispatcher deadpanned. "Engine 1, Engine 6, Engine 12, Engine 13, Ladder 1, Ladder 5, Rescue 1, Car 3."

McNamee and Zinkus stared at each other, brows arched, eyes wide. "That's a bad building," McNamee said. He let out a breath, said it again. "Bad building."

Two-sixty-six Franklin. Everyone in Worcester knew that building, if not by the address then by the shadow it had cast over downtown longer than anyone could remember. It was a hulk of brick and mortar rising eighty-five feet above an old industrial park immediately east of Interstate 290, eight elevated lanes that cut through the heart of the city. Civilians knew that building because of the giant words painted in white on the wall and underlined by the freeway: WORCESTER COLD STORAGE AND WAREHOUSE CO. Firefighters knew that building, dreaded it, because it sat there like a colossal chimney. No windows interrupted the endless rows of brick, save for a few tiny panes on the second floor, which meant there were no easy vents to bleed out heat and smoke and, if things got really hairy, no obvious escape hatches for anyone trapped inside. Hardly any of the firefighters had ever been in it, except for a few old-timers who'd cleaned up gas leaks or doused spot fires before the warehouse was abandoned in 1987 and, later, a captain named Robert A. Johnson, who got lost in a maze of meat lockers during a routine inspection. "Jesus," he had whispered to himself then. "We'd better never get a fire in here."

They would talk about it now and again the way firefighters will, guessing at a danger that might come to pass and, at the same time, hoping they won't be on duty if it does. Only two weeks earlier, driving through town in his gold Buick, McNamee had nudged his wife and pointed at Worcester Cold Storage. "You see that building?" he asked her, for no reason he can remember now. "It scares me. That building scares the shit out of me."

.   .   .

After Captain Johnson decided the beef had been roasted to a proper shade of pink, Paul Brotherton grabbed a knife from the rack above the sink in the Central Station kitchen and started carving it into neat, thin slices. For Brotherton, this was risky business. In five years on Rescue 1, pulling people (and, once, a parrot) out of fires, he'd never so much as twisted his ankle. But at the station, he could bust himself up good. He'd needed his hand sewn back together once after he lost control of a chopping knife in the kitchen, and he almost tanked his career when he slipped on a patch of ice in the back lot, landing so awkwardly and hard that he tore his thumb clean out of its socket. The doctors thought he might have to retire. Brotherton rehabilitated himself by playing video games with his sons.

Now he had Yogi growling at him. His given name is Steve Connole, but everyone calls him Yogi in homage to his bearish girth and bottomless gut, which once got him booted from an all-you-can-eat buffet before he'd had all he could eat. Yogi likes his meat in big pieces. "For chrissakes," he groused, his walrusy mustache curling with his snarl. "Cut it like a man, will ya? What's with the women's portions?"

"What are *you?*" Brotherton popped back. "The fuckin' portion police?"

The first tone sounded before Yogi could answer. A second, then a third. "Striking box 1438, Franklin and Arctic . . ." And fifteen men were moving, stepping into their gear, before the next syllable came out. In three quick motions—step through the trousers and into one boot, then the other, pull up the pants and snap the suspenders over the shoulders—each man was half dressed for battle.

Yogi and four other men clambered onto Ladder 1; Brotherton piled into the back of Rescue 1 with Jerry Lucey, his partner for the night, and three others; and Captain Johnson, whom everyone calls Robert A., hoisted himself into the front passenger side of Engine 1.

The sirens were on as soon as the yellow doors to the garage bays opened. Ladder 1 turned left onto Central Street, the rescue and engine trucks right behind. They roared two blocks to Summer Street, turned right, and screamed into the rotary at Washington Square. Robert A. could see smoke blowing from the top of the warehouse, now less than an eighth of a mile away.

Seconds later, Robert A. hopped down from Engine 1 to the pavement, turned his face to the sky, and saw nothing but clear night air. Maybe his perspective, staring straight up a wall of bricks, was too steep to bring the smoke into view. Or maybe the wind had shifted, blowing everything over the back side of the building. Or maybe the old warehouse had sucked the entire cloud back inside, as if holding back a secret.

"What the fuck?" Robert A. muttered to no one in particular. "Hey. Which fuckin' building's on fire?"

.　　.　　.

At the turn of the last century, keeping a few thousand sides of beef from spoiling required an enormous amount of insulating materials, layered one on top of another, to hold in the chill generated by massive blocks of ice and the wheezing coils of primitive refrigeration systems. The brick walls for Worcester Cold Storage and Warehouse Company, then, were laid eighteen inches thick and coated on the inside with a half foot of cork infused with asphalt. Chicago Dressed Beef, down the block at 256 Franklin Street, was constructed in a similar fashion, part of a complex of eleven buildings that a Lithuanian immigrant named Max Jacobson built after settling in the Blackstone River valley with his wife, Lena, in 1905.

As the years went by and the business changed hands, newer and better insulation was added. Polystyrene and polyurethane and Styrofoam, all derived from petroleum, were layered and sprayed over the cork and, in some spots, coated with a smooth laminate.

The building itself was shaped like a stout capital L, 150 feet on its long edge, along Franklin Street, and roughly 100 on the short side, parallel to I-290. A fire wall—solid brick punctured by a handful of fireproof doors—split the building in half where the base of the L met the spine, a line of demarcation drawn perpendicular to Franklin Street.

Inside, though, those dimensions and shapes were meaningless, lost to a jumble of narrow hallways and catacombed meat lockers. The doors were spring-loaded and heavy, designed to fall shut automatically, and the door handles were thick iron rings that nestled into round pockets, leaving the walls flush and smooth. One freezer might open into three others, all with identical doors. Even employees would get lost in Worcester Cold Storage, opening a wrong door that looked like the right door and every other door. Only the lower floors, where the forklifts operated, were different: At the top of the L, in the half of the building left of the fire wall, the first and second floors were open caverns, fifty feet deep and twice as wide, broken only by six cement columns, three on each side.

Chicago Dressed Beef closed in 1983. Worcester Cold Storage limped along for another four years before it, too, was emptied. The building was never completely abandoned, though. As late as

April 1999, after firefighters drowned a minor blaze on the roof of an adjacent building, the city's Fire Prevention Unit complained that homeless people could easily find their way inside that building and Worcester Cold Storage, and ordered that both be more solidly secured. By June 7, the owner, a developer named Ding On "Tony" Kwan, had finally sealed the warehouse tight.

Thomas Levesque still figured out a way to get inside. He was a thirty-seven-year-old drifter with a history of mental illness, a veteran of Worcester's soup kitchens and homeless shelters. In the spring of 1999, he met Julie Ann Barnes, a waif with dirty-blond hair and hollow eyes who'd dropped out of Wachusett Regional High School after her sophomore year. She was nineteen when she became pregnant with Thomas's child. The two of them took their meals at the Mustard Seed, a soup kitchen, and spent their nights on the second floor of Worcester Cold Storage, minding Julie's cat and dog. Julie loved animals.

Their relationship was fluid at best, volatile at worst, imploding one day, rekindling the next. The night of December 3, they were officially broken up but still huddling together inside the warehouse against the chill. Thomas wanted to have sex. Julie didn't. They squabbled, then tussled. A candle, the only light they had in the meat locker where they were, tipped over. The wick brushed a pile of clothing. Orange flames began dancing across the cloth, higher and faster, then leaped to a pile of old papers. Thomas and Julie tried beating the fire to death, flailing at it with a pillow. Flushed with air, it only continued to spread. Then they gave up, making their way down a narrow stairway to the street. Once outside, they walked along Franklin Street and under the elevated highway to the Worcester Common Outlet, a mall where the music store has headsets attached to terminals so customers can sample new releases. Thomas and Julie each slipped a pair over their ears and listened to CDs.

They never reported the fire. It burned for nearly two hours before the first puffs of smoke pushed up four floors and out through the roof.

. . .

Mike McNamee and George Zinkus were running four minutes behind the rest of the crews, barreling south on the interstate, the Expedition following a rise in the pavement that brought it parallel to Worcester Cold Storage. At that point, the fire was only a one-alarm blaze, meaning only the initial response units—four trucks from Central Station and four from three other stations—had been dispatched. At 6:20, as Zinkus wheeled down an exit ramp and into Posner Square, McNamee eyed the plume of smoke seeping from the roof and considered how bad a building Worcester Cold Storage could be. He decided to strike a second alarm, calling the order over his radio. In fire stations across the city, three sharp tones sounded, followed by dispatch ordering two more engines and another ladder truck to the scene.

The first wave of firefighters was already attacking the building. Captain Mike Coakley and Bert Davis positioned Ladder 1 on Franklin Street, put the jacks down to stabilize the truck, and started stretching 110 feet of high-tensile aluminum ladder from a turntable on the back of the truck toward the roof. Yogi and his partner, John Casello, trotted down Franklin Street to their left, toward a pair of loading-dock doors. To simplify things in the chaos, firefighters reduce the contours of a building to the first four letters of the alphabet, starting with A for the front wall and moving clockwise around the structure. Yogi and Casello headed toward the AB corner, where they forced open two doors near the bottom of a stairwell. They made a quick sweep of the first floor, which was huge and empty and quiet, bounded at the far end by the brick fire wall. No sign of flames. They backtracked to the stairwell and climbed to the second floor, hustling up three short, twisting risers of black steel steps.

Other firefighters had followed them to the same loading-dock doors and were already piling up the stairs. Robert A. and one of his men went all the way to the top, spot-checking for fire at every landing, poking their heads in to look for flames, before forcing open a bulkhead to the roof. Four men from Rescue 1 were right behind. Lieutenant Dave Halvorsen and one of his men stopped at the third floor for a more thorough search. Paul Brotherton told Halvorsen that he and Jerry Lucey were going up to the roof with Robert A.

On the roof, the top of the fire wall poked up as a short parapet, cutting the building in half from the A wall to the C wall and promising to contain any fire to one side or the other. The problem was, no one knew which side the fire was on. Near the back, along the C wall close to the parapet, was a glass cubicle fifteen feet wide and fifteen feet deep, reinforced with wire mesh, that capped a double elevator shaft. It would make a fine vent. "Clean it out," Robert A. told Brotherton.

Every firefighter carries a tool. Some have hoses and ropes, but everyone else wields a piece of medieval hardware—a flat-head ax, for instance, or a Boston Rake, which looks like an old vaudeville hook, except it's made of solid iron and can rip out a plaster ceiling in three swift strokes. Brotherton's weapon of choice was a Haligan, a rod of hardened steel roughly the size of a baseball bat, with one end flattened into a two-pronged claw. The other end, a flat wedge that can slip between a door and a jamb to pry it open, is attached perpendicularly to the shaft. Next to that, also at a 90 degree angle to the shaft, is an adze, a pear-sized steel point that can puncture the most solid walls and doors.

Thirty-eight-year-old Jerry Lucey was carrying a flat-head ax. He and Brotherton destroyed the glass cap in seconds, smashing it to bits before Coakley and Davis even made it up the ladder to the roof. They still didn't know where the fire was, but they knew something was burning: Smoke pulsed out of the hole in fast, wispy streams.

At about the same time, down on the street, Bill McNeil, who runs an all-night diner just on the other side of I-290, grabbed a cop directing traffic. "Hey," he told the cop, "some homeless people live in there."

The message that there might be people inside was relayed over the fire-department radios. Brotherton and Lucey walked back across the roof to the AB stairs, tromped down one flight, and started searching the top floor for people. Routine. At 6:22, only the thinnest haze of smoke hung in the corridors. More than two dozen men were in the warehouse, looking either for homeless people or flames. Each man had a tank strapped to his back filled with oxygen compressed to forty-five hundred pounds per square inch—enough for thirty minutes of relaxed breathing, half as long humping through a burning building—and connected to a plastic face mask. But the air was so clear that no one had bothered to put his on.

.   .   .

If a shift is fully staffed, which few shifts in the Worcester Fire Department ever are, thirty-seven men and seven trucks, plus a district chief and his driver, will respond to every working fire. Each engine truck carries one officer and four fighters. Assuming no one is trapped inside—saving people is always the first order of business—the first engine on the scene searches for the flames and lugs hoses toward them. The second engine taps a hydrant, and men from the third and fourth engines flank the blaze, positioning themselves above, beneath, behind, or to the side, depending on the circumstances.

Two ladder companies bring another ten men, who have two

main tasks. One is to open the building—forcing doors, bashing windows, smashing holes through walls—so the engine crews can drag their hoses inside. "We always bring the keys," Yogi likes to say. "And we haven't found one we couldn't get into yet." The ladder crew's other job is to ventilate the building. In any structure fire, the flames generate an enormous amount of smoke, which consists of carbon monoxide and a myriad of poisonous compounds. Because they are hot—plain old cotton cloth burns at roughly 400 degrees—those gases rise, collecting at the highest point in the room. If they aren't allowed to escape through a broken window or a hole sawed through the roof, they will linger, absorbing more heat from below until they explode.

District Chief McNamee once witnessed such a blast. He was in an old millhouse on Jacques Street back in 1982, when he was still a lieutenant on Engine 4, edging forward with a hose toward an orange roar at the far end of a long, narrow room. The ceiling, thick with smoke, quivered with a deep lemon glow and then erupted, a wall of flame racing above and toward him, the way a wave hurls itself upon a beach, and dropping to the floor when it reached the wall at his back. Firefighters call that a rollover because the flame rolls over—or, if the fates allow, above—anything in its way. A decent countermeasure, McNamee found, was to drop flat on his back and point his hose straight up, splashing 250 gallons on the ceiling every long minute until the flames finally washed away.

Even more dangerous than a rollover is a flashover. The principle behind it is the same: Trapped gases are heated until they reach what's called the ignition temperature, the point at which they spontaneously ignite. Unlike a rollover, however, a flashover happens everywhere at once; every molecule of atmosphere, every object in the vicinity, instantly turns to fire. A man at the edge of a room about to flash has maybe two seconds to run; a man inside that room is going to die.

On the other hand, opening a vent in the wrong place can trigger a backdraft, a massive explosion of raw and violent heat. A seasoned firefighter can usually see a backdraft coming. The first clue is the color of the smoke, a sickly shade of brownish yellow. The second is the way the smoke moves, puffing out of windows and under doors, then being sucked back inside, as if the fire were gasping for more fuel upon which to feed. If the wrong door is opened or the wrong window bashed out, the flame will draw in a great breath of air, hold it for an instant, then exhale in one lethal blast.

While the engine crews are attacking the fire and the ladder crews are venting, the rescue squads are crawling through smoke-filled rooms, looking for flames that may have spread and people who might be trapped, and hoping—*knowing*, really, because firefighters would be paralyzed with fear if they didn't trust their mates to do their jobs properly—that nothing will explode or collapse or flash. Rescue guys move on all fours, sweeping with their hands for bodies, or on one knee, shuffling one foot ahead to feel their way through the dark. It doesn't matter which way they move so long as they stay low, since the difference between two and five feet above the floor can be 400 degrees.

Firefighters like to tease each other about who has the toughest job. "A rescue guy," a man from a ladder truck might announce one night during a game of cards at the station, "is nothin' but a ladder guy who's afraid of heights." "Yeah? Well, fuck you," an engine guy might say, " 'cause a ladder guy ain't nothing but a fresh-air firefighter." And everyone laughs, because everyone has balls big enough to be busted or else he wouldn't survive long in the firehouse. But if firefighting were a war, and some nights it is, the rescue guys would be walking point.

.　　.　　.

The only thing Jeremiah Lucey ever wanted to be was a Worcester firefighter, and the only kind of firefighter he wanted to be was a rescue man. That's how he got assigned to Rescue 1 to begin with, back when he still carried the green shield of a rookie. After only nine months on the job, he called Randy Chavoor, the captain of the rescue truck, and told him he heard the squad was looking for a new man.

Chavoor took him on. There was some griping, veterans demanding to know what a green shield was doing on their truck. Chavoor had to admit he'd never heard of such a thing. On the other hand, he'd never known a rookie with the stones to call a captain and ask for a job, either.

Lucey was nothing if not tenacious, at least when he wanted something. Like when he was a teenager stocking shelves at the Big Y, the cashiers all giggled about how handsome he was—with his dark Celtic eyes and a tousle of jet-black hair, he was a dead ringer for a young Tom Hanks—but the one he really wanted was Michelle, a brunette who, as is usually the case in such matters, wanted nothing to do with him. After a few weeks, he asked her out, which, at that age, meant drinking a six-pack in a parked Pontiac.

"Can my girlfriend come?" Michelle asked, a question most men would have taken for outright rejection. Jerry said okay.

So the three of them sat in his car, sipping beer and talking. At the end of the evening, Jerry drove Michelle home and asked if they could go on a real date sometime, just the two of them. She said yes. Four and a half years later, in May 1985, they were married.

The fire department had tried to reject his advances, too. In 1990, Jerry scored high enough on the civil-service test to earn a seat in the drill school. But the city of Worcester was planning layoffs for the following year—last in, first out, which meant Jerry's entire class would be out of work the moment it graduated. He had a good job already, driving a truck for Coca-Cola, and, with two young boys, Jeremiah III and John, he couldn't afford to be out of work long. But Jerry wanted to fight fires, wanted action, so he and Michelle calculated how much she could make cutting hair part-time and pared down the family budget. Somehow the numbers worked. Jerry quit driving the truck, learned the basics of fighting fires, and then was promptly unemployed.

He stuck it out for a year, doing odd jobs on the side, until July 1992, when he was called back to the fire department. The job seemed a part of him, like his Irish blood, only one generation removed from the Ould Sod. Firefighting isn't so much a job as an identity, and Jerry wrapped himself in the trappings. If a memorial was to be dedicated—like, for instance, the one in Boston for nine firefighters who had died when a burned-out hotel collapsed on them in 1972—Jerry would march in the color guard. He lined the walls of his basement family room with photos of raging blazes, including one in which he appears as a fuzzy blur, a vague, dark outline behind a sheet of flame. At the bottom of the stairs, he framed a poster from *Backdraft*, a movie that always used to annoy him. "That's so fake," he would tell Michelle during the fire scenes, all orange light and pale smoke. "That's not what it's like at all."

Then he would tell her what it was really like in a burning building, how the smoke would be so black that he could find his partner only by feeling for his shape in the dark, how sometimes he stopped believing he would squirm out alive.

Paul LaRochelle, Jerry's partner for most of the past decade, remembers crawling through the kitchen of an apartment in a triple-decker with Jerry, the linoleum melting from the flames one floor below. "I can't find the door," he shouted at Jerry, his voice muffled by his mask. "Where's the damn door?"

"I got it," Jerry yelled back, reaching for his partner in the dark. "It's this way."

Jerry and Paul, along with their wives and children, spent as much time together off duty as they did on the job. They developed a shtick, Paul introducing the two of them as Sick and Twisted. "I'm Sick," Paul would say, "and he's Twisted."

Paul wasn't working December 3. Both he and Jerry were assigned to Group III, which was off duty that day, but Jerry had decided to work a swap for a guy from Group II on Engine 1 who was on an early-winter cruise. Another firefighter, an engine man by trade, was filling in for Joe LeBlanc, who was Paul Brotherton's partner on the rescue squad. Early in the evening, Jerry and the other fellow asked McNamee if they could switch, Jerry joining Brotherton on the rescue truck, the other guy going to Engine 1.

McNamee told them that was all right by him.

.   .   .

With the first floor clear, Yogi and Casello went up to the second floor. Yogi could hear the fire before he could see it, a ferocious snapping and popping behind the bricks on the far side of the room. He walked fifty feet to the door in the center of the fire wall and pushed it open into a thick forest of flames. "Hey, chief, I got it," he hollered into his radio. "I need a line up here."

Casello retreated down the stairs to get a two-and-a-half-inch hose. Robert A., meanwhile, followed the stairs from the roof down to the second floor, where he found Yogi wrestling with the door in the fire wall, trying to keep it from being sucked open toward the flames. Yogi didn't know that the only vent, the open elevator shaft, was *behind* the fire on the C side of the building. With the loading doors open at the AB corner of the building and another door open near the southwest corner, on the C wall, the

warehouse was becoming a giant stove, drawing air up the stair-
wells, across the floor, and through the fire wall, feeding a torch
that raced up the shaft toward the sky. All Yogi knew was that the
door insisted on swinging open toward the fire.

"Hey, Yoge," Robert A. said, "that don't look too good."

"No, it don't," he told the captain. "Come look what I found."
He was smiling, playful, like a kid who'd just found a steep and
bumpy hill to roll down on his bike. Sure, it looked dangerous. But
that was the fun of it.

Within seconds, Yogi and Robert A. were joined by four other
men and three hoses. A crew from Engine 13 had already tromped
up the stairs on the C side of the building, next to the shaft that was
venting the flame, and started soaking the fire from the south side.
"Better put your masks on, boys," Yogi said, still grinning. "This
could get ugly." Then he let the door swing open, and he stepped
toward the fire.

They moved to their right with two lines, each spitting 250 gallons a minute into the fire. They knocked down the first bank of
flames quickly enough, then moved through a burned-out doorway toward a second front, a howling orange wind. The hoses were
useless against something this hot; the streams were vaporized
into steam only inches out of the nozzle and were whooshed away
by flames that moved like the afterburners of a jet, streaked with
blue contrails and screaming horizontally into the elevator shaft.

The fire was eating through the ceiling, melting away the staples and joists that held the electrical system in place. Yogi was
near the fire wall when a tangle of wires fell from above, knocking
him off balance. He stumbled backward through the door, away
from the flames, and landed on his back. Above him, he saw smoke
streaming into the fire, like thick ribbons of a thunderhead racing
into a funnel cloud. "Hey, Cap," he hollered to Robert A. "Something don't look right. Everything's moving the wrong way."

.   .   .

By 6:35, McNamee had four hoses attacking the fire—"Pissing into a furnace, really," Robert A. says—two threaded up the AB stairwell and two up the C stairs. He also had more than a dozen men scattered on other floors, working in groups of two and three, searching for the homeless people who might be trapped inside.

McNamee was working alone. With the lines in place, he climbed to the third floor, pushed open a door, and stepped into a labyrinth of empty meat lockers and freezers. The smoke was still light, just dense enough to be smelled but not to sting his eyes or scratch his throat. He pushed through a second door, then a third. He was wandering deep into a burning maze, with no hose to lead him back if things turned bad, no partner to watch his ass. He told himself, This is a bad idea.

McNamee turned around. In front of him were three identical doors. His stomach tightened. He opened all three doors, one at a time. Behind each, he saw another room. His gut twitched again. He stood stone still, listening for boots clomping up stairs, for men hollering, for axes and Haligans bouncing against railings and walls.

The sounds were loudest through the middle door, which led to another door and, finally, the stairway. The smoke was still only a haze, visibility good, so McNamee turned up the stairwell, planning to search the fourth floor. He took one step, raised his foot to the next riser.

At that instant, smoke began to fall around him, pouring down from the floors above, thick and oily, like a predatory fog. It fell suddenly and without warning. In less than five seconds, everything—the walls, the stairs, even his own hand held less than an inch from his face—had disappeared into darkness.

McNamee had heard no sound, no loud pop or explosion over

the roar of the flames. He wondered if the top floor had flashed, if hot gases had pushed into rooms coated with asphalt-infused cork and Styrofoam until everything had ignited. All he knew for sure, though, was that the smoke had pushed into the hallways and lockers, overflowing and pushing, pushing out until it collapsed down the stairwell, a force seemingly overwhelming physics, a searing, noxious mist settling in on the floors below.

"I want everyone on the upper floors down to the ground now!" he hollered up the stairwell. "And I want head counts. I want everyone accounted for." Then he gave the same command over the radio, fumbling for his face piece in the dark.

A parade of firefighters traipsed down the AB stairs and gathered at the bottom. Then Paul Brotherton, still searching for homeless tramps with Jerry Lucey, keyed his radio for the first time, answering his chief from somewhere high up in the warehouse. *We're deep in the building, he said, and we don't know which way to go to get out.*

"Interior Command to Paul Brotherton," McNamee radioed back. "What floor are you on?"

We're two floors below the roof.

Brotherton and Lucey were counting down from the top, not up from the bottom, where the search teams would have to start. McNamee sprinted out of the loading-dock doors, working his eyes up and down the building. No windows. No way to tell how many fucking floors were in the building. No way to know for sure where two of his men were trapped.

At 6:37, with two men missing, a third alarm was struck. Twelve more men, five on Engine 3, three on Engine 7, and another four on Ladder 2, would arrive within minutes.

.   .   .

Paul Brotherton was supposed to paint the room he shared

with his wife in their neat ranch house in Auburn, a bedroom town southwest of Worcester. Denise, his wife and the mother of his six boys, had stripped the wallpaper, and she thought December 3 would be a fine night for Paul to call in sick and start painting.

"Absolutely not," he told her when she called, shortly before five o'clock, from her job as a pediatric nurse. "I'm not calling in sick to paint a room."

He was crankier than usual. He'd worked an overnight shift the night before, then spent the day shuttling his boys from appointments to practices and back again. "You know what?" Denise finally told him. "Go to work. I don't want you home tonight."

It was a minor spat as marital squabbles go. After everything they'd been through, an unpainted bedroom was barely a ripple, not worth the calories required to complain about it. They met in the early 1980s, when she was a nurse and Paul was an orderly at Worcester City Hospital, where, in the spring of 1983, Paul's father happened to be dying of cancer. It was a terrible death, long and slow, and Denise felt so sorry for Paul that she convinced fourteen coworkers to take him out for a night on the town to help take his mind off things.

On the appointed night, June 6, 1983, all fourteen people canceled. "Jeez, Denise," Paul said, "I'm still game if you are."

They went to Tammany Hall, a local juke joint that Denise remembers so precisely because Paul kept the ticket stubs in his wallet for the next seventeen years. Nothing was supposed to come of it. They were both engaged to other people. But that night, something clicked. Somehow, and in similar ways, they both realized they were planning to marry the wrong people. As it happened, a few weeks after their first date, they ended up on separate phones at the hospital, each taking grief from their spouses-to-be. They were in sight of each other, rolling their eyes back and forth. "On the count of three," Paul mouthed to Denise. He raised his index finger, then his middle finger, and when he straightened his ring finger, he and Denise both hung up.

A week after their first date, Paul was appointed to the fire academy. One month later, they decided to marry. They told Paul's mother on July 13, 1983. She was still grieving for her husband, her heart so badly broken she knew it would kill her. "That's nice," she said, managing a weak smile. "But I'm afraid I won't be there."

She suffered a massive coronary the next day and died before the ambulance got her to the hospital.

Paul's sister, Kim, was only ten at the time. The responsibility of raising her fell to Paul, who was twenty-four, and Denise, who would spend the night when Paul worked the evening shift. The wedding was moved up to February 1984, mainly so Paul and Denise could set a proper example for Kim.

The new family—Paul and Denise and Kim—moved into the home Paul's parents had left. If becoming a father to his sister before his own first son was born ever wore on Paul, he never let on. When she was a teenager, Kim's friends used to tell her how lucky she was to be raised by her brother. She would shake her head and tell them they didn't know the half of it. Paul and Denise were still young enough to know what teenagers did in Worcester, about the keggers down in Burncoat Park, about what went on all night after the senior prom. Which is why Paul told Kim she couldn't, and which is why he grounded her for five weeks when she rolled home past dawn anyway.

In 1992, Denise and Paul moved to Auburn. Kim came with them, staying until 1998, when she got married. Paul walked her down the aisle. By then, Paul and Denise had six boys, the oldest twelve and the youngest four. At the beach last summer, Paul lined them all up in a row, from youngest to oldest, with himself anchoring the end, facing the ocean with their backs to a camera, their trunks pulled down below the cracks of their asses. He titled the photo *Beach Bums* and hung it in the family room.

In the firehouse, Paul's one-liners were legendary. One afternoon in the shower room, he eyed one of his colleagues, working from the top of his bald head down his hirsute back. "Jeez," he muttered, "God sure has a weird sense of humor, huh?"

The other thing the guys knew about Paul Brotherton was how much he adored Denise. "I want you to meet my wife," is how he would introduce her, choosing his words deliberately, because he wanted people to know whom he'd been lucky enough to marry. Every Sunday morning, assuming his shift wasn't on, he brought her breakfast in bed. If she decided a half dozen friends should come over for a Saturday-night cookout, Paul wouldn't blink twice. And if she also happened to mention, as she did on a Tuesday last summer, that she wished they had a deck on which to entertain those friends, he would dig the holes for the footings that afternoon. By Saturday, he'd finished the entire deck, twenty-two feet long and twenty feet deep.

Paul taught his boys about fire. "You need to respect it," he told them. "It can warm your house and cook your food. But it'll destroy you in nothing flat if you don't respect it."

· · ·

Randy Chavoor left the rescue squad in 1994 when he was promoted to district chief, commanding Group II in the southern half of the city. "The forgotten station," he calls it, because there isn't much reason for anyone except firefighters to pass through south Worcester. The houses are crowded more closely there, the tenants poorer, the wiring and gas older and more rickety. Lots of action down south.

December 3 was a slow night for Chavoor's troops, so Chavoor ran some administrative errands, which took him to headquarters on Grove Street shortly after 6:00. At 6:12, dispatch reached him there and asked if 266 Franklin was in the southern district.

Chavoor knew it wasn't. But he also knew his buddy McNamee would steal a call from him in a heartbeat. He keyed his radio, planning to claim the fire for himself, but the battery was out of juice. Thirty seconds later, he heard dispatch sending McNamee and the other crews, including five men on Engine 13, who worked under Chavoor, to the warehouse.

Once he'd finished at headquarters, Chavoor and his driver headed for the southern-district station, following a route that crossed Franklin Street just west of Worcester Cold Storage. Chavoor told his driver to park near the corner. He sat and watched for a few minutes, seeing only a thin tail of smoke escaping from the roof. Bored, Chavoor told his driver to head back.

At 6:37, Chavoor heard the third alarm. He also heard Paul Brotherton say he was lost with Jerry Lucey. Chavoor shook his head, smiled. Tonight he would bust some balls. "Didn't I teach you better than that, Jerry?" he would say once the fire was under control. "*Real* rescue guys don't get lost." And then everyone would laugh, even if the sting from the smoke made their throats hurt.

.　　.　　.

A diabetic lifting weights at a local gym on December 3 forgot to eat after taking his insulin and passed out, at which point someone dialed 911. One tone was sounded. Engine 3, from the Grove Street Station, was dispatched. A milk run before suppertime.

Engine 3 was back in the station a few minutes before six o'clock. On the way back, Lieutenant John Sullivan, riding shotgun, had given the air an exaggerated sniff. "There's gonna be a big one tonight," he'd told the firefighter behind the wheel, a thirty-four-year-old bachelor named Jay Lyons. "Yep." Big sniff. "Three alarms. I can smell it." He'd sniffed again, deeper this time, like an old salt smelling the morning tide.

Sullivan did that almost every night. It was sort of a running gag. "Yeah," Jay answered, same as always. "And it'll be on the south side and we won't be going."

Jay wanted to go. Jay wanted the biggest flames, the thickest smoke, the hottest gases. He'd been chasing fires his whole life, ever since he was ten years old and listening to his Bearcat 210XL eighteen-channel scanner, waiting to hear three tones so he could jostle his father and say, "C'mon, Dad, we're going to a fire."

His parents never understood where Jay's fascination with firefighters had come from. Jay's father was a junior high school history teacher, his mother a nurse. But when he was twelve years old, a young lieutenant from the Worcester Fire Department named Mike McNamee bought the house across from Jay's on Saxon Road. Jay would listen for hours to McNamee's stories, and, later, McNamee would take him to the station to hang out with the guys, maybe ride along on a few runs, even spend the night in a spare bunk. In return, Jay delivered McNamee's newspaper every afternoon and baby-sat his two daughters. "If one of my girls ever brings home a boy half as nice as Jay," McNamee's wife, Joanne, used to say, "I'll be a happy woman."

Jay saw his first fatal fire in high school, when a short circuit lit up an old man's house early one morning on the next block over. "I watched these firefighters rush into this house filled with flames and smoke and carry an elderly gentleman from a rear door," Jay wrote in an essay for his application to Clark University in 1983. "Why did these men risk their lives for someone they didn't even know? . . . The answer itself is very simple. This is their life, the life of saving others."

Clark accepted Jay, and in 1987 he graduated with a degree in history. He had no intention of using it, though. He'd already taken the test for the fire department—hell, he took it for the first time when he was still in high school—and a few weeks after graduation, he started a twelve-week crash course in firefighting at the drill school. Mike McNamee was his training officer.

Jay liked taking tests and always scored well. He got a 99 on the test for the New York Fire Department, the Green Berets of the trade. And he'd scored pretty high on the test for the Massachusetts State Police, who offered him a job in 1992.

He agonized over the decision. "Stay with the fire department," his mother advised him. "That's what you've always wanted to do." But Jay wanted a new challenge, never wanted to be stuck wondering if he should have at least tried being a cop, so he resigned from the fire department that year and entered the police academy.

Following graduation, Jay was assigned to the Shelburne Falls barracks in western Massachusetts. But after eighteen months of chasing speeders and patrolling the drowsy hamlets just south of the Vermont border, he was granted a transfer to Martha's Vineyard.

To be young and single on Martha's Vineyard during the swarming summer tourist season is one thing. To be a cop stuck there alone after Labor Day, when only the fishermen and tradesmen and drunkards remain, is quite another. Businesses shut down, the cool summer breezes turn into bitter winter winds, and the island turns into an isolated cage. One year into his stint, Jay was stir-crazy. He requested a transfer to Cape Cod and the suburbs south of Boston. His request was denied. He would spend another winter on the island.

Jay started drinking at about four o'clock that afternoon, throwing back beers in frustration. At ten o'clock, he drove to the corner of Lake and Ocean avenues, in Oak Bluffs, where a man he had once arrested on a drug charge lived. Jay pointed his gun at the house and fired two shots. Both crashed through the siding, one lodging in a couch. Then he drove back downtown and swallowed a few more beers before climbing back into his car and wheeling through the center of Oak Bluffs, waving his pistol out the window and shooting six more rounds into the air.

He was arrested, of course, and suspended from the force. Eventually he was found guilty of assault and sentenced to two years in jail, with all but ninety days of it suspended. Jay was released from the Dukes County House of Correction in February 1997, with twenty-two days knocked off his sentence for good behavior.

He hadn't taken a drink for more than two years by then. He found work driving a school bus, manning the door at a nightclub, substitute teaching. But he still wanted to fight fires.

In August 1997, Worcester Fire Department chief Dennis Budd gave him a second chance. The city manager and mayor signed off on it. Jay told the chief, You won't be disappointed.

A few of the other firefighters were, though. They didn't like having an ex-convict on the job. "Hey, you don't fuckin' like it?" Jay would snap if anyone said it to his face. "Tough shit. I'm here. Deal with it."

.   .   .

Back at Grove Street, Jay Lyons heard the third alarm and scrambled behind the wheel of Engine 3 at 6:37. John Sullivan rode next to him, working the siren and yanking the cord that sounds the horn. Behind them, in a separate compartment rattling with axes and Haligans, were three other firefighters. One of them, Joe McGuirk, was thirty-eight years old but had been on the job only two years. Worcester Cold Storage would be his first big fire.

Most of the men were fully dressed before Lyons wheeled the truck into Lincoln Square, about halfway to the warehouse. They'd stepped into their trousers and boots before climbing into the truck, where their ten-pound heat-proof Nomex coats were draped on the backs of their seats, the sleeves already threaded through the harnesses of air tanks, arranged so they could slide into them with two quick dips of their shoulders. A light is clipped to one breast, and attached to the other is a PASS alarm, or Personal Alert Safety System. If a firefighter remains motionless for forty-five seconds, it emits a shrill chirp. If he doesn't jiggle the system to reset it, it produces a continuous piercing tone that other firefighters can follow. Whacking a panic button on the PASS sets off the same alarm.

Lyons had to wait to suit up, since the driver can't very well steer while he's squirming into the harness of an air tank. As Sullivan buckled up, he kept his ear to the radio, monitoring McNamee's orders. The district chief wanted the third-alarm companies en route, engines 3 and 7 and Ladder 2, to stop a half block from the warehouse until he figured out what to do with them. Lyons pulled over at the corner.

Thirty seconds later, McNamee ordered everyone to the base of the AB stairway to organize a search for Brotherton and Lucey. He told them to bring ropes that could be tied to railings as lifelines, something to hold on to in the dark. And he told them to go up in shifts, three or four at a time, rotating so he wouldn't lose track of anyone.

"Jay, shut it down," Sullivan ordered, meaning the engine. "You're coming in."

"Okay," Lyons answered, grabbing his coat. "I'll take Joe with me."

Sullivan and his other two men headed toward the warehouse. McGuirk waited at the engine while Lyons pulled on his gear.

.   .   .

There was never any question what Joe McGuirk would grow up to be. Ever since he was a kid, Joe knew he wanted to fight fires, just as his father had, just as his older brother did, just as his cousins did.

He knew it by the time he met Linda Howe at a nightclub in 1980, when he was only eighteen years old. He rushed home, called her house at two-thirty that morning, woke her father up, and stammered, "Please let this be Linda Howe's number." Mr. Howe hung up. Joe called back later that morning, at eight o'clock, convinced Linda to go see *The Rose* with him, and then saw her nearly every night for the next six years. They married in 1986.

Through all that time, and for eleven years after the wedding, Joe took the civil-service test every chance he got, never scoring high enough to earn a seat in drill school. He worked as a handyman for a while, then started painting houses. He studied at night to become a contractor, got his license in 1989, and opened his own business. He called it McGuirk & Son, which made the company sound bigger and was, in fact, technically accurate, since Linda had given birth to Everett two months earlier. A daughter, Emily, came along three years later.

In 1997, Joe passed the test for the fire department. He started training in September and was assigned to Engine 3 out of headquarters on Grove Street. His first week on the job, he worked three fires that were smoky enough to lure the local television cameramen and newspaper photographers, who all managed to frame Joe in their best shots. The guys at the station started calling him Hollywood Joe, but Linda started to worry, thinking maybe firefighting was a lot more dangerous than contracting.

After that first week, though, the job quieted down. If Joe left the station, it was almost always to chase car wrecks and stabilize coronary patients, none of which he particularly enjoyed. Joe wanted the rough-and-tumble of the job. He signed up for scuba classes, hoping he might make the underwater rescue team someday. Short of that, he wanted a spot on a ladder truck, smashing doors and sawing roofs and plucking people from ledges. Maybe when Jay Lyons was promoted to lieutenant, he'd be assigned to a ladder truck, Joe thought. Maybe he'd take Joe with him. Lyons was aggressive, liked the action. "Balls-in," Sullivan used to say about him. Joe liked that. He wanted to be balls-in, too.

.   .   .

Mayday, mayday. It sounded like Brotherton's voice. There was no echo of fear, no quiver of panic. But McNamee knew he was scared. Firefighters are loath to use that word, Mayday, ashamed to call for help, to admit that the smoke and the heat and the flames might be tougher than they are. To call a Mayday—or, worse, to hear one—is to know that death is no longer a theory but a probability.

Mayday. We're running out of air, can't find the way out. We're near a window.

McNamee bolted outside and scanned the warehouse walls. No windows.

"Paul," McNamee hollered into his radio, "activate your PASS system."

Long moment of silence. McNamee was anxious. Then Brotherton's voice came over the radio again. *We're on the floor, he said. We're buddy-breathing. Hurry.*

One air tank was dead, leaving only a few wisps of oxygen for Lucey and Brotherton to share, alternating shallow breaths through one mask. When a tank has two minutes of air left in it, the mask vibrates like a gentle air hammer. When the last breath is absorbed, the mask immediately turns into a vacuum, sucking hard against the face and tearing at the lungs, forcing a man to yank it off or die gasping. Once it's off, the only thing left to breathe is smoke, which consists of carbon monoxide and, depending on what's burning, anywhere from a few dozen to a few thousand toxic chemicals, including hydrogen cyanide and hydrochloric acid.

A heavy concentration of carbon monoxide alone will reduce a man to a paralytic stupor in five breaths, the carbon monoxide bonding to red blood cells and starving the body of oxygen. The brain, in an attempt to save itself, shuts down the least important parts of the body—essentially everything except itself, the heart, and the lungs.

While carbon monoxide is shutting down the body, the other poisons are destroying the airways. At room temperature, smoke particles irritate the bronchial tubes and lung tissues. Superheated, they scorch the deepest parts of the lungs, burning all the way into the tiniest air sacs. In response, the throat begins to close, swelling shut from the trauma in much the same way a finger swells when it's slammed in a door. The room where Brotherton and Lucey were trapped had already reached 200 degrees.

McNamee knew he had only minutes to find them or they would die. The search teams he'd dispatched were still circling through the building, and the crew from Ladder 2 headed toward the stairs. McNamee locked eyes with Lieutenant Tom Spencer. Behind him, Tim Jackson was tightening his mask. If they were scared, neither man showed it.

Dispatch came on the radio. "Fire alarm to command. We have an emergency alarm going off for radio 6004."

Brotherton had managed to hit the panic button on his radio as he ran out of air, which means he'd likely set off his PASS alarm as well. If he hadn't been trapped in a meat locker and lost behind two feet of brick and burning insulation, one of the search teams might have heard the squeal over the thunder of the fire.

At 6:38, Paul Brotherton keyed his radio one last time. *Hurry,* he rasped. *Please hurry.*

.   .   .

The blue spruce in front of Tim Jackson's house is almost fifteen feet tall now and nearly as wide, big enough to block out most of the traffic from Route 16 on the edge of Hopedale, a half hour southeast of Worcester. Tim planted it after Christmas in 1988. At the time, it was only a sapling that he and his wife, Mary, had decorated for their first holiday together.

He'd been a firefighter for sixteen years by then, having qualified for the job after a tour in Vietnam with the 101st Airborne. He'd come home with a tattoo of his company's insignia on his right bicep, pieces of shrapnel in his arms and leg from a mortar shell that pulverized three of his buddies, and a Purple Heart.

He met Mary in 1985 and married her on Easter Sunday three years later. It was Mary's second wedding, Tim's third. After the wedding, they moved into her house on Route 16, a pale-yellow bungalow that backs up to the Hopedale Village Cemetery. It was the first real house Tim had ever lived in. To him, it was a playground. He built a deck under a pergola outside the kitchen and grafted an addition onto the side, next to the dining room, with a planked ceiling and a fieldstone fireplace and a wide window in the front where he could sit in an armchair and watch his blue spruce grow. "God's country," he called his little plot of land.

Tim kept his magazines and newsletters—*Hog Tales* and *Cruising Rider* and the newsletters from HOG, the Harley Owner's Group—in a wicker basket on the floor to the left of his chair. Mary worried more about Tim's riding his bike with his brain-bucket helmet than she ever did about his fighting fires. He rode a Triumph when she met him but then converted to Harleys, trading a blue one for a red one for a black one, a fully dressed Electra Glide. Tim was meticulous with his bike, keeping the chrome on the turnout pipes polished, washing it during the quiet hours at the station house, and blowing the last droplets of water off the engine with the hose from a tank of compressed air.

Winter was the worst time of year for Tim. He couldn't ride his bike, for one thing, and none of his flowers were in bloom. The only thing that he liked about winter was the holidays, when he would drag a plastic snowman out of storage to decorate the front lawn and wrap a long string of blue lights around the spruce. Come spring, Tim was in the garden, digging a hole for a Korean lilac or pruning the azaleas out front. He kept his gardening magazines and books—*Essential Shrubs* and *Family Circle*'s 1996 gardening supplement—on a small table to the right of his chair. And when the new buds began to curl up from the hydrangeas, Tim and Mary would sit on the deck, Tim drawing in a great breath of spring air and smiling. "Well," he'd say, "we made it through another one."

Mary didn't know much about firefighting, mainly because Tim didn't tell her much. "How was your night?" she'd ask him when he came home in the morning. "Long and hard," he'd tell her.

"So you slept all night, huh?"

"Yeah," he'd answer. "It was pretty quiet."

.   .   .

McNamee was stationed at the bottom of the AB stairwell, waiting for firefighters as they came down from searching the upper floors for Brotherton and Lucey. Every few minutes, he would scramble outside again, working his eyes up and down the rows of bricks, searching for a clue—a window he'd overlooked, a break in the pattern where a floor joist might be—that might tell him how many floors were in the building, that might help him know for sure where his two men were trapped. Each crew that stumbled down the stairs briefed him on the conditions above, everyone giving the same basic report, which was growing worse by degrees: The heat was hotter, the smoke thicker, the situation more perilous.

Worcester Cold Storage had tried to swallow men for the past hour, erasing instinct and years of training in a ferocious black swirl. Firefighters are taught to maintain their bearings in the dark either by counting their steps—two forward, one left, three forward—and then backtracking, or by feeling for walls that, in most buildings, will lead them back to a door or a window. Robert A. tried the first method on the fourth floor, pacing carefully while he searched for his colleagues. He began retracing his steps even before the alarm on his tank went off, allowing himself more time than usual to find his way out. He would need it. He'd crawled only a few feet when he ran into a column where his memory told him there was clear space. Then a beam. Then a pole. His face mask started vibrating.

"This way! This way out!" Robert A. heard someone screaming over the fire, and then he heard the sharp clang of a Haligan banging against the stairwell. "This way!"

Robert A. took a deep breath. "Keep doing that!" he bellowed as loud as he could. "Keep doing that!" He followed the sound to the stairs. His tank emptied before he made it down to the bottom.

Captain Mike Coakley and Bert Davis tried following the walls to find their way out of the fifth floor. Clinging to each other in the blackness, feeling their way along the wall, they turned one corner, a second, a third, a fourth. "I think we're in a locker," Coakley told Davis. The two men crawled around the square again, the captain groping for the flush-handled door, wondering if he might die. By chance, they were next to the door when a hard puff of heat nudged it open, pushing it in less than an inch but enough for Coakley to feel the edge.

McNamee kept monitoring the stairway as searchers descended, emerging like wraiths from the oily fog. He knew that Tim Jackson and Lieutenant Tom Spencer were making their way across the fifth floor, feeling their way along the walls, working deep into the building in search of Brotherton and Lucey. They were almost to the fire wall in the center when Spencer keyed his radio. *We're running out of air,* he said. There was no panic, no urgency in his voice; in the chaos, McNamee never even heard the transmission.

By 7:30, McNamee could no longer deny his worst fears. The rescue, he realized, had become a recovery. Brotherton and Lucey were gone. The Worcester Fire Department hadn't lost a man since Tony Annunziata got lost in a furniture warehouse in 1962, and now McNamee was looking at two gone in one night. "We always win," McNamee used to say. "The whole building might burn to the ground, but everyone goes home."

But McNamee had never seen a building deteriorate so rapidly and so viciously as this one. He worried that if the smoke ignited, he could lose more men in an instant. And even if nothing exploded, there were too many ways for firefighters to lose their bearings in the chambers above. For the first time, he considered calling off the search.

But first, he would bolt up the stairs again for a final view of the conditions. When he was between the second and third floors— *Kawoooooomph!*—something blew up. The sound was the same as when a match touches the pilot light of a stove, only louder and deeper, a spasm of air expanding so fast and hard against the warehouse walls that the whole building shuddered and shook.

"Engine 1 to Interior Command," Robert A. barked into his radio. "Can you confirm or deny that part of this building just collapsed?"

"Robert A.," McNamee yelled back, "no, I don't think so. But I think a large area just lit off."

McNamee scrambled back down the stairs. Then another call came over the radio.

"Ladder 200 to Ladder 2." It was the ladder truck's senior man calling Tom Spencer.

Silence.

"Ladder 200 to Ladder 2," he heard again. More silence. The last anyone knew, Spencer had been on the fifth floor with Jackson, the highest the searing clouds would allow any man to climb in the building.

"Ladder 200 to Ladder 2!" Higher this time, louder, terror in the words. "Ladder 200 to Ladder 2! Ladder 200 to Ladder 2! Answer me!" A scream now, a choking, sobbing shriek. No one answered.

.   .   .

After Tim Jackson strung his blue Christmas lights around his blue spruce, Tom Spencer planned to sneak over to Hopedale, unscrew the bulbs one by one, and replace them with white lights. He wouldn't even have to see the look on Jackson's face the next morning—just imagining it was good enough. Spencer might not have been the funniest man in the Grove Street Station line for line, but he was the most elaborate prankster.

He was a small man, only 150 pounds, but tough and nearly vibrating with energy. He walked up mountains for fun and had ever since he was a boy. In 1999, for their twentieth wedding anniversary, Tom and Kathy Spencer drove to Camden, Maine, and climbed Mount Battie. And when, well into his thirties, he decided to start playing a team sport, he chose fast-pitch hardball. "None of that sissy softball," he'd say. Tom loved baseball, knew everything about it, and what he didn't know he would look up in the encyclopedias in the basement family room.

He also loved to travel. When he was a boy, his family never had much money, and vacations meant day trips to a state park. As a grown man, he wanted to make sure his own kids had the chance to see the world. Last year, he took them—Patrick, Casey, and Daniel—hiking through the Grand Canyon; in 1997, they spent fourteen days in England and France, Tom carefully recording each day's details—the weather, what Daniel had for lunch, the names of their hotels—in a small spiral notebook he carried in his breast pocket.

When his boys got involved in Boy Scouts, so did Tom. He taught his kids to kayak and how to find constellations in the night sky and how to lay HO-scale train tracks on a plywood platform in the basement. "I would never use my job as an excuse not to do anything with my kids," he'd tell Kathy.

He had more than one job, too, working part-time as a stage-hand at the Worcester Centrum and twelve hours a week cleaning office suites for a friend's company. And then there was music. He'd learned to play the piano in his thirties, and he became an opera aficionado. He made an annual pilgrimage to the Metro-politan Opera in New York City, and some nights he'd take his opera CDs to the Grove Street Station, torturing the men with Italian tenors and sopranos. Some of the guys would retaliate by making up their own opera, belting out the only Italian words they knew, which happened to be types of pasta. *Vermicelli, linguine, fett-ah-cheee-nee,* they'd sing. They called it *The Spaghetti Opera.*

Tom took it in stride. He had a gentle nature, drawn in no small part from religion. He was a liturgical minister at St. Charles Bor-romeo, where Kathy served communion and the kids did altar service. In May 1999, when the annual mass for firefighters in the Worcester diocese was held, Tom was asked to read the names of all the men, both active and retired, who'd passed away the previ-ous year, pausing after each one for the tolling of a bell. Tom showed up an hour early, studying the list and practicing the syllables. Mispronouncing a name, he believed, would be dis-respectful.

·   ·   ·

As the search for Brotherton and Lucey went on, the fire con-tinued to spread, feeding on the fresh air sucked up from below and on cork and polystyrene on the floors above. In one spot, near the front wall along Franklin Street, the temperature soared to 3600 degrees, twice as hot as in a crematorium.

As the heat, smoke, and steam descended, the search was forced lower, floor by floor. The sixth floor had been impenetrable since McNamee encountered the flood of smoke on the AB stairwell around 6:35. The fifth floor, where Spencer and Jackson had been lurching blindly through a miasma of burning petroleum products—the industrial equivalent of napalm—was lost shortly after 7:30. Then, at 8:00, a panting firefighter emerged at the bottom of the stairs. "It's too hot, chief," he told McNamee. "I couldn't make it past the third floor."

McNamee took another look at the smoke roiling above him and ran through the situation in his head. Brotherton and Lucey were probably dead, Tom Spencer wasn't answering his radio, and Tim Jackson was with him. The warehouse was winning, taking his men two by two. Sending another man up, McNamee realized, would be sending him to die. He turned his back to the stairway. Fifteen firefighters were crowded in front of him, ready to climb back into a solid wall of black heat.

"No more," McNamee said.

For one stunned second, no one said anything. The only sound McNamee heard was the deafening white noise from above, punctuated by snaps and pops and hisses. Then the men started yelling, surging forward, bellowing at the chief. "They're still up there, goddammit! They're still in there!"

McNamee stood his ground, guarding the stairs, pushing his hands into the chests of the men. "Listen to me!" he hollered. "You listen to me! We've already lost four. We're not going to lose any more."

McNamee watched as his men collapsed, their shoulders slumping, their heads bowing, as if he had thrown a great crushing weight down upon them. "I want the building evacuated," he told them. "I want everybody out."

Firefighters filed out the door, each marching back to his assigned truck for a head count. Then they fell back into a defensive posture, arranging the ladder trucks on Franklin Street and on I-290 so they could raise their hoses above the warehouse. Nine trucks started pouring seven thousand gallons a minute into the inferno, most of which turned to steam before reaching the building. Flames started shooting through the roof like a torch, illuminating the night sky.

The trucks were still moving into position when Lieutenant John Sullivan ran up to McNamee. "Mike, I can't find Jay and Joe," he said. "I've been around this building three times and I can't find them."

No one had seen Jay Lyons or Joe McGuirk since Sullivan had left them at the truck. Some of the men had heard one radio call from Spencer, saying he'd hooked up with Engine 3 on the fifth floor, which would have been McGuirk and Lyons. But McNamee had ordered everyone to wait at the bottom of the stairs, rotating through in organized shifts so he could keep track of them. Lyons and McGuirk must have slipped past McNamee when he was outside trying to figure out how tall the goddamned building was.

At that moment, Sullivan knew two more were gone. The same phrase scratched through his mind over and over: "They're fucking dead. They're fucking dead. All those guys, they're all fucking dead."

.   .   .

By the time District Chief Randy Chavoor returned to the warehouse, the three-alarm fire had escalated to a five-alarm furnace. Worcester firefighters were being called in on their days off to cover the station houses, Chief Dennis Budd had been paged away from dinner with his wife, and suburban departments were sending reinforcements. A big, nasty fire, sure, but after twenty-three years on the job, Chavoor knew how to handle a burning warehouse. "Surround and drown," the firefighters say—just keep spraying water until the flames go out. Assuming, of course, that you don't think anyone is lost inside.

He walked past McNamee on his way toward the building, never breaking stride as he patted him on the shoulder. "Hey, Mike," he said, "you got those two guys out, right?"

"Randy, no."

Chavoor stopped hard, turned around. He felt like he was moving in slow motion. "*What?*"

"It's not two," McNamee said, his voice weak. "It's six."

The two chiefs stared at each other, Chavoor trying to catch his breath, trying to form words in his throat. Then he slumped, the same heaviness pulling at his shoulders that McNamee had seen crush fifteen men at the bottom of the stairs. For two decades, Chavoor had believed firefighters were immortal. In one instant, they no longer were. In one instant, six were gone.

Chavoor's mind reeled, but there wasn't time to dwell on it. Chief Budd wanted two teams to make a final sweep as far into the building as they could go, and Chavoor and three of his men were ordered in with a rope. Chavoor told the lead man to tie the rope to the railing on the third landing. All four dropped to their knees and started crawling, moving single file, each man holding on to the one in front, the lead man carrying the rope. Chavoor could hear the fire roaring like an army of dragons, snarling and spitting, all around him. He couldn't see anything except blackness, couldn't feel anything but a sheet of steaming velvet wrapped around his face, swirling around him like a heavy cloth. Thirty feet from the stairwell, he ordered his men to stop. "Let's go!" he yelled. "We don't belong in here."

The crawl was longer on the way out. Chavoor felt the smoke reaching over him, and he half believed it was a giant black claw that was trying to pull him back into the bowels of the warehouse. This is it, he told himself. You're gonna die in here.

Then they were out, feeling their way through the door, tramping down the steps, finding each one by banging their heels against the treads. At the bottom of the stairs, Chavoor found one of Tom Spencer's men sobbing, trying to push his way back into the building to find his lost lieutenant. Chavoor wouldn't let him up. They huddled there for a moment, the firefighter heaving with sobs, Chavoor trying to calm him enough to retreat. They were the last two firefighters to walk out of the building.

.   .   .

Since 7:30, the fire had been playing out live on television, broadcast from microwave trucks scattered on the blocks around Franklin Street. A helicopter hovered above, taking thermal-imaging readings of the inferno's temperature. It was a spectacular scene, an orange plume raging one hundred feet above the interstate. Reporters monitoring the radio chatter already knew two men were missing, and it was only a matter of time before the full body count leaked out.

Official protocol is for the chaplain and the chiefs to deliver the news to the widows at their homes. But as the night wore on, phones started ringing all over the city, worried wives dialing fire stations, nervous relatives trying to figure out who was missing. So fire-department brass decided to gather everyone at a downtown church for a meeting. James Lyons, Jay's father, drove over, as did Kathy Spencer, who'd been told to go there by her in-laws. McNamee and Chavoor, however, didn't know that, so they divvied up the addresses and started making their awful rounds.

McNamee went to the Lyons home first, a tidy white colonial

across the street from his own house, the same one he'd seen framed in his living-room window for twenty years. Joan Lyons, Jay's mother, heard the Expedition pull up. She watched from the open doorway as McNamee forced his feet to keep moving across the lawn and up the brick walk. "Michael," she said, her voice already quaking, "do you have bad news for me?" She'd never called him Michael before.

The words stuck in McNamee's throat. "Joan," he whispered, "Jay's missing."

Joan nearly collapsed in shock. Racked with sobs, she tried dialing her daughter's phone number, but her fingers kept missing the buttons. McNamee, moving mechanically now, took the phone from her and dialed. His mind flashed back exactly two years to December 3, 1997, the night he dialed his own sisters' numbers to tell them their father was dead, killed when his car was crushed by a truck at exactly 6:10 in the evening.

He went to Tom Spencer's house next. Kathy had left the three kids at home. Patrick, the oldest boy, charged across the lawn in his stocking feet. "Mike, where's my dad? Where's my dad?" McNamee wrapped his arms around him, the boy screaming the same phrase over and over into the district chief's sooty coat. Behind him, still on the stoop, Casey wrapped her arms tight around her sides and sobbed. McNamee was too numb to cry.

Chavoor went to the other four houses He took Paul LaRochelle, Jerry Lucey's partner of five years, with him. "No one's going to tell Michelle but me," Paul told the chief. Michelle was waiting inside with her brother and sister, hoping no one would knock on her door, when she heard a noise outside. "Just don't tell me there's a chief's car in the driveway," she said. "Please just don't tell me that."

Her brother sucked in a short, shallow breath. "Oh, my God," he said.

Denise Brotherton had been monitoring the fire all night and had even called the station around eight o'clock, after everyone knew that Paul was dead. "Is he in?" she'd asked the firefighter manning the phone. "Nope," he'd deadpanned. "He's out on a run."

Friends had been trickling into the house all night for support. The congestion was making her more nervous. Still in her green scrubs from her shift at the hospital, she cracked a beer to calm her nerves and snuck a cigarette in the garage. Every few minutes, someone would ask her if she wanted to go to the warehouse to check things out. "No," she'd say. "Paul always told me if anything happens, the fire department will come to the house. So this is where I need to be. So far, no news is good news."

At about ten o'clock, the local news anchor announced that six Worcester firefighters were missing. All the families, the woman on the television said, had been notified.

Denise felt a wave of relief rush through her, her muscles and emotions uncoiling all at once. It lasted less than a second. Before she could take one calm breath, two Auburn police cruisers and the chief's car pulled in front of her house.

.   .   .

McNamee and Chavoor spent the rest of the night at the warehouse, watching a flood of water spraying into the flames, then rising into the darkness in a steamy mist. McNamee stayed straight through the next day, until the fire had been beaten back far enough for a forty-five-hundred-pound wrecking ball to swing into the B wall, starting a demolition job that would last more than two months. The ball swung once and bounced off the wall. After two more mighty wallops against the eighteen inches of brick, a smattering of mortar tumbled to the ground.

Thirty-two hours after the first alarm sounded, McNamee went home and collapsed into an easy chair. The phone rang. He picked it up, heard his daughter's voice, and started to weep.

.　　.　　.

By late Saturday, most of the B wall had been ripped down to the second floor. Once tons of rubble had been cleared away, some of the building's secrets were revealed. The fire wall was still standing, and the firefighters could count the number of openings spaced vertically along the wall—the remnants of doorways. For the first time, they knew for certain the building had six floors, which meant Brotherton and Lucey had been lost on the fifth. And they knew they'd at least looked in the right place.

It took eight days to recover all the bodies. Chavoor and McNamee worked the deck—which is what everyone called the second floor—watching men dig with their hands through wet ashes and hot bricks, a mountain of burnt offerings ten feet deep. It was miserable work, especially in the December chill, but firefighters from all over the state volunteered to help, and dozens more staffed the station houses so the Worcester men could recover their own. When they had to stand aside so a bucket crane could scoop tons of detritus away, they fidgeted, antsy. The crane would swing clear, Chavoor would yell, "Go!" and a dozen men would sprint back to the rubble and dig like mad. "Ho!" meant the crane was coming back, but no one ran away as quickly.

Cadaver-sniffing dogs, including a Black Lab named Izzie, pawed the ruins. When they smelled something human, they would take one step backward and sit. Most times, they would find only a nozzle or a buckle or a scrap of hose. On Sunday morning, December 5, one of them found Tim Jackson's body. No one can be sure exactly where he died—when the floors collapsed, the bodies slid around—but he appeared to have been about twenty-five feet from the AB stairwell. If the fifth floor had flashed and turned to fire, he might have had one second to take three or four giant strides away from the blast. But then the smoke around him would have exploded into flames, the heat and the concussion crushing him to the floor.

With Jackson's body, the firefighters employed a protocol they would follow five more times that week. All but the Worcester firefighters were cleared from the deck. A body bag and red firehouse blankets were lugged up, the blankets used to fill out the bag if the fire had severely damaged the corpse and to cover the stretcher carrying the body. Four firefighters from the dead man's station—Grove Street, in Jackson's case—lined the sides of the stretcher, an officer walked behind, and McNamee marched in front. They carried each man to the B wall, where two ladders were angled from the ground up to the deck. At the bottom of the ladders, a double line of firefighters formed a corridor to the ambulance. From the time he died until the time the doors closed on the ambulance, only Worcester firefighters touched the body.

They found Jackson's wedding ring the following Friday, the day he was waked, while they were sifting broken bricks and ash through a screen of quarter-inch mesh. The next morning, at the parlor before Jackson's funeral, a firefighter asked Mary if she could describe her husband's ring. "It's just a plain gold band," she said. "But inside, it's inscribed with my name."

The fireman broke into a smile. "I've got it," he said.

The diggers found Jay Lyons on Tuesday night. He died near the front wall, along Franklin Street, on the B side of the fire wall, in the area where the temperature had flashed to 3600 degrees. But the sterling-silver medallion Jay wore around his neck survived intact. It depicts Saint Florian, the patron saint of firefighters. PROTECT US, it says in relief.

Tom Spencer and Joe McGuirk were found next, near each other on the D side of the fire wall, as if they'd groped their way through the door together in the dark, then couldn't feel their way back. Jerry Lucey was dug out on Saturday afternoon, December 11, near the CD corner. When the building first filled with smoke and visibility was cut to zero, he and Brotherton were as far away as possible from the only stairwell that could have led them to safety, too far for searchers to hear their PASS alarms.

Denise Brotherton had been standing outside the warehouse since 2:20 that afternoon, after she'd heard on TV that Lucey's body had been found. She knew Paul would be nearby. She waited through the afternoon and into the evening, her white coat smudged to black by all the men who embraced her. Darkness fell. High on the D wall, which was still looming, unbroken, eighty-five feet above the ground, a piece of cork sparked to life like a struck match, a tongue of orange flame glowing directly over the men digging. "Oh, look," she said to herself, "it's back on fire. At least it's keeping Paul warm." She considered that for a moment. Yeah, right, she thought, like he needs to be kept warm.

Minutes later, one of the guys working the deck told her, "I think we've got a hit. What should we be looking for?"

"Dog tags," Denise said. "Paul always said to look for his dog tags." They were a souvenir from his four years in the Air Force, which he joined to see the world, even though he never got past Valdosta, Georgia.

Another hour passed. At 9:20, Denise told someone to bring a beer up to the deck. "Put a Sam Adams on the deck and say, 'Hey, Paul, we've got a Sam Adams up here for you.' He'll hear that." She managed to smile when she said it.

Forty minutes later, Chief Budd asked her into one of the tents set up outside the wreckage. "This is the hardest job I've ever had to do," he said, "but I want you to have these." He laid Paul's dog tags in her hand gently, as if they were fine and fragile things that might shatter.

It was nearly eleven o'clock on Saturday night when the procession formed around Brotherton's body. McNamee wasn't leading this time. He was home, collapsed in bed, after eight endless days at the site.

As the body neared the ladders at the B wall, the cork flickered; when Brotherton was safely on the ground, it went out, as quickly and quietly as it had ignited.

.   .   .

"People ask us if it's easier now," James Lyons is saying one afternoon in early March, three months after his son, Jay, died in the warehouse fire. "It's not. It's harder. In the beginning, there was so much going on, you didn't have time to think about it. Now we do."

For months, there were luncheons and benefits and honors. James Lyons got mail from as far away as Hawaii and Alaska, huge stacks of condolence cards piled in the den. His daughter, Kathryn, had Jay's Saint Florian medal cleaned and strung on a new silver chain, which she wears around her neck now. Denise Brotherton filled fifteen twenty-two-gallon plastic tubs with the poems and trinkets and notes delivered to her house. When Kathy Spencer accepted a flag at the memorial service, she whispered to a firefighter how Tom had always wanted a flagpole in front of the house. The next morning, a backhoe was digging a hole in her lawn and a flag dealer from suburban Boston was driving west with a twenty-five-foot pole. He wouldn't even tell Kathy his name.

The fire had claimed more than just six men. Captain Mike Coakley inhaled so much poison that night that the doctors think he might never go back to fighting fires. Captain Robert A.'s throat was burned so badly, he couldn't speak for six weeks. Lieutenant John Sullivan transferred out of Grove Street, off of Engine 3, to the drill school. He'd always been an instructor in one academy or another, and Jay Lyons used to tease him about how those who can't do, teach. For now, at least, it's not such a funny joke.

Paul Brotherton's usual partner, Joe LeBlanc, was on vacation on December 3, floating on a cruise ship in the middle of the Caribbean. He had a souvenir for Paul: two beaded braids he'd let an islander twist into his short gray hair just to prove he wasn't as uptight as Paul used to teasingly insist he was. He left the beads on Paul's casket. LeBlanc still shoots the shit with the guys at Central Station, still scrambles into Rescue 1 every time the bell goes off, and the adrenaline still courses through him. But on a rainy night in March, he's relieved when a reported fire turns out to be a malfunctioning smoke alarm. "It'll never be the same," he says, pulling off his gear back at the station. "The only fucking fire I want to see anymore is on a Sunday afternoon in my living room. I've been on this truck for twenty-four years, and it'll never be the same."

Mike McNamee doesn't think so, either. He still doesn't know exactly what happened. The contents of all the radio transmissions have been sealed by investigators, and the people who started the fire, who have pleaded not guilty to six counts of manslaughter, won't stand trial for months to come. In the meantime, McNamee's been to every counseling session, every crisis debriefing he could find, mostly so he won't feel a steamy hand on his shoulder a decade from now—the warehouse disaster coming back to haunt him. He knew all of these men too well. He was in the same drill class as Jackson. He trained Brotherton in 1983, and he was the only chief Joe McGuirk had ever had.

His men tell him he was a hero, that he stood up to a crowd of firefighters blinded by desperation and determination and told them, "No more," and that, by doing so, he saved all of their lives.

In March, James Lyons wheeled his son's prized possession, a 1995 black-on-charcoal Harley-Davidson Heritage Softail, across the street and gave it to the man who taught Jay how to fight fires, the man who was in charge the night Jay died. "It was nice," McNamee says, "to know they don't blame me."

He knows all of this in his head, yes. But he doesn't believe it, not in his gut. "We did everything right," he says. There is no defensiveness to the words. He sounds bewildered, as if he's trying to convince himself more than anyone else. "We entered, we vented, we attacked the fire. We did everything by the numbers," he says. "And the building beat us."

The New Yorker

WINNER, PROFILES

The Pitchman

You've seen him on TV. You've bought the Pocket Fisherman. Now read the profile. This story is a gleeful portrayal of infomercial maestro Ron Popeil. The author doesn't just tell the story of the Veg-O-Matic and Chop-O-Matic; he also provides cultural context for hucksterism throughout history.

Malcolm Gladwell

The Pitchman

Ron Popeil and the conquest of the American kitchen.

The extraordinary story of the Ronco Showtime Rotisserie BBQ begins with Nathan Morris, the son of the shoemaker and cantor Kidders Morris, who came over from the Old Country in the eighteen-eighties, and settled in Asbury Park, New Jersey. Nathan Morris was a pitchman. He worked the boardwalk and the five-and-dimes and county fairs up and down the Atlantic coast, selling kitchen gadgets made by Acme Metal, out of Newark. In the early forties, Nathan set up N. K Morris Manufacturing—turning out the KwiKi-Pi and the Morris Metric Slicer—and perhaps because it was the Depression and job prospects were dim, or perhaps because Nathan Morris made such a compelling case for his new profession, one by one the members of his family followed him into the business. His sons Lester Morris and Arnold (the Knife) Morris became his pitchmen. He set up his brother-in-law Irving Rosenbloom, who was to make a fortune on Long Island in plastic goods, including a hand grater of such excellence that Nathan paid homage to it with his own Dutch Kitchen Shredder Grater. He partnered with his brother Al, whose own sons worked the boardwalk, alongside a gangly Irishman by the name of Ed McMahon. Then, one summer just before the war, Nathan took on as an apprentice his nephew Samuel Jacob Popeil. S. J., as he was known, was so inspired by his uncle Nathan that he went on to found Popeil

Brothers, based in Chicago, and brought the world the Dial-O-Matic, the Chop-O-Matic, and the Veg-O-Matic. S. J. Popeil had two sons. The elder was Jerry, who died young. The younger is familiar to anyone who has ever watched an infomercial on late-night television. His name is Ron Popeil.

In the postwar years, many people made the kitchen their life's work. There were the Klinghoffers of New York, one of whom, Leon, died tragically in 1985, during the Achille Lauro incident, when he was pushed overboard in his wheelchair by Palestinian terrorists. They made the Roto-Broil 400, back in the fifties, an early rotisserie for the home, which was pitched by Lester Morris. There was Lewis Salton, who escaped the Nazis with an English stamp from his father's collection and parlayed it into an appliance factory in the Bronx. He brought the world the Salton Hotray—a sort of precursor to the microwave—and today Salton, Inc., sells the George Foreman Grill.

But no rival quite matched the Morris-Popeil clan. They were the first family of the American kitchen. They married beautiful women and made fortunes and stole ideas from one another and lay awake at night thinking of a way to chop an onion so that the only tears you shed were tears of joy. They believed that it was a mistake to separate product development from marketing, as most of their contemporaries did, because to them the two were indistinguishable: the object that sold best was the one that sold itself. They were spirited, brilliant men. And Ron Popeil was the most brilliant and spirited of them all. He was the family's Joseph, exiled to the wilderness by his father only to come back and make more money than the rest of the family combined. He was a pioneer in taking the secrets of the boardwalk pitchmen to the television screen. And, of all the kitchen gadgets in the Morris-Popeil pantheon, nothing has ever been quite so ingenious in its design, or so broad in its appeal, or so perfectly representative of the Morris-Popeil belief in the interrelation of the pitch and the object being pitched, as the Ronco Showtime Rotisserie & BBQ, the countertop oven that can be bought for four payments of $39.95 and may be, dollar for dollar, the finest kitchen appliance ever made.

A Rotisserie is Born

Ron Popeil is a handsome man, thick through the chest and shoulders, with a leonine head and striking, over-size features. He is in his mid-sixties, and lives in Beverly Hills, halfway up Coldwater Canyon, in a sprawling bungalow with a stand of avocado trees and a vegetable garden out back. In his habits he is, by Beverly Hills standards, old school. He carries his own bags. He has been known to eat at Denny's. He wears T-shirts and sweatpants. As often as twice a day, he can be found buying poultry or fish or meat at one of the local grocery stores—in particular, Costco, which he favors because the chickens there are ninety-nine cents a pound, as opposed to a dollar forty-nine at standard supermarkets. Whatever he buys, he brings back to his kitchen, a vast room overlooking the canyon, with an array of industrial appliances, a collection of fifteen hundred bottles of olive oil, and, in the corner, an oil painting of him, his fourth wife, Robin (a former Frederick's of Hollywood model), and their baby daughter, Contessa. On paper, Popeil owns a company called Ronco Inventions, which has two hundred employees and a couple of warehouses in Chatsworth, California, but the heart of Ronco is really Ron working out of his house, and many of the key players are really just friends of Ron's who work out of their houses, too, and who gather in Ron's kitchen when, every now and again, Ron cooks a soup and wants to talk things over.

In the last thirty years, Ron has invented a succession of kitchen gadgets, among them the Ronco Electric Food Dehydrator and the

Popeil Automatic Pasta and Sausage Maker, which featured a thrust bearing made of the same material used in bulletproof glass. He works steadily, guided by flashes of inspiration. This past August, for instance, he suddenly realized what product should follow the Showtime Rotisserie. He and his right-hand man, Alan Backus, had been working on a bread-and-batter machine, which would take up to ten pounds of chicken wings or scallops or shrimp or fish fillets and do all the work—combining the eggs, the flour, the breadcrumbs—in a few minutes, without dirtying either the cook's hands or the machine. "Alan goes to Korea, where we have some big orders coming through," Ron explained recently over lunch—a hamburger, medium-well, with fries—in the V.I.P. booth by the door in the Polo Lounge, at the Beverly Hills Hotel. "I call Alan on the phone. I wake him up. It was two in the morning there. And these are my exact words: 'Stop. Do not pursue the bread-and-batter machine. I will pick it up later. This other project needs to come first.'" The other project, his inspiration, was a device capable of smoking meats indoors without creating odors that can suffuse the air and permeate furniture. Ron had a version of the indoor smoker on his porch—"a Rube Goldberg kind of thing" that he'd worked on a year earlier—and, on a whim, he cooked a chicken in it. "That chicken was so good that I said to myself"—and with his left hand Ron began to pound on the table—"This is the best chicken sandwich I have ever had in my life." He turned to me: "How many times have you had a smoked-turkey sandwich? Maybe you have a smoked-turkey or a smoked-chicken sandwich once every six months. Once! How many times have you had smoked salmon? Aah. More. I'm going to say you come across smoked salmon as an hors d'oeuvre or an entrée once every three months. Baby-back ribs? Depends on which restaurant you order ribs at. Smoked sausage, same thing. You touch on smoked food"—he leaned in and poked my arm for emphasis—"but I know one thing, Malcolm. *You don't have a smoker.*"

The idea for the Showtime came about in the same way. Ron was at Costco about four years ago when he suddenly realized that there was a long line of customers waiting to buy chickens from the in-store rotisserie ovens. They touched on rotisserie chicken, but Ron knew one thing: they did not have a rotisserie oven. Ron went home and called Backus. Together, they bought a glass aquarium, a motor, a heating element, a spit rod, and a handful of other spare parts, and began tinkering. Ron wanted something big enough for a fifteen-pound turkey but small enough to fit into the space between the base of an average kitchen cupboard and the countertop. He didn't want a thermostat, because thermostats break, and the constant clicking on and off of the heat prevents the even, crispy browning that he felt was essential. And the spit rod had to rotate on the horizontal axis, not the vertical axis, because if you cooked a chicken or a side of beef on the vertical axis the top would dry out and the juices would drain to the bottom. Roderick Dorman, Ron's patent attorney, says that when he went over to Coldwater Canyon he often saw five or six prototypes on the kitchen counter, lined up in a row. Ron would have a chicken in each of them, so that he could compare the consistency of the flesh and the browning of the skin, and wonder if, say, there was a way to rotate a shish kebab as it approached the heating element so that the inner side of the kebab would get as brown as the outer part. By the time Ron finished, the Showtime prompted no fewer than two dozen patent applications. It was equipped with the most powerful motor in its class. It had a drip tray coated with a non-stick ceramic, which was easily cleaned, and the oven would still work even after it had been dropped on a concrete or stone surface ten times in succession, from a distance of three feet. To Ron, there was no question that it made the best chicken he had ever had in his life.

It was then that Ron filmed a television infomercial for the Showtime, twenty-eight minutes and thirty seconds in length. It was shot live before a studio audience, and aired for the first time on August 8, 1998. It has run ever since, often in the wee hours of the morning, or on obscure cable stations, alongside the get-rich schemes and the "Three's Company" reruns. The response to it has been such that within the next three years total sales of the Show-time should exceed a billion dollars. Ron Popeil didn't use a single focus group. He had no market researchers, R.&D. teams, public-relations advisers, Madison Avenue advertising companies, or business consultants. He did what the Morrises and the Popeils had been doing for most of the century, and what all the experts said couldn't be done in the modern economy. He dreamed up something new in his kitchen and went out and pitched it himself.

Pitchmen

Nathan Morris, Ron Popeil's great-uncle, looked a lot like Cary Grant. He wore a straw boater. He played the ukulele, drove a con-vertible, and composed melodies for the piano. He ran his busi-ness out of a low-slung, whitewashed building on Ridge Avenue, near Asbury Park, with a little annex in the back where he did pio-neering work with Teflon. He had certain eccentricities, such as a phobia he developed about travelling beyond Asbury Park with-out the presence of a doctor. He feuded with his brother Al, who subsequently left in a huff for Atlantic City, and then with his nephew S. J. Popeil, whom Nathan considered insufficiently grate-ful for the start he had given him in the kitchen-gadget business. That second feud led to a climactic legal showdown over S. J. Popeil's Chop-O-Matic, a food preparer with a pleated, W-shaped blade rotated by a special clutch mechanism. The Chop-O-Matic was ideal for making coleslaw and chopped liver, and when Mor-ris introduced a strikingly similar product, called the Roto-Chop,

S. J. Popeil sued his uncle for patent infringement. (As it happened, the Chop-O-Matic itself seemed to have been inspired by the Blitzhacker, from Switzerland, and S. J. later lost a patent judgment to the Swiss.)

The two squared off in Trenton, in May of 1958, in a courtroom jammed with Morrises and Popeils. When the trial opened, Nathan Morris was on the stand, being cross-examined by his nephew's attorneys, who were out to show him that he was no more than a huckster and a copycat. At a key point in the questioning, the judge suddenly burst in. "He took the index finger of his right hand and he pointed it at Morris," Jack Dominik, Popeil's longtime patent lawyer, recalls, "and as long as I live I will never forget what he said. 'I know you! You're a pitchman! I've seen you on the boardwalk!' And Morris pointed his index finger back at the judge and shouted, 'No! I'm a manufacturer. I'm a dignified manufacturer, and I work with the most eminent of counsel!'" (Nathan Morris, according to Dominik, was the kind of man who referred to everyone he worked with as eminent.) "At that moment," Dominik goes on, "Uncle Nat's face was getting red and the judge's was getting redder, so a recess was called." What happened later that day is best described in Dominik's unpublished manuscript, "The Inventions of Samuel Joseph Popeil by Jack E. Dominik—His Patent Lawyer." Nathan Morris had a sudden heart attack, and S. J. was guilt-stricken. "Sobbing ensued," Dominik writes. "Remorse set in. The next day, the case was settled. Thereafter, Uncle Nat's recovery from his previous day's heart attack was nothing short of a miracle."

Nathan Morris was a performer, like so many of his relatives, and pitching was, first and foremost, a performance. It's said that Nathan's nephew Archie (the Pitchman's Pitchman) Morris once sold, over a long afternoon, gadget after gadget to a well-dressed man. At the end of the day, Archie watched the man walk away, stop and peer into his bag, and then dump the whole lot into a nearby garbage can. The Morrises were that good. "My cousins could sell you an empty box," Ron says.

The last of the Morrises to be active in the pitching business is Arnold (the Knife) Morris, so named because of his extraordinary skill with the Sharpcut, the forerunner of the Ginsu. He is in his early seventies, a cheerful, impish man with a round face and a few wisps of white hair, and a trademark move whereby, after cutting a tomato into neat, regular slices, he deftly lines the pieces up in an even row against the flat edge of the blade. Today, he lives in Ocean Township, a few miles from Asbury Park, with Phyllis, his wife of twenty-nine years, whom he refers to (with the same irresistible conviction that he might use to describe, say, the Feather Touch Knife) as "the prettiest girl in Asbury Park." One morning recently, he sat in his study and launched into a pitch for the Dial-O-Matic, a slicer produced by S. J. Popeil some forty years ago.

"Come on over, folks. I'm going to show you the most amazing slicing machine you have ever seen in your life," he began. Phyllis, sitting nearby, beamed with pride. He picked up a package of barbecue spices, which Ron Popeil sells alongside his Showtime Rotisserie, and used it as a prop. "Take a look at this!" He held it in the air as if he were holding up a Tiffany vase. He talked about the machine's prowess at cutting potatoes, then onions, then tomatoes. His voice, a marvellous instrument inflected with the rhythms of the Jersey Shore, took on a singsong quality: "How many cut tomatoes like this? You stab it. You jab it. The juices run down your elbow. With the Dial-O-Matic, you do it a little differently. You put it in the machine and you wiggle"—he mimed fixing the tomato to the bed of the machine. "The tomato! Lady! The tomato! The more you wiggle, the more you get. The tomato! Lady! Every slice comes out perfectly, not a seed out of place. But the thing I love my Dial-O-Matic for is coleslaw. My mother-in-law used to take her cabbage and do this." He made a series of wild stabs at an imaginary cabbage. "I thought she was going to commit suicide. Oh, boy, did I pray—that she wouldn't slip! Don't get me wrong. I love my mother-in-law. It's her daughter I can't figure out. You take the cabbage. Cut it in half. Coleslaw, hot slaw. Pot slaw. Liberty slaw. It comes out like shredded wheat . . . "

It was a vaudeville monologue, except that Arnold wasn't merely entertaining; he was selling. "You can take a pitchman and make a great actor out of him, but you cannot take an actor and always make a great pitchman out of him," he says. The pitchman must make you applaud *and* take out your money. He must be able to execute what in pitchman's parlance is called "the turn"—the perilous, crucial moment where he goes from entertainer to businessman. If, out of a crowd of fifty, twenty-five people come forward to buy, the true pitchman sells to only twenty of them. To the remaining five, he says, "Wait! There's something else I want to show you!" Then he starts his pitch again, with slight variations, and the remaining four or five become the inner core of the next crowd, hemmed in by the people around them, and so eager to pay their money and be on their way that they start the selling frenzy all over again. The turn requires the management of expectation. That's why Arnold always kept a pineapple tantalizingly perched on his stand. "For forty years, I've been promising to show people how to cut the pineapple, and I've never cut it once," he says. "It got to the point where a pitchman friend of mine went out and bought himself a plastic pineapple. Why would you cut the pineapple? It cost a couple bucks. And if you cut it they'd leave." Arnold says that he once hired some guys to pitch a vegetable slicer for him at a fair in Danbury, Connecticut, and became so annoyed at their lackadaisical attitude that he took over the demonstration himself. They were, he says, waiting for him to fail: he had never worked that particular slicer before and, sure enough, he was massacring the vegetables. Still, in a single pitch he took in two hundred dollars. "Their eyes popped out of their heads," Arnold recalls. "They said, 'We don't understand it. You don't even know how to work the damn machine.' I said, 'But I know how to do one thing better than you.' They said, 'What's that?' I said, *'I know how to ask for the money.'* And that's the secret to the whole damn business."

.   .   .

Ron Popeil started pitching his father's kitchen gadgets at the Maxwell Street flea market in Chicago, in the mid-fifties. He was thirteen. Every morning, he would arrive at the market at five and prepare fifty pounds each of onions, cabbages, and carrots, and a hundred pounds of potatoes. He sold from six in the morning until four in the afternoon, bringing in as much as five hundred dollars a day. In his late teens, he started doing the state- and county-fair circuit, and then he scored a prime spot in the Woolworth's at State and Washington, in the Loop, which at the time was the top-grossing Woolworth's store in the country. He was making more than the manager of the store, selling the Chop-O-Matic and the Dial-O-Matic. He dined at the Pump Room and wore a Rolex and rented hundred-and-fifty-dollar-a-night hotel suites. In pictures from the period, he is beautiful, with thick dark hair and blue-green eyes and sensuous lips, and, several years later, when he moved his office to 919 Michigan Avenue, he was called the Paul Newman of the Playboy Building. Mel Korey, a friend of Ron's from college and his first business partner, remembers the time he went to see Ron pitch the Chop-O-Matic at the State Street Woolworth's. "He was mesmerizing," Korey says. "There were secretaries who would take their lunch break at Woolworth's to watch him because he was so good-looking. He would go into the turn, and people would just come running." Several years ago, Ron's friend Steve Wynn, the founder of the Mirage resorts, went to visit Michael Milken in prison. They were near a television, and happened to catch one of Ron's infomercials just as he was doing the countdown, a routine taken straight from the boardwalk, where he says, "You're not going to spend two hundred dollars, not a hundred and eighty dollars, not one-seventy, not one-sixty . . ." It's a standard pitchman's gimmick: it sounds dramatic only because the starting price is set way up high. But something about the way Ron did it was irresistible. As he got lower and lower, Wynn and Milken—who probably know as much about profit margins as anyone in America—cried out in unison, "Stop, Ron! Stop!"

Was Ron the best? The only attempt to settle the question definitively was made some forty years ago, when Ron and Arnold were working a knife set at the Eastern States Exposition, in West Springfield, Massachusetts. A third man, Frosty Wishon, who was a legend in his own right, was there, too. "Frosty was a well-dressed, articulate individual and a good salesman," Ron says. "But he thought he was the best. So I said, 'Well, guys, we've got a ten-day show, eleven, maybe twelve hours a day. We'll each do a rotation, and we'll compare how much we sell.'" In Morris-Popeil lore, this is known as "the shoot-out," and no one has ever forgotten the outcome. Ron beat Arnold, but only by a whisker—no more than a few hundred dollars. Frosty Wishon, meanwhile, sold only half as much as either of his rivals. "You have no idea the pressure Frosty was under," Ron continues. "He came up to me at the end of the show and said, 'Ron, I will never work with you again as long as I live.'"

No doubt Frosty Wishon was a charming and persuasive person, but he assumed that this was enough—that the rules of pitching were the same as the rules of celebrity endorsement. When Michael Jordan pitches McDonald's hamburgers, Michael Jordan is the star. But when Ron Popeil or Arnold Morris pitched, say, the Chop-O-Matic, his gift was to make the Chop-O-Matic the star. It was, after all, an innovation. It represented a different way of dicing onions and chopping liver: it required consumers to rethink the way they went about their business in the kitchen. Like most great innovations, it was disruptive. And how do you persuade people to disrupt their lives? Not merely by ingratiation or sincerity, and not by being famous or beautiful. You have to explain the invention to customers—not once or twice but three or four times, with a different twist each time. You have to show them exactly how it works and why it works, and make them follow your hands as you chop liver with it, and then tell them precisely how it fits into their routine, and, finally, sell them on the paradoxical fact that, revolutionary as the gadget is, it's not at all hard to use.

Thirty years ago, the videocassette recorder came on the market, and it was a disruptive product, too: it was supposed to make it possible to tape a television show so that no one would ever again be chained to the prime-time schedule. Yet, as ubiquitous as the VCR became, it was seldom put to that purpose. That's because the VCR was never pitched: no one ever explained the gadget to American consumers—not once or twice but three or four times—and no one showed them exactly how it worked or how it would fit into their routine, and no pair of hands guided them through every step of the process. All the VCR-makers did was hand over the box with a smile and a pat on the back, tossing in an instruction manual for good measure. Any pitchman could have told you that wasn't going to do it.

Once, when I was over at Ron's house in Coldwater Canyon, sitting on one of the high stools in his kitchen, he showed me what real pitching is all about. He was talking about how he had just had dinner with the actor Ron Silver, who is playing Ron's friend Robert Shapiro in a new movie about the O. J. Simpson trial. "They shave the back of Ron Silver's head so that he's got a bald spot, because, you know, Bob Shapiro's got a bald spot back there, too," Ron said. "So I say to him, 'You've gotta get GLH.'" GLH, one of Ron's earlier products, is an aerosol spray designed to thicken the hair and cover up bald spots. "I told him, 'It will make you look good. When you've got to do the scene, you shampoo it out.'"

At this point, the average salesman would have stopped. The story was an aside, no more. We had been discussing the Showtime Rotisserie, and on the counter behind us was a Showtime cooking a chicken and next to it a Showtime cooking baby-back ribs, and on the table in front of him Ron's pasta maker was working, and he was frying some garlic so that we could have a little lunch. But now that he had told me about GLH it was unthinkable that he would not also show me its wonders. He walked quickly over to a table at the other side of the room, talking as he went. "People always ask me, 'Ron, where did you get that name GLH?' I made it up. Great-Looking Hair." He picked up a can. "We make it in nine different colors. This is silver-black." He picked up a hand mirror and angled it above his head so that he could see his bald spot. "Now, the first thing I'll do is spray it where I don't need it." He shook the can and began spraying the crown of his head, talking all the while. "Then I'll go to the area itself." He pointed to his bald spot. "Right here. O.K. Now I'll let that dry. Brushing is fifty per cent of the way it's going to look." He began brushing vigorously, and suddenly Ron Popeil had what looked like a complete head of hair. "Wow," I said. Ron glowed. "And you tell me 'Wow.' That's what everyone says. 'Wow.' That's what people say who use it. 'Wow.' If you go outside"—he grabbed me by the arm and pulled me out onto the deck—"if you are in bright sunlight or daylight, you cannot tell that I have a big bald spot in the back of my head. It really looks like hair, but it's not hair. It's quite a product. It's incredible. Any shampoo will take it out. You know who would be a great candidate for this? Al Gore. You want to see how it feels?" Ron inclined the back of his head toward me. I had said, "Wow," and had looked at his hair inside and outside, but the pitchman in Ron Popeil wasn't satisfied. I had to feel the back of his head. I did. It felt just like real hair.

The Tinkerer

Ron Popeil inherited more than the pitching tradition of Nathan Morris. He was very much the son of S. J. Popeil, and that fact, too, goes a long way toward explaining the success of the Showtime Rotisserie. S. J. had a ten-room apartment high in the Drake Towers, near the top of Chicago's Magnificent Mile. He had a chauffeured Cadillac limousine with a car phone, a rarity in those days, which he delighted in showing off (as in "I'm calling you from the car"). He wore three-piece suits and loved to play the piano. He smoked cigars and scowled a lot and made funny little grunting noises as he talked. He kept his money in T-bills. His philosophy was expressed in a series of epigrams: To his attorney, "If they push you far enough, sue"; to his son, "It's not how much you spend, it's how much you make." And, to a designer who expressed doubts about the utility of one of his greatest hits, the Pocket Fisherman, "It's not for using; it's for giving." In 1974, S. J.'s second wife, Eloise, decided to have him killed, so she hired two hit men—one of whom, aptly, went by the name of Mr. Peeler. At the time, she was living at the Popeil estate in Newport Beach with her two daughters and her boyfriend, a thirty-seven-year-old machinist. When, at Eloise's trial, S. J. was questioned about the machinist, he replied, "I was kind of happy to have him take her off my hands." That was vintage S. J. But eleven months later, after Eloise got out of prison, S. J. married her again. That was vintage S. J., too. As a former colleague of his puts it, "He was a strange bird."

S. J. Popeil was a tinkerer. In the middle of the night, he would wake up and make frantic sketches on a pad he kept on his bedside table. He would disappear into his kitchen for hours and make a huge mess, and come out with a faraway look on his face. He loved standing behind his machinists, peering over their shoulders while they were assembling one of his prototypes. In the late forties and early fifties, he worked almost exclusively in plastic, reinterpreting kitchen basics with a subtle, modernist flair. "Popeil Brothers made these beautiful plastic flour sifters," Tim Samuelson, a curator at the Chicago Historical Society and a leading authority on the Popeil legacy, says. "They would use contrasting colors, or a combination of opaque plastic with a translucent swirl plastic." Samuelson became fascinated with all things Popeil after he acquired an original Popeil Brothers doughnut maker, in red-and-white plastic, which he felt "had beautiful lines"; to this day, in the kitchen of his Hyde Park high-rise, he uses the Chop-O-Matic in the preparation of salad ingredients. "There was always a little twist to what he did," Samuelson goes on. "Take the Popeil automatic egg turner. It looks like a regular spatula, but if you squeeze the handle the blade turns just enough to flip a fried egg."

Walter Herbst, a designer whose firm worked with Popeil Brothers for many years, says that S. J.'s modus operandi was to "come up with a holistic theme. He'd arrive in the morning with it. It would be something like"—Herbst assumes S. J.'s gruff voice—"'We need a better way to shred cabbage.' It was a passion, an absolute goddam passion. One morning, he must have been eating grapefruit, because he comes to work and calls me and says, 'We need a better way to cut grapefruit!'" The idea they came up with was a double-bladed paring knife, with the blades separated by a fraction of an inch so that both sides of the grapefruit membrane could be cut simultaneously. "There was a little grocery store a few blocks away," Herbst says. "So S. J. sends the chauffeur out for grapefruit. How many? Six. Well, over the period of a couple of weeks, six turns to twelve and twelve turns to twenty, until we were cutting thirty to forty grapefruits a day. I don't know if that little grocery store ever knew what happened."

S. J. Popeil's finest invention was undoubtedly the Veg-O-Matic, which came on the market in 1960 and was essentially a food processor, a Cuisinart without the motor. The heart of the gadget was a series of slender, sharp blades strung like guitar strings across two Teflon-coated metal rings, which were made in Woodstock, Illinois, from 364 Alcoa, a special grade of aluminum. When the rings were aligned on top of each other so that the blades ran parallel, a potato or an onion pushed through would come out in perfect slices. If the top ring was rotated, the blades formed a crosshatch, and a potato or an onion pushed through would come out diced. The rings were housed in a handsome plastic assembly, with a plunger to push the vegetables through the blades. Technically, the Veg-O-Matic was a triumph: the method of creating blades strong enough to withstand the assault of vegetables received a U.S. patent. But from a marketing perspective it posed a problem. S. J.'s products had hitherto been sold by pitchmen armed with a mound of vegetables meant to carry them through a day's worth of demonstrations. But the Veg-O-Matic was *too* good. In a single minute, according to the calculations of Popeil Brothers, it could produce a hundred and twenty egg wedges, three hundred cucumber slices, eleven hundred and fifty potato shoestrings, or three thousand onion dices. It could go through what used to be a day's worth of vegetables in a matter of minutes. The pitchman could no longer afford to pitch to just a hundred people at a time; he had to pitch to a hundred thousand. The Veg-O-Matic needed to be sold on television, and one of the very first pitchmen to grasp this fact was Ron Popeil.

In the summer of 1964, just after the Veg-O-Matic was introduced, Mel Korey joined forces with Ron Popeil in a company called Ronco. They shot a commercial for the Veg-O-Matic for five hundred dollars, a straightforward pitch shrunk to two minutes, and set out from Chicago for the surrounding towns of the Midwest. They cold-called local department stores and persuaded them to carry the Veg-O-Matic on guaranteed sale, which meant that whatever the stores didn't sell could be returned. Then they visited the local television station and bought a two- or three-week run of the cheapest airtime they could find, praying that it would be enough to drive traffic to the store. "We got Veg-O-Matics wholesale for $3.42," Korey says. "They retailed for $9.95, and we sold them to the stores for $7.46, which meant that we had four dollars to play with. If I spent a hundred dollars on television, I had to sell twenty-five Veg-O-Matics to break even." It was clear, in those days, that you could use television to sell kitchen products if you were Procter & Gamble. It wasn't so clear that this would work if you were Mel Korey and Ron Popeil, two pitchmen barely out of their teens selling a combination slicer-dicer that no one had ever heard of. They were taking a wild gamble, and, to their amazement, it paid off. "They had a store in Butte, Montana—Hennessy's," Korey goes on, thinking back to those first improbable years. "Back then, people there were still wearing peacoats. The city was mostly bars. It had just a few three-story buildings. There were twenty-seven thousand people, and one TV station. I had the Veg-O-Matic, and I go to the store, and they said, 'We'll take a case. We don't have a lot of traffic here.' I go to the TV station and the place is a dump. The only salesperson was going blind and deaf. So I do a schedule. For five weeks, I spend three hundred and fifty dollars. I figure if I sell a hundred and seventy-four machines—six cases—I'm happy. I go back to Chicago, and I walk into the office one morning and the phone is ringing. They said, 'We sold out. You've got to fly us another six cases of Veg-O-Matics.' The next week, on Monday, the phone rings. It's Butte again: 'We've got a hundred and fifty oversold.' I fly him another six cases. Every few days after that, whenever the phone rang we'd look at each other and say, 'Butte, Montana.'" Even today, thirty years later, Korey can scarcely believe it. "How many homes in total in that town? Maybe several thousand? We ended up selling two thousand five hundred Veg-O-Matics in five weeks!"

Why did the Veg-O-Matic sell so well? Doubtless, Americans were eager for a better way of slicing vegetables. But it was more than that: the Veg-O-Matic represented a perfect marriage between the medium (television) and the message (the gadget). The Veg-O-Matic was, in the relevant sense, utterly transparent. You took the potato and you pushed it through the Teflon-coated rings and—voilà!—you had French fries. There were no buttons being pressed, no hidden and intimidating gears: you could show-and-tell the Veg-O-Matic in a two-minute spot and allay every-one's fears about a daunting new technology. More specifically, you could train the camera on the machine and compel viewers to pay total attention to the product you were selling. TV allowed you to do even more effectively what the best pitchmen strove to do in live demonstrations—make the product the star.

.   .   .

This was a lesson Ron Popeil never forgot. In his infomercial for the Showtime Rotisserie, he opens not with himself but with a series of shots of meat and poultry, glistening almost obscenely as they rotate in the Showtime. A voice-over describes each shot: a "delicious six-pound chicken," a "succulent whole duckling," a "mouthwatering pork-loin roast . . ." Only then do we meet Ron, in a sports coat and jeans. He explains the problems of conven-tional barbecues, how messy and unpleasant they are. He bangs a hammer against the door of the Showtime, to demonstrate its strength. He deftly trusses a chicken, impales it on the patented two-pronged Showtime spit rod, and puts it into the oven. Then he repeats the process with a pair of chickens, salmon steaks gar-nished with lemon and dill, and a rib roast. All the time, the cam-era is on his hands, which are in constant motion, manipulating the Showtime apparatus gracefully, with his calming voice leading viewers through every step: "All I'm going to do here is slide it through like this. It goes in very easily. I'll match it up over here. What I'd like to do is take some herbs and spices here. All I'll do is slide it back. Raise up my glass door here. I'll turn it to a little over an hour. . . . Just set it and forget it."

Why does this work so well? Because the Showtime—like the Veg-O-Matic before it—was designed to be the star. From the very beginning, Ron insisted that the entire door be a clear pane of glass, and that it slant back to let in the maximum amount of light, so that the chicken or the turkey or the baby-back ribs turning inside would be visible at all times. Alan Backus says that after the first version of the Showtime came out Ron began obsessing over the quality and evenness of the browning and became convinced that the rotation speed of the spit wasn't quite right. The original machine moved at four revolutions per minute. Ron set up a comparison test in his kitchen, cooking chicken after chicken at varying speeds until he determined that the optimal speed of rotation was actually six r.p.m. One can imagine a bright-eyed M.B.A. clutching a sheaf of focus-group reports and arguing that Ronco was really selling convenience and healthful living, and that it was foolish to spend hundreds of thousands of dollars retooling production in search of a more even golden brown. But Ron understood that the perfect brown is important for the same reason that the slanted glass door is important: because in every respect the design of the product must support the transparency and effectiveness of its performance during a demonstration—the better it looks onstage, the easier it is for the pitchman to go into the turn and ask for the money.

If Ron had been the one to introduce the VCR, in other words, he would not simply have sold it in an infomercial. He would also have changed the VCR itself, so that it made sense in an infomercial. The clock, for example, wouldn't be digital. (The haplessly blinking unset clock has, of course, become a symbol of frustration.) The tape wouldn't be inserted behind a hidden door—it would be out in plain view, just like the chicken in the rotisserie, so that if it was recording you could see the spools turn. The controls wouldn't be discreet buttons; they would be large, and they would make a reassuring click as they were pushed up and down, and each step of the taping process would be identified with a big, obvious numeral so that you could set it and forget it. And would it be a slender black, low-profile box? Of course not. Ours is a culture in which the term "black box" is synonymous with incomprehensibility. Ron's VCR would be in red-and-white plastic, both opaque and translucent swirl, or maybe 364 Alcoa aluminum, painted in some bold primary color, and it would sit on top of the television, not below it, so that when your neighbor or your friend came over he would spot it immediately and say, "Wow, you have one of those Ronco Tape-O-Matics!"

A Real Piece of Work

Ron Popeil did not have a happy childhood. "I remember baking a potato. It must have been when I was four or five years old," he told me. We were in his kitchen, and had just sampled some baby-back ribs from the Showtime. It had taken some time to draw the memories out of him, because he is not one to dwell on the past. "I couldn't get that baked potato into my stomach fast enough, because I was so hungry." Ron is normally in constant motion, moving his hands, chopping food, bustling back and forth. But now he was still. His parents split up when he was very young. S. J. went off to Chicago. His mother disappeared. He and his older brother, Jerry, were shipped off to a boarding school in upstate New York. "I remember seeing my mother on one occasion. I don't remember seeing my father, ever, until I moved to Chicago, at thirteen. When I was in the boarding school, the thing I remember was a Sunday when the parents visited the children, and my parents never came. Even knowing that they weren't going to show up, I walked out to the perimeter and looked out over the farmland, and there was this road." He made an undulating motion with his hand to suggest a road stretching off into the distance. "I remember standing on the road crying, looking for the movement of a car miles away, hoping that it was my mother and father. And they never came. That's all I remember about boarding school." Ron remained perfectly still. "I don't remember ever having a birthday party in my life. I remember that my grandparents took us out and we moved to Florida. My grandfather used to tie me down in bed—my hands, my wrists, and my feet. Why? Because I had a habit of turning over on my stomach and bumping my head either up and down or side to side. Why? How? I don't know the answers. But I was spread-eagle, on my back, and if I was able to twist over and do it my grandfather would wake up at night and come in and beat the hell out of me." Ron stopped, and then added, "I never liked him. I never knew my mother or her parents or any of that family. That's it. Not an awful lot to remember. Obviously, other things took place. But they have been erased."

When Ron came to Chicago, at thirteen, with his grandparents, he was put to work in the Popeil Brothers factory—but only on the weekends, when his father wasn't there. "Canned salmon and white bread for lunch, that was the diet," he recalls. "Did I live with my father? Never. I lived with my grandparents." When he became a pitchman, his father gave him just one advantage: he extended his son credit. Mel Korey says that he once drove Ron home from college and dropped him off at his father's apartment. "He had a key to the apartment, and when he walked in his dad was in bed already. His dad said, 'Is that you, Ron?' And Ron said, 'Yeah.' And his dad never came out. And by the next morning Ron still hadn't seen him." Later, when Ron went into business for himself, he was persona non grata around Popeil Brothers. "Ronnie was never allowed in the place after that," one of S. J.'s former associates recalls. "He was never let in the front door. He was never allowed to be part of anything." My father, Ron says simply, "was all business. I didn't know him personally."

Here is a man who constructed his life in the image of his father—who went into the same business, who applied the same relentless attention to the workings of the kitchen, who got his start by selling his father's own products—and where was his father? "You know, they could have done wonders together," Korey says, shaking his head. "I remember one time we talked with K-tel about joining forces, and they said that we would be a *war machine*—that was their word. Well, Ron and his dad, they could have been a war machine." For all that, it is hard to find in Ron even a trace of bitterness. Once, I asked him, "Who are your inspirations?" The first name came easily: his good friend Steve Wynn. He was silent for a moment, and then he added, "My father." Despite everything, Ron clearly found in his father's example a tradition of irresistible value. And what did Ron do with that tradition? He transcended it. He created the Showtime, which is indisputably a better gadget, dollar for dollar, than the Morris Metric Slicer, the Dutch Kitchen Shredder Grater, the Chop-O-Matic, and the Veg-O-Matic combined.

When I was in Ocean Township, visiting Arnold Morris, he took me to the local Jewish cemetery, Chesed Shel Ames, on a small hilltop just outside town. We drove slowly through the town's poorer sections in Arnold's white Mercedes. It was a rainy day. At the cemetery, a man stood out front in an undershirt, drinking a beer. We entered through a little rusty gate. "This is where it all starts," Arnold said, by which he meant that everyone—the whole spirited, squabbling clan—was buried here. We walked up and down the rows until we found, off in a corner, the Morris headstones. There was Nathan Morris, of the straw boater and the opportune heart attack, and next to him his wife, Betty. A few rows over was the family patriarch, Kidders Morris, and his wife, and a few rows from there Irving Rosenbloom, who made a fortune in plastic goods out on Long Island. Then all the Popeils, in tidy rows: Ron's grandfather Isadore, who was as mean as a snake, and his wife, Mary; S. J., who turned a cold shoulder to his own son; Ron's brother, Jerry, who died young. Ron was from them, but he was not of them. Arnold walked slowly among the tombstones, the rain dancing off his baseball cap, and then he said something that seemed perfectly right. "You know, I'll bet you you'll never find Ronnie here."

On the Air

One Saturday night a few weeks ago, Ron Popeil arrived at the headquarters of the television shopping network QVC, a vast gleaming complex nestled in the woods of suburban Philadelphia. Ron is a regular on QVC. He supplements his infomercials with occasional appearances on the network, and, for twenty-four hours beginning that midnight, QVC had granted him eight live slots, starting with a special "Ronco" hour between midnight and 1 A.M. Ron was travelling with his daughter Shannon, who had got her start in the business selling the Ronco Electric Food Dehydrator on the fair circuit, and the plan was that the two of them would alternate throughout the day. They were pitching a Digital Jog Dial version of the Showtime, in black, available for one day only, at a "special value" of $129.72.

In the studio, Ron had set up eighteen Digital Jog Dial Showtimes on five wood-panelled gurneys. From Los Angeles, he had sent, via Federal Express, dozens of Styrofoam containers with enough meat for each of the day's airings: eight fifteen-pound turkeys, seventy-two hamburgers, eight legs of lamb, eight ducks, thirty-odd chickens, two dozen or so Rock Cornish game hens, and on and on, supplementing them with garnishes, trout, and some sausage bought that morning at three Philadelphia-area supermarkets. QVC's target was thirty-seven thousand machines, meaning that it hoped to gross about $4.5 million during the twenty-four hours—a huge day, even by the network's standards. Ron seemed tense. He barked at the team of QVC producers and cameramen bustling around the room. He fussed over the hero plates—the ready-made dinners that he would use to showcase meat taken straight from the oven. "Guys, this is impossible," he said, peering at a tray of mashed potatoes and gravy. "The level of gravy must be higher." He was limping a little. "You know, there's a lot of pressure on you," he said wearily. "'How did Ron do? Is he still the best?'"

With just a few minutes to go, Ron ducked into the greenroom next to the studio to put GLH in his hair: a few aerosol bursts, followed by vigorous brushing. "Where is God right now?" his co-host, Rick Domeier, yelled out, looking around theatrically for his guest star. "Is God backstage?" Ron then appeared, resplendent in a chef's coat, and the cameras began to roll. He sliced open a leg of lamb. He played with the dial of the new digital Showtime. He admired the crispy, succulent skin of the duck. He discussed the virtues of the new food-warming feature—where the machine would rotate at low heat for up to four hours after the meat was cooked in order to keep the juices moving—and, all the while, bantered so convincingly with viewers calling in on the testimonial line that it was as if he were back mesmerizing the secretaries in the Woolworth's at State and Washington.

In the greenroom, there were two computer monitors. The first displayed a line graph charting the number of calls that came in at any given second. The second was an electronic ledger showing the total sales up to that point. As Ron took flight, one by one, people left the studio to gather around the computers. Shannon Popeil came first. It was 12:40 A.M. In the studio, Ron was slicing onions with one of his father's Dial-O-Matics. She looked at the second monitor and gave a little gasp. Forty minutes in, and Ron had already passed seven hundred thousand dollars. A QVC manager walked in. It was 12:48 A.M., and Ron was roaring on: $837,650. "It can't be!" he cried out. "That's unbelievable!" Two QVC producers came over. One of them pointed at the first monitor, which was graphing the call volume. "Jump," he called out. "Jump!" There were only a few minutes left. Ron was extolling the virtues of the oven one final time, and, sure enough, the line began to take a sharp turn upward, as all over America viewers took out their wallets. The numbers on the second screen began to change in a blur of recalculation—rising in increments of $129.72 plus shipping and taxes. "You know, we're going to hit a million dollars, just on the first hour," one of the QVC guys said, and there was awe in his voice. It was one thing to talk about how Ron was the best there ever was, after all, but quite another to see proof of it, before your very eyes. At that moment, on the other side of the room, the door opened, and a man appeared, stooped and drawn but with a smile on his face. It was Ron Popeil, who invented a better rotisserie in his kitchen and went out and pitched it himself. There was a hush, and then the whole room stood up and cheered.

The American Scholar

FINALIST, ESSAYS

Mail

As the world goes ever more digital, Anne Fadiman, editor of The American Scholar, *celebrates the vanishing art of snail mail—lovingly described both at its origins and at its greatest flowering. This touchingly personal essay contrasts the lost world of hourly deliveries and the penny post with the current e-mail-a-minute.*

Anne Fadiman

Mail

Some years ago, my parents lived at the top of a steep hill. My father kept a pair of binoculars on his desk with which, like a pirate captain hoisting his spyglass to scan the horizon for treasure ships, he periodically inspected the mailbox to see if the flag had been raised. When it finally went up, he trudged down the driveway and opened the extra-large black metal box, purchased by my mother in the same accommodating spirit with which some wives buy their husbands extra-large trousers. The day's load—a mountain of letters and about twenty pounds of review books packed in Jiffy Bags, a few of which had been pierced by their angular contents and were leaking what my father called "mouse dirt"—was always tightly wedged. But he was a persistent man, and after a brief show of resistance the mail would surrender, to be carried up the hill in a tight clinch and dumped onto a gigantic desk. Until that moment, my father's day had not truly begun.

His desk was made of steel, weighed more than a refrigerator, and bristled with bookshelves and secret drawers and sliding panels and a niche for a cedar-lined humidor. (He believed that cigar-smoking and mail-reading were natural partners, like oysters and Muscadet.) I think of it as less a writing surface than a mail-sorting table. He hated Sundays and holidays because there was nothing new to spread on it. Vacations were taxing, the equivalent of forced relocations to places without food. His homecomings were always followed by day-long orgies of mail-opening—feast after famine—at the end of which all the letters were answered; all the bills were paid; the outgoing envelopes were affixed with stamps from a brass dispenser heavy enough to break your toe; the books and manuscripts were neatly stacked; and the empty Jiffy Bags were stuffed into an extra-large copper wastebasket, cheering confirmation that the process of postal digestion was complete.

"One of my unfailing minor pleasures may seem dull to more energetic souls: opening the mail," he once wrote.

> Living in an advanced industrial civilization is a kind of near-conquest over the unexpected. . . . Such efficiency is of course admirable. It does not, however, by its very nature afford scope to that perverse human trait, still not quite eliminated, which is pleased by the accidental. Thus to many tame citizens like me the morning mail functions as the voice of the unpredictable and keeps alive for a few minutes a day the keen sense of the unplanned and the unplannable. The letter opener is an instrument that has persisted from some antique land of chance and adventure into our ordered world of the perfectly calculated.

What chance and adventure might the day's haul contain? My brother asked him, when he was in his nineties, what kind of mail he liked best. "In my youth," he replied, "a love letter. In middle age, a job offer. Today, a check." (That was false cynicism, I think. His favorite letters were from his friends.) Whatever the accidental pleasure, it could not please until it arrived. Why were deliveries so few and so late (he frequently grumbled), when, had he lived in central London in the late seventeenth century, he could have received his mail between ten and twelve times a day?

.   .   .

We get what we need. In 1680, London had mail service nearly every hour because there were no telephones. If you wished to invite someone to tea in the afternoon, you could send him a letter in the morning and receive his reply before he showed up at your doorstep. Postage was one penny.

If you wished to send a letter to another town, however, delivery was less reliable and postage was gauged on a scale of staggering complexity. By the mid-1830s,

> the postage on a single letter delivered within eight miles of the office where it was posted was . . . twopence, the lowest rate beyond that limit being fourpence. Beyond fifteen miles it became fivepence; after which it rose a penny at time, but by irregular augmentation, to one shilling, the charge for three hundred miles. . . . There was as a general rule an additional charge of a half-penny on a letter crossing the Scotch border; while letters to or from Ireland had to bear, in addition, packet rates, and rates for crossing the bridges over the Conway and the Menai.

So wrote Rowland Hill, the greatest postal reformer in history, who in 1837 devised a scheme to reduce and standardize postal rates and to shift the burden of payment from the addressee to the sender.

Until a few years ago I had no idea that if you sent a letter out of town—and if you weren't a nobleman, a member of Parliament, or other VIP who had been granted the privilege of free postal franking—the postage was paid by the recipient. This dawned on me when I was reading a biography of Charles Lamb, whose employer, the East India House, allowed clerks to receive letters gratis until 1817: a substantial perk, sort of like being able to call your friends on your office's 800 number. (Lamb, who practiced stringent economies, also wrote much of his personal correspondence on company stationery. His most famous letter to Wordsworth, for instance—the one in which he refers to Coleridge as "an Archangel a little damaged"—is inscribed on a page whose heading reads "Please to state the Weights and Amounts of the following Lots.")

Sir Walter Scott liked to tell the story of how he had once had to pay "five pounds odd" in order to receive a package from a young New York lady he had never met: an atrocious play called *The Cherokee Lovers*, accompanied by a request to read it, correct it, write a prologue, and secure a producer. Two weeks later another large package arrived for which he was charged a similar amount. "Conceive my horror," he told his friend Lord Melville, "when out jumped the same identical tragedy of *The Cherokee Lovers*, with a second epistle from the authoress, stating that, as the winds had been boisterous, she feared the vessel entrusted with her former communication might have foundered, and therefore judged it prudent to forward a duplicate." Lord Melville doubtless found this tale hilarious, but Rowland Hill would have been appalled. He had grown up poor, and, as Christopher Browne notes in *Getting the Message*, his splendid history of the British postal system, "Hill had never forgotten his mother's anxiety when a letter with a high postal duty was delivered, nor the time when she sent him out to sell a bag of clothes to raise 3s for a batch of letters."

Hill was a born Utilitarian who, at the age of twelve, had been so frustrated by the irregularity of the bell at the school where his father was principal that he had instituted a precisely timed bell-ringing schedule. In 1837 he published a report called "Post Office Reform: Its Importance and Practicability." Why, he argued, should legions of accountants be employed to figure out the

Byzantine postal charges? Why should Britain's extortionate postal rates persist when France's revenues had risen, thanks to higher mail volume, after its rates were lowered? Why should post-men waste precious time waiting for absent addressees to come home and pay up? A national Penny Post was the answer, with postage paid by the senders, "using a bit of paper . . . covered at the back with a glutinous wash, which the bringer might, by the application of a little moisture, attach to the back of the letter."

After much debate, Parliament passed a postal reform act in 1839. On January 10, 1840, Hill wrote in his diary, "Penny Postage extended to the whole kingdom this day! . . . I guess that the number despatched to-night will not be less than 100,000, or more than three times what it was this day twelve-months. If less I shall be disappointed." On January 11 he wrote, "The number of letters despatched exceeded all expectation. It was 112,000, of which all but 13,000 or 14,000 were prepaid." In May, after experimentation to produce a canceling ink that could not be surreptitiously removed, the Post Office introduced the Penny Black, bearing a profile of Queen Victoria: the first postage stamp. The press, pondering the process of cancellation, fretted about the "untoward disfiguration of the royal person," but Victoria became an enthusiastic philatelist, and renounced the royal franking privilege for the pleasure of walking to the local post office from Balmoral Castle to stock up on stamps and gossip with the postmaster. When Rowland Hill—by that time, *Sir* Rowland Hill—retired as Post Office Secretary in 1864, *Punch* asked, "SHOULD ROWLAND HILL have a Statue? Certainly, if OLIVER CROMWELL should. For one is celebrated for cutting off the head of a bad King, and the other for sticking on the head of a good Queen."

The Penny Post, wrote Harriet Martineau, "will do more for the circulation of ideas, for the fostering of domestic affections, for the humanizing of the mass generally, than any other single measure that our national wit can devise." It was incontrovertible proof, in an age that embraced progress on all fronts ("the means of locomotion and correspondence, every mechanical art, every manufacture, every thing that promotes the convenience of life," as Macaulay put it in a typical gush of national pride), that the British were the most civilized people on earth. Ancient Syrian runners, Chinese carrier pigeons, Persian post riders, Egyptian papyrus bearers, Greek *hemerodromes*, Hebrew dromedary riders, Roman equestrian relays, medieval monk-messengers, Catalan *troters*, international couriers of the House of Thurn and Taxis, American mail wagons—what could these all have been leading up to, like an ever-ascending staircase, but the Victorian postal system?

And yet (to raise a subversive question), might it be possible that, whatever the profit in efficiency, there may have been a literary cost associated with the conversion from payment by addressee to payment by sender? If you knew that your recipient would have to bear the cost of your letter, wouldn't courtesy motivate you to write an extra good one? On the other hand, if you paid for it yourself, wouldn't you be more likely to feel you could get away with "Having a wonderful time, wish you were here"?

.   .   .

I used to think my father's attachment to the mail was strange. I now feel exactly the way he did. I live in an apartment building and, with or without binoculars, I cannot see my mailbox, one of thirteen dinky aluminum cells bolted to the lobby wall. The mail usually comes around four in the afternoon (proving that the postal staircase that reached its highest point with Rowland Hill has been descending ever since), which means that at around three, *just in case*, I'm likely to visit the lobby for the first of several reconnaissance missions. There's no flag, but over the years my fingers have become postally sensitive, and I can tell if the box is full by giving it the slightest of pats. If there's a hint of convexity—it's very subtle, nothing as obvious, let us say, as the bulge of a can that might harbor botulism—I whip out my key with the same excitement with which my father set forth down his driveway.

There the resemblance ends. The thrill of the treasure hunt is followed all too quickly by the glum realization that the box contains only four kinds of mail: 1) junk; 2) bills; 3) work; and 4) letters that I will read with enjoyment, place in a folder labeled "To Answer," leave there for a geologic interval, and feel guilty about. The longer they languish, the more I despair of my ability to live up to the escalating challenge of their response. It is a truism of epistolary psychology that, for example, a Christmas thank-you note written on December 26 can say any old thing, but if you wait until February, you are convinced that nothing less than *Middlemarch* will do.

In October of 1998 I finally gave in and signed up for e-mail. I had resisted for a long time. My husband and I were proud of our retrograde status. Not only did we lack a modem, but we didn't have a car, a microwave, a Cuisinart, an electric can opener, a cellular phone, a CD player, or cable television. It's hard to give up that sort of backward image; I worried that our friends wouldn't have enough to make fun of. I also worried that learning how to use e-mail would be like learning how to program our VCR, an unsuccessful project that had confirmed what excellent judgment we had shown in not purchasing a car, etc.

As millions of people had discovered before me, e-mail was fast. Sixteenth-century correspondents used to write "Haste, haste, haste, for lyfe, for lyfe, haste!" on their most urgent letters; my "server," a word that conjured up a delicious sycophancy, treated *every* message as if someone's life depended on it. Not only did it get there instantly, caromed in a series of analog cyberpackets along the nodes of the Internet and reconverted to digital form via its recipient's modem. (I do not understand a word of what I just wrote, but that is immaterial. Could the average Victorian have diagrammed the mail coach route from Swansea to Tunbridge Wells?) More important, I *answered* e-mail fast—almost always on the day it arrived. No more guilt! I used to think I did not like to write letters. I now realize that what I didn't like was folding the paper, sealing the envelope, looking up the address, licking the stamp, getting in the elevator, crossing the street, and dropping the letter in the postbox.

At first I made plenty of mistakes. I clicked on the wrong icons, my attachments didn't stick, and, not having learned how to file addresses, I sent an X-rated message to my husband (I thought) at gcolt@aol.com instead of georgecolt@aol.com. I hope Gerald or Gertrude found it flattering. But the learning curve was as steep as my father's driveway, and pretty soon I was batting out fifteen or twenty e-mails a day in the time it had once taken me to avoid answering a single letter. My box was nearly always full—no waiting, no binoculars, no convexity checks, no tugging—and when it wasn't, the reason was not that the mail hadn't *arrived*, it was that it hadn't been *sent*. I began to look forward every morning to the festive green arrow with which AT&T WorldNet welcomed me into my father's "antique land of chance and adventure." Would I be invited to purchase Viagra, lose thirty pounds, regrow my thinning hair, obtain electronic spy software, get an EZ loan, retire in three years, or win a Pentium III 500 MHz computer (presumably in order to receive such messages even faster)? Or would I find a satisfying little clutch of friendly notes whose responses could occupy me until I awoke sufficiently to tackle something that required intelligence? As

Hemingway wrote to Fitzgerald, describing the act of letter-writing: "Such a swell way to keep from working and yet feel you've done something."

My computer, without visible distension, managed to store a flood tide of mail that in nonvirtual form would have silted up my office to the ceiling. This was admirable. And when I wished to commune with my friend Charlie, who lives in Taipei, not only could I disregard the thirteen-hour time difference, but I was billed the same amount as if I had dialed his old telephone number on East Twenty-second Street. The German critic Bernhard Siegert has observed that the breakthrough concept behind Rowland Hill's Penny Post was "to think of all Great Britain as a single city, that is, no longer to give a moment's thought to what had been dear to Western discourse on the nature of the letter from the beginning: the idea of distance." E-mail is a modern Penny Post: the world is a single city with a single postal rate.

Alas, our Penny Post, like Hill's, comes at a price. If the transfer of postal charges from sender to recipient was the first great demotivator in the art of letter writing, e-mail was the second. "It now seems a good bet," Adam Gopnik has written, "that in two hundred years people will be reading someone's collected e-mail the way we read Edmund Wilson's diaries or Pepys's letters." Maybe—but will what they read be any good? E-mails are brief. (One doesn't blather; an overlong message might induce carpal tunnel syndrome in the recipient from excessive pressure on the Down arrow.) They are also—at least the ones I receive—frequently devoid of capitalization, minimally punctuated, and creatively spelled. E-mail's greatest strength—speed—is also its Achilles' heel. In effect, it's always December 26; you are not expected to write *Middlemarch*, and therefore you don't.

In a letter to his friend William Unwin, written on August 6, 1780, William Cowper noted that "a Letter may be written upon any thing or Nothing." This observation is supported by the index of *The Faber Book of Letters, 1578–1939*. Let us examine some entries from the *d* section:

damnation, 87
dances and entertainments, 33, 48, 59, 97, 111, 275
dentistry, 220
depressive illness, 81, 87
Dictionary of the English Language, Johnson's, 61
Diggers, 22
dolphins, methods of cooking, 37

I have never received an e-mail on any of these topics. Instead, I am informed that Your browser is not Y2K-compliant. Your son left his Pokémon turtle under our sofa. Your column is 23 lines too long. Important pieces of news, but, as Lytton Strachey (one of the all-time great letter writers) pointed out, "No good letter was ever written to convey information, or to please its recipient: it may achieve both these results incidentally; but its fundamental purpose is to express the personality of its writer." *But wait!* you pipe up. *Someone just e-mailed me a joke!* So she did, but wasn't the personality of the sender slightly muffled by the fact that she forwarded it from an e-mail *she* received, and sent it to seventeen additional addressees?

I also take a dim, or perhaps a buffaloed, view of electronic slang. Perhaps I should view it as a linguistic milestone, as historic as the evolution of Cockney rhyming slang in the 1840s. But will the future generations who reopen our hard drives be stirred by the eloquence of the e-acronyms recommended by a Web site on "netiquette"?

    BTDT   been there done that

FC	fingers crossed
IITYWTMWYBMAD	if I tell you what this means will you buy me a drink?
MTE	my thoughts exactly
ROTFL	rolling on the floor laughing
RTFM	read the f. . . . . . manual
TAH	take a hint
TTFN	ta ta for now

Or by the "emoticons," otherwise known as "smileys"—punctuational images, read sideways—that "help readers interpret the e-mail writer's attitude and tone"?

:-)	ha ha
:-(	boo hoo
(-:	I am left-handed
%-)	I have been staring at a green screen for 15 hours straight
:-&	I am tongue-tied
{:-)	I wear a toupee
:-[	I am a vampire
:-F	I am a bucktoothed vampire with one tooth missing
=| :-)=	I am Abraham Lincoln

"We are of a different race from the Greeks, to whom beauty

was everything," wrote Thomas Carlyle, a Victorian progress-booster. "Our glory and our beauty arise out of our inward strength, which makes us victorious over material resistance." We have achieved a similar victory of efficiency over beauty. I wouldn't give up e-mail if you paid me, but I'd feel a pang of regret if the epistolary novels of the future were to revolve around such messages as

Subject: R U Kidding?
From: Clarissa Harlowe <claha@virtue.com>
To: Robert Lovelace
                  <lovelaceandlovegirlz;@vice.com>
hi bob, TAH. if u think i'm gonna run off w/u, :-F. do u really think i'm that kind of girl?? if you're looking 4 a trollop, CLICK HERE NOW: http://www.hotpix.html. TTFN.

.   .   .

I own a letter written by Robert Falcon Scott, the polar explorer, to G.T. Temple, Esq., who helped procure the footgear for Scott's first Antarctic expedition. The date is February 26, 1901. The envelope and octavo stationery have black borders because Queen Victoria had died in January. The paper is yellowed, the handwriting is messy, and the stamp bears the Queen's profile—and the denomination ONE PENNY. I bought the letter many years ago because, unlike a Cuisinart, which would have cost about the same, it was something I believed I could not live without. I could never feel that way about an e-mail.

I also own my father's old wastebasket, which now holds my own empty Jiffy Bags. Several times a day I use his stamp dispenser; it is tarnished and dinged, but still capable of unspooling its contents with a singular smoothness. And my file cabinets hold hundreds of his letters, the earliest written in his sixties in small, crabbed handwriting, the last in his nineties, after he lost much of his sight, penned with a Magic Marker in huge capital letters. I hope my children will find them someday, as Hart Crane once found his grandmother's love letters in the attic,

> pressed so long
> Into a corner of the roof
> That they are brown and soft,
> And liable to melt as snow.

The Atlantic Monthly

FINALIST, PROFILES

The Million-Dollar Nose

Critic Robert Parker Jr. is the most influential man in the heady world of wine. This deftly nuanced character study documents the steadying effect that one incorruptible person can have on an industry. Dozens of articles have been written about Parker, but none has so aptly captured the man behind the nose.

William Langewiesche

The Million-Dollar Nose

With his stubborn disregard for the hierarchy of wines, Robert Parker, the straight-talking American wine critic, is revolutionizing the industry—and teaching the French wine establishment some lessons it would rather not learn

The most influential critic in the world today happens to be a critic of wine. He is not a snob or an obvious aesthete, as one might imagine, but an ordinary American, a burly, awkward, hardworking guy from the backcountry of northern Maryland, about half a step removed from the farm. His name is Robert Parker Jr., Bob for short, and he has no formal training in wine. He lives near his childhood home, among the dairies and second-growth forests in a place called Monkton, which has a post office but no town center. A new interstate highway has reduced the drive to Baltimore to merely thirty minutes, but otherwise has had little effect. Monkton remains rural and bland—a patch of forgotten America as culturally isolated and nondescript as the quietest parts of the Midwest. Parker likes it that way. He is married to his high school sweetheart, Pat, with whom he has a teenage daughter named Maia, adopted as an infant from a Korean orphanage. The family has a quiet and apparently idyllic domestic life. Parker seems to be a happy man. In repose he has the staid face of an affluent farmer. In his baggy shirts and summer shorts, with his heavy arms hanging wide, he looks as if he could wrestle down a cow.

He couldn't, because at age fifty-three he has a bad back. But here's how strong he has become: many people now believe that Robert Parker is single-handedly changing the history of wine. That's saying a lot. There are more than forty wine-producing countries in the world today, of which France is the first and the United States is the fourth; China is on the list. These countries have planted 30,000 square miles of vineyards and are making the equivalent of 35 billion bottles of wine every year. Parker directly controls the merest patch of all this—a micro-winery called Beaux Frères, near Newburg, Oregon, which he owns with his brother-in-law and refuses to promote. The wines produced there (from pinot noir grapes) are not necessarily among the best, but they keep Parker from sounding off about winemaking as, he says, a eunuch might sound off about sex. He is not an exporter, an importer, or a money man. He is a self-employed consumer advocate, a crusader in a peculiarly American tradition. It's really very simple, or so it seems at first. Parker samples 10,000 wines a year. He sniffs and sips them, and scribbles little notes. Some of the wines are good, and some are not—according to Parker. If he is changing wine history, as people claim, it is purely through the expression of his taste.

His base is a cramped two-room office in his house in Monkton, where the family's bulldog and basset hound like to lie on the tile floor and sleep and fart and snore. Parker has an acute sense of smell, but unless he is tasting wine, he enjoys their presence. The two secretaries who work in the outer office are less understanding. They told me that they, too, like the dogs but often usher them outside. The older of the secretaries has worked for Parker for years, but has never learned to enjoy wine. She is dedicated to Parker, as women close to him tend to be, in a protective and motherly way. Parker's real mother, who handles the office mail, has a different approach. She is said to be tough and unimpressed. One afternoon Parker, in a self-pitying mood, mentioned to her that for years he had received only letters of complaint. She fixed him with a stare and said, "That's because they're the only ones I've let you see."

Her instincts were probably good. Parker seems to have trouble distinguishing friends from sycophants, and he sets too much store by the compliments he receives. He does his best work not in public but in his private inner office, where he is left mostly alone. That office has a messy desk and a computer, a stereo stacked with CDs (Bob Dylan, Neil Young), a countertop crowded with bottles, a rack of clean wine glasses, and a sink that is deep enough to allow for spitting without splattering. There he writes and publishes an un-illustrated journal called *The Wine Advocate,* subtitled "The Independent Consumer's Bimonthly Guide to Fine Wine."

The Wine Advocate accepts no advertising. A subscription costs $50 a year. Each issue consists of an editorial or two and about fifty-six pages of blunt commentaries on wines that Parker has recently tasted. The commentaries are short, usually two or three sentences, grouped by region and winery, and associated with

"Parker Points," which are scores on a scale of 50 to 100. One of the lowest scores Parker ever gave a new vintage was 56, for 1979 Lambert Bridge Cabernet Sauvignon, about which he wrote, "One has to wonder what this winery does to its cabernet to make it so undrinkable. . . . This wine has an intense vegetative, barnyard aroma and very unusual flavors." But generally, poor wines score in the 70s, adequate ones in the 80s, and really good ones in the 90s. There are significant gradations within those ranges. Rarely, Parker has given a wine a perfect score of 100—seventy-six times out of 220,000 wines tasted. He always lists an approximate retail price and provides an opinion about when the wine will be ready to drink. He works hard to avoid conflicts of interest: he pays his own way, accepts no gifts or payoffs, and does not speculate financially on wine. As a result he has an unimpeachable reputation for integrity in an industry that does not.

The Wine Advocate has 40,000 subscribers, in every U.S. state and thirty-seven foreign countries. These are influential readers, and they pass the issues around, igniting the markets of Asia, the United States, and now even Europe, where collectors and wealthy consumers can be counted on to search out wines on the basis of Parker's recommendations. The effects are felt on store shelves, where retailers display Parker's comments or scores, and up the supply chain, influencing speculation, negotiation, and price-setting, until even the producers of mass wines feel the weight of Parker's opinions. The trade has never known such a voice, such a power, before. When it comes to the great wines—those that drive styles and prices for the entire industry—there is hardly another critic now who counts.

The effects are global. As wines rise and fall on the basis of Parker's judgments, and as producers respond to his presence, the industry worldwide is moving in an unexpected direction, toward denser, darker, and more dramatic wines. It would be simplistic to believe that the movement is entirely due to Parker: he may just be its most effective agent. In any case, these denser, darker wines are the wines that Parker and now much of the world prefer to drink. Because they require intensive thinning and pruning of the vines, hand harvesting, and at the winemaking stage the sort of attention to detail that can be achieved only one vat at a time, they lend themselves to production on a reduced scale. At the extreme they are known as "garage wines," smaller-scale even than "micro-wines"—so small that some are produced in garage-size buildings. Such wines are often absurdly expensive, because they are rare and fashionable. That's the bad side. But they allow producers without much money (or the ability to attract large investments) to make a living by making wine. That's the surprise. With his single-minded concentration on taste and his unique ability to communicate his opinion, Parker may be pioneering a new kind of globalization—not the monolith that the world dreads but the monolith's counterforce: a boutique economy that is American in inspiration, individualistic, and anti-industrial at the core.

In France especially—the country, ironically, that fights against the McDonald's-ization of the world—this new form of entrepreneurial winemaking is being resisted. It's easy to understand why. France has long been the bastion of big-time wines. Parker threatens these wines, and the companies and families that produce them. Particularly in Bordeaux, the culturally conservative city that is widely considered to be the world capital of wine, winemakers are engaged in an increasingly bitter fight against Parker and his influence. This year the fight has broken into the open.

"A Democratic View"

It's a strange position for a man from Monkton. One commonly heard explanation for it is that Parker writes in English at a time when English use is increasing around the globe. But the

British, who are the traditional wine critics, write in English too, and they don't enjoy anything like Parker's clout. Many of them have a diploma called the Master of Wine, or M.W., for which they've been required to pass tests—based largely on the identification of obscure or antique wines—that Parker would probably fail. Parker's eminence is therefore annoying to them. They see Parker, correctly, as an American upstart. They see him as a heathen.

Lineage counts for a lot with the British critics and is accorded proper deference. At their worst they seem to practice criticism as an excuse for Continental excursions: the villages were picturesque, the peasants were quaint, and the wines were "noble" above all. In contrast, Parker's criticism sounds like his mother's—direct and pointed, like one American talking straight to another. There are other American critics too, of course, but none who has been able to equal the directness and authenticity of Parker's voice. Last April, after tasting the most recent offering of Canon, a famous producer in Bordeaux, Parker gave the wine a score of 84–85 and wrote,

> Once again, this renowned estate appears to have badly missed the mark. Undoubtedly, part of the difficulty in 1999 was the fact that the vineyard was hit by the hail storm that punished a small zone of vineyards on September 5th. This medium dark ruby-colored effort reveals soft, berry flavors with steely/mineral-like notes in the background. Some of the vineyard's pedigree comes through, but this uninspiring, medium-bodied wine possesses little depth or length. Anticipated maturity: now–2008.

It's an intentional style, and more difficult to achieve than it seems—prose so plain and clear that it reads like a subway map. It is also a particular outlook. Last spring in Monkton, Parker said to me, "What I've brought is a democratic view. I don't give a shit that your family goes back to pre-Revolution and you've got more wealth than I could imagine. If this wine's no good, I'm gonna say so."

That's the sort of English everyone can understand—and the big French winemaking families don't like it at all. Those families are some of the most conservative in Europe, masters of understatement and judgmental silence. They are epitomized by the wine aristocrats of Bordeaux, who pioneered the production of modern red wine 300 years ago, and who ever since have been able, on the basis of their wines' lineage alone, to set the standards and prices for the industry worldwide: traditionally, if they declared that their wine was the most desirable in the world, then whatever its real merits, it was accepted as such. Anyone who disagreed, said the Bordelais, simply did not know wine. The magic here lay, of course, in the tight control of definitions. It provided for an enviable commercial position, and allowed the Bordelais to pull off a double trick—producing very large quantities of very high-priced wines. But Parker is changing all that. It is getting harder for the Bordelais to disregard the laws of supply and demand, or the fact that their great wines aren't always very good.

Bordeaux is the key to understanding Parker's role in the world. It produced many of the truly fine wines on which he built his reputation, yet as a place that has come to rely on the techniques of modern high-yield production, it stands as the most important example of the industrialization in wine that he has been fighting against. Bordeaux is big business in disguise. The composition of the aristocracy there has changed over time, but outsiders who have bought into it have always eagerly adapted, mimicking the old families so willingly that by the second generation their carpetbagging is almost forgotten. In recent years a slew of publicly held corporations have bought in as well, and even they have played along, furnishing their chateaux with antiques and hiring the second sons of the aristocracy to make their wines in imitation of tradition. This is considered respectable, civic-minded behavior—and indeed it is, in a place that has staked its fortunes on its power to define the meaning of taste.

In Bordeaux the wines are made not of single grape varietals but of ever-changing combinations. Those combinations have been based on the cabernet sauvignon grape, with varying amounts of merlot, cabernet franc, and another, rarer grape, petit verdot, mixed in according to each winemaker's calculation, to provide a bit of "depth," or to intensify the wine. The result has traditionally been complex, light-colored wines, epitomized by the elegant "clarets" produced by the old vineyards north of the city, in an area called the Médoc, on the left bank of the river Gironde. The British have traded in claret since the 1700s, and they have long understood the rules of the game. There are unfortunate years of too much cold or rain, but if the wine is thin, then it is subtle or laudably austere. If it is undrinkably acidic or astringent when young, then, like a family inheritance, it is not intended to be consumed soon but to be put away to mellow, for future generations to enjoy.

But now comes this Parker, a man as naive as America, with his raw talent, his disproportionate weight, and his stubborn disregard for the hierarchy of taste. It is maddening to the Bordelais that even in France consumers increasingly are using him as a reference. The Bordelais believe Parker favors dark and dramatic wines—wines that they claim are at their most impressive when they are young in the glass, or competing in organized wine tastings, and that, more ominously, may well lack a pedigree. Wines like these depend more heavily on the merlot grape than on the cabernet sauvignon. To some degree they have long existed on the Gironde's right bank, around St.-Emilion and Pomerol, areas that in the context of the Médoc are considered to be newcomers, producing plebeian and somewhat simplistic wines. The new small wines are like those right-bank wines, only more so—darker, more intense, and, to the untutored palate, more accessible. These are the boutique growths, the so-called garage wines, that are starting to command the highest prices, and they are spreading like a rot through the region. Parker is to blame.

The old families try to hold steady. Last spring when I went to Bordeaux to ask them about Parker, they told me that he is deferential, that he visits twice a year, that he maintains a small Bordeaux office from which he publishes *The Wine Advocate*'s only foreign-language edition, and that he pays homage to the region as the reference point for the world. But they also admitted, when pressed a bit, that he terrifies them. When Parker criticizes their wines, they see their prices tumble. When he compliments their wines, they can't resist using this to their advantage and proclaiming their scores. In private they complain that he is playing them like puppets. In public, for business reasons, they smile and pretend to be his friends. The duplicity is humiliating—and worse, it signals their loss of control.

You have to admire these people for their sense of irony. In the region of Bordeaux one day, one of them—impeccably dressed in jacket and tie, in an office where Thomas Jefferson went to taste wine, with portraits of ancestors hanging on the walls—made the argument to me, with just the slightest hint of humor in his eyes, that Bordeaux should erect a statue of Parker in honor of his contributions. It was the sort of dry joke he might have made to his patrician friends. Twice in the past ten years the Bordelais have arranged through local politicians to award Parker a national medal, the more recent of which was the Legion of Honor—France's highest award. It was presented to Parker at a ceremony in Paris in June of last year, by President Jacques Chirac, for having promoted French wines. Parker accepted the medal with tears in his eyes.

If reform is a form of promotion, Parker *has* promoted French wines—and perhaps some families felt that he deserved credit for that. But more likely they intended the medal as a public acknowledgment that they would have to find some way to live with him. The impulse is well known: you give a man a badge when you can't shut him up. Not that they hadn't tried. By the time of the Paris ceremony the French had sued Parker for what he had written, sued him for what he had not written, and even sued him for something in between—a mistake in translation. (A cellar that Parker called "disgusting" became "*dégueulasse*"—literally, "nauseating," which was more than he'd meant to say.) They had forced him into formal public apologies. They had cost him hundreds of thousands of dollars in legal fees. They had banned him from their estates, fired his friends, mounted whispering campaigns against him, and pilloried him numerous times in French newspapers and magazines. To top it all, through blacklisting and a coordinated effort to render him useless to his readers, they had exploited a series of mistakes that Parker had made and had almost managed to run him out of Burgundy. The story of Parker's failure in Burgundy is long and complicated and not particularly relevant to Bordeaux. But in no country other than France has anything similar happened to him. Parker told me that he didn't want to sound like Oliver Stone, though he seemed sometimes to believe in conspiracies. And maybe for good reason. His life is not at risk, of course, but people in Bordeaux talked openly to me about setting him up for a drunk-driving arrest. Parker told me that several years ago one of them attacked him with a dog.

It was a small dog, but aggressive. Parker was in his hotel room in Bordeaux one night, working on the day's notes, when he got a phone call from Jacques Hébrard, the family manager of a famous chateau called Cheval Blanc, whose recent vintage Parker had described as a disappointment. Because Hébrard was very angry, Parker agreed to visit the chateau the following night, after his regular schedule of work, in order to retaste the wine. At the agreed-upon time he knocked on the chateau door. When it opened, a snarling schnauzer came out, leaped into the air, and clamped onto Parker's leg. Hébrard stood in the doorway, staring into Parker's face and making no attempt to intervene. After several attempts Parker managed to shake off the dog, which went tumbling into the night. Parker followed Hébrard into an office, where he saw that his pants were torn and blood was running down his leg. He asked Hébrard for a bandage. Hébrard came across the room and glanced disdainfully at the wound. Without saying a word, he went to the far side of a desk, pulled out a copy of *The Wine Advocate*, and slammed it down hard. He said, "*This* is what you wrote about my wine!"

In his simplified French, Parker said, "That's why I'm here. To retaste it. Because you think I'm wrong."

"Well, I'm not going to let you retaste it."

Parker got as belligerent as he gets. He said, "Look. I came here at the end of the day. You said I could taste your wine. I've been bitten by your dog. If I was wrong about this wine, I will be the first to say so."

Hébrard stalked out of the office. Parker thought he would have to get up and leave. But then Hébrard came back and said, "Okay, let's go taste the wine." Parker limped after him to the tasting room. He was quick, as he always is; he tasted the wine twice to be sure, as is his habit, and realized to his chagrin that Hébrard was right—the wine was better than he had thought. He returned to his hotel to wash his wound. As a critic who often has to condemn the efforts of people he likes, he now had the equally hard task of admitting that Hébrard's work was top-notch. For the families of Bordeaux it was satisfying: Parker had been punished for his judgment. With luck he would have a little scar as a souvenir.

10,000 Wines a Year

Parker's house in Monkton stands in the woods on a hummock, off a narrow road next to a state park. It is an anonymous structure, somewhat like others scattered nearby, and according to Parker, it's just about right. When I went to see him, he told me that he does not like to stand out, that he's glad for his fame but relieved that it is contained within the tight circles of wine. He said he is reluctant to appear on television or the radio, because he has learned how bad it can be. Once, after an hour of waiting, he had an interview that consisted entirely of this: "Welcome to the show, Bruce, we don't have a lot of time, but, real quick here, what's your favorite white zinfandel?" Monkton is a shelter from all that. After Parker was written up in the Baltimore *Sun*, one of his neighbors said, "Hey, Bob, I didn't know you were some sort of *wine* expert." Parker answered "Yeah" with a shrug, because he wants to be a regular guy.

But of course he's not a regular guy—not anymore. Parker's success has taken him around the world and widened his view. It has taught him to believe in the idea of live and let live—except for anyone making bad wine. Simultaneously it has narrowed him, encouraging a peculiar single-mindedness that sustains his work but seems to have closed him off to topics beyond his immediate concerns. He can mingle with his neighbors at the post office and talk about politics and the weather, but even then what he's really thinking about, according to his wife, is food or wine. Given the chance, he becomes hard to follow, talking excitedly about obscure vintages and elaborate dishes with piled-up names—but he also runs on about plain old Maryland crab. He is a professional critic with strong opinions, and also simply a glutton. His enthusiasm permeates his work. He loves to eat. He loves to drink. And he can't stand moralists who say this is wrong.

He means the temperance crusaders and righteous nutritionists who are given so much attention in the United States—people he calls the Pleasure Police. When he was with me, he lacked the nerve to take on Mothers Against Drunk Driving. Instead he went after their natural allies at the Washington-based Center for Science in the Public Interest, which he described as being in the business of "the taboo of the week."

He said, "Fettuccine Alfredo is dangerous for your health. Kung pao chicken will destroy your life. Holy shit, the first week it's one of the classics of Italian cooking, the next week it's one of the staples of Chinese cooking! These are the people who do studies that your carry-out Chinese meals are saturated in fat. . . . I'd just like to *meet* them! I mean, what do they do for pleasure?"

I asked him whether in a world so full of hunger it didn't seem self-indulgent to worry over the choices on a menu. This was a backhanded way of getting at a question that still concerns me: how anyone could dedicate his life to something as superfluous as the taste of wine. Ultimately it was not an answerable question— and Parker didn't pursue my line of thought. Later he told me about losing his temper at a reporter who had asked him how he could possibly spend so much time tasting wine: "I said, 'Look, I don't have an argument for you. I'm a common-sense kind of guy. I wouldn't sit here unless I could do it. I know you can't do it, and don't want to do it. But I *can* do it, and I *want* to do it.'"

He was in a more reflective, less defensive mood with me. He said, "Part of life is to live it, and enjoy it, and seize the moments that you find particularly pleasing." He meant, of course, pleasure as defined by dining. I realized I couldn't blame him for this orientation after all: he was born with such strong taste buds that it seemed to be a biological thing.

He kept calling himself a hedonist. That's a philosophical thing. He gave me a book called *Between Meals,* a profound little memoir by the late A. J. Liebling, the celebrated *New Yorker* writer, who died in 1963, at the age of fifty-nine. Liebling, too, was a glutton, and a famously defiant one. *Between Meals* was his argument for the uncomplicated pleasures of neighborhood bistros in France. He began it with what must have seemed to Parker like words meant for him:

> The primary requisite for writing well about food is a good appetite. Without this, it is impossible to accumulate, within the allotted span, enough experience of eating to have anything worth setting down. Each day brings only two opportunities for field work, and they are not to be wasted minimizing the intake of cholesterol.

Liebling believed that it was equally important to research the subject of wine. He grew fat without flinching, and although he suffered a difficult last few years, disfigured by gout, he continued working until the end without expressing regret. He wrote, "No sane man can afford to dispense with debilitating pleasures; no ascetic can be considered reliably sane. Hitler was the archetype of the abstemious man. When the other krauts saw him drink water in the Beer Hall they should have known he was not to be trusted."

Parker gave me Liebling's book because he would like someday to write such a memoir. But the two men are very different. Liebling was a literary acrobat, a sophisticate, and ultimately a nihilist of the boozy kind. Parker is none of that. He is a technical writer faced with tight deadlines. Nonetheless he shares with Liebling an unabashed enthusiasm for dining. He said to me, "I've always followed the rule that anything worth doing is worth doing excessively."

He sees the consequences in the mirror. He was a good runner once, but is too heavy for it now. He rides a mountain bike for exercise, and tries furiously to overtake younger bikers on the trails, and only sometimes succeeds. People in the wine business like to talk about his health. In California recently I heard that he has cancer of the mouth, which he does not. In Bordeaux people told me that he has a bad heart. This stems from an episode three years ago, at a French restaurant in New York, when during a ten-course meal Parker grew gray, sweaty, and weak, heard a high-pitched whine in his ears, and even lost his appetite. A cardiologist who was there thought he was having a heart attack. Parker somehow knew that he was not. His friends waited anxiously while an ambulance rushed to the scene. The rescue team laid Parker on a stretcher and carried him outside. At that point a man identified to him as the governor of New York, George Pataki, arrived for a meal, and Parker, looking up from the edge of death, gave his last good advice. He said, "Don't eat the scallops!" It would have made a nice epitaph, but at the hospital the doctors discovered that he had a bleeding ulcer, and they easily patched him up.

Otherwise Parker shows no signs of slowing down. Not only does he taste 10,000 wines a year, but he stores the sensation of each one into a permanent gustatory memory. When I asked him about the mechanical aspects of his work, he told me in a matter-of-fact way that he remembers every wine he has tasted over the past thirty-two years and, within a few points, every score he has given as well. That amounts to several hundred thousand relevant memories, which apparently he can summon up at will. He said he has no idea how he does this, except perhaps through intense concentration while tasting wine. He said, "A wine goes in my mouth, and I just see it. I see it in three dimensions. The textures. The flavors. The smells. They just jump out at me. I can taste with a hundred screaming kids in a room. When I put my nose in a glass, it's like tunnel vision. I move into another world, where everything around me is just gone, and every bit of mental energy is focused on that wine." Afterward he can't help it—he just remembers.

As a result, he has a breadth of knowledge beyond that of any other critic alive: he remembers not only every French wine he has tasted but also every wine from Germany, Spain, Italy, Chile, Australia, the United States, and New Zealand, among other countries. As a single judge awarding scores across the board, he implicitly compares all these wines with one another—just as a consumer might in a store. That is where his experience gives him an intellectual advantage: many of the other critics also issue scores, but they are hemmed in by the narrowness of their experience or neutered by the consensus of committees. They make bitter puns about Parker's "critical mass," because, it's true, he is a force running wild in their midst, one man dominating their field. It's easy to see why they would distrust him. But when they accuse him of despotism, that's a harder fit.

He seems to vacillate between regret and arrogance about the position he is in. In principle he does not believe in imposing his will on others, but in practice he often does so. He told me that he is aware of the contradiction, and agrees with the people who question whether any one man should hold such power. His commentaries have become complicated by the certainty that they will be read as more than frank opinions. When he writes that a wine is "an insider's secret," it instantly becomes just the opposite. A positive review and a score over 90, especially for a wine that is produced in small quantities, can ignite speculation that sends the price rocketing and clears the wine out of the stores—just the sort of thing that Parker, as a consumer advocate, would like to fight. Worse, a critical comment or a poor score can also be blown out of proportion, and may be financially devastating to the producer. That's the unhappy side of Parker's achievement. Either way, Parker seems to wish that the world wouldn't take him quite so seriously. But, of course, he won't just back down and go away.

Technically, he would not be the world's greatest taster, if such a person could exist. There are other tasters with palates just as good, who are better trained in viticulture or enology, or who have read more history. But wine is a subject so large that expertise within it has to be defined by boundaries: there are specialists in regions who can identify wines more precisely than Parker, and specialists in subregions who can do even better. Parker is the practical one. Ten thousand is a small number of wines in an industry that produces 12,000 wines in Bordeaux alone: the ones he concentrates on are the sort of fine wines—usually costing more than $20 a bottle—that Americans can buy and might want to drink. It is only within that category that Parker is one of the best tasters alive.

That's still a big claim. In recognition of his special talent, Parker has managed to add a clause to his disability insurance—a paragraph that insures his olfactory sense, his "nose," for a million dollars. He told me he had taken out the policy after meeting a European critic who had lost his ability to smell and therefore to taste. I mentioned that given the scale of Parker's career, a million dollars seemed like a small sum. He agreed and said he had been unable to get the underwriter to agree to a higher amount. He laughed and said, "I'm sure if I put in a claim saying I couldn't taste anymore, they'd give me some pretty smelly tests." The kind of tests, he said, that would curl a man's nose.

For now, his senses are healthy. Given a choice, he prefers to taste tannic or complex red wines in the morning, when he is at his best, and to finish the day with relatively simple white wines. He stands, in order to be alert. He checks the cleanliness of the glass. If he has doubts, he breathes moisture into it and sniffs for any residual odors—soap, chlorine, wood, or cardboard. He calls this "the Parker exhale test," as if he had copyrighted the term. If the glass is not clean, he rinses it with bottled water and dries it. He pours the wine. Then, with his hand on his hip, he lifts the glass, looks at the wine, smells the wine, swirls the wine, puts the wine in his mouth, curls his tongue around it, sucks in air noisily to agitate it, distributes the wine throughout his mouth, and forces the vapors into the back of his nose. He hesitates for just an instant and then spits the wine out and concentrates on its residual tastes.

He jots a few notes, or mumbles his comments into a tape recorder, and then repeats the process to verify his impressions.

Even his detractors admit that he is phenomenally consistent—that after describing a wine once he will describe it in nearly the same way if he retastes it "blind" (without reference to the label), and that these descriptions fit among others he makes in the constellation of wines. In theory such steadiness allows experienced readers to calibrate their palates against his, and to make informed choices even when they disagree with him. In reality most readers probably just look at the scores. Parker has become so confident in his judgments that he likes to point out his mistakes—in part because he doesn't make many. Stories about his natural abilities abound. I was told, for instance, that at an informal get-together in Bordeaux recently, someone handed Parker a glass of Sauternes, and he casually remarked after taking a sip that it reminded him of a certain wine he had tasted ten years before—or at least of how that wine might have evolved. The point of the story, of course, was that he got it right, and that this was an ordinary occurrence for him. The Bordelais would like to believe that his talent is disconnected from his knowledge or intelligence. They would like to believe that Parker is an idiot savant.

The characterization annoys Parker, who points out that he was once an attorney for the Farm Credit Banks of Baltimore—a notably weak defense, undermined by his admission that the job was a bore. It seems likely that the Bordelais are at least partly right—that Parker does have a freakish genius for smell and taste, which by luck he discovered about himself. He calls it a "privileged ability," but as a true American, he wants to be very clear that he has exploited it too. That's fair enough, because he's a hard worker. For about a fourth of the year he travels to the world's important wine areas, where he shrugs off the impulse to socialize or sightsee and gets down to intensive wine tasting all day, every day. He visits the vineyards and also has the wines brought to a central point—a hotel, for instance—where he can go through more than a hundred in a day without wasting time on the road traveling to vineyards.

There is a machine-like quality to what he does. When at home in Maryland, he continues to work at least six days a week, tasting, grading, and writing notes at a furious pace. This is out of necessity. Having set himself up as a watchdog, and having committed himself to the rigors of a regular publishing schedule, Parker has been trapped by the math of expanding expectations: not only must he taste the ever-greater number of wines in each new vintage, but, because wines in the bottle endure and evolve, he must also retaste a growing number of old wines. Of course, he does drop some wines along the way, but still the obligations build. Moreover, for the sake of valid comparisons—the across-the-board scoring that is so useful to his readers—he is condemned to work largely on his own. His publisher in Paris told me that he sometimes thinks of Parker as a tragic figure, like a character in a classic play. When I asked Parker about this later, he said that his publisher was wrong. Indeed, one of the keys to his success is his sustained and almost childlike enthusiasm for his job. But it's true that he faces quandaries.

The math that traps him helps him too. Parker's output is huge as a result of it. Beyond the nearly 350 pages of new material required annually for *The Wine Advocate*, he compiles and expands on his notes to create bulky wine-buying guidebooks, of which eleven have so far been published in various editions, on various regions. These books have been translated into five languages and have hit the best-seller lists in several countries, including France. For Parker they have been a windfall—generating more income than *The Wine Advocate* does, at little extra expense, and making him a rich man by his own measure. He is frank about his good fortune: he was poor before, and he is glad that he no longer is. Nonetheless, what's unusual about Parker—

this American at work in the world—is that for him money remains intrinsically uninteresting.

The Dark Side of Wine

The person who made that point most clearly to me was Pierre-Antoine Rovani, a thirty-six-year-old man with a reputation as a brilliant taster, who hired on with Parker four years ago, partly to cover hostile Burgundy, where Parker himself now rarely ventures, and who has been grappling ever since with the perhaps impossible job of establishing an independent yet integrated voice within *The Wine Advocate*. Rovani is a sardonic fellow with a goatee and sparkling eyes—the son of French officials, raised and educated in Washington, D.C., where he lives today. Money is intrinsically interesting to him. He earned a degree in economics, and worked as a business consultant for several years (also, improbably, as the White House correspondent for the Saudi press agency) before moving into the retail wine business and then making the leap to Parker's side. When I met him, last spring in Georgetown, he told me that he had burned his bridges and would never be able to go back to retailing. I didn't doubt it, because he seemed to have a skeptical view of the business and a habit of speaking his mind. For several hours he told me about the dark side of wine—kickbacks, payoffs, and frauds of many kinds. He saw the humor in it. He said, "You dump the bad stuff on Park Avenue. If the bottle says 'Grand Cru,' or 'Premier Grand Cru,' or 'Pomerol,' or, you know, if there's a word on there that some rich guy recognizes . . . "

"You can sell it," I suggested.

He nodded. "In small quantities. In a place like New York. Where there are *lots* of idiots. You can get away with it."

You can also, if you have a stock of bad wine, take out your scissors, find a relevant issue of *The Wine Advocate*, and, with a bit of tape and a copy machine, improve the score. Rovani mentioned a New York store that had recently done just that, sending out altered scores and tasting notes with its promotional literature. The work was so shoddy in this case that the doctored print lay crooked on the page.

Rovani seemed amused by this. I got the impression that he sympathized with the store's owner. In any case, he seemed to have a better feel than Parker for commercial realities on the front lines, where one of the big problems is how to handle an annual over-production of wine worldwide that amounts to roughly 25 percent. The surplus has not been allowed to drive down prices, as it should have to provide for a healthy industry in the long term. This is in part because of wine's residual status as an elite drink. For those in the business, maintaining that image is important not only for commercial reasons but also for reasons of personal prestige. Every stage of the trade is involved in establishing the high prices, but ultimately those prices can be sustained only through the retailers and their sales efforts. The problem for the retailers is that wine—unlike luxurious hotel rooms and other hyperinflated products generally covered as business expenses—is usually paid for directly out of the consumer's pocket. This makes for a scary business, especially toward the high end, where *The Wine Advocate* roams. The truth is that even the best wines cost only about $10 a bottle to produce, and they are not inherently rare. If the initial cost is tripled to allow for profits along the path of distribution, one can reasonably conclude that retail prices above $30 are based on speculation, image, and hype.

Rovani mentioned a Bordeaux called Le Pin, which sells in recent vintages for $600 to $1,000 a bottle. I asked him what kind of person would buy it. He shrugged. "Look, it's a game. Why is it that at a certain age men start buying little sports cars, or the cigar boat that makes so much noise—or they get the trophy wife. How many of these guys don't even drink the wine? They call you up and they say, 'I've got twenty cases of Lafite, I've twenty cases of Le Pin . . .' These are trophies that they're collecting." He described conference calls with three or four competing stockbrokers, made when he was a retailer, in which he sold half a million dollars' worth of wines.

Those men are extreme cases, as is Le Pin, but they set the tone for the business of fine wines. Parker publicly denounces the high prices as "the legalized mugging of the consumer," but in private he admits that the victims are usually all too willing to be mugged. He said, "I know collectors with forty thousand bottles who if you poured them a glass of Gallo Hearty Burgundy wouldn't know the difference. I know collectors who, believe me, if you mixed Kool-Aid into cheap Chilean merlot, they'd taste it and say, 'Well, yeah . . .'"

In a world like this a little doctoring of the tasting notes hardly seems important. Rovani described the industry as a game of musical chairs, in which the players throughout the chain of distribution all scramble to avoid getting stuck with the stock. I asked him about being an importer. He said, "What's it like? You sweat. Very early in the morning, because of the time differences, the faxes start coming in, and you have to gamble your entire business because the figures are so high. If it's a good vintage, you can't sit it out, because you'll lose your customer base. So you gamble."

He offered to show me what the gamble looks like: in Washington alone there are a couple of big warehouses stacked floor to ceiling with overpriced wines that cannot be returned and will soon begin to decline. For anyone interested in money, it's an impressive sight. The only way out is bravely forward again, and into the stores, where finally the customer is left standing and blinking at the price he just paid for the bottle in his hand. Retailers are thankful for the strong economy. Fine wines are selling well, but the structure that sustains them is flimsy. All along the chain of supply people fear a collapse, because they have had to invest heavily in what everyone knows is vastly overpriced stock. A collapse wouldn't look like much in the store. But a reduction of just a few dollars in the price the market is willing to pay would crush businesses around the world.

Rovani would welcome such a "correction," because he is an economist who believes in market necessities. Parker would welcome it, because he is an ethicist who opposes the speculation in wine. This highlights a basic difference between the two men. Rovani, who is a salaried employee, sometimes chafes at what he sees as Parker's lack of interest in building the value of his own business. He mentioned to me, for instance, that *The Wine Advocate* has never had a marketing budget, that it has not been significantly promoted even in Parker's guidebooks, and that in his opinion the royalties that Parker has agreed to for his foreign book sales are ridiculously small. He said, "Bob is extremely hardworking, extremely loyal, honorable, a great parent, a brilliant wine taster. But he just doesn't get excited by business. When I try to talk to him about the French *Wine Buyer's Guide*, or the contract issues, he'll talk about it for two or three minutes, and then you can see he's bored by it. He'll change the subject to when we can get together and go eat dim sum." Rovani seemed regretful rather than upset. He knew that the weakness he was describing was also Parker's strength. He was resigned to this frustration. He shrugged and said, "Money is not what he's passionate about. And the key to Bob Parker is passion."

An Innocent Abroad

Parker was born in 1947 into a family of dairy farmers, just a few minutes' drive from where he lives today. His parents did not drink wine. They did not drink milk. They drank soda pop. Parker was their only child. When he was four, they built a house down the road and left the farm. Parker's father went to work selling heavy construction equipment, a job he excelled at because he was good with people and didn't mind driving. He was a regular guy with one unusual quality: he had an acute sense of smell. He could pick up garlic on a person's breath from across a room. Young Parker had the same gift, but he didn't realize it was anything special.

He had a typical American childhood. He attended public schools, had a few bicycles, and played a lot of soccer. At the right age he discovered girls and learned to drive. He went to Washington a few times. He went to Baltimore. But Monkton was his world. And it was not a fine-wine kind of place. The high school was called Hereford. It was a plain brick building in a field, a school attended by front-yard mechanics and Future Farmers of America. Parker was not quite like them, but he played soccer well, and he had a normal number of friends. He was one of the "smart kids" enrolled in a small program for college-bound students whose main qualifications seemed to be that their fathers did not work with their hands. In the tenth grade Parker fell in love with a fellow student, a lively girl named Pat Etzel, who is now his wife. They graduated together in the class of 1965—a typical Monkton vintage of no great distinction, soon diminished by the loss of two boys in Vietnam. On Pat Etzel's eighteenth birthday Parker had his first taste of wine. It was sweet, bubbly, fortified cold duck, and it made him throw up.

Pat went off to a women's college in Frederick, Maryland, to study French. In order to stay close to her, Parker accepted a soccer scholarship for one year at a college in northern Virginia, and then transferred to the University of Maryland at College Park, where he dabbled in history and art appreciation. He was a strapping young man with sideburns and longish hair—a solitary but affable guy who, like many men at his age, was having to wait around to grow up. He vaguely opposed the war in Vietnam. On the basis of a temporary injury to his knee he got himself permanently excused from the draft. He finally found the courage to tell his father that he didn't enjoy hunting. For lack of genuine academic interests, he decided on a career in law. He sometimes had a surprising seriousness about him that hinted at his powers of concentration. But it would have been difficult to judge his intelligence. He got good grades, but he was an empty page.

Then came the autumn of 1967, when Pat left for a junior year abroad in Strasbourg, France. Parker told me that Pat's parents did not then approve of her relationship with him, and they hoped that this separation would persuade her to break it off. Parker worried that she might. His pretty girlfriend had matured into a strikingly beautiful woman, slender and graceful, with a lively angular face set off by mischievous green eyes, and now she had ventured out into an unseen world full of foreign men. Parker had little contact with her through the fall—a few delayed letters and hurried telephone calls—and he was increasingly unsure of her feelings. Still, they had a plan to meet in Paris for the December holidays.

The trip was a huge idea for Parker. He still gets excited when he talks about it. Until then he had traveled only as far away as New York, by train, and he had never before flown in an airplane. His father, who had often preached to him about the importance of having shined shoes, made Parker buy a white shirt and a dark three-piece suit for the flight. During the short hop from Baltimore to New York, Parker spilled coffee on himself. During the long flight across the North Atlantic he sat next to a casually dressed Harvard student, who had the good manners not to comment on Parker's stains. This fellow spoke impeccable French and had a mother who was waiting for him in some well-known neighborhood of Paris. He was able to offer Parker fascinating opinions about the best European destinations. He was very depressing. It was beyond his imagination that Parker had never flown before.

As the day turned into night, Parker began to brood. What if he missed Pat in the crowd at the airport? Worse, what if she didn't even bother to show up? Or what if she did show up but didn't love him anymore? Parker didn't know much about the world, but he had heard about French lovers. He figured these were the same guys who had developed the French kiss—and that was probably just the start. He ordered a couple of whiskeys and drank himself to sleep.

The flight was due to arrive in Paris at 10:30. Parker woke up at 10:45. When he saw the time, he jumped into the aisle and yelled, "Shit, I've missed my stop!" The Harvard fellow looked at him in disbelief. A stewardess came up and informed him that an airplane is not a train. He sat again. The Harvard fellow said, "You really *haven't* flown before." Then the captain announced that Paris was fogged in and the flight was being diverted to Rome. Parker panicked again. He said, "How am I supposed to get from Rome to Paris? I don't even speak Italian!" The Harvard fellow laughed and assured him that there would be a flight to Paris in the morning. In the meantime he would have a night to explore Rome. Parker decided then and there to put aside his fears and to embrace this unexpected experience. It was an important moment for him. He was becoming a traveler.

The airline gave him a hotel room in Rome, but he was too wide awake to stay in it. He visited a bar. He wandered the streets. It's characteristic of Parker that his first strong impression of Europe was a smell, and that he identified it precisely. It was the stench of horse urine emanating from a Gypsy encampment by the Coliseum. At dawn he watched Rome come alive for another chaotic day. He was enthralled by the density of the street culture, and by its casual connection to history. He was enthralled by the people, the sounds, and the architectural mixture. He did not shy away from the strangeness of the scene, as provincials often do, comparing Rome with home, or wrinkling their noses. He opened himself completely. He inhaled Europe. He drank it in.

The mood endured, and became in some ways a permanent thing. It helped that a few hours later the airline was able to deliver him to a still-foggy Paris and that his beautiful Pat was waiting there for him and that she loved him very much, spoke good French, and wanted to serve as his guide. She took him by subway to the Trocadéro, led him backward up the steps to the street, and spun him around for his first clear sight of the city: it was a view of the Eiffel Tower, rising gracefully on the opposite bank of the Seine. "Wow!" Parker said, as he often still does.

The young couple stayed in a cheap hotel in the Latin Quarter, a dingy little place called the Danube. For several days they walked through Paris. Parker told me that he couldn't get enough of it. He was in heaven. In the evenings at neighborhood restaurants Pat playfully ordered snails, frogs' legs, mussels, fatty pâtés, and smelly cheeses—foods that should have disgusted a kid from Monkton but in this case did not. Neither of them would have guessed that Parker had one of the world's great palates, or that with these intimate little meals he might be starting down a path toward fame and power. That would have been ridiculous. About the food Parker said, "This stuff is *good!*" and left it at that, as a regular guy would.

He was alone with Pat Etzel in Paris and ferociously in love. Is it surprising that he learned to like the wine? The wine they ordered with their meals was the cheapest they could find, served in carafes, pale red, pleasantly alcoholic, and unremarkable by Parker's present standards, but it was unlike anything he had tasted before. Parker told me he was immediately fascinated by it. Here was a beverage that seemed to complement food and promote conversation, that gave him a buzz but did not make him drunk, and that never blurred his vision like liquor or bloated him like beer. It's hard to imagine his sensations the first few times he put it in his mouth. It was not sweet like bourbon or soda pop. Did it taste of fruit, as people said? It was maybe a little astringent. Parker lacked the vocabulary necessary to sort out the confusion of tastes. He idealized the wine at first. He liked the thought that it was a product of French culture, an artifact that was authentic yet accessible and meant to be shared. As it passed over his tongue, he sensed that it was loaded with meanings he didn't understand. But his immediate reactions were typically straightforward. Every night the wine was different, and every night it seemed to work. "This stuff is *good!*" Beyond that, he knew little.

Pat took him to Strasbourg, where his education continued. Parker described to me how in the cold, gray countryside of northeastern France he was shocked by the lingering evidence, after so many years, of the two world wars—the buildings still pockmarked or lying in ruin, the cripples in the cafés and on the trains, the village monuments engraved with long lists of the dead, grouped by family name. The destruction was worse than anything Parker had imagined, and it made him realize how sheltered he had been. He knew that the United States had fought hard and well to liberate this ground, but he did not swell with national pride or indulge, as others do, in the sly denigration of the French for their claims about *résistance.* He realized that battles alone could not explain such scars. The significance of *résistance* was not martial—it was the underlying stubbornness that had allowed the ordinary French to emerge from an apocalypse with their attitudes toward life still largely intact. Parker admired them for it, and had all the more reason every night to appreciate their wine.

Pat had met a doctor in Strasbourg, who invited the young couple to share a few meals with him in the best local restaurants. The doctor was a gourmet and a generous man, and he enjoyed introducing them to the tradition of the three-hour dinner, and to tastes that lay beyond their means. For Parker, with his acute sensitivities, the meals were not just pleasures but profound revelations. He began to concentrate on food in a way that he had not previously known was possible. He also had his first few bottles of really fine wine. Already he was beginning to sort out the tastes. In France today the story goes that he looked up after sipping a certain wine and said, "Oh, that's good! There's a little taste of grapefruit there, and a little taste of lemon, and a little taste of . . ." The doctor is said to have gazed at him and remarked, "Do you know that you have just defined the main components of a Riesling?" And Parker is said to have understood at that moment that he had the talents of a prodigy.

The story is too tidy to be quite true, but in essence it is correct: after those meals in Strasbourg there was no turning Parker back. His visit to France lasted six weeks, with an unpleasant interlude of bad food in Germany. When it was time for him to go home, he and Pat returned to Paris, intent on spending the last of his holiday money on a final gourmet meal. They chose Maxim's, a three-star restaurant on the rue Royale, which was known as a bastion of classic French cuisine. They checked into their cheap hotel. In preparation for the dinner, Pat pressed the collar of Parker's washed white shirt between two books, and brushed the wrinkles from their best clothes. Parker dutifully shined his shoes.

They arrived at Maxim's, and after a typically disdainful attendant hung Pat's cloth coat on a rack loaded with furs, the couple was banished to a secondary dining room full of foreigners, and assigned to a table with a flickering electric lamp. When Parker complained about the lamp, a disapproving waiter tried to fix it and received a shock that knocked him to the floor. It didn't help matters that the two Americans could hardly keep from laughing. But they settled down, and after a while they ordered their meal. The restaurant photographer came along and took a picture, which they kept, of a smiling Pat and a more somber Parker in his suit, gazing down and away with a shy, thoughtful expression on his face. Maxim's was turning into another lesson for him. The wine they drank was overpriced. The food looked better than it tasted. The dessert was a pretty little tart so tough that it shot out from under Parker's knife, flew off the table, and stuck to the pants of a passing waiter. When Parker took Pat to dance on the restaurant's small dance floor, the maitre d'hôtel came up and explained with regret that the color of Parker's polished shoes was an inappropriate brown. Pat led Parker back to their table. Then came the bill.

Terroir and Tradition

Thirty-two years later there are wine families in France who feel that Parker is still making them pay. Near the city of Bordeaux last spring I talked to one of the most powerful producers in the trade, a businessman with formal manners, who did not want me to use his name. He pretended for a while to be Parker's friend, but finally could not keep his anger from showing. He shut his office door against the secretaries outside, turned to me, and said, "*Monsieur*, do you know Robert Parker? Have you met him?" His voice was deep and resonant. "*Monsieur*, you surely do not believe that such a man is simply *tasting wines!* You do not believe that he ignores the *political* context of his work! *Non, monsieur*, Robert Parker knows precisely what he is doing. And he has his reasons."

I was intrigued. Was he going to tell me that Parker was in it for the money after all? That he had hidden allies? Secret meetings? Understandings with governments? I asked him to explain.

From a stack of papers on his desk he slid me a fax that someone had just sent him. It was a page from a recent *Wine Advocate*, a survey of Australian wines. He made a steeple of his hands and watched me darkly while I glanced over what Parker had written.

It didn't take long. He had liked some Australian wines so much that he had scored them in the nineties. I looked up and said, "But your own wines score well too."

That was not the point. His own wines were traditional, and these most certainly were not. He saw the very comparison as a betrayal of Bordeaux. He said, "Bob is a big, dramatic man, with big, dramatic tastes. But our wines are supposed to be *red*, not *black*." He held up his pen, a shiny black Mont Blanc, to show me the color of the wines that he thought Parker favors. He said, "I have known him for twenty years, but I will no longer read what he writes. He wants to lead us down a path to destruction."

That's Bordeaux—a place so steeped in tradition that it's not unusual to find people who go around actively regretting the French Revolution. When I told the story of the Australian wines to Rovani, he said, "What did you expect? Those people *own* the town. The bottom line is, when that's your business, how much do you like the big, goofy northern-Maryland guy who rates you? Because your game is control."

Rovani does not cover Bordeaux, but he knows it well and seems to enjoy the scene. He told me about a conversation he had one day with a powerful chateau owner there. "I asked him how he got interested in wine and he said, 'After I finished school, my father had really nothing of importance to give me as a gift, and so he gave me . . .'" Rovani named a famous chateau. He laughed. "I mean, the thing's worth millions!"

I said, "And when he says that to you, does he realize that he's . . . "

Rovani interrupted. "That he's talking to a guy who plays with his credit-card debt? It's beyond that. It doesn't matter. I'm not in his life—you know what I mean?"

"Yes, but does he realize he's playing a role?"

"I always wonder. I always wonder how far over the line these people get."

In Bordeaux the answer to that question is all about a person's connection to the right class of wine. This is a place where strangers ask you your birth year to establish not your age but the associated vintage. Among the great wine families, I met one man who smiled about his position in life—but he had just gotten remarried. The others did not smile. They belonged to a rigid and self-referential society, similar to a hereditary aristocracy but mercantile in its essence, and shaped in a peculiar way by the formal rankings of the nearly two hundred top chateaux, the so-called "classified growths." The language is confusing, because "growth" refers not to the vines or even to the individual wines but to the participating chateaux, each of which has been assigned a more or less permanent ranking according to traditional perceptions of its relative prestige and quality. The first classifications were created in the nineteenth century as marketing tools to justify the prices that the top Bordeaux wines were already commanding. They were a huge success, allowing consumers to sort through the confusion of labels, and providing the producers with price-setting structures and a stability that had been lacking in the business. But they went too far. The great weakness of the Bordeaux classification system is that it allows for little or no change. And so it has had the effect of ossifying the entire industry of Bordeaux wines and with it the structure of society.

Parker is a revolutionary because he disregards the traditional rankings and simply tastes the wines. He has in practice created an entirely new and simplified classification system, based upon his own judgment. This is of grave concern to Bordeaux, and especially to the Médoc, which has the most important and prestigious of the classified growths, and where traditionally the most expensive wines have been made. The Médoc is a rolling expanse of vineyards punctuated by overblown manors and occasional impoverished villages (some of them largely inhabited by Moroccan field workers) from which the life seems to have been sucked.

It is not an attractive place, but because of its famous wines, it thinks highly of itself. I had been warned that the families there would close their doors on me, as they would close them on Parker if they could. They did not. They guided me through the intricacies of the business, introduced me to their friends, and patiently explained the error of Parker's ways. But nowhere among them was I able to find the person I sought—someone with the humor and perspective necessary to make a persuasive argument for the preservation of their world. These people were not playing roles. They had crossed a line at birth.

Among them I found a man who seemed to embody their fears—Bernard Ginestet, the aging scion of a once-great family, an aristocrat fallen from the heights, who in his loss is said to have become a philosopher of wine. I met him for lunch in Bordeaux, in the medieval center of the city. He was a gaunt, gray, unshaven man with heavy-lidded eyes and the voice of a chain smoker; I thought he looked a bit roughed up by life, and probably for the better. He had the demeanor of a disillusioned aristocrat, at once detached and self-abandoned. When he smiled, his face remained serious. When he said, "In every family there are people who are failures," I could not tell if he was referring to himself. Years before, he had inherited and then been forced to sell the historic Chateau Margaux, a large estate in the Médoc that has been making wines for centuries and that stands at the very peak of the classification system, as one of only five classified "first growths" in the Médoc. When he lost the property, in 1977, the Bordelais were horrified by the depth of his fall.

After honoring the family debts Ginestet had little left. He was elected mayor of the local village, also named Margaux. To make a living he became a writer and an editor, and produced a series of narrowly focused books, each on the subject of a single official wine-production area, known as an *appellation*, often of only a few square miles. Because of the geographic concentration of such work, he became an authority on the central concept of the Bordelais culture: a belief in the fundamental significance of what is called *terroir*. The word *terroir* has no concise translation but relates strongly to history, class, and pedigree; it means the soil both real and metaphorical from which a vine, a wine, or a person emerges. Ginestet told me I could spend days trying to understand it. Because weather matters too, as do changes brought about by economics and technology, there is a need to consider the vintage. But for the aristocracy of Bordeaux *terroir* matters most of all.

My conversation with Ginestet did not go well. He had lived for a while near San Francisco, and he thought he knew the American mind. Few of his books had been translated. I asked him why. He waved his fork vaguely, and in English he said, "Too *Frenchy*," as if that explanation were enough. He thought my questions about Bordeaux were simplistic. He denied every premise. But rather than clearly expressing himself, he grimaced and shrugged in the Gallic manner, lapsed into silences, worked the food on his plate, glanced at the elegant women at the next table, sipped his water, sipped his wine. He erected barriers. He was very relaxed, but he seemed to feel he was under attack.

I was able to draw him out only on the subject of Parker. He acted fond of him, as an uncle might act toward an obstreperous nephew. Parker had dedicated a book to him, but had also given his wines some very poor scores. Ginestet said, "Bob has succeeded in providing the image that fits today."

"What image is that?"

"The guru. The one who knows."

"Wasn't there a need for a guru before?"

"Yes, but it was fragmented by country, or zone of influence. Today there is the 'globalization.'" He thought it through, and coined a nice phrase. He said, "Bob is an artisan in the globalization of wine."

He meant globalization by the French definition—the imposition of an American style. Like a lot of Frenchmen, he seemed to see the United States as a single, unified culture. He had lived there, but possibly had not understood its true dimensions—the coexistence within it of so many different nations. He knew something about San Francisco and New York, and had a superficial view of the rest.

He said, "The American taste is very standardized. Price-conscious. Unsubtle. And that is where Bob excels. He has understood it—partly by intuition, partly by deduction. Americans like simple things. 'Square.'" He drew a square in the air. "And Bob has a 'square' taste."

I mentioned that Parker's books sell well in France. But Ginestet wanted to keep talking about the United States. He said, "What bothers Americans is, they like certainty. If wine contains a truth, it is the *absence* of certainty. But one of the reasons Bob has succeeded is that he knows no doubts."

"And the French—what do they like?"

This was a more complicated thing. He didn't exactly say that the French like uncertainty. He said, "My personal philosophy is, you can be sure of nothing." Then he chose to give a little. He lit a cigarette and inhaled. His voice softened. He said, "Lighter wines. Wines of pleasure. Wines of . . . emotion." I wanted to try him again on the idea of *terroir*, but he closed up when I fumbled for definitions, and so I called for the bill.

Waiting for Parker

It was a rough spring in Bordeaux. Parker had left town after a ten-day stay, during which he had tasted the wines made just a few months before, in the fall of 1999. The early sale of such very young wines, two years before they can be bottled (let alone consumed), is considered to be a prerogative of Bordeaux's top chateaux, most of which now try to sell their entire production this way. These wines are known as "futures." They provide the chateaux with obvious financial advantages, and with the valuable appearance of enjoying a frantic demand for their wines. They provide consumers with the pleasure of playing an insider's role, and with early access to wines that in theory will become more expensive when they mature. The process is extraordinarily complicated. It kicks off each spring with a wild scramble that lasts for several weeks, during which the chateaux sell the fall's vintage in allocations to the traditional traders in Bordeaux—the *négociants*, who enjoy exclusive purchasing rights and have maintained a lock on the business for a few hundred years. Each chateau negotiates its own prices—but as much in jealous relation to the prices that its neighbors are getting as in anticipation of the market. This is more rational than it might seem, because prices help to determine prestige, and prestige is always relative. Each spring, when it's time to start over again, no one wants to go first. One of the smart new winemakers told me that Bordeaux is like *barbichette*, a schoolyard game in which children hold one another by the chin to see who laughs first. The child who loses gets a slap in the face.

Parker makes it worse. When he is in Bordeaux, he keeps mostly to himself, and though the city studies his every gesture during the tastings, hoping for some indication of his thoughts, he keeps his face neutral and his notes private, and he goes home to Monkton without expressing his opinions. The business then plays *barbichette* for several weeks while waiting for *The Wine Advocate*'s regular Bordeaux edition to appear, in late April. Last spring, after Parker left, the wait was said to be more intense than ever before. All of Bordeaux knew that 1999 had been at best an average year, and that the market was already flooded with overpriced and mediocre 1997s and the uneven and still more expensive 1998s. Retailers worldwide were rebelling against an allocation system that, rather than being a privilege, felt like a feeding tube shoved down their throats.

Back in Bordeaux the production levels were very high. Chateau Margaux alone was making 440,000 bottles a year—of what was supposed to be expensive stuff. At a similar chateau in the Médoc, a place called Léoville-Barton, the owner told me he sometimes wistfully considers that if he could just get each person in Bordeaux to drink one bottle of his wine every year, he could sell out his entire stock right there. But of course that would include children, practicing Muslims, and a sizable population on welfare. Short of such reveries, some chateau owners hoped that an economic bridge could be maintained to what was likely to be the sought-after vintage of 2000.

It was obvious to everyone that deep and wide price reductions would soon be needed. It was also obvious that Parker would agree, and that in the coming issue of *The Wine Advocate* he would advise his readers to stay away from 1999 futures in general. Still . . . again . . . *barbichette*. Who would reduce his prices first? Who would give that tactical advantage to his neighbors, allowing them to set their prices higher than his—if only just slightly? Moreover, who among Bordeaux's natural leaders would ignore the certainty that Parker would celebrate some of the wines and score them, perhaps, merely one point beyond 89 and into the magic 90s? For those wines the prestige would be all the greater in a year of general decline. So Bordeaux waited.

One afternoon I went to a professional tasting at Chateau Pavie, a revitalized winery near the hilltop village of St.-Emilion, where several hundred buyers from around the world were milling about in an elegant vaulted hall, sampling a selection of about forty 1999s, which were being presented by a Bordeaux trade association, the Union des Grands Crus. The buyers kept to themselves in groups of two or three, and wandered among the offerings, spinning and sloshing the wines, tasting them, and leaning forward to spit them into centrally placed porcelain funnels. The funnels drained into buckets encased in wooden barrels. The buckets were carried off by young men slipping quietly through the crowd.

A lot of thought had gone into that setting. The lighting was cool but not cold. The art was bright and modern. The floors were a lovely tile, a shade of desert tan. A few steps away, wide doors opened into a still-larger vaulted hall—Pavie's lavish temperature-controlled production room, which was three stories high and had double walls and a viewing platform overlooking lines of dramatically lit oak barrels: a fortune in new wine. But the buyers seemed hardened to any such efforts, whether in architecture or in wine. They were not aesthetes. They were not dilettantes. They were professional skeptics, people who made their living by being unimpressed. Now, like everyone else, they were stuck having to wait for Parker in order to come to terms on prices. They jotted disgruntled little notes about the tastings. But mostly they were just biding time.

Our host was the president of the Union des Grands Crus, a vocal Parker supporter named Alain Raynaud, who at his property in nearby Libourne was making some of the best wines in Bordeaux. Raynaud was aware of his guests' frustration, and he blamed the *négociants*, the traders in Bordeaux. He said, "If Parker has too much influence, it's the fault of the traders. They have the chance right now, while their clients are here, to decide for themselves what they think of these wines. If they want to, they can make the deals. But whether because they are cowards or lack the will, instead they will wait. I find it completely surprising, and I know that Parker does too."

I said, "But Parker is not just some critic. The traders have to take into account that he makes the market."

Raynaud said, "Last year I brought my 1998 right here, to show it to Bordeaux. I was very proud of it. And I said, "*Voilà!* I propose this wine at one hundred francs a bottle, before tax. Everybody said—*everybody!*—'This is very great wine that you've made! But you've raised your price too much, and we won't buy it.'

"And I said, 'Okay, very good, we'll just wait until Bob Parker gives it a score.'

"Parker scored it ninety-three to ninety-five. That very day I could easily have asked two hundred francs for it, and it would have been snapped up. I didn't do that. I sold it at a hundred and twenty-five francs. But the last I heard is that in the dealing between the traders just here in Bordeaux it's now going for three hundred francs a bottle."

Raynaud was not simply gloating. His point was that the traders had profited more by waiting for Parker than they would have by fulfilling their traditional role, negotiating prices and investing in wines on the basis of their own independent judgments. In other words, Raynaud believed that the traders were shirking their duties. He was probably right, but he was also being unfair. What he left unsaid is that because of Parker—this one man with so much power—the terrain has become much less certain for the Bordeaux traders. The critical decisions are made not about the ordinary wines but about the very best, especially those that when tasted young might qualify for a Parker score in the 90s. Yes, there is money to be made by exploiting the advantage that traders have of being first in line and simply following Parker's lead. But there is also money to be lost by moving out in front of Parker. If a trader decides that a wine is very good and agrees with the chateau on a moderately high price for it, he runs the significant risk that Parker might score the wine at 89 as opposed to 90 or 91—and that in a generally skittish market the price for it will tumble. That is one of the ironies of Parker's role. He regrets the skittishness of the market. He opposes speculation of any kind. But inevitably he fuels it.

The Rocky Balboa of Wine

Parker says that he never intended any of this. When he went home from his first trip to France, he got together with a few college friends and began drinking wines for fun. He read some British wine books, which he found interesting on historical topics but strangely impractical on the subject of taste. What did it mean when a wine had a hint of Russian leather? Worse, what did it mean when a wine elicited metaphors? "This wine is a beautiful lady in the last years of her life, wearing a bit too much makeup, perhaps, who can no longer hide all the wrinkles she has. . . ." What Parker wanted to know about a wine was whether to buy it or not.

He took a class from Gordon Prange, the author of *At Dawn We Slept*, who taught him the discipline of writing short, clear sentences. He kept tasting wines. When he was twenty-two he married Pat and went back to Europe with her for the summer. After finishing college, he started law school, still at the University of Maryland. The young couple moved into a cheap basement apartment that they kept at a constant 55°, just perfect for wine. Parker was becoming more serious about his hobby. Pat was willing to go along with it because she was young, but she sometimes quarreled with Parker about the money he was spending on wine. She had a job teaching French in a public school. Parker told me he was known as the phantom of law school, because he liked to stay up late watching Dick Cavett and then needed to sleep through the morning. But one class started with a roll call, so he usually managed to show up for it. The class was about conflict of interest—a hot topic in the early 1970s—and was taught by the Watergate counsel Sam Dash. Parker thought it was fascinating, and he began to think of wine in these new terms, to wonder why so many famous wines were watery and bland but were written about as if they were not. As a budding consumerist, he began to feel indignant. He felt he had been ambushed too often.

Parker passed the bar in 1973 and dutifully took a job in Baltimore, which soon confirmed his suspicion that legal work would bore him. As often as possible he escaped with Pat to Europe. They concentrated on France, where she could serve as his translator and charm the chateaux into letting them inside to talk and taste wine. Parker was very serious, and he took notes; Pat enjoyed looking after him. With a hobby as expensive as wine, they did not have much money to spare. They traveled light, and in the evenings ate cheaply. They managed Europe on ten dollars a day. It was a simple time for them. They look back on it now with nostalgia.

By 1978 Parker was ready to put his experience to use. He typed up the first issue of *The Wine Advocate*, including on the front page a consumerist manifesto. He bought a few mailing lists from wine retailers and sent out 6,500 free copies. Six hundred people subscribed—a disappointment for Parker at the time, but by direct-mail standards a success. In the second issue (the first for which people had paid) he wrote a scathing critique of the industrialization of California vineyards—a trend that he blamed for producing bland, sterile, and overly manipulated wines that tasted alike and seemed designed to survive the rigors of mass distribution and generally to minimize business risk. It was a battle cry heard initially by very few people, but they must have welcomed it. The circulation of *The Wine Advocate* began to climb. Parker still needed his earnings as a lawyer to pay the bills, but he consoled himself that the journal allowed him his independence of mind.

Such independence was not a hallmark of most other critics—a collection mostly of ineffectual men whom Parker in his moral rigidity and his ambition began to despise. The feeling was soon reciprocated, dividing the wine press into camps so hostile that the slick New York–based *Wine Spectator* has never run a profile of Parker and will barely mention his name. But in the early days, before Parker was known, a British critic came up to him in London and said, "Living in America, how hard is it for you to get your cases of first-growth claret?"

Parker said, "What do you mean?"

The critic looked confused. "Don't you get a case of Latour, Lafite, and Margaux sent every year?"

"No," Parker said. "Maybe I should be insulted."

He meant insulted on behalf of his readers. But he cannot have been surprised. The setup is an open secret. In Bordeaux people say that the critics' car trunks automatically pop open at the famous estates, and just can't be closed until they are full of bottles. Some critics are consultants. Some are importers. Some simply write for magazines that depend on wine advertising. The problem they all have is how to make a living. In English this generally leads to a critical technique known as "varying the degrees of 'wonderful.'" In French the relevant technique is called "drowning the fish"—a slightly different thing, which contributes to the tendency toward bewildering complexity in French prose.

At one of the middle-ranked chateaux in the Médoc, during the wait last spring for Parker's declarations, an iconoclastic winemaker named Olivier Sèze called most French critics "odious." He said, "They use our wines as a pretext for their writings. 'Look— what I write is good! Look—what I write is intelligent!' But you read a full page of it and you say, 'What was that about? About wine? About a car? Perfume?'"

With Parker there was never any question. By 1982, after four years in existence, *The Wine Advocate* had a circulation of 7,000. Then came the Bordeaux vintage of 1982, whose young wines were unusually dark, powerful, and fruity. When Parker flew home from tasting those "futures" in the spring of 1983, he was so eager to get back and write about what he had found that he worried uncharacteristically that the airplane might crash. This was the scoop of a lifetime, a vintage that he was convinced would become one of the greatest in history, and that the other critics, within their variations of "wonderful," seemed to have underestimated. Parker advised his readers to buy the wines, and many did so—in large quantities. A lot of money was at stake. The established critics attacked, arguing that the young 1982s lacked acidity and therefore would not age well. They were saying, in essence, that these wines tasted too good too soon—an argument related to the traditional one that bad wines require age to become better. Parker suspected the opposite—that the greatest vintages (he thought of '61 and '49 and '47) are so seamless and free of imperfections that they are balanced from birth—and that 1982 was just such a vintage.

With his career on the line, he returned to Bordeaux and started asking about the past. In the archives of Chateau Haut-Brion he found an old diary that expressed concern about the famous vintage of 1929—that the then-young wines were too intense, and would not endure. Parker knew those wines after fifty years, and considered them to be excellent still. He retasted the 1982s and was again astonished by their splendor. He went home to Monkton, and reiterated his earlier judgments. By 1984, when the wines were being bottled, it was obvious to everyone that he was right. Most of the opposing critics began to back down. One who didn't was forced into an increasingly untenable position, and finally lost his job. *The Wine Spectator* eventually came out with an issue celebrating the 1982 vintage, but by then those wines were hard to find and very expensive. Parker's reputation was made. Some of his readers had gotten rich on his advice. Others simply had picked up good wine at a good price. *The Wine Advocate*'s circulation jumped past 10,000. Parker quit his job as a lawyer. Several weeks later he signed his first book contract in New York. He told me that going home on the train, he felt like Sylvester Stallone in *Rocky*.

Saving Bordeaux From Itself

Last spring, when the annual Bordeaux issue of *The Wine Advocate* finally came out, the Bordeaux establishment lashed back angrily. In a campaign led by some of the large chateaux, people attacked Parker in the local press, accusing him not only of undue influence and technical incompetence but also of cronyism and, by innuendo, of malice. The Bordeaux newspaper, *Sud-Ouest*, published several articles laying out the accusations, and a wider press spread the story—through Europe and to the United States. These accusations were for the most part unfounded, but they were serious enough to leave Parker feeling wounded and perhaps genuinely threatened. He took the unusual step of writing letters in his own defense—but he was hampered by a lack of detail in the accusations, and by the fact that during his last stay in Bordeaux he had indeed not handled himself well. It was a matter of appearances: he had gone for a private dinner with Alain Raynaud at a remote country hotel, and the next day had tasted the wines of the Union des Grands Crus and rated Raynaud's very high.

A well-known chateau called Bouscaut ran a sarcastic advertisement for its 1999 wines, including a defiant proclamation of its score of only 79–82. In the ad a cartoon depicted a retailer saying to a customer, "A good wine with a real *terroir*? An individualistic wine? No hesitation—find one with a bad Parker score!!!!" Parker's response was typically blunt. To a query from a London wine magazine he responded, "The cartoon was a splendid idea. Given the wine Bouscaut has made, I would resort to humor, too, if it helped to sell the wine. But purchasers of it will find out who the joke is really on." As a consumerist, Parker naturally is self-righteous and maybe too easily aggrieved. His mother could have told him just to smile and sit tight.

At first glance Bordeaux seemed to be upset about very little. In his April issue Parker praised some producers for their 1999s but reported, accurately, that the year had been excessively wet and hot, resulting in few compelling wines and little reason to buy futures. This was hardly a surprise. But then Parker went further. He wrote a few paragraphs that were unusual for him, in which he expressed his thoughts about Bordeaux's business side and discussed the global glut in its wines. He said the retail trade worldwide would have to cut its losses by dumping the 1997s en masse and skeptically judging each wine from 1998. Then, while scolding the Bordeaux producers for their "egregious blunder" and foolish greed, he called for a reduction in the prices for the 1999s by 30 percent or more. He wrote, "If arrogance prevents them from understanding this, they will see the irresponsibility of their ways . . . sooner rather than later."

This was getting closer to a reason for a fight. A 30 percent reduction in prices? The producers choked at the very thought, and they knew that Parker's opinions, once expressed, are not just abstractions: this issue of *The Wine Advocate* would be wielded by the disgruntled buyers, who were already murmuring about a boycott. Parker had the audacity to claim that he was trying to save Bordeaux from itself. Those few paragraphs of his were going to cost Bordeaux a lot.

But the truth is that the chateaux have the financial reserves to ride out a downturn in the market—along with the cushion that the 2000 vintage is likely to provide. They are not, in other words, so obviously beleaguered that they need to fear Parker's frank assessment. Their reaction to it, therefore, can only be understood as an expression of a deeper problem: what they are really worried about is the accelerating movement toward the garage wines, those dark, dramatic, small-production wines that are being made with fanatical devotion to detail.

The garage phenomenon began in Bordeaux less than a decade ago as a novelty, but it seems now to be evolving beyond mere fashion, and taking shape as one of the more important changes of the past 200 years. The competitive advantages are clear: the garage wines do not require large vineyards, big crews, a manor house, or a classic patch of *terroir*—and they are now fetching the highest prices in Bordeaux. This is extremely threatening to the established families, whose very society requires them to hold stiffly to the idea that price is a reflection of quality. Privately, the families claim that the "*garagistes*" are cheating—that because of the ultra-small quantities involved (for any label, typically less than 15,000 bottles a year), the new producers are able to manipulate their prices in the most cynical ways, buying back significant percentages of their own stock in order to stimulate the market, or working through unnamed agents to ratchet up demand artificially at the famous London and New York auction houses. In some ways the big families are right. It is certainly true that many of the garage wines are terrible buys and that if a wine-drinker wanted one rule for Bordeaux it would be to stay away from them entirely. Another rule, however, might be to stay away from the famous chateaux as well. For the established families it's a predicament: after so much market manipulation of their own, they are hardly in a position to complain on behalf of the consumers. Meanwhile, the garage wines are spreading through the cracks and odd parcels of the best wine-growing region in the world, the finite realm of Bordeaux, where rapidly and insidiously they are subverting the structures on which the great families rely.

It's no wonder those families fear Robert Parker. He is indeed the man to blame. He claims to disapprove of the prices for the garage wines, but insists on judging such wines as a purist would, concentrating entirely on their taste. It is true that the garage wines are dense, impressive, and often extremely good. Parker likes the idea of them, and in the new Bordeaux *Wine Advocate* he said so more clearly than ever before.

There's an argument now that the *garagistes* are making wines to suit Parker's taste, and that therefore the world is getting smaller here, too. I heard it many times. Parker is a monopolist, the Bill Gates of wine; Bordeaux must follow the example of José Bové, the French anti-globalist, and fight back against Parker's domination. The image of one American with so much power seems valid from a distance. But up close it tends to fall apart. No two fine wines are ever the same. I moved for weeks among the *garagistes*, and even I, with my lack of knowledge and my dull palate, would never have mistaken any one of their wines for any other. Parker is making the world not smaller but larger. Bordeaux distrusts him for that reason. After 300 years he is breaking up the *terroir*.

The leading *garagiste* is a brash, self-confident man named Jean-Luc Thunevin, who with his wife, Murielle, makes a ripe red wine called Valandraud, one of the stars of the region. The Thunevins are seen in Bordeaux as the ultimate outsiders. He is a "*pied-noir*," the son of refugees from the Algerian war for independence, an outsider who worked in a bank for thirteen years and nearly went broke in the restaurant business before acquiring a scrap of ground and getting into wine in 1991. Until a few years ago she was a nurse's assistant.

The Thunevins do not have a chateau, though they could almost afford one by now. They live in the center of St.-Emilion, in bright and minimally furnished quarters directly above their wine-production rooms. One evening over dinner there he said to me, "People think our wine is a product of Parker—but it's not true. Parker is prudent. He didn't know if we were going to keep producing good wines—if we were serious, if we were honest. He started grading only after four years, when he had tasted our wines in the bottle. For the first few years he gave us scores only in the eighties. But the effect of Parker was to accelerate things. Before, we would have required fifty years to be recognized—and, of course, we would never have been able to survive. But thanks to Parker, we needed only four years. It was his willingness to taste our wines, and the speed of the information, that mattered."

Thunevin is openly despised by the old families of Bordeaux, who call him "*Tue-le-vin*," a shortened form of "He who kills the wine." I asked him what he thought about them in return. He said, "I'm not trying to be accepted. People have problems because they absolutely want to enter a milieu that is not theirs. I have the advantage that I don't care. When I started into the business, I had a friend who warned me. He said, 'In Bordeaux they don't like newcomers. They're going to break you.'" Thunevin smiled, as if to say, "And now look who is afraid."

The subversion has spread even into Bordeaux's heart, the Médoc, where Murielle Thunevin in 1999 starting making a new garage wine, called Marojallia, in a neglected patch of vineyard, with a little stone shed, a little tractor, and not much else. Every day through the summer she drove there in her jeans and rough shirts, and worked side by side with two Moroccan women to tend the vines. In the fall, with a slightly larger crew, she harvested the grapes and made the first wine. Her powerful neighbors at the surrounding chateaux were shocked and outraged, and came by to peer into the shed, but they could do nothing about her presence.

During Parker's tastings last spring the current owner of Chateau Margaux, a woman named Corinne Mentzelopoulos, wanted to talk to Parker only about the Thunevins' new wine. Parker later told me that she was resentful, and viewed the innovation as dangerous. She said, "We believe in *terroir*."

Parker refused to accept the traditional meaning of that word. He said, "Well, it is a *terroir*. It doesn't have a history of three hundred years, like Chateau Margaux, but it's a *terroir*. Why shouldn't someone try to improve the quality of wine that comes from this parcel of land?" She retreated to the old answer—that no one knew how the wine would evolve.

Parker, for his part, refused to budge. In *The Wine Advocate* he discussed Murielle Thunevin's new wine, which he had tasted as a future. He wrote,

> This is the first of what will likely be an increasing move toward limited production "garage" wines in the Médoc (something the powers in the appellation are totally against). An impressive first effort, it has the potential to merit an outstanding rating after bottling. There are nearly 600 cases of this saturated purple-colored offering, which exhibits low acid, sweet blackberry aromas backed by chocolate and toast. In the mouth, the wine is voluptuous, opulent, pure, and harmonious. My rating is conservative since this is the debut release, but this 1999 has enormous potential, and since it is likely to be bottled without fining or filtration, it should merit an outstanding score.

He gave it 89–91, neatly signaling his view of the years to come. The message to the old families was clear.

In the essay accompanying the tasting notes, Parker professed astonishment that anyone might fear the *garagistes*. He wrote,

> There is no stopping this new phenomenon in spite of the hostility it has received from *négociants*, the Médoc's aristocracy, and those reactionaries in favor of preserving Bordeaux's status quo. These wines are not the destabilizing influence many old timers would have consumers believe. What's wrong with an

energetic person taking a small piece of property and trying to turn out something sensational?

But Parker knew perfectly well that a fundamental change was under way—that a vast industrial structure seemed about to break apart. When I saw him again at home in Monkton, with his dogs snoring in a corner of the office, he admitted that these might be the final years for the old families of Bordeaux. Olivier Sèze, the iconoclastic winemaker in the Médoc, had been gleeful at that possibility. He had said, "If people start to make better wines than the first growths, the whole system falls apart. It becomes a revolution. It *is* a revolution!" Parker, too, sometimes used that word. The coming vintage of 2000, he told me, would strengthen the great chateaux, but only temporarily. He had a long-term view. He said, "A hundred years from now the garage wines won't be a separate category. They will be up and down the Médoc. Everyone will be making wines that way. And if someone wants to go back over the history, Thunevin will be seen as the pioneer who totally changed the system."

"And Parker?"

"My name might come up too—maybe as a footnote."

He pretended to have a workman's view of himself in history. He said, "I'm an anti-industrial kind of guy." As if he were just another critic expressing an opinion, he said, "I don't like manipulation, compromise, or interventionistic winemaking—unless something goes wrong. I believe that the responsibility of the winemaker is to take that fruit and get it into the bottle as the most natural and purest expression of that vineyard, of the grape varietal or blend, and of the vintage." He also said, "When I started tasting wines, in the 1970s, we were on a slippery slope. There was a standardization of wines, where you couldn't tell a Chianti from a cabernet. That's pretty much stopped now." He refused to say it had stopped because of him. I figured he was being willfully modest. His own mother seems to believe he has developed a big ego. But the furthest he would go now was to express surprise that the logo he had chosen for *The Wine Advocate* had long been overlooked. It is a corkscrew in the form of a crusader's cross, and he admitted almost shyly that at last it has been noticed.

GQ

FINALIST, PROFILES

The Ghost

Elizabeth Gilbert's profile of Hank Williams III is at once sympathetic and unflinching, a candid look at a musician burdened with his own demons and also oppressed by the tortured legacy of his father and grandfather. Gilbert uses uncommon insight and her own rich voice to really make this story sing.

Elizabeth Gilbert

The Ghost

I say, "Just speak your mind, Hank-3. Don't let me stop you."

Me and the grandson of Hank Williams are sitting in some honky-tonk dive in downtown Nashville, listening to some mediocre band churn through some weepy old set of country-music standards. The grandson of Hank Williams bears the Christian name Shelton Hank Williams, but he is better known around these parts as Hank-3, so that's why I call him that. Me and everyone else in this bar. Who have all recognized him on sight. Hank-3 is a little hard to miss, mind you. He's the only six-foot-two-inch, 144-pound, twangy-voiced, heavily tattooed, longhaired skeleton walking around Nashville these days who looks exactly like Hank Williams. And you cannot hide the face of Hank Williams in this town. It would be like if Elvis Presley had a dead-ringer grandson who someday tried to walk around Memphis without getting any attention. Not a chance. Heads would turn, jaws drop.

Tonight the grandson of Hank Williams is perched on a barstool, balancing on his bony ass, smoking cigarettes as if there were some kind of contest for it and drinking whiskey just as competitively. And he's bitching about his recording label, Curb Records. He's griping about what a hard time he had getting Curb to put even a measly three of his own songs on his debut album (which is a very impressive and totally rocking country production called *Risin' Outlaw*—and the three original cuts are the very best part of it, thank you very much). Hank-3 seems to have never heard that tenet about not telling journalists every single little thing you think, do or want, which is why he's saying, "These people at Curb are all fucking assholes. The next album I'm doing, it's all gonna be filled with all my own songs, or fuck them and I'll see you in court. Because this is fucking bullshit. They tried to make my album commercial and radio-friendly, and that is not what I am all about, man. And now the radio doesn't even play my shit anyhow. So what was the fucking point?"

I say, "Just speak your mind, Hank-3. Don't let me stop you."

Hank-3 is very fidgety with his ponytail tonight. He's very flinchy, very dodgy. It's six o'clock in the evening, and he just woke up. This is a perfectly typical timetable for his vampiric existence. His stomach kills from the flu, an ailment he gets, according to his calculations, "once every five fucking weeks." His complexion? Consumptive. His demeanor? Exhausted. And here's why: Hank-3 has been on the road nonstop for five years now, swilling booze, smoking drugs, reconceiving American country music, sleeping on a bus with five other guys and singing his guts out in low-down bars where rednecks spend their evenings kicking each other's dumb redneck asses. And now he's dog-tired. Dog-tired and 27 years of age.

The grandson of Hank Williams continues, "I got this new song I just wrote. It's about how much I hate the modern Nashville establishment. It's called 'I Put the Dick in Dixie and the Cunt in Country,' but my label hates that shit. They'll never let me record it. So fuck them. Fuck them all. They can all go fucking fuck themselves."

I say, "Don't sugarcoat things for my benefit, Hank-3."

"Yeaaahhhh," he drawls. "I know I should shut my fucking mouth. My producers hate it when I talk in public like this. They keep trying to get me to shut up. They tried to send me to media school six fucking times."

Media school?

"Yeaaahhhh . . . that's where all the big Nashville stars go these days, to learn how to turn questions around and act like they love that family-values shit and deflect subjects about drugs and whoring, but I can't do that. I can't play those games. I'll tell you what, man. I am not a motherfucker who does fucking *lunch*."

Up onstage the band starts playing a song called "I'm So Lonesome I Could Cry." This is one of Hank-3's granddaddy's sweetest and best tunes, but Hank-3 doesn't even look up. This is a truly great song, perhaps even the saddest song in the whole Hank Williams canon. But what we have here tonight, folks, is not perhaps the most inspired rendition of it. The beat is dragging behind the attractive blond singer like a bum leg. Still, she has a poignant enough tremor to her voice to convey the point of the song just fine, and here's the point of the song: Life is endless pain. The bar gets real quiet. The singer's eyes are closed. She sways. Her short denim dress and red cowboy boots are very sexy. At last Hank-3 manages a look up at that cute young thing onstage, singing his grandfather's most mournful dirge.

"OK, OK," he mutters under his breath. "You look great, honey, and you got a nice voice. Now go home and write your own goddamn songs."

.   .   .

It cannot honestly be said that Hank-3 looked exactly like his grandfather from birth. But that's only because newborns are not generally tall, gaunt, pallid individuals with hollowed-out cheekbones and haunted eyes. No, the healthy baby boy who was named Shelton Hank Williams was just a regular-looking infant, chubby and pink. His mama and his daddy loved baby Shelton very much. Baby Shelton's mama was a pretty lady with green eyes and a face shaped like a valentine. She grew up on a farm in Jane, Missouri, where, every Saturday night of the summer, the whole family used to sprawl out on the cool hardwood floor of the living room and listen to the Grand Ole Opry coming in live on the radio all the way from distant Nashville.

Baby Shelton's daddy was a good-looking young man named Hank Williams Jr., who was trying to make a distinctive name for himself as a country-music star. Although making such a distinction was perhaps not the easiest thing in this world to attempt if your name happened to contain the words *Hank* and *Williams*.

Because that's who baby Shelton's grandfather was—Hank Williams himself.

The Hillbilly Shakespeare. A tall, gaunt, pallid individual with hollowed-out cheekbones and haunted eyes, who wrote close to 150 songs before murdering himself with alcohol, drugs and sorrow at the age of 29. A dirt-poor, ignorant child born in 1923 to a dirt-poor, ignorant, drunk father (who swiftly abandoned him) on a grim chunk of tenant farmland in rural Alabama, Hank Williams was a most unlikely genius. A dreadful failure in school and too sickly for manual labor (Hank suffered lifelong crippling pain from undiagnosed spina bifida), the kid learned how to play guitar because it was the one thing that came easy for him. His teacher was an illiterate black singer named Tee-Tot, who worked the streets of Georgiana, Alabama, and who educated Hank in the mournful sound of deep-ass Delta blues. Hank took this sound and blended it—using the intuition of a natural-born alchemist—with the emotional gospel strains of Baptist hymns and the simple, fiddle-driven dance tunes of the dirt-poor, ignorant white folk he knew all too well, thereby inventing modern American country music. Hank Williams wrote every kind of country song there is, and he did it with a grace, a purity and a deceptive simplicity that made his work just plain better than the work of any country artist who has ever followed. He wrote drinking songs, train songs, jail songs, mama songs, honky-tonk songs, cowboy songs, Jesus songs and Devil songs. He wrote dozens upon dozens of meetin', cheatin' and retreatin' songs. He wrote "Hey, Good Lookin'." He wrote "There's a Tear in My Beer." He wrote "I Saw the Light." He wrote songs in ten minutes that were immediately chiseled into our collective cultural consciousness and haven't budged since.

He became the biggest musical star of his day, but he also fucked up every good break he ever got: Married a woman who drove him insane. Verbally abused his most steadfast audiences. Drove away his dearest friends. Pissed off every executive who tried to manage his career. Got fired from the Grand Ole Opry for being an alcoholic lowlife, got beat to pieces in stupid fights, got tossed in stupid jails for stupid displays of public drunkenness. He had, as his Nashville publisher, Roy Acuff, put it, "a million-dollar voice and a 10-cent brain." Hank Williams sped toward death like Jimmy Dean heading for that car wreck, and on New Year's Eve, 1952, he finally got where he was always destined to go. Died in the back of a Cadillac, on his way to a show, bundled up in blankets like a plague victim. Skinny and wasted (did I mention he was only 29 years old?), his spirit broken by mean women and melancholy, his body destroyed by booze, painkillers and excess, his lonesome heart just quit.

Exact cause of death? Well, you might say: inevitability.

So Hank Williams died, and he left behind him a dazzling musical legacy but also an ambitious young widow and a fatherless toddler son, whose name was Hank Williams Jr. And this poor kid got shoved out on the road at the earliest age by his mother, who put him out there onstage to make money for the family, obediently singing his dead father's songs. Hank Williams Jr. grew up starved for light under the long shadow of his father, a man he has referred to as being "something between God and John Wayne." He worked the lone road hard, putting on concerts and signing photographs for fans who would say to him, night after night,

"You're pretty good, kid. But you're not as good as your daddy." Then, when he was still just a teenager, he met that pretty farm girl with the face shaped like a valentine. He married her, and they had their own boy, Shelton Hank Williams. Things were nice for a while, but then it all went to hell. There was a quick divorce. Then there was a terrible accident, when Hank Williams Jr. fell off a mountaintop and had his face torn off and had to spend three years in and out of the hospital, getting his head completely rebuilt. Then came his own epic period of drinking, drugs, whoring, pissing off the Nashville establishment and fucking up. Out of which came his incredibly lucrative new career as Bocephus, a Dixie-fried, hell-raising southern-rock redneck icon. The critics tended to hate him, but he was a big commercial star. And not much of a father to his little boy.

So that brings us right up to Shelton Hank Williams. The most recent Hank. Hank-3. Fatherless child, as per the timeworn Williams family custom.

Shelton grew up in Nashville with the dimmest sense that there was something special about his name. Knew he had a dead, famous grandfather. Saw his daddy on TV all the time, but rarely in person. Shelton himself had been completely cut off from the fortune of both Hank Williamses. The mama with the valentine-shaped face raised her son as best she could, all by herself and on a retail store clerk's salary. She was a good Christian woman who loved her boy. But here's what young Shelton loved: music. And he wasn't into that corny old-timey Nashville shit, either, but the hardest, scariest music he could find. Even when he was 4 years old, he was already whaling on his drums to Kiss albums. When he got older, the music he loved got even harder—Henry Rollins, Black Sabbath, the Sex Pistols, the Misfits. ("If Marilyn Manson was around when I was a kid," Hank-3 says, "I would have listened to *that* and my mom would've shit even more bricks.") He got kicked out of a decent private school because his grades sucked, and once he hit the public-school system, he just quit on the whole education thing and started hanging out with the really bad kids. Grew his hair down to his ass but shaved his head on the sides. Got tattoos he liked to think his mama didn't know about. Joined up with some local punk bands with names like Bedwetter, Buzzkill, Rift. His mama sent him to Christian camps, where they tried to exorcise the Devil from him. They tried to scare him by telling him how listening to this satanic music would doom his soul to burn in hell for eternity. Shelton believed every last word of it, but that only made him more attracted to the angry music because he wanted to be scared.

All the while, though, there was this physical change coming over his whole being. His mama started to notice it when Shelton Hank Williams was about 12 years old. He got real tall on her all of a sudden. Starvation-skinny. And then there was something about the big Adam's apple growing out of his long throat, something about the endless thin line of a mouth, the arresting cheekbones, the tragic and cavernous eyes. He was starting to look just like his grandfather, and—believe you me—this is no kind of look for any little kid to have. Shelton seemed to be morphing back in time, reaching back into some lost genetic history book for his identity. And odd, too, that despite all his fascination for satanic music, he was always nagging his mother to tell him stories about Hank Williams Sr. And his mama tried to oblige, but there was only so much she herself knew. The man was a legend, she told Shelton, and so you'll always hear legendary stories about his legendary talent, his legendary drinking, his legendary downfall. If you want to truly understand the man, though, Shelton's mama said, make sure you seek out the people who actually knew him personally. Ask them what he was like.

And so, when Shelton Hank Williams was 15 years old—an angry, sensitive, scrawny, fatherless boy with a bony body and eardrums numbed by the unremitting screams of thrash punk music—he decided he wanted to meet Minnie Pearl. He'd heard that Minnie Pearl was one of his grandfather's best friends in the Nashville music scene of the 1950s, and he wanted to know who exactly his grandfather was as a person. So he called up Minnie Pearl, and she said, sure, she'd meet him at her Methodist church in Nashville. His mama drove him over there on the appointed day. Shelton stepped out of the car. He was an absolute calamity of a teenager, dressed in some aggressive heavy-metal concert T-shirt, with long and dirty hair and a dope smoker's bloodshot eyes. Minnie Pearl walked over to greet him. She was an old, sweet-faced lady, wearing a prim gingham dress and one of her famous Hee Haw hats with the dangling price tag. She took one close look at this kid and went stark pale. And it wasn't because of the way he was dressed, either.

"Lord, honey," Minnie Pearl said to Shelton Hank Williams. "You're a *ghost*."

.   .   .

The manner by which Hank-3 became a country-music artist is such a perfectly classic country-music story (full of dirtbaggery, poverty, woe, booze, out-of-wedlock births and sheriffs) that it almost feels like a jukebox wrote it. Dig this. Shelton Hank Williams hit his early twenties. And nobody was ever less connected to country music than he was. The guy was playing in punk bands, living with friends, making about $30 a night off his music, doing all kinds of drugs and screwing all kinds of girls. (Well, one kind.)

He'd been in trouble with The Law, but only for "stupid shit" that he doesn't want to discuss because "they cleared my record, and nobody would ever understand anyhow." But life was sweet. Playing on the bill with bands like Corrosion of Conformity, Bad Religion and Fugazi while doing drugs and chicks—that was about the breadth of the ambition of the grandson of Hank Williams. ("I never did figure on being a college man," he makes clear.) So one night he was playing a punk show, and "here come these two pigs, with a bunch of punk kids following behind to see what the fuck is up. The cops ask me if I'm Shelton Williams, and I say, yeah, I'm Shelton Williams. And then they serve me with the fucking papers."

Seems Shelton had enjoyed a one-night stand with some girl about three years ago, and she'd waited until now to let him know there had been a child born as a result. Cute little boy. Kid was 3 years old now, and the young mother wanted some child support paid. Not just in the future, but back into the past. To the tune of $24,000. Now, where the hell is a punk lowlife like Shelton Hank Williams supposed to come up with $24,000?

Clearly, it was time to cash in on the name. There was nothing to it but pure mercenary need at first. He strode into a showbiz manager's office in Nashville and introduced himself. He basically said, "My name is Hank Williams the third, and I need to raise some money." He probably didn't even have to say all that; his arresting physical resemblance to Hank Williams Sr. was his real calling card. No problem. The manager promptly sent Hank-3 off to Branson, Missouri—the kitsch-country capital of the world— and got him an act. Put him in a white hat and a white suit (that nicely covered up the tattoos) as if he were the Ghost of Hank Williams. The act sold out every day, rudimentary as it might have been.

Shelton was barely a guitar player at that time, and he knew virtually nothing about the country genre, so he had to learn the old Hank Williams songs as he went. Any educated Nashville audience would have hurled him off the stage in disgust, but the retirees and Korean War veterans and grandmotherly tourists of Branson ("Hell," Hank-3 recalls, "those people were all damn near asleep!") were perfectly nice to him. Of course, when Shelton's punk friends found out what he was up to, they were as horror-struck as snooty debutantes: "Omigod, Shelton! How could you?!" But Shelton told them, "Look, it's about a fucking paycheck to fix a fuckup that I gotta take care of, so shut the fuck up." It was like he'd always told them: "I wasn't gonna put on that fucking cowboy hat until I really needed to milk the money."

It was almost like a reprise of what had happened to Hank Williams Jr. all those years ago—a young boy pushed into the public eye to make money by singing an older man's tunes. But there was something different about this situation. Namely, that Hank-3 wasn't some reluctant 8-year-old kid out there onstage. Here instead was a young man with a heartily intact self-identity, who already had formed a sophisticated (although completely "other") musical aesthetic. Shelton Hank Williams, a genuine student of rock and punk, was clearly a person capable of being moved by music. As such, what else could he do but fall in love with his grandfather's work? It was inevitable. Because it's not as if they were making him sing Don Ho tunes up there; these were the songs of Hank Williams, which are (and I can't imagine anybody in the world contradicting me on this) the best songs ever written. Therefore, what happened to Hank-3 in Branson was not a humiliation; it was an education.

His managers paired him up with a young guy named Jason who played stand-up bass and who, like Shelton, was raised on hard rock like it was mother's milk. The two of them strapped on their hillbilly spelunking gear and climbed deep, deep down into a full-out study of the dark and rich caves of old-time country music.

"What you have to understand," Jason says today, "is that, even to punks, Hank Williams Sr. is revered in a manner that is beyond reproach. He's seen as a broken hero. He was an individualist who fought the commercial Nashville system. He was a genius who transcended genre, on the level of a Miles Davis or a Robert Johnson. Of course, me and Shelton fell in love with him. We were both so green back then, but doing that show in Branson was how we learned to play country music. Shelton's tribute to Hank Senior became a real tour de force. It all came so natural to him. He could automatically do what Hank Senior could do. I think maybe it's because he's so similarly constructed genetically. He could just sound like him, yodel like him, play guitar like him with such ease. Or maybe he has some of Hank's soul in him, I don't know. But he got it down fast."

Look, it would have been enough just to have been a great impersonator. What a gimmick! There's a woman wandering the world right now named Jett Williams, who, after years of ugly lawsuits, has finally been able to prove that she is the illegitimate daughter of Hank Williams Sr. These days Jett Williams travels all over the country, singing the songs of the daddy she never met, backed by a band that has featured members of the Drifting Cowboys, Hank's original band. And it's a good living, even if it's not the most original or dynamic act in the world. (Here's Hank-3's critique of Jett Williams, as delivered with his usual gentle decorum: "She's fucking bullshit. She's not even a real musician. I'm sorry, but if you're 50 years old and you can't sing a fucking note and you got something to say about your life or your family, then go write a fucking book, but get off the fucking stage.") OK, point taken. But the truth is that Hank-3 could have done this act just as easily, or even more easily, than Jett Williams. If all he was really after was the fast money, then he could have decided to be the Ghost of Hank Williams forever, wearing the white suit and singing the old songs and cashing checks at the First National Bank of Branson until the end of time.

Instead, this.

Shelton Hank Williams took on the mantle of country music as if it were the natural inheritance fate had always had in mind for him. He started writing his own country songs. He wrote drinking songs, train songs, jail songs, mama songs, honky-tonk songs, Jesus songs and Devil songs. He wrote meetin', cheatin' and retreatin' songs. It came so easy to him, this songwriting. And what little about it didn't come easy, he studied with a deliberation and a focus that damn near made a college man out of him after all.

He took one quick look around Nashville and recognized there was nothing being recorded in Music Square these days worth listening to for more than three minutes. What the hell are you supposed to make of modern country music, anyhow, when the biggest star of the day is that abs-of-steel spokesmodel Shania Twain? The whole commercial pop-crossover sanitized machine of Nashville made Hank-3 instinctively barf. So he officially named his grandfather as the center of his musical universe and then set out to explore the grizzled stellar bodies that orbit Hank William Sr.: Johnny Cash, Merle Haggard, Waylon Jennings, Willie Nelson, Buck Owens, George Jones, Wayne Hancock. He immersed himself in all of it. And then this child of punk took his studies on the road, perfecting his country style as he embarked on a punishing and apparently everlasting tour schedule, playing every venue there is—small towns, punk clubs, honky-tonk bars, redneck joints, county fairs and even the Grand Ole Opry. He played every weekend and four nights a week for five years, building up his fan base and honing his own musical style.

Furthermore, as part of his training to be a classic country-music star, he started living the classic country-music-star lifestyle, big-time. First thing he did was deliberately step up the drinking. "I never drank at all hardly before I started playing country music," he explains. "I just smoked a ton of pot and did drugs with my punk friends. But when I started playing country, I just had to become a fucking drunk. Just so I could understand the music, you know? Just so I could understand all the other old fucking drunks."

He also left his girlfriend of seven years, not because he didn't love her but because he wanted to experience "that kind of pain, so I could have something to write about." He was miserable without her, precisely as planned, and got a whole heap of songs out of it. He pushed his body to the edge of collapse with hooch, drugs, insane hours, shit food and every other manner of abuse. It got so bad that when his girlfriend staged an intervention, Hank-3's father and his father's good buddy Waylon Jennings (speaking of old fucking drunks) showed up, deeply concerned. And that's saying something, folks, because Hank Williams Jr. had not exactly been playing the role of doting parent thus far in the kid's life. Still, even the old man got worried and stuck Hank-3 into rehab in California. Hank-3 enjoyed rehab immensely, in that he met "some really cool motherfuckers in there," but he got fed up with the program and walked out one day. Walked out and informed the adorably concerned Bocephus and Waylon Jennings that he had no intention of returning to rehab for years yet, if ever.

"You guys just gotta give me time to max out," he told them. "I'm just doing the same thing you fuckers did."

Wretched, lonely, broke, drunk, physically depleted—it was all coming together for Hank-3. And then, just to make things even more country-music perfect, he actually had to sell off his pickup truck in order to pay his bills. And then his dog up and died on him one day. Right there in front of his very own eyes. The kindly gods of Nashville were obviously smiling down on him.

Hank Williams III, country-music star, had arrived.

And, my God, were people ever ready for him. With the release of that rocking debut album, Hank-3 became a critics' beloved darling overnight. They loved his authentic hillbilly sensibility and his hard-core, boss lyrics. (*I been roughed-up, beat up, I've been cut, I got a tattoo at a tender age. . . .*) The critics, full of nostalgia for his grandfather (and full of irritation over decades of his father's lowest-common-denominator are-you-ready-for-some-football musical shenanigans), tripped over their own tongues trying to articulate their praise. They said that Hank-3 had "the songwriting skills and raw appeal of his forebears," that he sang "like he was born at a roadhouse," that he was "goose-bumpy good," that his songs suggested Hank Sr.'s "emotional ache and longing, and they do it over a most refined sense of melody," that "talent skips a generation."

It all may sound hyperbolic, but truly, the album swings. And as for the live act? There's nothing like it. Because Hank-3 has never left his punk roots behind him. Sometimes, if the mood is right, he plays one set of his extraordinarily good country music and then he graciously warns all the older folks in the crowd that they might want to get the hell out before it gets too loud and then he kicks into a hard, angry thrash-metal punk set. The line dancing stops abruptly, and the mosh pit forms, and the night turns very surreal indeed. Hank-3 and his band are equally comfortable in both styles of music. And the crazy thing is, they don't even change their instruments when they change their form. The very same stand-up bass, fiddle, guitar and drum that created a smooth, authentic Texas honky-tonk sound one minute transform into a tightly rendered, pounding buzz saw of screaming rage the next. Hard to even know what to call this transformation. I've heard it described as punkabilly, psychobilly, hellbilly, cow punk. . . . It kind of defies description.

It's something that only Shelton Hank Williams can do. And it's kind of unbelievably great.

.   .   .

The way he lives? Oh boy.

Hank-3 uses as his address this ramshackle old house outside Nashville that he shares with a bunch of other people. Hard to tell who really lives in this house and who's merely dropping by this house for the evening to sell pot or eat pizza or have sex with someone who actually does live in the house. Hank-3 himself is hardly ever home, since he basically lives on his tour bus. But he does have a bedroom here, which looks like the bedroom of a disgruntled teenager—all posters and porn and filthy laundry. He's "home" right now, for what that's worth. He's had three days off from his tour, although he hasn't enjoyed it much, since he's been puking in agony from the flu the whole time. Hank-3's tour bus is parked in the front yard of the house at the moment, resting in the uncut grass amid the crickets and fireflies, waiting for him. The band members are gradually gathering at Hank-3's house, slowly rejoining after their time off. They're all showered and rested, for now and for once. The plan is to leave around midnight for the fourteen-hour drive to Texas and the next leg of this endless Hank Williams III tour.

As for Hank-3 himself, he's in his skanky bedroom, hidden behind a closed door, deep in a business meeting with his entertainment lawyer. Hank-3's entertainment lawyer is an intelligent young woman named Elizabeth Gregory, who might appear to have the toughest client in all of Nashville. (Consider this typically discreet Hank-3 nugget of wisdom: "I have the respect of all the players and old hands, but not the lawyers and businessmen, and that's fine. I give them the finger, and that's exactly what they need—more people giving them the finger.") So, yes, he's a bit of a pain in the hole, what with his knee-jerk, punk-rock, white-trash distrust of anything corporate and his reactionary refusal to acknowledge that anybody who holds a real job could ever possibly hold a real opinion. And that does tire out Elizabeth Gregory and make her lawyering pretty hard. But she deals with Hank-3 nonetheless, for two reasons. First of all, she adores him. She adores him for the same reason everyone who works with Hank-3 ultimately adores him: because he's such a funny, strange, renegade but oddly tenderhearted character. He's such a vulnerable doofus, under his fuck-this, fuck-that exterior. Very sweet and polite, in his way—"always jumping up to get the door for you or give you his seat," says his best friend, Jason. With that physical frailty about him (his body has no more meat on it than a broken umbrella) and with that face (the baby-soft skin looks as if it's never been shaved, but the eyes are famished), he begs to be cared for.

Hank-3's grandfather inspired this same kind of affection in people, using that same trick of appealing helplessness hidden under outrageously bad behavior. Everyone who worked with Hank Williams Sr. adored him, too, even when he was in full-out fuckup form. ("I am trying to be your friend 'cause I know you need a friend," wrote Fred Rose, Hank's famously steadfast manager, in a heartbreaking 1948 letter to the nose-diving hillbilly genius. "The guys that are drinking with you are not your friends, they just like the whiskey you buy and when you run out of money enough to buy them whiskey they will leave you all by yourself and tell everyone you are a drunk. . . . Don't get the idea I'm trying to bawl you out because I'm just trying to see you become what I know you can become.")

And that brings us to the second reason Hank-3's entertainment lawyer, the very intelligent Elizabeth Gregory, ultimately sticks around: because she's just trying to see him become what she knows he can become. Because she happens to believe he's a genius.

"I think we're all kind of afraid to say what we think he could become," Elizabeth tells me later that evening, when Hank-3 has holed up in his room all alone to smoke pot and pack up his clothes for the ride to Texas. "He's making music here that simply does not sound like anything else anyone has ever done. It's not only that he plays punk and country separately; he's starting to combine them more and more into something totally new. That's what his next album will be all about. Think about it—a hard-rock sound with that twangy country voice of his? It's incredible. My secret belief is that he's capable of becoming another American icon, someone whose magnetism is so powerful and whose individual musical style is so immune to the fads of time that he could endure forever. I think he could become a legend."

Legend, of course, is not a word to be tossed around like some cheap Frisbee. Although it is tempting to imagine legendary status for Hank-3, because he damn sure has the pedigree for it. And then there's what Merle Kilgore said. Merle Kilgore is a famous songwriter and Nashville legend in his own right. He traveled with Hank Williams Sr. back in the 1950s, and he's handled the career of Hank Williams Jr. for decades now.

"What do I think of Hank Williams III?" says Merle. "I think he's very talented, and I think he'll make it big. If he doesn't die."

Yeah, well. He's got the pedigree for that too.

.　　.　　.

Living on a tour bus is like living in a submarine. Smells like it, feels like it. A compact, airtight metal confine, rocking gently in the deep currents of travel. Each guy in the band has his own coffin-size berth on the bus with a curtain for privacy and a wee reading light to make it feel all homey. The front of the bus is a common living space, where the guys sit and drink beer and tell stories. The back of the bus is a dark little caboose of a room, and that's where Shelton Hank Williams lives. He spends his life back there, working on new songs and listening to tapes of past shows to puzzle out improvements. He's got a good stereo system in this little room, along with guitars and a TV and a VCR and bottles of whiskey and tons of pot. It's not that I want to harp on the pot, but it is absolutely amazing how much pot this guy smokes. He smokes joints the way chain-smokers smoke cigarettes—one after another after another after another—and he chain-smokes cigarettes too. I honestly don't know where he finds the time for it all.

The bus leaves Nashville for Terrell, Texas, around one o'clock in the morning, which is only the beginning of a new day for Hank-3. Once we're on the road, I hang out back there in his room with him for a good long while. We drink some whiskey together. And I don't generally indulge, but we smoke a whole lot of pot together, too. (What the hell, I figure. When in Nashville . . .) Also, I'm hoping if I get plenty doped up, it'll help me shake off the chilly edginess I still have around this guy. After two days of being around Hank-3, I'm still unable to get over the feeling that I'm in the room with a phantasm. That hungry face, that skeletal form, that twangy Depression-era country voice with so much drawl in it that it sounds like he's pulling taffy with every word, that pallor, that weariness, that undertone of melancholy—it's all so *Hank Williams.*

It's a personal curse of Shelton Hank Williams that he tends to freak people out like this. He was booked once to play on *Late Night With Conan O'Brien,* and during the sound check he lit into an old Hank Senior song to warm up. One of the guys from Conan's road-weary crew just lost his shit when he heard that voice and saw that face. This big, strong man came up to Hank-3's manager, all shaken and pale, rolling up his sleeves to show off his goose bumps.

"Hey, man," he said, and he was almost angry about it. "That just ain't *right.*"

.   .   .

In the back of his bus, Hank-3 is fidgety as ever. He's still complaining of stomach cramps, and his sinuses are bothering him from the change in climate, and he keeps trying to arrange his body comfortably around his brittle, yard-long femurs. He puts in a CD of one of his heroes—a mournful hillbilly freak named Hasil Adkins who plays the rawest, most haunted music I've ever heard outside the Mississippi Delta. While Hasil Adkins moans, wrestles with the Devil and howls at Jesus, Hank-3 explains how he loves the guy "for outdrinking, outfucking, outfighting anyone and for being a total white-trash alcoholic motherfucker who dedicates his music to every state prison he's ever been in."

Here's what's on Hank-3's mind tonight—music, God, death and his ancestors. Hank-3 tries to explain how much he needs both kinds of music he plays; the punk to exorcise his rage, the country to bring him some kind of sad peace. He tells me about how he doesn't own anything of his grandfather's except one necktie, which he made the curators of a museum at the Grand Ole Opry give him after a show: "I was like, 'Come on! You all got a whole shitload of Hank's stuff here, and the guy is my fucking grandfather, and I got nothing!'" And then, God. Hank-3 definitely has some things to say about God tonight. First of all, about how completely he believes in all of it—in Jesus, in the dark forces of evil, in the reality of possession, in heaven and hell. "I know I'm a sinner," he says. "Look at me. I drink. I do drugs. I don't know my own son. I cuss all the fucking time. I live wild and free and reckless, but that's the price you have to pay to rock. I just hope I'll live to 60, and then I'll turn to the Lord and say, 'I'm ready for you now. I got all the time in the world to start making it up to you now.'"

(For an example of how just such a plan can work successfully and on this exact time frame, see: Johnny Cash. For an example of how it can backfire horribly, see: Hank Williams Sr.)

Hank-3 talks about the elderly people who come to his shows sometimes just to touch him or to deliver him messages from his grandfather that they claim have come to them in dreams. A lot of times, he says, they bring warnings from Hank Sr. to take it easy on the drinking and the drugs. But Hank-3 talks about his own drinking and his drug use with a resigned lack of concern. "If you're on the road, that's the price you have to pay," he says. "Just subtract fifteen years from your life and fucking deal with it." And anyhow, he says, he's got it under control. He loves his life and doesn't want to die, and he's careful not to mix different drugs together, and he's never missed a show because he was too fucked-up to play. Of course, it hurts him to know that his mom isn't "too happy right now" with him, what with the substance abuse and all the raw shit he says in public, but that's the reality of being a rock star's mom. Certainly, he muses, "Marilyn Manson's mom must go through the same thing." I tell Hank-3 this is the first time I have ever considered the concept "Marilyn Manson's mom," and he sighs and says, "Yeaaahhhh . . . well, everybody's got one."

But it's not true that his mom isn't too happy with him. Gwen Williams is proud of Shelton. Loves him immensely. Still sees him as a sweet and fun boy. She's just worried. She believes "there's a gift that runs through this family, but the abuse is always there, too. It's almost like a destiny with these men."

What really makes her angry, though, is the way the world seems to want to push her fragile young son into that devastating lifestyle. There's such an alluring symmetry to the idea of Hank-3's being as self-destructive as Hank–1 and Hank–2 that people actually try to encourage it. At every Hank Williams III show, there's no end of people lining up to buy him shots of whiskey as he performs. They all want to participate in this dynastic downfall. When he slams back the shots, the crowd cheers and Hank-3 always says grimly, "Thank you, everyone. Thank you for applauding my addiction."

As the bus rolls on, Hank-3 sets to talking about his dad. I mention that Hank Jr. wouldn't be interviewed for this story, and Hank-3 says, yeah, well, what can you expect? Typical. He admits he got a shitty deal from Hank Jr. as a kid. Yeah, he was the dumped son. Yeah, he barely knows the guy at all. He remembers visiting with his dad once when Bocephus was on tour, back when Shelton wasn't more than 11 years old. The wildness and thrill and terror of it. All those drugs and women everywhere. Roadies used to give

Shelton "finger sips" of their drinks—letting him dip his little fingers in their bourbon and lick it off. They'd leave him in a room with a half-dressed woman and tell her to "let the kid have some fun." He remembers another time, when arrangements were made for him to meet his father at some airport for a brief once-a-year rendezvous and "I made my mom stop to buy me a cowboy hat so he would be proud of me, and just that one stop made us ten minutes late. So he was already gone by the time I showed up. And then I was left to cry all day about it." He remembers asking his dad for a material possession only once—a new drum set. Hank Jr. said, "Geez, son, I don't know. That sounds pretty expensive." And this, Shelton says, "from a guy who was making $80,000 a night in concessions alone!"

All of which makes it even stranger that the position Shelton Hank Williams always takes with his father in the end is that of defensive linebacker.

Conceding his own sadness at not having a dad to speak of, he then steps up to defend Hank Jr.'s character. ("Think of how hard it was for him to grow up under that shadow!") He defends Hank Jr.'s music. ("He can play every instrument on that stage, and he's a great performer.") He even defends Hank Jr.'s decision to cut baby Shelton out of his existence. ("How could he know how to treat me? He never had a father. And with me being the kid of the divorce, he's always bound to have some resentment about me.")

Such a weird, sympathetic stance. But if you take a closer look at Hank Jr., you'll see that he is the person here most in need of a sympathetic perspective. Consider the difficulty of his situation. He spends his life struggling to create a self-identity in country music despite having a father whose discography is the very King James Bible of country music. He finally gets out from under his daddy's firm thumb by becoming his own musician. OK, so he's no Hillbilly Shakespeare, but he is the crown prince of beer-swilling redneck anthems and he is his own man at last. But no sooner does Hank Jr. get himself all commercially successful and separated from the original icon than this abandoned son of his shows up on the music scene, looking and sounding just like the old man, and creates a phenomenally good debut album. And every serious music critic in the country suddenly starts saying, "Looks like talent skips a generation." What an unexpected blow. What a cruel double-whammy ego slam. *You're pretty good, boy. But you're not as good as your daddy.*

Oh, and by the way—*you're not as good as your son, either.*

And what a psychic earthquake this must create for Hank-3, too! To be killing off his father even as he resurrects his grandfather? It's all too much. It's no wonder the boy drinks.

OK, now I really *am* stoned.

The little back room of this bus is blue with smoke, and so is my brain. So now I'm finally in a place where I can dare to ask Shelton Hank Williams the awkward but essential question I've been mulling over since I first heard him singing so dolefully and beautifully.

"Listen," I say. "Forgive me for asking, and I'm not sure how to bring this up. But are you the ghost of Hank Williams? Do you ever wonder that? Do you ever wonder if you might be . . . um . . . *him?*"

He doesn't answer at first. The road rolls by below us. Hasil Adkins wrestles with the Devil in the background of our silence.

I say, "Just speak your mind, Hank-3. Don't let me stop you." He cranks his skinny neck around and looks up at the ceiling. He says, "I don't know. I could be. Maybe. I definitely feel him with me sometimes, when I'm writing country songs and everything is going good. I can feel him there, at least."

"And what does that feel like?"

The grandson of Hank Williams smiles his tired, ancient smile and says . . .

"Warm."

Terrell, Texas.

A flat brown map spot outside Dallas. There's a bar here called Rustlers, where Hank Williams III is booked to play tonight. It's one of those huge-ass Texas productions of a bar, with a dance floor as big as any pasture. There's weather brewing. Tornado clouds. Hank-3's fiddler says, "I got a bad feeling about this. Texas dance hall? Low-pressure system building? I bet we see at least four brawls tonight."

By 7 P.M. Shelton Hank Williams has not woken up yet. Fanbelt, the bus driver, says, "He won't get up until ten minutes before the show. Never does. The boy doesn't hardly ever see daylight."

By 8:00 there is noise coming from Hank-3's little room at the back of the bus. Hard, loud punk music is playing. I hear a string of muffled yodels. He's warming up back there.

At 8:30 the owner of the dance hall walks bowleggedly out across the parking lot to the bus. He knocks on the door and asks if he can meet Hank Williams III in person. Hank-3 emerges from his back room at last, looking like he's limping out of a hospital after a long stay. The owner of the dance hall welcomes him to Terrell, Texas. Hank-3 graciously thanks him for the welcome. The owner asks if Hank-3 wouldn't mind signing this old record album he's got of Hank Williams songs, and Hank-3 graciously obliges. And then the owner of the dance hall busts forth a huge grin and pulls out a nice, big bottle of Jack Daniel's.

"And this here's a little present for you," he says. "Hell, you can't very well sing like your granddaddy without getting all lickered up, now, can you?"

"No, I guess not," says Hank-3, and he graciously thanks the dance-hall owner for the kind and thoughtful gift.

The bar is full of rawboned country people. The men have faces like saddle leather, and the women are wearing their once-a-week makeup. There are a lot of elderly people here tonight. One old man tells me he's come out on a rare public appearance because "country music is all about a story to tell, about the good and bad of life. The real times. Telling those stories is what made Hank Williams Sr. so good. I hear this boy does the same kind of thing as his granddaddy, and I hope to find it's true."

I ask the old guy if he's heard that Hank-3 also sings hard punk music, and he shakes his head and says, "Well, shit-damn!"

Hank-3 comes onstage without any showy moves. He's wearing a cool old cowboy shirt and a beat-to-shit cowboy hat. His boots are held together with duct tape. His hair hangs down his back in a thin braid, like a whip. He just steps into the light and starts singing. The band is tight as a screw, and it doesn't take but half a song for the old man beside me to realize that what he had hoped to find true *is* true. Ghost-white Shelton Hank Williams is singing in that voice as sharp and chilling as a train whistle. He sings an interesting mix. He sings more of his granddaddy's songs tonight than I might have expected—giving us wonderful versions of "Your Cheatin' Heart" and "Lovesick Blues." He even throws in one of his dad's shit-kicking tunes, "Women I've Never Had," to satisfy that kind of fan. He plays a few old Johnny Cash classics, just because they rule. It's his own songs, though, that really kill tonight. They are so good. So original and familiar at the same time. As the first strains begin, you can see people hesitating on the dance floor. You can almost hear them thinking, *What Hank Williams song is that? How is it I've never heard that Hank Williams song before?* They cock their heads and listen close, and then it dawns on them: They have never heard this Hank Williams song before because it's *new*.

I'm gonna do some drinkin', Hank-3 wails. *I'm gonna drink all the whiskey I can find. . . .*

The grateful, rawboned country people partner up and spin around and take a break from their two-stepping only to stare at the young man on the small stage. They look up at him frequently,

as though to check their eyesight. As though to reassure themselves that what they see is real. They all seem a little spooked. But
if they should step outside for a moment to breathe some fresh air
or to privately kiss one another, they will see something even more
spooky—the pale and boiling storm clouds, which have moved so
low to earth tonight you'd swear to God they were trying to touch
the very roof of this sprawling Texas dance hall.

Zoetrope: All-Story

WINNER, FICTION

Fair Warning

In this award-winning short story, Pulitzer Prize-winning author Robert Olen Butler creates a confident young woman auctioneer who can sell just about anything, but is unlucky in love. As she meets and captures the man of her dreams, Butler takes readers along for the raucous ride.

Robert Olen Butler

Fair Warning

Perhaps my fate was sealed when I sold my three-year-old sister. My father had taken me to a couple of cattle auctions, not minding that I was a girl—this was before Missy was born, of course—and I'd loved the fast talk and the intensity of the whole thing. So the day after my seventh birthday party, where Missy did a song for everyone while I sat alone, my chin on my hand, and meditated behind my still uncut birthday cake, it seemed to me that here was a charming and beautiful little asset that I had no further use for and could be liquidated to good effect. So I gathered a passel of children from our gated community in Houston, kids with serious money, and I had Missy do a bit of her song once more, and I said, "Ladies and gentlemen, no greater or more complete perfection of animal beauty ever stood on two legs than the little girl who stands before you. She has prizewinning breeding and good teeth. She will neither hook, kick, strike, nor bite you. She is the pride and joy and greatest treasure of the Dickerson family and she is now available to you. Who will start the bidding for this future blue-ribbon winner? Who'll offer fifty cents? Fifty cents. Who'll give me fifty?" I saw nothing but blank stares before me. I'd gotten all these kids together but I still hadn't quite gotten them into the spirit of the thing. So I looked one of these kids in the eye and I said, "You, Tony Speck. Aren't your parents rich enough to give you an allowance of fifty cents?" He made a hard, scrunched-up face and he said, "A dollar." And I was off. I finally sold her for six dollars and twenty-five cents to a quiet girl up the street whose daddy was in oil. She was an only child, a thing I made her feel sorry about when the bidding slowed down at five bucks.

Needless to say, the deal didn't go through. Missy tried to go get her dolls and clothes before she went off to what I persuaded her was a happy, extended sleep-over, and Mama found out. That night my parents and Missy ate dinner in the dining room and I was put in the den with a TV tray to eat my spaghetti alone. If I wanted to sell one of them then I wanted to sell them all, they claimed, and eating alone was supposed to show me how it would feel. I was supposed to be lonely. Of course, they were wrong. It was just my sister I wanted to dispose of. And all I was feeling was that somehow Missy had done it to me again. She was at my daddy's elbow in the other room, offering her cheek for pinching. I felt pissed about that but I also felt exhilarated at the thought of what I'd done at the sale. I figured she wasn't worth even half the final bid.

And so I sit now, at another stage of my life, at another pasta dinner with much to think about, and I am forty years old—which is something to think about in and of itself. But instead I go back only a few weeks, to the Crippenhouse auction. Near the end of the morning, after I'd gaveled down dozens of lots of major artwork for big money from a big crowd that nearly filled our Blue Salon, a tiny, minor Renoir came up. Barely six inches square. One fat naked young woman with a little splash of vague foliage behind her. Generic Impressionism on a very small scale. Like a near-sighted man looking through the knothole in a fence without his glasses. And yet I stood before these wealthy people and I knew them well, most of them, knew them from playing them at this podium many times before and meeting them at parties and studying the social registers and reading their bios and following their ups and downs and comings and goings in the society columns and the *Wall Street Journal* and even the *Times* news pages. I stood before them and there was a crisp smell of ozone in the air and the soft clarity of our indirect lights and, muffled in our plush drapery and carpeting, the rich hush of money well and profusely spent. I looked around, giving them a moment to catch their breath. The estimate on the Renoir was $140,000 and sometimes we'd put a relatively low estimate on a thing we knew would be hot in order to draw in more sharks looking for an easy kill, and if you knew what you were doing, they wouldn't even realize that you'd actually gotten them into a feeding frenzy until they'd done something foolish. But this was one of those items where we'd jacked up the estimate on a minor piece that had one prestige selling point in order to improve its standing. Renoir. He's automatically a big deal, we were saying. In fact, though, we were going to be happy getting 80 percent of the estimate. I had just one bid in the book lying open before me—mine was bound in morocco with gilt pages—which is where an auctioneer notes the order bids, the bids placed by the big customers with accounts who are too busy sunning themselves somewhere in the Mediterranean or cutting deals down in Wall Street to attend an auction. And for the little Renoir, the one book bid wasn't even six figures, and I knew the guy had a thing for fat women.

So I looked out at the bid-weary group and I said, "I know you people," though at the moment I said this, my eyes fell on a man on the far left side about eight rows back who, in fact, I did not know. There were, of course, others in the room I didn't know, but this man had his eyes on me and he was as small-scaled and indistinct to my sight as the fat girl in the painting. But he was fixed on me and I could see his eyes were dark and his hair was dark and slicked straight back and his jaw was quite square and I know those aren't enough things to warrant being caught stopping and looking at somebody and feeling some vague sense of possibility—no, hardly even that—feeling a surge of heat in your brow and a little catch and then quickening of your breath.

I forced my attention back to the matter at hand. "I know you," I repeated, getting back into the flow that had already started in me. "You're wearing hundred-dollar underpants and carrying three-thousand-dollar fountain pens."

They laughed. And they squirmed a little. Good.

I said, "You will not relinquish even the smallest detail of your life to mediocrity."

Now they stirred. I am known for talking to my bidders. Cajoling them. Browbeating them, even. At Christie's and Sotheby's they would grumble at what I do. But they value me at Nichols and Gray for these things. And my regulars here know what to expect.

I said, "But there is a space in the rich and wonderful place where you live that is given over to just such a thing, mediocrity. A column in the foyer, a narrow slip of wall between two doors. You know the place. Think about it. Feel bad about it. And here is Pierre-Auguste Renoir, dead for eighty years, the king of the most popular movement in the history of serious art, ready to turn that patch of mediocrity into a glorious vision of corporeal beauty. Lot One-fifty-six. Entitled 'Adorable Naked French Woman with Ample Enough Thighs to Keep Even John Paul Gibbons in One Place.'" And with this I looked directly at John Paul Gibbons, who was in his usual seat to the right side in the second row. He was as famous in the world of these people for his womanizing as for his money. I said, "Start the bidding at forty thousand, John Paul."

He winked at me and waved his bidder's paddle and we were off.

"Forty thousand," I said. "Who'll make it fifty?"

Since John Paul was on my right, I suppose it was only natural for me to scan back to the left to draw out a competing bid. I found myself looking toward the man with the dark eyes. How had I missed this face all morning? And he raised his paddle.

"Fifty thousand . . ." I cried, and I almost identified him in the way I'd been thinking of him. But I caught myself. ". . . to the gentleman on the left side." I was instantly regretful for having started this the way I had. Was Renoir's pudgy beauty his type?

My auctioneer self swung back to John Paul Gibbons to pull out a further bid, even as thoughts of another, covert self in me raced on.

"Sixty from Mr. Gibbons," I said, thinking, *If she is his type, then I'm shit out of luck. All my life I've been in desperate pursuit of exactly the wrong kind of butt.*

And sure enough, Dark-Eyes bid seventy. I was happy for womanhood in general, I guess, if this were true, that men were coming back around to desiring the likes of this plumped-up pillow of a young woman but I was sad for me and I looked over my shoulder at her and my auctioneer self said, "Isn't she beautiful?" and my voice betrayed no malice.

John Paul took it to eighty and Dark-Eyes took it to ninety while I paused inside and grew sharp with myself. You've become a desperate and pathetic figure, Amy Dickerson, growing jealous over a stranger's interest in the image of a naked butterball. "Ninety-five to the book," I said.

And there was a brief pause.

I swung back to John Paul. A man like this—how many times had *he* merely seen a woman across a room and he knew he had to get closer to her, had to woo and bed her if he could? Was I suddenly like him? "A hundred? Can you give me a hundred? No way you people are going to let a Renoir go for five figures. You'd be embarrassed to let that happen."

John Paul raised his paddle. "A hundred thousand to John Paul Gibbons."

The bid had run past the order bid in my book and a basic rule for an auctioneer is to play only two bidders at a time. But I didn't want to look at Dark-Eyes again. I should have gone back to him, but if he had a thing for this woman who looked so unlike me, then to hell with him, he didn't deserve it. If he was bidding for it—and this thought made me grow warm again—if he was bidding for it merely out of his responsiveness to me, then I didn't want him to waste his money on a second-rate piece. "One ten?" I said, and I raised my eyes here on the right side and another paddle went up, about halfway back, a woman who lived on Park Avenue with a house full of Impressionists and a husband twice her age. "One ten to Mrs. Fielding on the right."

She and John Paul moved it up in a few moments to the estimate, one forty. There was another little lull. I said, "It's against you, Mrs. Fielding." Still she hesitated. I should turn to my left, I knew. Dark-Eyes could be waiting to give a bid. But instead I went for all the other Mrs. Fieldings. I raised my hand toward the painting, which sat on an easel behind me and to my left. My auctioneer self said, "Doesn't she look like that brief glimpse you had of your dearest aunt at her bath when you were a girl? Or even your dear mama? Her essence is here before you, a great work of art." But the other me, with this left arm lifted, thought—for the first time ever from this podium, because I was always a cool character in this place, always fresh and cool—this other me that had gone quite inexplicably mad thought, *My God what if I'm sweating and he's looking at a great dark moon beneath my arm?*

This man had gotten to me from the start, unquestionably, and this thought snaps me back to the trendiest Italian restaurant in Manhattan, where I sit now waiting for my pasta. There are impulsive attractions that make you feel like you're in control of your life somehow—here's something I want, even superficially, and I'm free to grab it. Then there are the impulsive attractions that only remind you how freedom is a fake. You might be free to *pursue* your desires, but you're never free to *choose* them.

And I had no choice that morning. I lowered my arm abruptly in spite of the fact I hadn't sweat from nerves since I was sixteen. But I'd already made my selling point. I'd stoked the desire of others and Mrs. Fielding took up the pursuit, as did another wealthy woman for a few bids and then another—I played them two at a time—and then it was one of the monied women against a little man who dealt in art in the Village and should have known better about this piece, which made me wonder if *he'd* had a life-changing glimpse of his corpulent mama at her bath, but that was the kind of thing my auctioneer self *rightly* ruminated on during the rush of the bidding and I had more or less put Dark-Eyes out of my mind and we climbed over a quarter of a million and my boss was beaming in the back of the room and then it stopped, with the little man holding a bid of $260,000. "It's against you," I said to the woman still in the bidding. She shook her head faintly to say she was out of it.

There is a moment that comes when you've done your work well when the whole room finally and abruptly goes, *What the hell are we doing?* I knew we had reached that moment. But I would have to look back to my left before I could I push on to a conclusion.

"Two sixty," I said. "Do I hear two seventy? Two seventy for your sweet Aunt Isabelle? Two sixty then. Fair warning."

Now I looked to him.

His eyes were fixed on me as before and then he smiled, and the unflappable Amy Dickerson, master auctioneer, suddenly flapped. I lost the flow of my words and I stopped. It seemed that he was about to raise his paddle. *Don't do it*, I thought, trying to send a warning to him across this space. I wrenched my attention away and cried, "Sold! For two hundred and sixty thousand dollars."

I normally use the lull after the gavel, while the lot just sold is taken away and the next one set up, to assess certain buyers that I've learned to read. One woman who sits perfectly still through the bidding for items she has no interest in will suddenly start shuffling her feet when something she wants is about to come up. Another starts smoothing her hair. One distinguished retired surgeon, who always wears a vest, will lift up slightly from where he's sitting, first one cheek and then the other, as if he's passing a perfect pair of farts. But on that morning I was still struggling with an unreasonable obsession. I thought of nothing but this complete stranger and I finally realized that the only way to exorcise this feeling was to confront it, but when at last I worked up the courage to look once more to my left, Dark-Eyes had gone.

.   .   .

"I was relieved," I told my sister the next day at a sushi lunch. "But damn if I wasn't wildly disappointed as well."

"So?"

"So? There sat a man like John Paul Gibbons and I'm suddenly acting like his dark twin sister."

"Is John Paul still after you?"

"You're missing the point," I said.

She shrugged. "I don't think so. You're forty, Amy. You're single. It's hormones and lifestyle."

"Yow," I cried.

"Did you get some wasabi up your nose?"

In fact I was merely thinking, *If you hadn't gone back for your dolls and your clothes I wouldn't be sitting here with you once a week out of familial devotion listening to your complacent hardness of heart.* Though I realized, trying to be honest with myself, that my alternative today—and most days—was eating lunch on my own, bolting my food, avoiding the company of men who bored me, a list that got longer every day, it seemed. I resented her stumbling onto a half-truth about me and so I leaned toward her and said, "You're thirty-six yourself. You haven't got much longer to be smug."

"That reminds me," Missy said. "Jeff mentioned he saw a poster up in Southampton for the charity auction you're doing."

"How does what I said remind you of that?" I put as much muscle in my voice as I could, but she looked at me as if I'd simply belched. She wasn't going to answer. She had no answer. I knew the answer: her loving husband was her shield against turning forty. Right. Maybe.

"Mama said she hoped you'd call sometime," Missy said.

I was still following the track under Missy's surface. Mama— still living on a street with a gate in Houston—thought that a beautiful woman like me, as she put it, was either stupid or a lesbian not to have been married when I hit forty. And she knew, as God was her witness, that I wasn't a lesbian.

"She hated Daddy by the time she was forty," I said.

"Calm down," Missy said. "Drink some green tea. It's like a sedative."

"And he hated her."

Missy looked away, her mouth tightened into a thin red line.

Okay. I felt guilty for rubbing this in. I'd arrived a couple of times myself at something like hatred for the man I was living with. In another era, I might have already gone ahead and married each of them—Max and Fred—and it would have been no different for me than for Mama.

I followed Missy's eyes across the room. She was looking at no one, she was just getting pissed with me, but there was a man leaning across a table for two touching the wrist of the woman he was with. He was talking quickly, ardently. I looked away, conscious of my own wrist. Whose gesture was that from my own life? Either Max or Fred. I twisted my mind away. *Who cares which one?* I thought. Whoever it was would say, Amy, Amy, Amy, you get so logical when you're angry. And yet the touch on my wrist meant he still thought I was a quaking bundle of nerves beneath the irrefutable points I'd been making against him. All he had to do was touch me there and he'd wipe the logic away and prevail. But no way, Mister. I never lost my logic in an argument, even though sometimes there were tears, as meaningless as getting wet for somebody you're just having sex with. I'm crying, I'd say to him, but don't you dare take it wrong, you son of a bitch. It was Max.

"I've got to go," my sister said, and I looked at her a little dazedly, I realized, and we both rose and we hugged and kissed on the cheek. We split the bill and my half of the tip was six dollars and twenty-five cents. I watched her gliding away out the door and then I stared at the money in my hand.

.   .   .

The auction business is built on the three Ds: debt, divorce, and death. The next morning Arthur Gray sat me down in his office with WQXR playing low in the background—some simpering generic baroque thing was going on—and he fluttered his eyebrows at me over the quarter of a million I'd gotten for the worst Renoir oil he'd ever seen and then he sent me off to an estate evaluation on Central Park West. The death of a reclusive woman who apparently had had an eye for Victoriana. Her only son would meet me.

The doorman had my name and I went up in an elevator that smelled faintly of Obsession and I rang the bell at the woman's apartment. And when the door swung open I found myself standing before Dark-Eyes.

I'm sure I let the creature beneath the auctioneer show her face in that moment: the little half smile that came over Dark-Eyes told me so. The smile was faintly patronizing, even. But I forgave him that. I was, after all, making myself a gawking fool at the moment. The smile also suggested, I realized, that he had requested me specifically for this evaluation. I focused on that thought, even as I put on my professional demeanor.

"I'm Amy Dickerson," I said. "Of Nichols and Gray."

He bowed faintly and he repeated my name. "Ms. Dickerson." He was a little older than I thought, from close up, and even handsomer. His cheekbones were high and his eyes were darker than I'd been able to see from the podium. "I'm Trevor Martin. Mrs. Edward Martin's son."

"I'm glad," I said, and to myself I said, *What the hell does that mean?* "To meet you," I added, though I fooled neither of us. I was glad he was here and I was here. The only thing I wasn't glad about was that his name was Trevor. It was a name made for a rainy climate, and spats.

"Come in," he said, and I did and I nearly staggered from the Victorian profusion of the place. The foyer was stuffed full: an umbrella stand and a grandfather clock and a stand-up coatrack and a dozen dark-framed hunting scenes and a gilt-wood-and-gesso mirror and a Gothic-style cupboard and a papier-mâché prie-dieu with shell-inlaid cherubs and a top rail of red velvet, and Trevor—I had to think of him as that now, at least till I could call him Dark-Eyes to his face—Trevor was moving ahead of me and I followed him into Mrs. Edward Martin's parlor—and my eyes could not hold still, there was such a welter of things, and I went from fainting bench to pump organ to the William Morris Strawberry Thief wallpaper—the walls were aswirl with vines and flowers and strawberries and speckled birds.

"I don't know where the smell of lilacs is coming from," he said.

I looked at him, not prepared for that cognitive leap. I looked back to a mantelpiece filled with parian porcelains of Shakespeare, General Gordon, Julius Caesar, Victoria herself threatening to fall from the edge where she'd been jostled by the crowd of other white busts.

"It's always in my clothes after I visit here."

"What's that?" I said, trying to gain control of my senses.

"The lilac. I never asked her where it came from, but now when I'm free to look, I can't find it."

"You must miss her," I said.

"Is that what I'm conveying?" His voice had gone flat.

I didn't even know myself why I'd jumped to that conclusion, much less expressed it. Maybe it was all her stuff around me. See me, love me, miss me, she was crying, I am so intricate and so ornamented that you can't help but do that. But Trevor clearly had seen her, and whether or not he'd loved her, I don't think he missed her much. Evidently he heard his own tone, because he smiled at me and he made his voice go so soft from what seemed like self-reflection that my hands grew itchy to touch him. "That must sound like an odd response," he said. "How could an only child not miss his mother?"

"I can think of ways."

He smiled again but this time at the room. He looked around. "Do you wonder if I grew up amidst all this?"

"Yes."

"I did."

"And you want to get rid of it."

His smile came back to me. He looked at me closely and he was no Trevor at all. "Every bit of it," he said.

.   .   .

That first day I sat at a bentwood table in the kitchen and he would bring me the things he could carry—a sterling silver biscuit box and a cut-glass decanter, a coach-lace coffee cozy and a silver-and-gold peacock pendant, and on and on—and I would make notes for the catalog description and I would give him an estimate and he never challenged a figure, never asked a question. At some point I realized it was past two and we ordered in Chinese and he had already rolled the sleeves on his pale green silk shirt and we ate together, me using chopsticks, him using a fork. In the center of the table sat a spring-driven tabletop horse-racing toy with eight painted lead horses with jockeys that circled a grooved wooden track. He had just put it before me when the doorbell rang with the food.

We ate in silence for a couple of minutes, a nice silence, I thought—we were comfortable enough with each other already that we didn't have to make small talk. Finally, though, I pointed to the toy and asked, "Was this yours?"

"Not really. It was around. I never played with it."

"Weren't you allowed?"

"How much will we get?" he said.

"Toys aren't a specialty of mine. I can only get you into the ballpark."

"Close enough."

"I think the estimate would be around three hundred dollars."

"And you'd work the bid up to six."

I looked at the row of jockeys. "We've got a couple of regulars who play the horses. And more than a couple are still kids at heart."

"You're scary sometimes, Amy Dickerson, what you can pick up in people." He was smiling the same smile I'd taken for self-reflection.

"This might be true," I said. I was up to my elbows here in mothers and children and my own mother thought the same thing about me, expecting all the good men in the world to be frightened away. Looking into Trevor's dark eyes I felt a twist of something in my chest that the cool and collected part of me recognized as panic.

"I mean that in an admiring way," he said.

"How come I didn't pick up on that?"

"I'm sorry. I scare people, too."

"But you don't scare me. See the problem I'm suddenly faced with? We have an imbalance here."

"In the courtroom," he said.

"You're a lawyer?"

"Yes."

"That *is* scary," I said, and part of me meant it.

"I only defend the poor and the downtrodden," he said.

"Not if you can afford silk shirts."

"That was two categories. I defend the poor and the downtrodden rich."

"Is there such a thing?"

"Ask any rich man. He'll tell you."

"What about rich women?"

The playfulness drained out of him, pulling the corners of his mouth down. I knew he was thinking about his mother again.

"Trevor," I said, softly. He looked me in the eyes and I said, "Play the game."

For a moment he didn't understand.

I nodded to the spring-driven tabletop horse-racing toy with eight hollow-cast, painted lead horses with jockeys and grooved wooden track, estimate three hundred dollars. He followed my gesture and looked at the object for a moment. Then he stretched and pulled it to him and he put his hand on the key at the side. He hesitated and looked at me. Ever so slightly I nodded, yes.

He turned the key and the kitchen filled with the metallic scrinch of the gears and he turned it again and again until it would turn no more. Then he tripped the release lever and the horses set out jerking around the track once, twice, a horse taking the lead and then losing it to another and that one losing it to another until the sound ceased and the horses stopped. Trevor's eyes had never left the game. Now he looked at me.

"Which one was yours?" I asked.

He reached out his hand and laid it over mine. Our first touch. "They all were," he said.

.　　.　　.

There was a time when I thought I would be a model. I *was* a model. I did the catwalk glide as well as any of them, selling the clothes, selling the attitude. And off the job—when I was in my own jeans and going, *Who the hell was I today?*—I had trouble figuring out how to put one foot in front of the other one without feeling like I was still on the runway. There was a time when I was an actress. I was Miss Firecracker and I was Marilyn Monroe and I was passionate about a shampoo and I was still going, *Who the hell was I today?* There were the two times when I lived with a man for a few years. It didn't help ease Mama's angst. People actually think to get married, in Texas, she'd observe. It didn't help ease my angst either. I was "Babe" to one and "A.D." to the other and one never made a sound when we had sex and the other yelled, "Oh Mama," over and over, and I found part of myself sitting somewhere on the other side of the room watching all this and turning over the same basic question.

So what was I reading in Trevor Martin, the once and perhaps future Dark-Eyes, that would make me hopeful? After he put his hand on mine he said, "I've been divorced for six months. My mother has been dead for six weeks. It feels good to have a woman look inside me. That's not really happened before. But I'm trying to move slowly into the rest of my life."

"I understand," I said, and I did. "For one thing, we have every object of your childhood to go through first."

He squeezed my hand gently, which told me he'd known I'd understand and he was grateful.

.　　.　　.

I left him on the first evening and went to a Thai restaurant and ate alone, as had been my recent custom, though I felt the possibilities with Dark-Eyes unfurling before me. But that didn't stop me from eating too fast and I walked out with my brow sweating and my lips tingling from the peppers.

And when I was done, I went to my apartment and I stepped in and when I switched on the lights I was stopped cold. My eyes leaped from overstuffed chair to overstuffed couch to silk Persian rug and all of it was in Bloomingdale's earth tones and it was me, it was what was left of me after I'd been dead for six weeks and somebody that wasn't me but was *like* me was here to catalog it all and there was a ficus in a corner and a Dali print of Don Quixote over the empty mantelpiece and a wall of bookshelves and I wanted to turn around and walk out, go to a bar or back to work, take my notes from the first day at Mrs. Edward Martin's and go put them in a computer, anything but step further into this apartment with its silence buzzing in my ears.

Then I saw the red light flashing on my answering machine and I moved into my apartment as if nothing odd was going on. I approached the phone, which sat, I was suddenly acutely aware, on an Angelo Donghia maple side table with Deco-style tapering legs, estimated value four hundred dollars. But the flashing light finally cleared my head: I had one message and I pushed the button.

It was Arthur Gray. "Hello, Amy," he said. "About the benefit auction. Woody Allen just came through with a walk-on part in his new film. *Postmodern Millie,* I think it is. And Giuliani's offered a dinner at Gracie Mansion. But I've had a special request, and since we're not being *entirely* altruistic here—rightly not—I really think we should do it. More later. You know how I appreciate you. Our best customers are your biggest admirers . . . Almost forgot. Do you need a lift to the Hamptons Saturday? We should get out there early and I've got a limo. Let me know. Bye."

All of which barely registered at the time. I realized it was the assumption that the red light was Trevor that had cleared the mortality from my head.

.　　.　　.

On that night I sat naked on the edge of my bed, my silk night-shirt laid out beside me, and I thought of Trevor, the silk of his shirt the color of a ripe honeydew, or the color—if green is the color of jealousy—of the pallid twinge I felt when I found Max, in the third year of our relationship, in a restaurant we'd been to together half a dozen times, only this time he had a woman hanging on his arm. He saw me. I saw him. It was lunchtime and I sat down at a table, my back to him, and I ate my lunch alone, which I'd planned to do, and very fast, faster than usual. I loved that Caesar salad and split-pea soup, in spite of the speed, perhaps because of it: I was furious. Only the tiniest bit jealous, surprisingly, but angry. I love to eat when I'm angry. He wouldn't talk about it that night. The one on his arm never argued with him, he said. She was just about as stupid and irrational as he was, he said, thinking, I suppose, that he was being ironic. But even at that moment I thought it was the first truthful thing he'd said in a long time.

I laid my hand on the nightshirt. The silk was cool and slick and I clenched it with my fingers like a lover's back. And then I let it go. It was Fred's shirt. It had been too big for pasty slender Fred. I looked at it. Periwinkle blue. White oyster buttons. Soft tip collar. Versace. Two hundred and fifty dollars. Who'll start the bidding at nothing? I looked at the shirt and wondered why I hadn't given it away or thrown it away from the negative provenance. But I didn't give a damn about that. It felt good to sleep in. That was a healthy attitude, surely.

I looked around the room. And my eyes moved to my dresser and found a silver tankard stuffed with an arrangement of dried flowers. I rose and crossed to it and picked it up. It was from Max. The tankard, not the flowers. It was Georgian with a baluster shape and a flared circular foot and a light engraved pattern of flowers and foliate scrolls. He'd been an ignorant gift-giver. Subscriptions and sweaters. I vaguely remembered challenging him about it and he'd bought me this for seven hundred dollars. On eBay, where every grandma and pack rat is her own auction house. And he'd gotten me a glorified beer mug. But I was grateful at the time. He wanted to use it himself, I realized. He said the silver was the only thing that would keep a beer cold in the Georgian era. Yum, he said. But I didn't let him use it even once. I put flowers in his beer mug and I kept it to this moment, standing naked and alone in my bedroom, my face twisted beyond recognition in the reflection in my hand. It was beautiful, this object, really. That's why I kept it. Both these men had vanished forever from this place. Exorcised. The objects they touched—a thing I would push like crazy in an auction if they'd been famous and dead—held not a trace of them. And I felt the chilly creep of panic in my limbs at this thought.

I put the tankard down and turned away. I crossed to the bed and I lifted this Versace shirt with soft tip collar and I let it fall over my head and down, the silk shimmering against me, and suddenly I felt as if I'd climbed inside Trevor's skin. Can you trust to know a man from a pair of dark eyes? From Chinese food and a child's game played by an adult after a lifetime of quiet pain inflicted by a mother? From the touch of a hand? Inside this draping of silk my body had its own kind of logic. These details *are* the man, my body reasoned, as surely as the buttons and the stitching and the weave of cloth are this $250 shirt. I raised my paddle and I bid on this man.

.　　.　　.

How do you assess the value of a thing? There are five major objective standards. The condition: the more nearly perfect, the better. The rarity: the rarer, the better. The size: usually neither too big nor too small. The provenance: the more intense—either good or bad—the better. The authenticity: though a fake may be, to any but an informed eye, indistinguishable from the true object, the world of the auction will cast out the pretender.

And so I turn my mind now to the fifth night, the Friday night, of my week of assessments in the apartment of the deceased Mrs. Edward Martin, mother of Trevor Martin. On this night he opened the door to the bell and this fifth silk shirt was bloused in the sleeves and open to the third button and his chest was covered with dark down and his smile was so deeply appreciative of my standing there waiting to be let in that I thought for a moment he was about to take me in his arms and kiss me, which I would have readily accepted.

But he did not. We spent the morning and the first hours of the afternoon working our way around the larger pieces in the foyer, the parlor, the library, the dining room. Then, after I'd assessed a beautiful mahogany three-pedestal dining table with brass paw feet, he said, "You're hungry." He was right. And for the second day in a row he did not even ask what I wanted but went to the phone and ordered my favorite Chinese dishes—though, in all honesty, I would have varied my fare if he'd asked—but I found myself liking his presumption, liking that he should know this domestic detail about me.

And after we ate, he took me to a small room lined completely with armoires in rosewood and mahogany and walnut, and filling the armoires was everything that could be embroidered—quilts and drapes and cushions and bellows and doilies and on and on, big things and small—and there were Persian rugs stacked knee high in the center of the floor and on top of them sat two open steamer trunks, overflowing with indistinguishable cloth objects all frilled and flowered.

"I'm surprised at her," I said without thinking. "She's out of control in here."

"This was my room," Trevor said.

I turned to him, wanting to take the words back.

"It didn't look like this," he said, smiling.

I had a strong impulse now to lean forward and lay my forehead against the triangle of his exposed chest. But I held still. I would not push him into the rest of his life. Then he said, "Let's leave this room for later," and he was moving away. I followed him down the hallway and he paused at a closed door, the only room I hadn't seen. He hesitated, not looking at me, but staring at the door itself as if trying to listen for something on the other side. I quickly sorted out the apartment in my head and I realized that this must have been her bedroom.

How long had it been since I'd made love? Some months. Too many months. One of the great, largely unacknowledged jokes Nature plays on women—at least this woman—is to increase one's desire for sex while decreasing one's tolerance for boring men. Horny and discriminating is a bad combination, it seems to me. And the situation before me—exceedingly strange though it was shaping up to be—was anything but boring. Still he hesitated.

I said, "This is hard for you."

He nodded.

He opened the door and I had no choice but to step to his side and look in.

There were probably some pots and pans, a telephone and a commode, some kitchen utensils, that were not Victorian in Mrs. Edward Martin's apartment. But almost nothing else. Except now I was looking at her bed and it was eighteenth-century Italian with a great arched headboard painted pale blue and parcel-gilt, carved with lunettes, and rising at each side was a pale pink pilaster topped not by a finial but by a golden cupid, his bow and arrow aimed at the bed. The smell of lilacs rolled palpably from the room, Trevor put his arm around my shoulders, and some little voice in my head was going, *How desperate have you become?*

Then he gave me a quick friendly squeeze and his arm disappeared from around me and he said, "Maybe I'll let you do this room on your own."

"Right," I said, and I sounded as if I was choking.

.   .   .

An hour later I found him sitting at the kitchen table, sipping a cup of coffee. I sat down across from him.

We were quiet together for a time, and then he said, "Do you want some coffee?"

"No," I said. "Thanks."

He stared into his own cup for a long moment and then he said, "She loved objects."

"That's clear."

"My childhood, her adulthood. It was all one," he said softly. "She had a good eye. She knew what she wanted and she knew what it would cost and she was ready to pay it."

He was saying these things with a tone that sounded like tenderness. On our first evening he'd taken pleasure in my being able to look inside him, but at this moment he seemed opaque. He felt tender about her shopping? But then it made a kind of sense. I, of all people, should understand his mother. I played people like her every day.

I made my voice go gentle, matching his tone. "What she saw and loved and bought, this was how she said who she was."

Trevor looked at me and nodded faintly. "Like style. We are what we wear. We are what we hang on our walls. Perhaps you're right. She was talking to me."

He looked away.

And I thought: the buying isn't the point; it's that we *understand* the objects. We love what we understand. And then I averted my eyes from the next logical step. But I can see it now, replaying it all: we love what we understand, and there I sat, understanding Trevor Martin.

I waited for him to say more but he seemed content with the silence. I was not. I was doing entirely too much thinking. I said, "I've solved your mystery."

He smiled at me and cocked his head. The smile was reassuring. It was okay to move on.

I said, "Her pillows—and there are a dozen of them—they all have lilac sachets stuffed inside the cases."

"Of course. I should have realized. She slept in it."

I found I was relieved that even in his freedom to search for the source of the scent he had avoided her bedclothes. And he had not made love to me on her bed. These were good and reassuring things. I was free now to relax with my pleasure in the way he lifted his eyebrows each time he sipped his coffee, the way he lifted his chin to enjoy the taste, the way his eyes moved to the right and his mouth bunched up slightly when he grew thoughtful, the way— for the second time—he reached out and laid his hand on mine. I was filled with the details of him. I could sell him for a million bucks. Not that I would. Clearly, part of me was beginning to think he was a keeper.

When his hand settled on my hand, he said, "I will sleep better tonight because of you."

I looked at him with a little stutter in my chest. I'd suddenly become what my daddy used to call "cow-simple." It was from his touch. It was from merely the word *sleeping*. It was stupid but I was having trouble figuring out what he was really trying to say.

And he let me gape on, as if I was out alone in a field, paused in the middle of chewing my cud, wondering where I was. Then he said, "The mystery. Solved."

"Of course," I said.

·　　·　　·

When this fifth work day was done, for the fifth time he walked me to the door and thanked me, rather formally, for all that I was doing. Tonight I stopped and looked into his eyes when he said this. "I've enjoyed your company," I said.

"And I've enjoyed yours," he said.

That's all I wanted to say. I turned to go.

"Amy," he said.

I turned back and my instinct said this was the time he would take me into his arms. My instinct was wrong. Was this another trend for the forty-year-old woman? Horny, discriminating, and utterly without sexual intuition? He simply said, "I'll see you down."

We went out the door together and along the hall and I pushed the down button on the elevator and a spark of static electricity bit at my fingertip. That was it, I thought. I've now discharged into the electrical system of the building elevators whatever that was I was feeling a few moments ago.

The doors opened. We stepped in. The doors closed. We were alone, and maybe the elevators did suck up the charge that was between us, because we descended one floor of the ten we had to go and Trevor reached out and flipped the red switch on the panel and the elevator bounced to a stop and a bell began ringing and he took me in his arms and I leaped up and hooked my legs around him as we kissed. He pressed me against the wall and he did not make a sound.

.   .   .

The next day I leaned into the tinted window of Arthur Gray's limo and faced the rush of trees and light standards and, eventually, industrial parks, along the Long Island Expressway. I never had understood what men saw in lovemaking in a standing position. Though Trevor had been strong enough, certainly, to hold me up without my constantly feeling like I would slip off him. He was silent, but he did not cry out, "Oh Mama," which would have been much worse, under the circumstances. We'd not had a proper date. We'd never even gone out for a meal. But that sounded like my mama talking. I was well fucked and unusually meditative.

When we were on Highway 27, out among the potato fields and vegetable stands and runs of quaint shops and approaching East Hampton, Arthur finally roused me from going nowhere in my head. He said, "Amy, there's one more item that I want you to put on your list. Okay?"

"Okay."

"It's the special request I mentioned on your machine." Arthur was shuffling his feet and talking all around something and he'd finally gotten me interested, even suspicious.

"What are you talking about, Arthur?"

"A dinner with you."

"With me?"

"At Fellini's. In SoHo. They've already donated the meal, with wine. Dinner for two with the most beautiful auctioneer in New York."

I was silent. This was really troubling for a reason I couldn't quite define.

"Come on," he said. "Think of the whales."

"This is for whales? I thought it was for a disease."

"Whales get diseases, too. The point is that your mystique, which is considerable, is Nichols and Gray's mystique, as well. Give somebody a dandy candlelit dinner. For us. Okay?"

There was no good reason to say no. I liked whales. I liked Arthur. I liked Nichols and Gray. But there was suddenly a great whale of a fear breaching inside me and falling back with a big splash: I was going to have to sell myself.

I looked out the window and across a field I saw a cow, standing alone, wondering where the hell she was.

. . .

We were set up in a four-pole tent on the grounds of an estate with the sound of the ocean crashing just outside. I stood on a platform behind a lectern loaned by the local Episcopal Church and I looked out at many of my regulars and some comparably affluent strangers and they were in their boaters and chinos and late spring silks and I looked at all their faces once, twice, and John Paul Gibbons was on the right side in the second row and he winked at me. This was becoming a discomforting motif. And suddenly I figured I knew whose request it was that I be auctioned off.

I began. To an ancient little lady I did not know—I presumed she was a permanent Hamptons resident—I sold the services of Puff Daddy to hip-hop her answering-machine message. I had an order bid in my book for $150 but I squeezed $600 from the old lady, invoking the great, thinking beings-of-the-deep in their hour of need. I'd gotten a cello lesson with Yo-Yo Ma up to $1,600—having ferreted out two sets of parents, each with a child they'd browbeaten into learning the cello—when Trevor appeared at the back of the tent. He lifted his chin at me, as if he were tasting his coffee.

We'd never spoken of this event during the week we'd just spent together. I didn't expect him. I felt something strong suddenly roil up within me, but I wasn't sure what. I focused on the next bid. "It's against the couple down in front. How about seventeen? Seventeen hundred? What if your child meets *their* child in a school music competition?"

They hesitated.

"Whose butt will get whipped?" I cried.

They bid seventeen hundred. But I felt it was over. The other couple was hiding behind the heads in front of them. I scanned the audience a last time. Trevor was circling over to my left. "Fair warning," I called.

There were no more bids and I sold Yo-Yo Ma for $1,700 as Trevor found a seat. Oddly, I still didn't know how I felt about his being here. I threw myself into the lots on Arthur's list and I was good, I was very good. The whales were no doubt somewhere off the coast leaping for joy. And then I reached Lot 19.

"The next lot . . ." I began, and I felt my throat seizing up. I felt Trevor's dark eyes on me, without even looking in his direction. I was breathless against the wall of the elevator and all I could hear was the bell and the pop of Trevor's breath as he moved and my mind had begun to wander a little bit and he was right about how he smelled whenever he visited his mother's apartment, he smelled of lilacs—no, not of lilacs, of lilac *sachet*—and my head thumped against the wall and I said "Oops" but he did not hear and I thought about her pillows and though I was glad I was not in her bed, I figured I'd accept those dozen pillows on the floor of the elevator so I could lie down in a soft place for this.

"The next lot . . ." I repeated, and I pushed on. "Number nineteen. Dinner for two at Fellini's in SoHo, with wine and your auctioneer."

There was a smattering of delighted oohs and chuckles.

I almost started the bidding at a measly $50. But this impulse did not come from my auctioneer self, I instantly realized. There was a shrinking inside me that I did not like and so I started the bid for what I thought to be an exorbitant amount. I'd simply go unclaimed. "Who'll open the bid for four hundred dollars?" I said.

I saw John Paul's head snap a little, but before I could congratulate myself, in my peripheral vision I could see a paddle leap up without pause. I looked. It was Trevor.

Suddenly there was something I had to know.

I said, "I'm sorry, ladies and gentlemen, let me stop right here for a moment. Before we begin, I need some more information on this lot."

There was a ripple of laughter through the tent and I stepped away from the lectern. Arthur was standing off to my right and I stepped down from the platform and I approached him.

He must have read something in my face. He blanched and whispered, "What is it? You're doing a smashing job."

"Who asked to put me up for bid?"

"Sorry, my dear," he said. "That's a bit of a secret."

"You always start sounding British when you know you're in trouble. And you are. Give it up."

He tried to wink and shrug and say nothing.

"Arthur," I said as calmly as I could. "I don't want to grab you by the throat and throw you to the ground in front of all these good clients. Tell me who."

This was convincing. "Trevor Martin," he said.

I felt a flash of anger. Why? I demanded explanations from myself as I stepped back up onto the platform: Surely this was something I wanted. I wanted Trevor to pay big bucks for me and take me to dinner like he should. But what's this "should" stuff about? Why *should* he do that? And why should *I* expect—as part of me did—a sweet and gentle invitation to dinner in an elevator instead of a hot five minutes of sex? I'd been thinking about the sex, myself. I'd been wanting it. I couldn't let myself be a hypocrite.

I cried, "We have four hundred from Mr. Martin. Who'll make it five hundred?" and all the explanations vanished in my head and I was left with an abrupt realization: there was something being put before this crowd that had a value in need of being articulated. I pointed to one of the paddles in the back, some elderly gentleman who I'd been pitting against Mrs. Fielding, who would want to talk about who knows what over dinner, maybe the time she'd seen her dear and pudgy aunt in the nude, after her bath. "Five hundred," I called, and that suddenly seemed way too low.

"I am not a Renoir," I said. "But I am . . . not six inches square, either."

It was a start.

"I am in excellent condition," I cried. "For an object my age. Who'll make it a thousand."

It was a big leap. But I found myself feeling ready for a big leap.

There was only a moment of hesitation and I saw a paddle go up to my right and I looked and it was John Paul Gibbons. All right. "A thousand dollars to John Paul Gibbons. Who'll make it eleven hundred?"

And now I looked to Trevor. He raised his paddle instantly. "Eleven hundred to Mr. Martin. And this is still an unconscionable bargain. I am rare. I am. Who else knows so many of you so well? Who else has filled your homes and emptied your wallets? Who'll make it fifteen hundred?"

I turned back to John Paul and he winked again and lifted his paddle and he glanced over his shoulder toward Trevor.

I said, "I am a perfect size, thanks to my ongoing efforts. Neither too big nor too small. Who'll make it two thousand?"

I, too, looked at Trevor and he smiled that faintly patronizing smile of his and he lifted his paddle and I was caught by his smile, the smile that he gave me the first time I saw him, the smile he'd given me as we walked past the doorman last night and into the warm evening air and he said, "I think I've begun to move into the rest of my life."

His life. But what did I want in the rest of *my* life? I'd like to have seen the inside of *his* apartment by this point. I'd like to have been asked to dinner, just the two of us, without a price put on anything. He takes his first step in the elevator, when it's least expected, and he arranges to *buy* his next step. This was his mother's way. I lowered my face. My book lay open before me. I lifted my face. "I am authentic," I said. "You must look into me now, as I've looked into you." And I took my own challenge. And I looked. And I said, "Three thousand to the book."

There was a little gasp. A private tour of Dollywood, Tennessee, with Dolly Parton herself as guide had gone for $2,800, the biggest bid of the auction.

I looked at John Paul. He blew me a little kiss and kept his paddle on his lap. I turned to Trevor. "It's against you, Mr. Martin," I said. "Thirty-five?"

The smile was gone. But he lifted his paddle.

"Three thousand five hundred to Mr. Martin," I cried, and I instantly added, "Four thousand to the book."

Now there was a great hum that lifted in the crowd, resonating, perhaps, with the one from the sea. "It's against you, Mr. Martin," I said. His face slowly eclipsed itself behind the face in front of him, a jowly man in a shirt and tie, a Wall Street lawyer who collected Stieff teddy bears.

"Fair warning," I cried, scanning the faces before me. I let the warning sit with them all for a long moment, and then I said, "Sold to the book for four thousand dollars."

.   .   .

And now I sit at this newest chic SoHo restaurant with the faces of Anita Ekberg and Marcello Mastroianni and Giulietta Masina and Signor Fellini himself all about me on the walls, and two places are set at the table. But I am alone and waiting for no one. And yet, I am lingering now over the linguini, eating it strand by strand, sipping my wine in tiny, dry sips. And I am feeling good. The book, of course, had been empty. I bid for myself, and I won.

TIME

WINNER, PUBLIC INTEREST

Big Money & Politics

How the Little Guy Gets Crunched

Soaked by Congress

Throwing the Game

Amid the recent avalanche of coverage about campaign finance reform, this concisely written series stands apart as a devastating indictment of a system run amok. By ferreting out individual stories of who gets hurt and why, Barlett and Steele bring the issue into crystalline focus, proving that there are real human costs to political influence peddling.

Donald L. Barlett and
James B. Steele

Big Money &
Politics

How the Little Guy Gets Crunched

*When powerful interests shower Washington with millions in cam-
paign contributions, they often get what they want. But it's ordinary
citizens and firms that pay the price--and most of them never see it
coming.*

I t was just your typical piece of congressional dirty work. As
1999 wound down, the House and Senate passed the District
of Columbia Appropriations Act. You might think that would
be a boring piece of legislation. You would be wrong. For buried
in the endless clauses authorizing such spending items as $867
million for education and $5 million to promote the adoption of
foster children was Section 6001: Superfund Recycling Equity. It
had nothing to do with the District of Columbia, nor appropriations, nor "equity" as it is commonly defined.

Instead Section 6001 was inserted in the appropriations bill by
Senator Trent Lott of Mississippi, the Senate majority leader, to
take the nation's scrap-metal dealers off the hook for millions of
dollars in potential Superfund liabilities at toxic-waste sites. In
doing so, Lott had the support of colleagues in both parties.

This early Christmas present to the scrap-metal dealers—who
contributed more than $300,000 to political candidates and com-
mittees during the 1990s—made them very happy. Others in the
recycling chain were not so happy. All of a sudden, they were

potentially responsible for millions of dollars in damages the junkmen might otherwise have had to pay.

While clever in its obscurity, Section 6001 is not an especially big giveaway by Capitol Hill standards. Rather, it is typical among the growing litany of examples of how Washington extends favorable treatment to one set of citizens at the expense of another. It's a process that frequently causes serious, sometimes fatal economic harm to unwary individuals and businesses that are in the way.

How do you get that favorable treatment? If you know the right people in Congress and in the White House, you can often get anything you want. And there are two surefire ways to get close to those people:

- Contribute to their political campaigns.
- Spend generously on lobbying.

If you do both of these things, success will maul you like groupies at a rock concert. If you do neither—and this is the case with about 200 million individuals of voting age and several million corporations—those people in Washington will treat you accordingly. In essence, campaign spending in America has divided all of us into two groups: first- and second-class citizens. This is what happens if you are in the latter group:

You pick up a disproportionate share of America's tax bill.

You pay higher prices for a broad range of products, from peanuts to prescription drugs.

You pay taxes that others in a similar situation have been excused from paying.

You are compelled to abide by laws while others are granted immunity from them.

You must pay debts that you incur while others do not.

You are barred from writing off on your tax return some of the money spent on necessities while others deduct the cost of their entertainment.

You must run your business by one set of rules while the government creates another set for your competitors.

In contrast, first-class citizens—the fortunate few who contribute to the right politicians and hire the right lobbyists—enjoy all the benefits of their special status. Among them:

If they make a bad business decision, the government bails them out.

If they want to hire workers at below-market wage rates, the government provides the means to do so.

If they want more time to pay their debts, the government gives them an extension.

If they want immunity from certain laws, the government gives it.

If they want to ignore rules their competitors must comply with, the government gives its approval.

If they want to kill legislation that is intended for the public good, it gets killed.

Call it government for the few at the expense of the many. Looked at another way, almost any time a citizen or a business gets what it wants through campaign contributions and lobbying, someone else pays the price for it. Sometimes it's a few people, sometimes millions. Sometimes it's one business, sometimes many. In short, through a process often obscured from public view, Washington anoints winners and creates losers. Among the recent winners and the wannabes, who collectively have contributed millions of dollars to candidates and their parties and spent generously on lobbying:

Tax-Free Profits

Last December, President Clinton signed into law the Ticket to Work and Work Incentives Improvement Act, hailing the legislation as providing "the most significant advancement for people with disabilities since the Americans with Disabilities Act almost a decade ago." He called it "a genuinely American bill."

Indeed so. For it also provided something quite unrelated to disabilities: a lucrative tax break for banks, insurers and financial-service companies. A provision woven into the legislation allowed the foreign subsidiaries of these businesses to extend the income-tax-free status of foreign earnings from the sale of securities, annuities and other financial holdings. Among the big winners: American International Group Inc., an insurance giant, as well as the recently formed Citigroup. Overall, the tax break will cost the U.S. Treasury $1.5 billion in the next two years, just as it did in the past two years. The amount is equivalent to all the income taxes paid over four years by 300,000 individuals and families that earn between $25,000 and $30,000 a year.

The Great S&L Giveback

Owners of savings and loan associations, many of whom are suing the Federal Government for clamping down on them during the S&L crisis in the 1980s, will benefit from a one-paragraph clause that was slipped into legislation that will hold the U.S. government liable for billions of dollars in damage claims because federal regulators nixed certain accounting practices. As is typical with special-interest measures, there were no hearings or estimates of the cost before the clause mysteriously showed up in the Omnibus Consolidated and Emergency Supplemental Appropriations Act of 1998. Among the potential beneficiaries: billionaires Ron Perelman and the Pritzker and Bass families. The losers: all other taxpayers, who will have to pick up the tab.

·   ·   ·

The future promises much more of the same. In this presidential election year, companies and industries that hope for special treatment in the new decade are busy making their political contributions and their connections. Examples:

A Longer Life For Golden Drugs

Major pharmaceutical companies will seek legislation to extend the patent life on their most valuable drugs. In the past, such giveaways were often inserted into unrelated legislation and covered a single drug or two. But this year, watch for heavy lobbying for the granddaddy of all patent extenders. It would protect pharmaceutical company sales of $3 billion annually and add years to the profitable life of at least seven expensive drugs, such as Schering-Plough's Claritin for allergies and Eulexin for prostate cancer, SmithKline Beecham's Relafen for arthritis and G.D. Searle's Daypro for arthritis. The big losers: patients, especially senior citizens on fixed incomes, who must buy expensive prescription drugs instead of cheaper generic versions. Estimates of the added cost run from $1 billion to $11 billion over the next decade.

Cars with a Checkered Past

The National Automobile Dealers Association is pushing for a federal law regulating the sale of rebuilt wrecked cars. Like a lot of special-interest legislation, the National Salvage Motor Vehicle Consumer Protection Act, as it's called, sounds good. No one is likely to argue with its call for federal standards to govern the sale of "nonrepairable and rebuilt vehicles." But look closely. The fine print actually provides minimal standards, gives states the option of ignoring these, applies to only half the cars on the road and keeps secret the history of near totaled vehicles. Sponsored by majority leader Lott, the bill has cleared the Senate Commerce Committee, whose chairman, presidential candidate John McCain, is a co-sponsor. Losers: consumers who unknowingly buy rebuilt wrecks at inflated prices.

.   .   .

Both the recipients of campaign contributions and the givers insist that no public official is for sale, that no favors are granted in exchange for cash. Few people believe that; U.S. Supreme Court Justice David Souter summed up the prevailing public attitude during arguments in a case that led the Justices last week to uphold the current $1,000 limit on individual campaign contributions. (Donations to parties are still unlimited.) Said Souter:

"I think most people assume—I do, certainly—that someone making an extraordinarily large contribution is going to get some kind of an extraordinary return for it. I think that is a pervasive assumption. And . . . there is certainly an appearance of, call it an attenuated corruption, if you will, that large contributors are simply going to get better service, whatever that service may be, from a politician than the average contributor, let alone no contributor."

Campaign-finance reform has emerged as an issue during the budding presidential race. Three of the four leading candidates are for it; one is against. McCain has made limiting campaign contributions his defining issue, although the Arizona Republican has accepted contributions from corporations seeking favors from his Commerce committee. Bill Bradley has also spoken out for reform, calling for public financing of elections. Vice President Gore, although involved in the Clinton Administration's 1996 fund-raising scandals, also advocates publicly funded campaigns. Only Texas Governor George W. Bush favors the status quo.

Just how obsessed with raking in cash are the 535 members of Congress?

A veteran Washington lawyer who once served an apprenticeship with a prominent U.S. Senator relates a telling experience. The lawyer, who represents an agency of a state government, visited the home office of a Congressman in that state to discuss a national issue affecting the agency and, indirectly, the Congressman's constituents. After an effusive greeting, the Congressman's next words were brief and to the point:

"How much money can you contribute?"

The stunned lawyer explained that he represented a state agency and that state governments do not contribute to political candidates. As if in response to hearing some programmed words that altered his brain circuitry, the Congressman changed his tone and demeanor instantly. Suddenly, he had more pressing obligations. He would be unable to meet with the lawyer. Rather, he said, an aide would listen to whatever it was the lawyer had to say.

Of course, those who give money to political candidates or their parties don't necessarily get everything they seek. Often the reason is that their opponents are just as well connected. But they do get access—to the Representative or Senator, the White House aide or Executive Branch official—to make their case.

Try it yourself. You won't get it.

Bits and pieces of the story of those who give the money and what they get in return have been told, here and elsewhere. But who gets hurt—the citizens and businesses that do not play the game—remains an untold story.

How to Become a Top Banana

When a fruit baron wanted to conquer more of the European market, he got Washington to launch a trade war for him. The victims of the cross fire? A bunch of ordinary Americans who never saw it coming

I n Summerville, S.C., Rick Reinert has built a small business called Reha Enterprises that sells bath oil, soap and other supplies. But now he is selling many of his products, imported from Germany, at no profit or at a loss. This is the result of an order by the U.S. government.

In New York City, Arthur Kaplan, owner of Galaxy of Graphics

Ltd., a retailer of decorative prints, has stopped selling the popular English lithographs produced for him by a venerable London art dealer for two decades. This is the result of an order by the U.S. government.

In Somerset, Wis., Timothy Dove, who heads a 17-year-old family business called Action Battery, which sells and installs industrial batteries, has lost a quarter-million-dollar account and faces the prospect of more losses to come. This is the result of an order by the U.S. government.

What's going on here?

Nearly a year ago, the Clinton Administration imposed a 100% tariff on the products these three businesses and hundreds of others like them import and sell. That's sort of like charging you $40,000 for a $20,000 Ford Taurus.

What did these folks do to encourage the wrath of the White House? Absolutely nothing. It was what they didn't do that matters. They neglected to make huge campaign contributions or hire high-powered Washington lobbyists to plead their case.

Reinert, Kaplan and Dove are what the military refers to as collateral damage—unwitting victims of what will go down in economic history as the Great Banana War. Except that for these victims, collateral is up close and very personal.

This is partly the story of Carl H. Lindner Jr. of Cincinnati, a certified member since 1982 of the Forbes list of the 400 richest Americans, who has a personal fortune estimated at $800 million and has been a very large contributor to political candidates, both Democratic and Republican.

But mostly this is a story about people who get hurt by contributions, who are paying a steep personal price because of the influence exercised by unlimited money in elections and lobbying. These human casualties are mostly unchronicled, but you can count them in the millions. They are your friends and neighbors.

In simplest terms, Lindner, whose company has dominated the

global trade in bananas for a century, was in 1993 frustrated because European countries limited imports of his bananas. He complained to the U.S. government, which complained to the World Trade Organization (WTO), which authorized the U.S. government to retaliate by imposing a stiff tariff—in effect, a tax—on select European goods shipped to this country.

So which goods to attack? President Clinton could have slapped the 100% tariff on, say, Mercedes-Benz autos imported from Germany, fine wines from France, or elegant women's shoes from Italy. But that might have provoked retaliation by the Europeans against major American exports. So instead the President chose to punish smaller and less important European companies—companies that furnished bath products to Reinert, prints to Kaplan and batteries to Dove. In short, the Administration came down with a heavy foot on relatively powerless citizens. People who, like 99% of the population, contribute little or no money directly to politicians.

How heavy was that foot? In Reinert's case, the U.S. government raised the tariff on his most popular product, an herbal foam bath, from just under 5% to 100%. His U.S. Customs bill for the last six months of 1999 spiraled to $37,783 from just $1,851— a 1,941% tax increase.

For a small business, that's strong poison. Indeed, when Reinert called the office of U.S. Trade Representative Charlene Barshefsky to describe his plight, an official there expressed amazement. "[They] were very surprised I was still importing," recalls Reinert. "They thought the tariff would cut off the industry—shut it down. That was their intention. They wanted to kill that industry, whatever industry it is." That, naturally, would have meant killing Reinert's business as well.

Reinert did have an option. He could have found a way around paying the tax. Except it would have been illegal. Sort of like people working off the books to avoid paying income tax on their earnings. That's what many small-business people in Reinert's position are doing—fudging their import records. It's polite language for falsifying government documents. Each distinct type of product imported into the U.S. is assigned an individual code number. The tariff is collected on the basis of the code numbers. Thus changing a single numeral in the code will convert a taxable product into one that is not subject to tax.

Are the people doing this comfortable with their deception, which an ambitious federal prosecutor could turn into a conviction accompanied by a large fine and prison sentence? Absolutely not. But it's a matter of survival. Further, they figure, if the U.S. government decides to take care of a multinational business whose owner, his family and his fellow executives contribute millions of dollars to political candidates and their parties—and to punish small businesses whose owners do not contribute—then why not cheat?

. . .

At age 80, Lindner sits atop a corporate agglomeration that includes American Financial Group, Inc., an insurance business (annual revenue: $4 billion); Chiquita Brands International, Inc., the fruit-and-vegetable giant ($2.7 billion); and an array of other businesses, including Provident Financial Group, Inc., a bank holding company (assets: $8 billion); and American Heritage Homes, one of Florida's largest builders.

At American Heritage, Lindner has been a business partner since 1996 with the king of Democratic fund raisers, Terence McAuliffe, described by an admiring Vice President Al Gore as "the greatest fund raiser in the history of the universe." McAuliffe has raised tens of millions of dollars for the Democratic Party, for President Clinton's 1996 re-election campaign, for the President's legal-defense fund, for the President's library and for Hillary Clinton's New York Senate run.

Since 1990, political contributions of $1,000 or more by Lindner, members of his family, his companies and their executives have added up to well over $5 million. Most of the money has gone to the Republican Party and its candidates. But at strategic moments, Lindner has made hefty contributions to the Clinton Administration.

The short version of the money story is this: Europe first offended Lindner when it imposed import restrictions on bananas from Latin America, where his plantations are located. Lindner then contributed a quarter of a million dollars to the Democrats. Gore called and asked for more money. Lindner gave it. And then some more. So much more that Lindner had dinner in the White House, attended a coffee klatch there for the truly generous and slept in the Lincoln Bedroom. Along the way, he periodically met with then U.S. Trade Representative Mickey Kantor and his staff, the officials who ultimately sought the trade sanctions intended to punish the Europeans and force them to give Lindner what he wanted.

Clinton's people weren't the only ones looking after Lindner. Members of Congress—Democrats and Republicans, fund raisers all, beneficiaries themselves of Lindner's largesse—called or wrote or met with Kantor and the President to encourage action on behalf of Chiquita. Trent Lott of Mississippi, the Republican majority leader in the Senate, did it. So did John Glenn, at the time a Democratic Senator from Ohio. And Republican Congressman Jim Bunning of Kentucky, now a Senator. And Charles Stenholm, the Democratic Representative from Texas. And Richard Lugar, the Republican Senator from Indiana. And Mike DeWine, the Republican Senator from Ohio. And, of course, Mitch McConnell, the Republican Senator from Kentucky, who is Congress's most strident advocate of unlimited money in elections.

On April 19, 1999, the U.S. Trade Representative imposed the punitive tariffs on nine types of European goods. To be sure, trade experts outside the European Union generally agree that the restrictive banana policies do violate free-trade rules. Indeed, four global trade panels have reached that conclusion over the years. But restrictive trade policies are hardly peculiar to Europe. The U.S. has its own, notably those that restrict the free access of sugar and peanuts to the American market.

The Clinton Administration has been less than forthcoming about its relationship with the banana baron. In response to repeated *Time* requests for documents relating to the decision to seek the WTO's help with the banana dispute, the U.S. Trade Representative's office stalled, saying it was having trouble coordinating its many files. When it finally began turning over documents last December, many were censored or blank, with the USTR claiming that release of the information would "constitute a clearly unwarranted invasion of personal privacy."

The Banana Baron's Lament

Carl Lindner began investing in bananas in the 1970s, and by 1984 he had acquired a controlling interest in one of America's enduring brand names. Lindner and his family, through their American Financial Group, own 40% of the outstanding shares in Chiquita Brands International, based in Cincinnati, Ohio.

Before Lindner bought in, Chiquita Brands was the old United Fruit Co., a ruthless buccaneer that earned a justifiable reputation as a tyrant that bribed officials of foreign governments, used armed force to keep its workers in line and generally mistreated its thousands of dirt-poor laborers on impoverished Caribbean islands and Central American plantations. All of which helps explain why Chiquita was—and is—the world's dominant banana producer.

But how did it come to pass that the U.S. government launched a trade war over bananas at the expense of small American businesses, especially since the U.S. does not export bananas and Chiquita employs no American production workers?

It started with bananas in Europe. After World War II, the continent's banana market divided into two kinds. Such countries as Britain, France and Spain limited imports and gave preferential treatment to bananas grown in their former colonies. Thus Britain encouraged banana output in Jamaica, Dominica, St. Lucia; France extended special treatment to bananas grown in the Ivory Coast and the Cameroons. At the other extreme, Germany offered a free market with no import restrictions or tariffs.

Britain and France took the position that banana production was essential for both the economic health and the social well-being of their former colonies. By the late 1980s, about one-third of the work forces on the small island nations were employed in banana production.

Protected banana production, that is. Most of the bananas were grown on small family farms and tilled by hand on hilly terrain and poor soil, with little or no mechanization or irrigation. Yields were far below those in places like Honduras, Guatemala and Ecuador. In fact, the cost of growing bananas in the Caribbean was twice that for bananas produced on Latin American plantations. Without their favorable entrée to Europe, the banana industries of these small islands might have disappeared.

Chiquita nevertheless cracked the British market through its ownership of a British subsidiary, Fyffes Ltd., which grew bananas in the former British colonies. British consumers paid a relatively high price for those bananas, but Chiquita's margin from this trade was still small compared with the profits from its efficient plantations in Latin America. By 1986, as the European Union began to take shape, Chiquita executives hoped the restrictions would be lifted and its low-cost bananas could take over the market. So Chiquita sold off its Fyffes subsidiary.

It would prove to be the first in a series of missteps by the Lindner-controlled company—suggesting at least the possibility that the ensuing banana war was really intended to bail out the Lindners from their costly business mistakes.

Meanwhile, in a tariff-free and quota-free Germany, Chiquita had seized 45% of the market. Envisioning the same potential for all of Europe, as well as the former Soviet satellites that were opening up, Chiquita and its chief competitor, Dole Food, decided in the early 1990s to pour more money into production and flood the European market with bananas. With more bananas than buyers, prices—and hence profits—plummeted.

Worse still, the E.U. announced that instead of an open market, which Chiquita had hoped for, it would expand the old system, with quotas and tariffs on bananas brought in from Latin America and preferential treatment for bananas grown in the former colonies. The new rules went into effect on July 1, 1993.

They certainly should not have come as a surprise to Chiquita, the U.S. government or anyone else. The signs had been clear for years that Europe intended to continue giving preferential status to bananas from its former colonies. An investment report prepared in October 1990 by the Wall Street firm of Shearson Lehman Bros., Inc., predicted that Europe, contrary to Chiquita's hopes, would maintain the status quo for years to come.

Even Chiquita knew at the time what it faced. In its 1992 annual report filed with the U.S. Securities and Exchange Commission, the company acknowledged that "although we will oppose these restrictive policies in the proper legal forums, we are prepared to adapt to this new regulated environment." By this time, Dole, the world's second largest banana producer and Chiquita's only real rival, had hedged its bets and arranged to acquire bananas from those countries with no tariffs and generous import quotas.

Meanwhile, Chiquita's business was tanking. From 1992 to 1994, the company racked up $407 million in losses. Its stock price plunged from $40 to $11 a share. In meetings with government officials, Chiquita laid the blame squarely on the E.U.'s trade restrictions. The U.S. Trade Representative and the rest of the Clinton Administration bought the line, at least officially. And to this day, Chiquita officials insist that's the case. Steven

Warshaw, Chiquita's president, told *Time*, "The E.U.'s illegal banana regime is the cause of the company's poor financial results since 1992. It would be absurd to conclude otherwise . . . It is well accepted that the E.U.'s banana regime was specifically designed to expropriate market share from U.S. banana interests to benefit European multinationals and other interests within the European market . . . Our stock price declined precipitously, and our industry has been substantially damaged."

While there is little question that Chiquita's sales would be higher were it not for Europe's quota and licensing system, a close look at company filings with the Securities and Exchange Commission over the past 15 years shows that a good portion of Chiquita's decline is attributable to other causes. In the years it posted record losses, Chiquita said in the SEC reports, its costs "were significantly impacted" by outbreaks of banana disease, bad weather, a strike by workers in Honduras, as well as shipping and operating losses from its "Japanese 'green' banana trading operations."

Banana pricing wars also took a toll, but even more telling, the company ran up its long-term debt so that cash payments for interest charges spiraled from $52.6 million in 1990 to $164.3 million in 1993. Even if Chiquita sales had reached the level the WTO said they would have in the absence of European restrictive policies, the company still would have recorded losses or, at best, a marginal profit. As a Wall Street investment analyst who tracked the banana industry put it in 1992, "we have serious doubts about the abilities of management to deal with the company's problems."

Over the 15 years ending in 1998, with the Lindners in control, Chiquita tallied total sales of $45 billion but profits of only $44 million. That's the equivalent of a $10,000 investment that returns 65¢ a year. Not surprisingly, the company's stock is now trading at less than $5 a share.

In an SEC filing last December, a minority shareholder of

Chiquita's reported that the Lindners were pondering an auction to sell off Chiquita. All of which may explain the money trail the Lindners left behind in Washington.

Throwing Money At The Problem

Lindner, a nonsmoking, nondrinking, nonswearing Baptist, has been a major supporter of the Republican Party, its candidates and causes. This may account for the less than enthusiastic response that Lindner received when he first took his banana case to the Clinton Administration early in 1993. In fact, at that time the U.S. Trade Representative's internal memos show that bananas were a low priority for the U.S. government. What's more, USTR and State Department officials had given—and would continue to give—repeated assurances to leaders of Caribbean governments that the U.S. supported European preferences for their bananas. And not without good reason. Everyone was fearful that islanders unable to grow and sell bananas would turn to a much bigger cash crop—drugs.

It was against this background that in June of that year, Keith Lindner, then president of Chiquita and one of Carl's three sons in the family businesses, wrote a "Dear Ambassador" letter to Mickey Kantor outlining concerns over Europe's import restrictions. There was little response.

That December, Carl Lindner contributed a quarter of a million dollars to the Democratic National Committee, establishing himself as a generous supporter of both political parties.

Through the early months of 1994, the Lindner lobbying juggernaut concentrated on building congressional support to pressure the Clinton Administration into action. From January to August, lawmakers of both parties bombarded Clinton and Kantor with letters demanding action.

Among the more strident and persistent correspondents were Bob Dole, who would eventually campaign for the presidency aboard Lindner's corporate jet, and John Glenn, who counted Lindner as a campaign contributor.

In January, Dole and Glenn, along with Senator Richard Lugar, wrote to the President calling for "sustained interventions" with European Union officials to make clear that export quotas and licensing "are not an acceptable solution." By August, Dole and Glenn demanded that Kantor initiate a so-called 301 investigation. The name comes from a section of the 1974 trade law that gives the USTR authority to investigate foreign trade practices and impose tariffs in retaliation.

On Sept. 13, Dole arranged a breakfast meeting with Kantor and Lindner. A day later, according to an internal USTR memo, Kantor and his staff had a follow-up meeting with Lindner and his colleagues to discuss "possible strategies" to overturn the European quotas.

Over the years, the USTR has averaged only about five 301 investigations annually. Even rarer are cases in which the USTR has recommended punitive tariffs on the imports of the offending nation. The Chiquita case was rarer still—an instance in which the complaining company was not even a U.S. exporter. Two USTR staff members acknowledged this in a memo to Kantor on Oct. 13, 1994, saying that "if initiated, this investigation would break new ground, as this would be the first time that USTR had ever used Section 301 in connection with a product not exported from the United States but from elsewhere." Nonetheless, the staff members said "we have been persuaded by Chiquita that the practices here do have a significant effect on U.S. commerce." Lawyers for other U.S. corporations disagreed strongly. Natalie Shields, tax and trade counsel for Black & Decker, later captured the logic of the USTR decision this way: "This would inflict substantial harm on one U.S. company in an effort to benefit other U.S. companies which export bananas from third countries."

But the Clinton Administration liked the notion. On Monday, Oct. 17, 1994, Kantor authorized the 301 investigation. That Thursday night Lindner was in the White House, attending a dinner as a guest of the President. And the following week, Al Gore called Lindner, asking for another major donation. Lindner delivered. On Nov. 3, Lindner's American Financial Corp. donated $50,000 to the D.N.C. His Great American Holding Corp. donated $25,000, and his American Money Management kicked in $25,000, bringing the one-day total to $100,000.

At the same time, Senators Dole and Glenn kept the pressure on, urging Kantor in another letter on Nov. 17 to retaliate against the Europeans.

The following month, on Dec. 10, the Lindners again met with Kantor, after which they fired off a "Dear Mickey" letter, thanking him for his efforts.

At year's end, on Dec. 30, James E. Evans, a Lindner executive, contributed $150,000 to the D.N.C., bringing to $250,000 the sum that in one year Lindner, his companies and their executives poured into Democratic coffers.

On Jan. 3, 1995, four days after the latest Lindner-related contribution, Kantor announced "a list of retaliatory actions that he [was] considering against the European Union to counter E.U. policies which discriminate against U.S. banana marketing companies." Specifically, Kantor said he was contemplating sanctions "that would directly hit E.U. firms providing air, maritime and space transportation services."

On Thursday of the same week, Terry McAuliffe, Bill Clinton's moneyman and Lindner's home-building partner, sent a memo to Nancy Hernreich, one of the President's administrative assistants, summarizing a conversation he had had with the President on fund-raising activities. McAuliffe asked that overnight stays at the White House be arranged for major contributors; that dates be scheduled for contributors to have breakfast, lunch or coffee with the President; and that other contributors be included in such presidential activities as golf and jogging.

The next day another aide passed along a memo to Harold Ickes, the President's deputy chief of staff, saying that "Nancy has asked us to follow up on this at the President's direction and his note indicates 'promptly.'" The memo called for "overnights for top top supporters." Accompanying McAuliffe's memo was a 10-person list of those "top top" supporters prepared by McAuliffe. Prominently holding down the No. 2 slot: longtime Republican Carl H. Lindner.

Five weeks later, on Feb. 9, Lindner was in the White House at a state dinner honoring German Chancellor Helmut Kohl. After entertainment by Tony Bennett and a German chorus, Lindner went upstairs to bed. Less than two weeks later, he was back in the White House for coffee.

Cranking Up The Pressure

Throughout this period, Lindner's allies in Congress kept the pressure on the Clinton Administration. On June 21, Senator Dole wrote to Kantor: "I am concerned that time is running out in the banana case. U.S. banana companies are on the verge of suffering even greater irreparable damage as a result of the E.U. and Latin practices."

Kantor scribbled a note in the margin of the letter, addressed to Jeff N.—Jeffrey Nuechterlein, senior counsel to Kantor—and Jeffrey L.—Jeffrey Lang, one of his top aides: "Please give me a way to proceed. Pressure is going to grow. MK."

Kantor says he has no recollection of the note. "I don't remember writing it," he says. Lang doesn't remember it either. He recused himself from the banana dispute, he says, because before his appointment as Deputy U.S. Trade Representative, he represented the European side in the WTO proceedings. Nuechterlein, likewise, doesn't remember anything about it. "I was not involved with bananas substantively," he says.

Dim memories aside, the pressure did indeed grow. On July 19 Carl and Keith Lindner wrote to Kantor again, expressing their dissatisfaction with proposals put forth by the Europeans to resolve the banana dispute. At least in the view of the Lindners, the war should be waged as a joint effort, with Chiquita and its ally, the U.S. government, on one side and the European Union Commission on the other.

On Aug. 3, the four-member Hawaiian congressional delegation sent a letter to Kantor saying they were prepared to talk about possible "international courses of action" against the E.U. As America's only state producing bananas—most were grown for consumption on the islands—Hawaii had an indirect stake in the outcome of the banana war; because Chiquita, Dole and other producers had flooded the European market, tariffs notwithstanding, the overflow had found its way back into the U.S., driving down retail prices.

The following day, Lindner's American Financial Corp. delivered an additional $100,000 to the D.N.C. A few days later, the Lindners met once again with Kantor. Two months went by. On Nov. 3, the Lindners advised Kantor's staff that it was "very important" they get together for 20 minutes. This particular meeting did not take place, but nine days later, on a Sunday night, Lindner was sitting behind Clinton at a presidential gala in Ford's Theatre.

As 1995 gave way to 1996, the money kept gushing from the Lindner empire, much of it in smaller, harder-to-trace donations. In February a Lindner executive gave $10,000 to the D.N.C., and American Financial Corp. contributed $15,000. In March, Lindner directed $10,000 each to the Minnesota, North Carolina, Tennessee and Iowa Democratic parties, $15,000 to the Michigan Democratic Party and $5,000 to the Connecticut Democratic

Party. In April he steered $10,000 to the Pennsylvania Democratic Party.

With at least an additional $95,000 of Lindner money in the Democratic Party's bank accounts, the U.S. Trade Representative on May 8 took its banana case to the WTO. At long last, the Clinton Administration was ready to mount a global trade war on Lindner's behalf.

A spokesman for Chiquita dismissed the suggestion that campaign contributions by Lindner had anything to do with the USTR's taking the case. "It is well known that Carl Lindner has been actively involved and a major contributor to candidates and other causes on a multipartisan basis for many decades," he said.

Former Trade Representative Kantor also insisted that contributions played no part in his decision. "The staff made a unanimous recommendation to me that we bring the case," he said.

Of Lindner's contributions, Kantor said, "I couldn't have cared less. It made no difference to us whatsoever. We didn't hear a word from the White House."

Be that as it may, the USTR decision to pursue a trade war over bananas was sharply at odds with its handling of similar agricultural issues. Consider this: today, even with the tough trade restrictions still in place, Chiquita controls 20% of the European market. By way of contrast, the USTR has negotiated with Japan to allow American companies a 3% share of the Japanese market for rice.

In other words, the U.S. went to war on behalf of one American company that already had 20% of a foreign market, and it negotiated to secure 3% of another foreign market for the benefit of seven to 10 American companies.

Over the next two years, Lindner continued to dispense cash to the Democrats. In June 1997, two installments of $10,000 each went to the Democratic National Committee Services Corp. In November he gave $75,000 to the D.N.C. and in February 1998 another $75,000. That was followed by contributions of $10,000, $10,000, $25,000, $50,000, $25,000 and $5,000.

Throughout this period, Lindner and Chiquita enjoyed a close working relationship with the USTR office. Copies of U.S. government correspondence with heads of state in other countries were voluntarily turned over to Lindner. Finally, on Nov. 10, 1998, the USTR proposed 100% tariffs on several dozen European imports. The agency said the increased tariffs would be imposed on March 3, 1999, if Europe did not relent and relax its restrictions on Latin American bananas.

The products included pecorino cheese, certain wines, apple juice, bath preparations, candles, furs, coniferous wood, paper boxes, lithographs, cashmere sweaters, women's suits, dresses, skirts, bed linens, scissors, sewing machines, vacuum cleaners, food grinders, windshield wipers, dolls, photographic equipment, chandeliers, glass Christmas ornaments, sweet biscuits, wafers, felt paper, plastic handbags, coffee or tea makers, electric toy trains, greeting cards, stoves and ballpoint pens.

In short, it was a list of products bearing absolutely no relation to bananas.

While government officials were assuring reporters that the tariffs would never be levied, the U.S.-based companies that would be affected were taking no chances. In all, 42 types of products were targeted for tariff increases and, as it had to do by law, the USTR asked interested parties to respond.

Respond they did, setting off a furious lobbying campaign to try to get off the banana hit list. Companies and politicians showered the agency with letters warning of potential job losses in their districts if the increased tariffs were imposed.

At a USTR hearing on Dec. 9 attended by trade associations and Washington lobbyists, various interest groups spoke out against the tariffs, saying they would cripple or possibly destroy their businesses.

"The imposition of a prohibitive duty on ballpoint pens would have a devastating effect on Gillette's writing-instruments business in the U.S.," a representative for the Gillette Co. warned.

"Subjecting these dolls to a 100% duty could well result in the collapse of the entire line of American Girl products," a representative for Mattel cautioned.

"The imposition of a 100% duty rate on articles of fur clothing and garments will seriously impact our members, making their garments outrageously expensive, even for a luxury product," declared a representative of the Fur Information Council of America.

Two weeks later, on Dec. 21, products imported by Gillette, Mattel and fur retailers, as well as those of some two dozen other trade groups and industries that testified at the hearing or lobbied the USTR, were dropped from the list.

More lobbying ensued. On April 19, when the final list was published, most of the goods once proposed for high tariffs had been stricken from the list. Only nine types of products were covered.

In announcing the final list, Barshefsky, who had replaced Kantor as U.S. Trade Representative, reiterated that the higher annual tariffs on European goods were in retaliation for Europe's refusal to change its import rules on bananas.

"It is proof that the system works," she said. "When members [of the WTO] refuse to live by the rules, they will pay a price." There was one major oversight in Barshefsky's reasoning: the wrong people were going to pay the price.

The Clinton Administration salvo aimed at giant European corporations hit Rick Reinert, Arthur Kaplan, Timothy Dove and other small entrepreneurs, whose only connection to bananas is to eat one every now and then.

"I Thought It Was A Joke"

Reinert is—or more accurately was—the typical American small-town, small-business success story. He grew up in LaPorte,

Ind., and attended Western Kentucky University before enlisting in the U.S. Army in 1975. He and his wife, whom he met during his Army stint in Germany, started their wholesale bath-supplies business in 1994 out of the family garage in Summerville, S.C., a pine tree–studded bedroom community of Charleston. "We began very meagerly," says Reinert. "We didn't have one account." By knocking on doors, attending an endless parade of trade shows and selecting the right representatives, they built a solid customer base of some 2,000 stores—gift shops, beauty salons, boutiques, grocery stores, independent pharmacies and a major drugstore chain. Their most popular items, which they buy from a German supplier and account for 60% of sales, are aromatic foam baths scented with herbs from lavender to rosemary. And these items were among the ones singled out by the USTR office for its trade war with Europe over bananas.

Reinert remained blissfully unaware until January 1999 that he was on his way to war. That's when he first heard about the proposed tariffs. "I was at a Portland [Ore.] gift show . . . and I happened to read this little blurb in *Time* about bath products. I thought it was a joke." He investigated. "It was no joke. We were on the potential hit list."

That's when Reinert started writing letters and calling everyone—his Congressman, his Senator, the USTR. It was during one of many conversations with a USTR staff member that he was told, in effect, it was his own fault that he had got caught up in the trade war. After all, the USTR had published a list of the targeted imports in the *Federal Register*. He should have attended the hearings in Washington, just like Gillette (annual sales: $10 billion) and Mattel ($5 billion). If he had, then Reha Enterprises (less than $1 million) might have been removed from the list as well.

Reinert is still fuming. "That's ridiculous. I mean, do you read the *Federal Register*? Does anybody in Summerville read the *Federal Register*?" The trade official suggested Reinert should have hired a lobbyist in Washington to keep him briefed. That one didn't go over well either. "I mean, we've got two kids. It's a small business," says Reinert. "Who in his right mind would come up with stuff like that?"

"We're only [six] years old," Reinert says. "Cash flow is always a problem. Finance is always a problem. But they are just destroying the base of our company."

What other advice has Reinert received from officials in the U.S. Trade Representative office and from the staffs of members of Congress?

He says one official urged him, off the record, to break the law—to change the number on the Customs invoice so it would appear that he was importing goods not subject to the tariff. Reinert demurred. "I could end up in jail for it," he says. "I don't want to be the only one without a chair when the music stops."

Another official chided Reinert for not buying American, a rebuke that angered him. Reinert responded, "'Why don't you go out in your parking lot and count all the Mercedes and Porsches, BMWs, Lexuses and Toyotas?' I mean, these are just ridiculous arguments."

In response to repeated calls and letters, Reinert heard personally from Barshefsky last August. The news was not good. Reinert, she suggested, was standing in the wrong place at the wrong time when the war started. She explained in her best bureaucratic language that it was legally impossible to remove Reinert's bath products from the tariff list. Said she: "We have examined the question of whether [the USTR office] has the authority to grant exemptions to small businesses, such as yours, that are severely harmed by the increased tariffs . . . We have concluded that the relevant statute . . . does not provide such authority to USTR."

Three months later, in November 1999, Barshefsky told quite a different story when she testified before the Senate Banking Committee concerning the upcoming WTO gathering in Seattle. In response to a committee member who suggested legislation that would rotate products on and off the tariff hit lists, Barshefsky asserted that "I have discretionary authority as it is to alter a retaliation list if that becomes necessary or advisable. So the authority is already there."

None of this is any help to Reinert, Kaplan, Dove and the hundreds of other small entrepreneurs like them, some of whom have already been forced out of business. Nor is it any consolation for all those who have been caught up in the ripple effect—the peripheral businesses, from trucking companies to local suppliers, who deal with those on the tariff list.

For his part, Reinert continues to wage his battle, writing letters to whoever he thinks just might take an interest in his case. "It's been mentioned to me, you know, from all levels of government, [that] you cannot fight the government. Well, I think you can. It's wrong what they're doing."

The USTR, for its part, insists that the products chosen for high tariffs were intended to "minimize the impact" on Americans and "maximize the impact on Europeans," in the words of Peter Scher, a special trade negotiator. As to how much pressure they have had on Europe, Scher said, "I think it has had an impact. Has it moved the E.U. as far as we want them? No. But it has certainly moved the E.U. to the negotiating table."

Might the tariffs that have squeezed Rick Reinert and other small businesses remain in place another year or two? "Anything is possible," said Scher. "The ball is in the E.U.'s court." Even Chiquita acknowledges that there is little movement toward a settlement. "There is no end in sight," said a company spokesman.

· · ·

So what does the battlefield look like as the Great Banana War's tariffs approach their first anniversary?

Well, the operators of some small businesses, like Reinert, are limping along from month to month. Other small-business people are filing fraudulent Customs documents to escape payment. Other businesses are doing just fine because their suppliers in Europe agreed to pick up the tariff or it applies to just a small percentage of the goods they sell. In Europe as in America, small businesses have been harmed by the U.S. tariffs. Larger companies have been mostly unaffected. And the European Union has kept in place its system of quotas and licenses to limit Chiquita bananas. Who, then, is the winner in this war?

That's easy. It's the President, many members of Congress and the Democratic and Republican parties—all of whom have milked the war for millions of dollars in campaign contributions—along with the lobbyists who abetted the process.

A final note. While Lindner had many areas of political interest beyond his battle with the European Union, a partial accounting of the flow of his dollars during the Great Banana War—as measured by contributions of $1,000 or more—as well as lobbying expenditures on the war, shows:

Republicans—$4.2 million

Democrats—$1.4 million

Washington lobbyists—$1.5 million

That's more money than a business like Rick Reinert's will earn in a lifetime.

Soaked By Congress

Lavished with campaign cash, lawmakers are "reforming" bankruptcy—punishing the downtrodden to catch a few cheats

Congress is about to make life a lot tougher—and more expensive—for people like the Trapp family of Plantation, Fla. As if their life isn't hard enough already. Eight-year-old Annelise, the oldest of the three Trapp children, is a bright, spunky, dark-haired wisp who suffers from a degenerative muscular condition. She lives in a wheelchair or bed, is tied to a respirator at least eight hours a day, eats mostly through a tube and requires round-the-clock nursing care. Doctors have implanted steel rods in her back to stem the curvature of her spine.

Her parents, Charles and Lisa, are staring at a medical bill for $106,373 from Miami Children's Hospital. Then there are the credit-card debts. The $10,310 they owe Bank One. The $5,537 they owe Chase Manhattan Bank. The $8,222 they owe MBNA America. The $4,925 they owe on their Citibank Preferred Visa card. The $6,838 they owe on their Discover card. The $6,458 they owe on their MasterCard. "People don't understand, unless they have a medically needy child, these kinds of circumstances," says Charles Trapp, 42, a mail carrier.

Why would Congress add to the burdens of folks like the Trapps? The family has filed for bankruptcy, and Congress wants to make it a lot more difficult for other Americans to do the same, a change that would hit especially hard at women. And poor people. And the recently jobless. And the sick.

Under legislation Congress is expected to take up soon, families like the Trapps will be required to go through a series of means tests to justify their medical and other expenses. That will cost them: more money in legal bills, more days lost from work, more mental aggravation. Even worse, in the end they still might not qualify for bankruptcy assistance.

Most members of Congress believe in what they are doing. Senator Charles Grassley, an Iowa Republican, speaks for many of his colleagues when he says, "I hope this bill does make bankruptcy more embarrassing—and more difficult. In fact, I plead guilty that that is a motive behind our legislation."

The House passed its version of the bankruptcy bill last year. The Senate enacted its bill in February. Now members of both chambers are meeting in secret to iron out differences and put their finishing touches on what they call the Bankruptcy Reform Act, which has the ostensible goal of curbing abuses.

What is the real reason Congress is doing this? Because the legislation is just what banks, credit-card companies, debt consolidators and other financial-services businesses ordered. To get it, they retained high-powered Washington lobbyists, among them Haley Barbour, former chairman of the Republican National Committee, and Lloyd Bentsen, onetime Senator and Treasury Secretary. The price tag for lobbying: more than $5 million.

At the same time, the lending industry poured contributions into the coffers of the national committees of both political parties and into the campaigns of individual lawmakers whose support was crucial. Some of the giving was appropriately timed. A $200,000 contribution to the National Republican Senatorial Committee by MBNA Corp.—which is to credit cards what Pepsi is to soft drinks—was delivered on the day of an earlier House vote on the bankruptcy bill. It passed handily, 300 to 125. The price tag for political contributions: more than $20 million. Says a Capitol Hill staff member who worked on the bankruptcy legislation: "If this were NASCAR, the members would have to have the corporate logos of their sponsors sewn to their jackets."

The Bankruptcy Reform Act is typical of legislation that Congress writes for the benefit of special-interest groups that are hefty campaign contributors—at the expense of ordinary Americans who contribute nothing. The proposed legislation would treat a bankrupt man's credit-card debt the same as his obligation to pay child support, meaning that MasterCard and an unmarried mother would compete for the same limited pool of cash. And the law would create hurdles intended to discourage or prevent people from filing for bankruptcy protection.

If, for example, a bankruptcy filer was left with more than $1,200 a year (beyond his basic expenses) over five years, that would be considered an abuse. If a mother tapped an ATM to buy necessities such as food or prescription drugs six weeks before filing for bankruptcy, the withdrawal could be considered a fraudulent transaction. If a family planned to file for bankruptcy, it would first have to undergo credit counseling, in some cases at its own expense. If a child or some other member of the family received medical treatment within 90 days before the bankruptcy filing, the bills could never be written off, no matter how poor the family.

To get into bankruptcy court, a filer would have to produce a variety of financial documents, including statements of projected monthly income and expected pay raises over the next year, and tax returns for the previous three years. No one of these requirements may look particularly onerous. But taken together, these and other provisions would impose additional burdens and legal costs on individuals and families already struggling to survive. "It's a thousand paper cuts," says Elizabeth Warren, a Harvard Law School professor and bankruptcy specialist. "And some people will bleed to death from a thousand paper cuts."

That includes people like the Trapps, who, after years of meeting their bills, were finally engulfed in a sea of debt through circumstances beyond their control. In that, they fit the classic image of a family seeking help in bankruptcy court. Contrary to the popular view of bankruptcy filers as free spenders who vacation in the Caribbean and buy expensive jewelry on their credit cards, the vast majority turn to bankruptcy court only after one of three events: loss of job, divorce or extraordinary medical expenses—in short, the kind of misfortune that can befall anyone. For the Trapps, it was two out of three. Just as the family was consumed by medical bills, Lisa Trapp had to give up her job as a mail carrier to manage her daughter's care.

Current bankruptcy law allows most individuals and families to file under Chapter 7. Here, assets—if there are any—are pulled together by a trustee and sold off. The bankruptcy filer may be able to keep his home and a few personal possessions. Retirement accounts and pensions also cannot be touched. Proceeds from the asset sale are divided among creditors. Outstanding debts, such as credit-card or medical bills, are discharged, meaning they do not have to be paid. Again there are certain exceptions: most taxes, child support, alimony and student loans cannot be discharged. Other individuals and families—those who are deemed able to pay back a larger portion of their debt—may file under Chapter 13. Here, the debtor agrees to pay a percentage of his income every month for up to five years to a trustee, who distributes the money to creditors.

During the 1990s, there were two filings under Chapter 7 for every one under Chapter 13. But the overwhelming majority of Chapter 13 bankruptcy cases ended in failure, with the debtors unable to complete the payment plan because they had insufficient income.

Under the legislation before Congress, new means tests would force more borrowers into Chapter 13—leading to still more failures—and would eliminate bankruptcy as an option for others. For this second group, life will be especially bleak. Listen to their future as described by Brady Williamson, who teaches constitutional law at the University of Wisconsin in Madison and was chairman of the former National Bankruptcy Review Commission, appointed by Congress in 1995: "A family without access to the bankruptcy system is subject to garnishment proceedings, to multiple collection actions, to repossession of personal property and to mortgage foreclosure. There is virtually no way to save their home and, for the family that does not own a home, no way to ever qualify to buy one." The wage earner will be "faced with what is essentially a life term in debtor's prison."

How did this come about? The credit-card industry seized on a sharp increase in bankruptcy filings in 1996 and 1997 to mount an intensive lobbying campaign for legislation that would make it easier to collect from borrowers who file for bankruptcy. A sophisticated public-relations blitz created the image of a bankruptcy system rife with abuse and in need of reform. That campaign told of rich people walking away from their debts, courtesy of bankruptcy court. It told of responsible families who paid their bills being forced to pick up the costs of more affluent Americans and others who were bilking the system. And it warned that bankruptcy had lost its "stigma."

The industry bankrolled studies to back its claims. In February 1998 the WEFA Group, a Philadelphia-based economics consulting firm, released a report contending that personal bankruptcies cost each American household an average of $400 a year. Paid for by MasterCard International and Visa USA, the WEFA study put the overall cost to the economy at $44 billion in 1997. Said Mark Lauritano, a WEFA senior vice president: "Clearly, the American consumer is facing a significant burden as the result of bankruptcy, both through higher prices and increased interest rates." The dollar-cost claims—which were disinguous at best— would become the most widely quoted statistics in the campaign that produced the legislation now before Congress.

To apply pressure on lawmakers, the industry ran a series of ads in newspapers calling for bankruptcy reform. "What Do Bankruptcies Cost American Families?" asked a typical ad in the Washington *Post* on June 4, 1998. The answer: "A month's worth of groceries." Sponsored by a consortium of credit-industry trade associations, the ad showed a shopping cart filled with groceries. "Today's record number of personal bankruptcies costs every American family $400 a year. Now Congress has an opportunity to enact bankruptcy reform that reduces this burden and is fair to everyone . . . while ensuring that people who can pay their debts do so."

Other Visa- and MasterCard-financed studies asserted that many whose debts are discharged in bankruptcy could actually pay some of their bills but don't. The Credit Research Center at Georgetown University estimated that 25% of the debtors who file in Chapter 7 could repay more than 30% of their nonhousing debt over five years. The study warned that the continuing rise in bankruptcy filings would increase the cost of credit. It concluded: "Our results imply that the bankruptcy system itself is contributing to these rising costs by offering the opportunity to wipe out debt with a single signature to many borrowers that have the ability to repay."

Industry lobbyists promoted the themes. George Wallace, a lawyer representing the American Financial Services Association, contended that there is "growing statistical evidence that there's a significant group of American consumers who are using bankruptcy when they have some ability to pay. We have a system today that is broken, a system that provides a welfare benefit without a means testing."

Members of Congress echoed the industry line. Declared Representative George Gekas, the Pennsylvania Republican who shepherded the legislation through the House (and who has collected $30,000 in political contributions since 1997 from bankers and credit-card companies): "In 1997 Americans filed an all-time record of 1.33 million consumer-bankruptcy petitions, which erased an estimated $40 billion in consumer debt. Those losses are passed on to [other] consumers, resulting in a hidden tax for every American household. The only reasonable explanation is that the stigma of bankruptcy is all but dead. It is simply too easy to file."

Representative Bill McCollum, a Florida Republican who has received $225,000 from the lending industry, upped the ante: "Bankruptcy will cost consumers more than $50 billion in 1998 alone. That translates into more than $550 per household in higher costs for goods, services and credit."

Senator Robert Torricelli of New Jersey, a strong advocate of the Senate bill and head of the Democratic Senatorial Campaign Committee, last year pocketed a $150,000 contribution from MBNA. "What every American needs to understand is that somebody is paying the price," says Torricelli. "I believe this is the equivalent of an invisible tax on the American family, estimated to cost each and every American family $400 a year."

There is only one problem with all this rhetoric: it's not true. That's the finding of a *Time* investigation based on interviews with those directly involved in the system—judges, lawyers, trustees, bankruptcy professors and the bankrupt themselves—along with an examination of court records across the country and an array of statistical evidence. While lenders do indeed lose money on those who fail to pay their bills, the U.S. Bankruptcy Court maintains no statistics on the types of debt written off—credit cards, medical, personal loans—or the total dollar amount discharged. But whatever that number may be, it misses the point: there is little more to be extracted from those in bankruptcy. Some people unquestionably use bankruptcy court to escape bills they could afford to pay, but their numbers are insignificant. The vast majority of bankruptcy filers have neither the income nor the assets to pay creditors. Most turn to bankruptcy as a last resort.

To understand how much at odds with the real world the bankruptcy scene imagined by Congress and the lending industry is, spend a moment with the people who have a street-level view of the system. Steven Friedman, a bankruptcy judge in West Palm Beach, Fla., describes the people who pass through his courtroom as "average citizens who have worked hard to obtain a decent standard of living and, through unfortunate circumstances such as medical problems or financial or job loss, are down on their luck." He adds, "The instances of abuse, where people who file bankruptcy are attempting to defraud their creditors or to be dishonest, are very [few]."

Says attorney Judith Swift, a former president of the bankruptcy bar in Dallas: "I keep a box of tissues in my office because people are mortified that they have to file bankruptcy. I've seen grown men break down. They take the financial crises as a sign of personal failure. A lot of people who come to my office have been holding down one full-time job and two piddly little part-time jobs, trying frantically not to have to file a bankruptcy. It's a very, very difficult decision for most people."

It was for Maxean Bowen, a single mother raising an 11-year-old daughter. A social worker in the foster-care system in New York City, Bowen helped rehabilitate parents with substance-abuse problems. In 1998 she developed a painful condition in both feet that made it difficult for her to walk. Because her job required her to make house calls, she had to give it up and go on unemployment, hoping the condition would ease up. Her take-home pay dropped from about $1,600 a month to $800. To get by, she borrowed from relatives and started using credit cards to pay for food, clothing, utilities and rent. "I thought, 'As soon as I get back to work, I'll try to pay these off,'" she says.

By 1999, when she got a job interviewing families in an office, she owed thousands of dollars to the credit-card companies— much of it in late fees. That's when the threatening calls and letters surged. "They would call me on the job," she says. "That was very embarrassing. They call you early in the morning. They call you late at night. Sometimes I get calls at 10 o'clock at night. And they are very nasty." To placate them, she sent $200 to $300 on occasion. "But when the bill came the next month, it seemed like it went higher," she says. "I was going crazy."

A co-worker suggested bankruptcy, and Bowen filed a petition in U.S. Bankruptcy Court in New York. She still gets calls demanding payment. At least now, she says, she knows her creditors can't attach her salary, no matter how ugly the conversation turns.

Bowen's discovery that she was treading water despite her partial payments—and that the outstanding balance never went down—is not unusual. A government study showed that by the time individuals and families seek bankruptcy protection, more than 20% of income before taxes is going toward paying interest and fees on their unsecured debt.

This helps underscore why the notion that debtors in bankruptcy court are sitting on many billions of dollars that they could turn over to their creditors is a figment of the imagination of lenders and lawmakers. Consider:

- A study of 1,955 Chapter 7 bankruptcy filers in 1997–98 by the Executive Office for U.S. Trustees, which monitors the bankruptcy system, concluded that "by the time they filed, they had little if any capacity to repay. In fact, most will have to increase income or reduce expenses to remain solvent after bankruptcy."

- The same study projected that the total amount that unsecured creditors, like credit-card companies, might be expected to collect from all Chapter 7 filers added up to "less than $1 billion annually."

- A study by two law professors at Creighton University, funded by the nonpartisan American Bankruptcy Institute, found that only 3.6% of Chapter 7 debtors would be able to pay more. "The vast majority belong in that chapter," the study stressed. "They have too little income after necessary expenses to repay unsecured debt. It is vital, therefore, that no undue burdens be thrust on that needy majority in order to flush out a small minority of abusers." The amount that might be collected: less than $1 billion.

- Congress's own investigative arm, the General Accounting Office, criticized two studies financed by the credit-card industry that purported to show that a substantial number of debtors could pay more. Questioning their assumptions, data and sampling procedures, the GAO said that "neither report provides reliable answers to the questions of how many debtors could make some repayment and how much debt they could repay."

As all of this suggests, there is little money to be squeezed out of those in bankruptcy, especially since trustees already collect about $4 billion from debtors each year, a sum that includes proceeds from liquidated assets. Even if they could find an additional $1 billion, the economic and emotional costs of doing so would far outweigh the return. To put it in perspective, the estimated $1 billion that might be collected would amount to two-tenths of 1 percentage point of outstanding revolving credit. If trustees were able to scare up another $4 billion—as the industry claims but few in the bankruptcy system believe possible—it would still amount to less than seven-tenths of 1 percentage point of revolving credit.

To further undercut claims by the lending industry that it needs get-tough legislation, 82 professors at 66 law schools, from Harvard to UCLA, last September signed a letter itemizing the consequences the proposed bankruptcy legislation would have on those in need of financial relief. It was sent to every U.S. Senator.

What would motivate a sizable majority of Congress to support such legislation? Money. Lots of it. In addition to the $5 million the lending industry spent on lobbyists who worked exclusively on pushing the bankruptcy bill through Congress, it shelled out $50 million that went to firms that lobbied on bankruptcy and other issues.

To be sure, some lawmakers who voted for the bill believe bankruptcy is out of control, that many filers just want to walk away from debts they can afford to pay. Some were angered by the procession of Hollywood entertainers and other wealthy prominent citizens who used the system in the 1990s. Some were annoyed by lawyers who advertised bankruptcy as an easy solution for overextended consumers. And some were troubled by what they saw as a decline in values. "We have had a general lack of shame or personal responsibility that used to be associated with paying bills or not paying bills and the filing of bankruptcy," said Senator Grassley, who has collected more than $100,000 in campaign contributions from credit-card companies and other lenders since 1997.

While the bill contains some genuine reforms, on balance the harm that it would do far outweighs the good. At the same time Congress has written legislation to make life more burdensome for low- and middle-income filers, it has declined to put any curbs on practices of the financial industry that are leading many individuals deeper and deeper into debt. Beverly Fox, a bankruptcy lawyer in Plantation, told *Time*: "[You] have a family with an annual gross combined income of $35,000. I see they owe Citibank $10,700. At the time Citibank gave them that credit limit, which is almost 33% of their annual gross income, Citibank looked at their credit report, or should have, and could see that they already owed three or four other credit cards $3,000, to $4,000, to $5,000. They were already $15,000 in debt, and the banks continued to raise [the family's] credit limits because they are making the minimum payments. Once a family is over 30%

debt-to-income ratio, it should stop using unsecured credit. But people don't know that. They think that because they've been approved for this higher credit limit, they can manage it." Because many people pay only the minimum amount due or a few dollars more, Fox says, they think everything is fine. But the balance on the cards "continues to grow, more as a result of the interest than the use of the cards."

Consumer advocates urged Congress to include in the legislation a provision requiring credit-card companies to spell out on each monthly statement the number of years it would take a cardholder to pay off the debt by making minimum payments, and how much that would cost overall. But that proposal went nowhere because it was opposed by the credit-card industry. The Senate version of the bill requires companies to include on monthly statements a toll-free number that cardholders can call to find out how long it would take them to pay off their loan.

Congress also turned back an amendment by Senator Paul Wellstone, a Minnesota Democrat, who proposed that lenders who charged more than 100% annual interest should be barred from collecting their debts in bankruptcy court. One-hundred percent interest? Actually, that's the bargain-basement rate. In some cases, interest rates run upwards of 1,000%.

Welcome to the world of payday lending, where annual interest rates would make Mob loan sharks of an earlier era blush in embarrassment. The business flourishes in working-class neighborhoods, where people run out of money before their next payday. The lender may charge up to $40 for a $200 loan to be repaid in two weeks. That's an annual interest rate of 521%. In exchange for the advance, the lender requires the borrower to write a check for $240, dated to coincide with his next paycheck. When the two weeks are up, the borrower may repay the loan or roll it over into a new one, further increasing the interest charges. If the borrower fails to do either, the lender cashes the postdated check. If it bounces, the lender sues and in some states collects up to three times the value of the check, plus interest.

An Illinois study found the average annual interest rate for such services in that state was 533%. One customer was charged 2,007%.

Senator Orrin Hatch, a Utah Republican who has championed the bankruptcy legislation, defended payday loans. Said Hatch: "These lenders provide a vital service to the poorest borrowers. With this check-cashing service, borrowers can get the emergency cash they need without telling the boss they need a cash advance or giving up their televisions and furniture."

The burgeoning payday-loan industry includes publicly owned companies. Ace Cash Express, Inc., of Irving, Texas, operates more than 900 stores in 28 states and the District of Columbia where it cashes checks, sells lottery tickets and provides money-transfer and bill-paying services. At a third of its stores, Ace offers payday loans. Its stock is traded on the NASDAQ.

For a fee of $30, Ace will advance cash for a $200 check for two weeks. That works out to an annual rate of 391%. Income from the company's lending operations jumped from 7% of its total revenue in 1997 to 12% in 1999.

The company's largest stockholder is Edward ("Rusty") Rose III of Dallas. Rose owns 11% of Ace's outstanding stock, according to documents filed with the U.S. Securities and Exchange Commission. Rose is the millionaire Dallas investor who helped George W. Bush turn a $600,000 investment in the Texas Rangers baseball team into $15 million—a 2,400% profit. Rose is one of the Bush Pioneers, the elite group of fund raisers who each promised to raise $100,000 for the Texas Governor's presidential race.

While Rose has done quite nicely from his investments, customers of Ace Cash Express and other payday lenders have not fared nearly so well. As you might expect, people who pay interest charges of 300% or more often end up in bankruptcy court. Says

David Nixon, a lawyer in Fayetteville, Ark.: "The kinds of people who use payday loans are just barely getting by. They have jobs. They work hard. They try to pay their bills, but they come up short. Here's an easy way to get cash fast—at least it seems easy. But it's like getting on a treadmill. Once they get on it, it's impossible to get off."

Sometimes the people on the treadmill aren't those you might expect. In Greenwood, Ind., one of Ace's customers was Eva Rowings, 60, a retired high school Latin teacher. In 1995 Rowings began teaching part time at a reduced salary. "I tried to make ends meet," she says, "and I did pretty well for a couple of years, but then it all went downhill." She had four operations, including gall bladder surgery and orthoscopic procedures on both shoulders.

The debts piled up. She owed $5,800 in medical bills, $5,900 on credit cards and $8,100 in loans, plus other miscellaneous bills. Her debts matched her total annual income.

She began borrowing at two other payday-lending firms before turning to Ace, where she was "astonished at the number of senior citizens that were coming in each month." In a typical transaction, she borrowed $200 for 12 days and paid a $30 fee—an annual interest rate of 456%. If she missed a payment, she says, she would owe an additional $30. "By the end of the month," she says, "I would have no money." Finally, a distressed Rowings, who had always believed in paying her debts but was worn down by the endless dunning calls from bill collectors day and night, decided there was never going to be an end. She filed for bankruptcy. "It was humiliating," she says. "I wished I had never stopped teaching full time."

Another point should be noted. Rowings did not contribute to the election campaigns of candidates for Congress. Nor did Charles and Lisa Trapp. Nor Maxean Bowen. Their creditors, on the other hand, have contributed millions and millions of dollars to get the legislation they want—from thousands of small donations of less than $5,000 to hundreds of large ones ranging from $5,000 to more than a quarter-million dollars. Since 1997 credit-card companies and other lenders have given $2.2 million to the House and Senate Judiciary Committee members responsible for drafting the legislation, according to data compiled by the Center for Responsive Politics.

While the industry got much of what it wanted, Congress thus far has sidestepped an opportunity to enact a genuine reform and end one of the most blatant bankruptcy inequities—the homestead provision.

If you live in a $2 million home in Texas or Florida and file for bankruptcy, you are guaranteed you can keep your home. If you live in a $75,000 home in Pennsylvania or Delaware and file for bankruptcy, you may lose it. How is this possible? People who file for bankruptcy claim their exemptions under state law. In the case of the homestead law, the provision varies from state to state. Five states—Florida, Iowa, Kansas, South Dakota and Texas—have unlimited exemptions. Whether a residence is worth $10,000 or $10 million, it can't be touched by creditors. Five other states— Delaware, Maryland, New Jersey, Pennsylvania and Rhode Island—along with the District of Columbia, have no homestead provision, meaning a person can lose his home in bankruptcy. The value of the exemption in the remaining 40 states ranges from $2,500 in Arkansas to $200,000 in Minnesota.

Advocates of bankruptcy overhaul outside Congress have argued for years that federal law should be amended so that all Americans are treated alike, no matter where they live. But Congress doesn't see it that way. The reason? States' rights. Says Senator Sam Brownback, a Kansas Republican: "What is being attempted here is to take a right away from states that they've had for over a hundred years. It's contrary to states' rights."

Not exactly. The Constitution expressly gives Congress the power to establish "uniform laws on the subject of bankruptcies throughout the United States." Both the House and Senate bills contain homestead provisions. Neither deals with the basic unfairness of the exemption. The Senate bill would permit bankruptcy filers to retain up to $100,000 in equity in their home. Any amount over that would go to creditors. The House bill would allow homeowners to retain up to $250,000 in equity. But that cap would be meaningless, since any state could opt out of it under the bill. Key members of Congress are on record as saying there will be no bill that limits the exemption.

To understand how the current system works, how it would work under "reform"—most likely the same—and how it should work if Congress were crafting a law that treated all people equally, let's consider the story of two homeowners in bankruptcy. One is James Villa, a 42-year-old onetime stockbroker who lives in a $1.4 million home in Boca Raton, Fla. The other is Allen Smith, a 73-year-old retired autoworker with throat cancer who lives in a deteriorating $80,000 home in Wilmington, Del.

Let's begin with Villa. Through most of the 1990s, he was president, chief executive officer and indirect owner of 99.5% of the stock of H.J. Meyers & Co., Inc., a brokerage firm based in Rochester, N.Y., with branch offices in more than a dozen cities. H.J. Meyers was a boiler room. Its most significant feature, according to an investigation by Massachusetts securities authorities, "was the high-pressure tactics of management continually exerted on brokers, who then used high-pressure tactics on their customers." Brokers cold-called people urging them to invest in speculative securities and initial public offerings underwritten by the firm. Brokers "implied to investors that they were in possession of important nonpublic information concerning an issuer."

One investor bought stock on his credit card after being assured that he would double his $25,000 investment and that "nothing can go wrong." He didn't and it did. He lost $15,000 and was forced to take out a home equity loan to cover his losses.

Villa profited handsomely from the business. For himself, he collected cigarette speedboats and vintage autos and racing cars, from a 1957 Cadillac to a 1990 Ferrari. For his wife, he collected jewelry—a $22,000 Rolex watch, a three-carat $44,000 wedding ring and $9,000 diamond earrings.

In October 1998, Massachusetts securities authorities ruled that H.J. Meyers had engaged in fraudulent and unethical practices. They revoked the broker-dealer registrations of the firm, Villa and four of his associates. Shortly before the crackdown, H.J. Meyers closed its doors, and in November 1998 Villa packed up and headed for Florida and its generous homestead exemption. He left behind a countryside littered with investors who had lost money, including some whose retirement savings had disappeared. Some of the unlucky H.J. Meyers clients took their cases to arbitration, won awards and filed claims in Villa's bankruptcy case.

How much the creditors will eventually receive is up in the air. Charles Cohen, Villa's lawyer, says that "obviously, Mr Villa is going to try to pay back everything he can. How much I can't tell you at this point." In the assets column, Villa's most valuable possession is his $1.4 million Boca Raton home. But it's beyond the reach of his creditors, thanks to the homestead exemption.

By contrast, 1,100 miles to the north, in Wilmington, Del., 73-year-old Allen Smith is about to lose his home in bankruptcy court. Smith was born in Birmingham, Ala., and served in the Coast Guard during World War II. After his discharge in 1945, he attended an auto-mechanics school in Detroit and then went to work as a metal finisher and body repairman for Chrysler. The company transferred him to its Delaware plant in 1959, where he worked until he was forced out after 35 years during one of the automaker's downsizings.

Smith bought his modest home in Wilmington in 1964. In 1970, at age 44, he married. His wife Carolyn worked at a neighborhood florist. "I was living good, having a good time," Smith told *Time*, "giving my wife everything she needed. Tried to make her happy."

When Smith lost his job at Chrysler in 1982, he was too young to collect Social Security so he took a new job as a security guard. Two years later, his world began to unravel. "Everything just went bad at one time. It waited until I got retired. If I had been working, it would have been different, but I had retired before everything started to happen."

"Everything" began with his wife's diabetes. "She just lost her toe in 1984," he says. Then "they had to cut her leg. And they had to keep cutting it off." Finally, they amputated both legs. To accommodate her wheelchair, Smith built a ramp and made other renovations. To pay for it all and to keep up with the monthly payments on all his credit cards, he borrowed against his house, which had been paid off. "I had what they called triple-A credit," he says.

Along the way, Smith's physical condition deteriorated, and he had to quit his security job. He developed throat cancer and now speaks through a voice box. "I got sick," he says. "I got a thyroid [condition], cancer, low sugar, high blood pressure, heart murmur. I got everything. I'm lucky to be alive."

In June 1998 the Smiths filed a bankruptcy petition under Chapter 13, with the understanding they would make $100 monthly payments to a trustee who would distribute the money to creditors. By that time, the loan against their home had swelled to $64,000, and they owed $51,000 on their credit cards and charge accounts, double their annual income. That November, Carolyn Smith died. With the loss of her Social Security income, Smith struggled. His situation was further complicated by a run of misfortune. He was hospitalized after a stroke; he had cataract surgery; the friend who promised to collect his pension and Social Security checks and make his mortgage payments didn't, and the mortgage company moved to foreclose. That's when his Chapter 13 case collapsed—as happens in two-thirds of all Chapter 13 proceedings—and he was switched to Chapter 7. Now he's awaiting his discharge. He will lose his home and move to Toledo, where he will live with a niece. "I wasn't planning to move," he says. "It hurts. I don't want to be nobody's responsibility because I've always been my own man all my life."

To create a level playing field for everyone, Congress would need to enact a flat exemption that covers all assets—from home to pension. Otherwise there is the kind of inequity described by A. Jay Cristol, the chief U.S. bankruptcy judge in Miami:

"Let's assume you have two very decent, honest people and one of them has a million-dollar home and one of them has a million dollars in cash and they go into bankruptcy. The one with the million-dollar home keeps a million bucks and the one with the million dollars in cash gives all but a thousand dollars in cash to the trustee."

The same scenario applies to retirement accounts. The wealthy investor who puts $1 million into a retirement plan gets to keep the money. The middle-income family with $10,000 in a savings account loses it.

The simple solution: Establish one exemption that covers all assets, from homesteads to pensions. Says Judge Cristol: "Why not just say you can have as a fresh start $55,000 or $100,000, or whatever the legislature decides is the right amount, and it doesn't make a difference if it's equity in your home or whether it's cash in the bank. That's what you get to keep. And that would be fairer and simpler, and the poorest people would be treated the same as the wealthiest people. But as it is now, the worse off you are, the worse you're treated."

Lenders and lawmakers maintain that the bankruptcy laws need to be toughened to reverse the sharp growth in filings during the 1990s. While bankruptcy cases did indeed rise through 1998, they fell in 1999. But what Congress and credit-card companies neglected to say was that the increase was largely attributable to one group—women with modest or low incomes. For this group, reform is going to be especially bad.

Although courts do not keep data on the number of men, women and couples who file for bankruptcy, academic studies have developed estimates. Research conducted by Elizabeth Warren, a Harvard law professor, and Teresa Sullivan, dean of graduate studies at the University of Texas, shows the pattern. From 1981 to 1999, bankruptcy filings by women shot up 838%—four times as fast as for all others—jumping from 53,000 to 497,000. In contrast, filings by husbands and wives rose just 138%, from 178,000 to 423,000. Once a small minority in bankruptcy court, women now comprise the largest single bloc—39% of all personal-bankruptcy cases—more than men or couples.

Despite all the glowing economic indicators that point up—stock-market indexes, employment, corporate profits—the income gap continues to widen, and those most often found toward the bottom are women. Even women in jobs that pay solid middle-class wages find themselves in financial trouble and must seek bankruptcy protection when they are overwhelmed by debt following a breakup or a divorce.

Women such as Lucy Garcia. The 26-year-old mother of two boys, ages 9 and 6, Garcia is a payroll coordinator at the Sheraton New York, one of midtown Manhattan's largest hotels. Assigned to the food-and-beverage department, she helps compute wages, overtime payments and other payroll items for the department's 800 employees. And she balances the department's checkbook.

But in her personal life, balancing finances hasn't been easy since Garcia and her sons' father separated more than a year ago. Family finances had always been tight, and with just one paycheck, Garcia found herself using credit cards to buy the basics. "Sometimes when you don't have money and you need to buy things for your kids, like food and stuff like that, you use the credit card because it's so easy," she says.

After payroll deductions for taxes and Social Security, she had about $1,850 a month to pay her bills. After her rent of $580, a car loan of $400 and an insurance premium of $200, she was left with $670 a month to feed and clothe the boys and herself and pay for her utilities, child care, other miscellaneous expenses—and her credit-card bills.

To bring the ballooning debt under control, she stopped using credit cards and made nominal payments on her accounts. "I thought if I sent them something, $10 or $20, they would leave me alone," she says. But she only fell further behind. Even in months when she didn't use the credit cards, the amount she owed rose because of late-payment penalties and interest charges. Before long, she needed to pay at least $300 a month just to stay even.

Unable to do so, she became increasingly short of cash and unable to pay her bills—rent, car, credit cards. She began alternating payments—the rent one month, credit cards the next, making a car payment after that. That didn't work either, and soon she was getting dunning letters and phone calls. One credit-card company threatened to attach her wages.

"It is just so frustrating to know you owe this much money," she says. "I wish I had the money to pay it off and be O.K. I can't sleep at night. I have tried to not let it affect me with my children. Kids don't know. They say, 'Mommy, I want this.' 'Can we do that?' My God, if they only knew."

When she fell behind in the rent and her landlord warned that he would evict her, she knew she had to do something. She turned to a Manhattan consumer-bankruptcy lawyer, Charles Juntikka. Garcia was typical of many of his clients—embarrassed by her debts, upset over not being able to pay her bills, not knowing where to turn. "There is this image of middle-class people running up huge debts, then declaring bankruptcy and laughing at everyone," he says. "I've just never seen that. These people hurt."

Juntikka filed a petition for Garcia under Chapter 7, seeking to have her unsecured credit-card debt discharged. Garcia says she intends to give up the car to further reduce her debt load, and Juntikka is optimistic she will get a fresh start. Now, for the first time in months, Garcia says, she can sleep at night.

But if the Bankruptcy Reform Act pending in Congress were the law, Garcia would not be able to rest so easy. "Lucy wouldn't be able to obtain a discharge under this bill," says Juntikka. "Under the new standards Congress has put in the bill, she earns too much money. She could not get a discharge. She would still be stuck with some of the credit-card bills she can't pay now."

The standards referred to by Juntikka concern the means testing that allocates a fixed amount of expenses to debtors in computing their ability to pay their debts. And as Juntikka interprets them, Garcia would not be able to seek relief in Chapter 7. Even if by some chance she could prove her case in court, he says, the process would be lengthy and costly. "People aren't going to be able to deal with these draconian measures," he says. As a result, some people will be permanently indebted to credit-card companies, others will see their wages attached, some may lose their homes. "This is going to cause so much misery," he says.

Warren, the Harvard law professor and longtime student of bankruptcy, marvels at how a piece of legislation that could penalize so many people has come this far. "This is one of those things with low visibility, and therefore it's easy to give in to the interest group," says Warren. "It all flies below the radar screen. That's the best place for the lobbyists. That's where the pickings are the fattest. The only way to explain it is campaign contributions."

Throwing The Game

Why Congress isn't closing a loophole that fosters gambling on college sports—and corrupts them

I s it possible that an industry in one state can stymie legislation sought by community leaders in the other 49?

You bet.

Not only is it possible. That's the way it works in the world of campaign contributions. Gambling on college sports is a case study of how Big Money runs Washington.

Eight years ago, at the urging of worried coaches and university presidents, Congress outlawed betting on collegiate sports in every state except Nevada.

Since then, the big money at stake has become a bad influence on campus, riddling college sports with such corruption as game rigging and point shaving. Dozens of athletes have been convicted or suspended. When you follow the money in these cases, it leads to one place: Nevada. That's because student athletes profit from legal bets placed in Las Vegas and Reno casinos, and, far more significantly, bookies in the other 49 states funnel illegal bets into those casinos to protect themselves from having to pay out on unlikely winners at high odds.

There has been an outcry from universities and even some alarmed members of Congress. But the 1992 law still holds, and gambling on college games is thriving as never before in Nevada. Legislation meant to deal with that problem, favored by a congressional majority, remains buried on Capitol Hill.

What gives?

Nevada gives, that's what. In particular, the gaming industry gives to Congress—and gives and gives, in the form of contributions to both political parties totaling more than $16 million over the past six years. That's four times as much money as the gaming industry sent to Washington in the previous six years. And it's enough, apparently, to persuade congressional leaders to band together to stop (so far) a proposed bill that would end the Nevada exemption from even reaching the floor of either the House or the Senate. If there is an object lesson here, it is this: Money talks in Washington, and it talks loud enough to drown out supporters of the most well-meaning legislation, no matter how large their numbers, no matter how influential they might seem to be. It's almost as if the gamblers are keeping prominent lawmakers of both parties on retainer.

And a lucrative retainer it is. In November 1997, Trent Lott, the Mississippi Republican and Senate majority leader, and Mitch McConnell, the Republican Senator from Kentucky who believes unlimited campaign cash is a free-speech right, flew to Las Vegas aboard the jet of casino impresario Steve Wynn to attend a gaming industry G.O.P. fund raiser. The Republicans left with $100,000—the start of something big. Within a year, additional casino contributions would boost that sum to nearly $1 million.

In May 1999, Richard Gephardt, the Democratic Congressman from Missouri and House minority leader, and his colleague Charles Rangel, New York Democrat, flew to Las Vegas to pick up a check from Wynn in the amount of $250,000. The money went to the Democratic Congressional Campaign Committee. And this week Gephardt and Rangel plan to return for yet another fund raiser, where they hope to raise $500,000.

For America's $30 billion-a-year gambling industry, the system has worked nicely. When some members of Congress tried to end the individual income tax deduction for gambling losses, key Republicans and Democrats buried the measure. Twice. Now casinos want to kill the legislation outlawing betting everywhere on collegiate and all amateur sports that would close the Nevada loophole. The legislation has the support of coaches and university administrators from Florida to Oregon. But it has been bottled up by the congressional leadership since April, despite growing pressure from reformers like Arizona Republican Senator John McCain.

In the 1990s, when gambling on college sports became a major attraction at Las Vegas casinos—the betting action topped $2 billion a year, and the NCAA basketball championship rivaled the Super Bowl as the single largest gambling event—more college athletes were involved in fixing games or wagering on college teams than in any of the decades before legalized gaming became popular. Some of that action flowed into Nevada from illegal gambling networks across the country. Among the college gambling cases since 1992:

The University of Maine suspended 19 members of its football and basketball teams for their roles in a $10,000-a-week gambling operation; the University of Rhode Island and Bryant College uncovered a gambling ring involving student athletes; a Northwestern University running back who became the school's career rushing leader fumbled the football on the goal line to ensure that his team would not beat the point spread and that he would win his $400 wager; a Central Florida student team manager was convicted in federal court of offering $15,000 in bribes to players to hold down scoring and cover the point spread in a basketball game with Stanford; Boston College suspended 13 members of its football team for betting on college sports, including three who reportedly bet against their own team; two Arizona State players were convicted and sent to prison for shaving points; two former Northwestern University basketball players were convicted of rigging games against Penn State, Wisconsin and Michigan, a scam organized by a former Notre Dame place kicker turned bookie; four former Northwestern football players pleaded guilty to perjury charges after lying to grand juries investigating sports betting at the school; and last year the University of Michigan released a study saying that nearly half of the male athletes in the survey acknowledged wagering on college sports. The study indicated that 1 of every 20 players shaved points, bet on his own games or leaked insider information about players to gamblers.

None of that's surprising, given the mixed message that Congress sends to student athletes; gambling on college sports is a federal crime in 49 states, but it's legal in Nevada. "People in general, college students in particular, have the belief that betting on college athletics is O.K. because it's legal in Nevada," said Lou Holtz, the former Notre Dame football coach now at the University of South Carolina, when he testified before the House Judiciary Committee in June. "We will do a great disservice to the youth of this country if we do not take action now . . . It's illegal to bet on college athletics in 49 states. Why isn't it in the 50th state as well?"

Think what would happen if Congress legalized the sale and use of marijuana in one state only. That's what lawmakers have done with sports gambling.

.   .   .

For a little more than two decades now, the sports books, as they are called in Nevada, have been an integral part of casinos large and small. Walk into any casino and you will see an area carved out for sports gamblers. There the legal gambler may spread his sports pages and tip sheets across one of the rows of desks usually found in college libraries, each individually lighted, or sit back in one of the dozens of plush chairs and, while being served drinks by a cocktail waitress, study the giant electronic board that covers the wall in front, offering information on the sporting events of the day, from the latest odds to reports on player injuries.

You can bet not only on who wins a game but also on the total points scored by individual players, most points scored by a player, total three-point field goals by one basketball team or both teams combined, total team points and rebounds combined, total points scored in the game, the half-time score—even the free-throw shooting percentage of individual players.

The most insidious aspect of legalized betting on college teams is the point spread. It raises dark questions where there should be none. For someone betting the spread, it matters not whether your favorite team wins, but rather by how much they win or lose. Las Vegas casinos set a point spread for each game. It's published in newspapers across the U.S. and used by illegal bookmakers. Over the years, college coaches have taken the news media to task for providing this bookmaking service. Only a handful of large publications have refused to print the collegiate betting lines, among them the *New York Times*, the *Washington Post*, the *Christian Science Monitor* and the *Sporting News*.

Here's how the betting lines work: say a casino's sports book favors the Duke basketball team to beat Florida State by 11 points. If you bet on Duke, but Duke wins by only 8 points, you lose. If you bet on Florida State, you win.

And that's the source of a nagging question—not just for gamblers but for fans, coaches and university administrators. If a team beats its opponents but not by the official Vegas spread, were the games fixed? Did players deliberately miss shots? Did they intentionally foul? Did they purposely fail to block shots?

Therein lies the sinister beauty of rigging a game by shaving points: It's nearly impossible to detect, as long as the players do some serious acting. In one fixed game, the gambler who engineered the point shaving complimented the players involved saying he "liked the way [they] made it appear that they were playing hard."

The perverse influence of the point spread is that it pressures teams to rack up enough points to beat the line. Says coach Holtz, "I have witnessed our football players be idolized, praised and cheered after a win. I've also witnessed them being ridiculed, demonized and ostracized after a win. The only difference was in one case we covered the point spread. In the other we didn't."

Thinking about such pressure can conceivably have a distorting influence on a coach's game strategy. Says Orlando ("Tubby") Smith, the men's basketball coach at the University of Kentucky: "What am I to do if I know that my team is favored by 17 points, and our outmanned opponent is trailing by 20 late? . . . Do I clear out my bench and play all my reserves or leave the regulars in a little longer? Just knowing the line as I make my decisions courtside could determine winners and losers across the country. It's a very disturbing situation . . . No longer is it a simple matter of winning or losing. The question begs, Did your respective team cover?"

And the questions don't go away. Such was the case with the California State University, Fresno, basketball team during the 1996–97 season, when it failed to beat the point spread in a number of games. The questions eventually led to a federal-grand-jury investigation in which witnesses and game films were subpoenaed. Three years later, the probe continues.

.   .   .

How did it get this way? With a lot of help from Congress. Until the mid–1970s, legalized sports betting in Nevada was confined to dimly lit, smoke-filled rooms in tiny turf clubs where the floor was the ashtray. Recalls Richard Davies, a history professor at the University of Nevada at Reno: "The aroma of stale cigar smoke, day-old spilled beer and greasy hot dogs generated an ambiance only a dedicated horse player could appreciate," which was appropriate, since most of the betting action was on horses, not sports. The casinos had no sports books.

The main reason: no money to be made. From 1951 to '74, the Federal Government levied a 10% excise tax on the amount of sports wagers. Since the profit margin before the tax was generally 5% or less, the tax made the business unprofitable. But in 1974, the Nevada congressional delegation helped persuade Congress to slash the tax from 10% to 2%. The rush was on. By 1988, wagers on all sports—professional and college—totaled $1.3 billion.

Other states joined in, after a fashion. Oregon passed a law permitting a state lottery keyed to professional football, while Montana approved betting on fantasy sports leagues. Professional sports teams and the NCAA grew alarmed and pressured Congress for a law banning all sports wagering. One of the more vocal supporters was Bill Bradley, the former basketball star and Democratic Senator from New Jersey: "State-sponsored sports betting could change forever the relationship between the player and the game, and the game and the fans. Sports would become the gamblers' game and not the fans' game, and athletes would become roulette chips," he said in 1992. Congress agreed and enacted the Professional and Amateur Sports Protection Act, the law prohibiting gambling on amateur sporting events in all states except Nevada.

The popular movement to make the ban universal gathered force last year when the National Gambling Impact Study Commission, which had been appointed by President Bill Clinton and congressional leaders, called for closing the Nevada loophole. Armed with the report, the NCAA went on the offensive, and sympathetic lawmakers in the House and Senate introduced bills to make it official. Coaches and university heads testified, including Graham Spanier, president of Penn State: "There has been a blurring of the line between legal and illegal sports gambling in this country. Sports gambling has become such a part of the glamour of Las Vegas that it is fairly safe to conclude that many do not know that gambling on college sports is an illegal activity in virtually every state in the United States." Dozens of other organizations outside the athletic community also urged Congress to act. They represented Republicans and Democrats; church, family and education groups, from the American Council on Education to a commission of the Southern Baptist Convention.

But they were fighting a formidable opponent. Over the past several years, the gambling industry and its trade association, the American Gaming Association, have emerged as a major influence group in Washington, doling out large campaign contributions and wining and dining lawmakers. Like many other special interests, they are equal-opportunity givers, as attested to by a sampling of contributions reported to the Federal Election Commission. In 1996, Sheldon Adelson, whose Las Vegas Sands Inc. owns the new Venetian Resort-Hotel-Casino on the Las Vegas Strip, contributed $100,000 to the Republican National State Election Committee and $105,000 to the Democratic National Committee. Steve Wynn's Mirage Resorts donated $226,500 to the Republican National Committee that same year. Wynn, who came late to bipartisan giving, would discover the Democrats a little later.

In both 1997 and '98, Adelson again gave $100,000 to the Republican National State Election Committee. In 1998, Mirage Resorts kicked in $300,000 to the National Republican Senatorial Committee, followed with $300,000 to the Republicans and $250,000 to the Democrats in 1999. In 1998, Circus Circus gave $285,000 to the same G.O.P. committee. The following year, Park Place Entertainment, the former gaming division of the Hilton Hotels, gave $100,000 to the Democrats and $75,000 to the Republicans, and MGM Grand gave $150,000 each to the Democrats and Republicans.

Sometimes all this money was delivered privately. Sometimes it was delivered at public fund raisers held along the Strip. In that November 1997 fund raiser, gaming executives paid at least $1,000 a person to rub shoulders with Republican leaders Trent Lott and Mitch McConnell, in an event that gaming officials characterized as a "tremendous success." Democrats received similar treatment in July 1999 when House minority leader Richard Gephardt of Missouri, Democratic Congressional Campaign Committee chairman Patrick Kennedy of Rhode Island and Ways and Means ranking member Charles Rangel of New York attended a Las Vegas luncheon.

With all that money flowing to lawmakers, you might guess what happened next. The NCAA-backed bills are stalled. But not because they lack the votes. "I would allege there would be a vote of 98 to 2 in this Senate, if it came to a vote," ventured the bill's key supporter, McCain of Arizona, in a July 18 speech on the Senate floor. Even critics of the legislation acknowledge it would pass if brought to a vote. But leaders of both parties have resisted bringing the legislation to the floor because of fear that the gaming industry will cut off its campaign contributions. Here's how that fear works:

Last year, when the NCAA first took its case to the Senate Judiciary Committee, the college-sports officials got a favorable reception. Committee staff members were confident their boss, Utah Republican Orrin Hatch, the committee chairman, would embrace the issue. After all, years earlier the Senator had made his feelings clear: "Sports gambling is bad for the country. It is bad for our young people. It is bad for everybody," he said in the Senate on June 2, 1992. Hatch said that perhaps the exemption for Nevada "will have to be revisited at some future time."

NCAA officials worked with Hatch's staff on drafting legislation and were told that Hatch would be a co-sponsor. The proposal also secured the support of two other key Senators, the ranking Democrat on the Judiciary Committee, Patrick Leahy of Vermont, and Kansas Republican Sam Brownback.

Then, all of a sudden, NCAA officials saw their calls go unreturned. Hatch, who had made suggestions during the drafting, suddenly let it be known he would not be a co-sponsor, and has since said the proposed bill does not go far enough to stop the problem. Kentucky's McConnell, a major recipient of gaming-industry contributions, had met with Hatch and other Republican Senators on the Judiciary Committee and asked them not to support the bill. "He told them it would impact his ability to raise money for [the G.O.P.'s Senate fund-raising committee] from the gambling industry," said a Capitol Hill observer familiar with the negotiations.

Eventually, the NCAA found in McCain a powerful advocate—but not powerful enough. The Senate Commerce Committee, over which he presides, held hearings, approved a bill and sent it to the Senate floor recommending passage. There it has languished, a victim of parliamentary maneuvering by the leadership. A similar bill was approved by the House Judiciary Committee last week, but its fate before the full House remains unclear.

Surely one reason is that the NCAA, which is a tax-exempt organization, cannot make campaign contributions. Even its lobbying budget is minimal by Washington standards, less than $200,000 a year. The American Gaming Association alone, on the other hand, spent $1.6 million last year.

As part of the lobbying campaign, Las Vegas casinos mounted a p.r. blitz to enlist the support of their customers. They distributed literature warning that "politicians want to snatch away your rights! . . . They want to take away your rights as an adult to come to Nevada and place a legal wager." The industry has also fought the bill on grounds that it would wipe out thousands of jobs in Nevada. (In fact, wagering on college sports amounts to less than 1% of casino business in that state.) But mainly the gaming industry has rested its case against the legislation on this:

It makes no sense to eliminate legalized sports gambling in Nevada because the amount wagered is dwarfed by illegal gaming in the other 49 states. Indeed, goes the argument, without a legal way to bet on college games, gamblers would wager illegally and contribute further to the growth in illegal gambling. To promote this view, the industry bought ads in newspapers warning of the consequences if Congress eliminates legal sports betting in Nevada. Under a headline declaring s. 2340: A "FIX" ONLY A BOOKIE COULD LOVE in the *Washington Post* on June 22, Harrah's Entertainment Inc. admonished, "If Congress bans legalized betting on college sports, it will make a lot of illegal bookies very happy. Because eliminating the only regulated, legitimate way to gamble on college games in the U.S. will do nothing but create a new business for illegal bookmakers."

Law-enforcement officials typically offer a different view: that legal sports betting actually fuels illegal gambling and provides two services for bookies everywhere. It gives them a reliable source for quoting the odds on a game and, more important, provides a convenient place to spread the risk on their bets. Says Wayne A. Johnson, chief investigator of the Chicago Crime Commission, the citizens watchdog committee that has been fighting organized crime since the days of Al Capone: "Legalized gambling only perpetuates illegal gambling. It does not displace it, as many people believe. That's a false assumption." Even Nevada's regulatory officials have acknowledged this connection. The chairman of the Nevada State Gaming Control Board, Steve DuCharme, said in a 1999 interview, "A lot of money made through illegal gambling is laid off in Las Vegas. If a bookie has a lot of money on one side of a bet, they bet the other one in Las Vegas to try and even the bet."

Years of wiretaps by federal and state law-enforcement authorities have repeatedly documented the links between legal and illegal gambling. Typical of this arrangement was a Schenectady, N.Y., gambling ring uncovered in 1997 by the New York State Organized Crime Task Force. In raids in July that year in Las Vegas and Schenectady, authorities arrested 15 bookmakers, confiscated $436,000 in cash and uncovered evidence of a multi-million-dollar betting ring. The Schenectady bookies ran a full-scale operation complete with computers and multiple phone lines. In one eight-week period, police wiretaps turned up 5,800 calls to their "wire room" near downtown Schenectady from gamblers placing bets on college and professional basketball games.

When the need arose, the Schenectady gamblers had their very own contact in Las Vegas. He was Thomas DiNola, a former Schenectady resident who fled New York State in 1989 to avoid a $250,000 civil judgment arising from another gambling case. He relocated to Las Vegas but kept up ties to the hometown bookies. As a local bookie told a potential customer, in a conversation picked up on wiretaps, "We're a pretty big operation. We're based in Las Vegas, and I work this local branch. We're a full-tilt operation."

DiNola gave the Schenectady bookies a commission for layoff bets they sent his way, and business was good. In one 19-day period during college basketball's March Madness in 1997, DiNola and his associates accepted 336 sports bets over the phone totaling $312,620. At his trial, DiNola testified that on one day he handled $80,000 in bets on 65 games. "I took all the bets and placed them with sports books in Las Vegas," he said. After deducting a commission, he wired any winnings to New York. When authorities raided his business and home in Nevada, they confiscated $286,000 in cash. DiNola eventually pleaded guilty and was sentenced to 1½ to three years in prison and fined $15,000. A dozen others also pleaded guilty and were given sentences ranging from probation to jail time.

No one believes closing the Nevada loophole would end gambling on college campuses. But should you have any doubt about the connection between the fixing of college games and the legal sports books of Nevada, consider the Northwestern University men's basketball scandal.

Two Northwestern players ultimately pleaded guilty to gambling charges growing out of a point-shaving scheme to fix three basketball games in 1995. In return for payoffs from gamblers, the players agreed to hold down the score so that Northwestern would lose by more than the oddsmakers' point spread.

At the center of the scandal was Kevin Pendergast, a former Notre Dame football star who had gained fame in 1992 when he was hurriedly pressed into action during the Sugar Bowl game after the team's place kicker was injured. He kicked one field goal and an extra point at a critical time, helping the Irish to a dramatic 39–28 come-from-behind upset victory over favored Florida. Two years later, he kicked the winning field goal for Notre Dame in the Cotton Bowl in a stirring 24–21 victory over Texas A&M. He had arrived at Notre Dame on an athletic scholarship and was, in the words of a Notre Dame official, "a man of good character and strong values."

After he graduated, Pendergast's life took a different turn. Determined to become an entertainer, he formed a band. Nightlife brought him into contact with gamblers, and before long he was nearly $20,000 in debt.

To help pay his bookies, Pendergast orchestrated the Northwestern point-shaving scheme. In February 1995 he made contact with Kenneth Dion Lee, 21, a starting guard on the Northwestern men's basketball squad. A three-point specialist who was one of the team's leading scorers, Lee had his own gambling problems. At one point Northwestern had suspended him for it. He had run up big debts too.

Pendergast promised to pay Lee thousands of dollars if he could hold down the score of certain Northwestern games. Lee agreed and later recruited starting center Dewey Williams and a third player. A college friend put Pendergast in touch with an acquaintance, Brian Irving, who lived in Reno and agreed to place the bets. Over the next few weeks, Pendergast and Irving put the plan into gear. Three Northwestern games were selected: against

Wisconsin on Feb. 15, Penn State on Feb. 22 and Michigan on March 1. Once the Nevada sports books set the line, Pendergast would telephone Lee with that number. Northwestern, the underdog in all three games, had to lose each by more than the spread.

While the spread varied with each game, one factor was constant—the pivotal role Nevada played in executing the scheme. After Pendergast raised money in Chicago, he wired it to Irving in Reno. For the Penn State game, Irving bet $4,400 with the sports book at the Reno Hilton. When Penn State, a 14-point favorite, won by 30 points, Irving collected the group's winnings and wired an initial $6,000 payment to Pendergast, who gave Lee $4,000 in cash as his share.

For the Michigan game, Pendergast and two friends flew to Las Vegas on March 1 and bet $20,150 with the sports book at Caesars Palace that Northwestern would lose that night by at least 25½ points. When Pendergast phoned Lee in Ann Arbor and conveyed that number, Lee was reluctant to go ahead because "the spread was too high." But Pendergast, according to court papers, was insistent, and to sweeten the deal offered to double Lee's take to $8,000. Only then did Lee agree.

As it turned out, Lee's misgivings were well placed. Northwestern lost, but by only 17 points, and Pendergast lost all his bets.

Ultimately, Pendergast, Irving, Lee and Williams would lose even more. When the game rigging was uncovered, they were sent to prison.

Since his release, Pendergast has become an advocate for the pending legislation that would end legal betting on college sports in Nevada. He has acknowledged his guilt and cooperated with authorities, but he has also singled out Nevada as the linchpin of the scheme. He told lawmakers and others on Capitol Hill in February, "Without Nevada, without the option of betting money in Nevada, the Northwestern basketball point-shaving scandal would not have occurred."

Gourmet

FINALIST, REVIEWS
AND CRITICISM

Paris on the Hudson

Restaurant critic Jonathan Gold takes readers inside the kitchens and onto the tables of some of New York's most popular restaurants, serving up frank, entertaining reviews without condescension. As editor Ruth Reichl says, "Reading him is like sharing that meal."

Jonathan Gold

Paris on the Hudson

Fake, fun, and fabulous with fat, Pastis riffs on a Gallic theme.

I t is practically bacchanalian inside Pastis early on a wintry Sunday night: air blue with cigarette smoke; Pernod-soaked miniskirts packed four-deep at the bar; rowdy young Wall Street dudes, who look buttoned down even in their anoraks, flicking at one another with the striped dish towels that pass for napkins in this grand café. Music, a weird blend of African pop and Grand Funk Railroad, blasts from speakers in the ceiling; coats are wadded under chairs, behind rails, between seats.

The main dining room off toward the rear of the restaurant has filled up with rather more sedately dressed downtown families, complete with what seems like at least one seven-year-old at each table who screams with delight when she discovers that the cheeseburgers actually cost one dollar less than the hamburgers. In one corner of the bar a party cranks up with serial canoodling, shrieks of cocktail-fueled laughter, and processions to the powder room that seem as relentless and unending as the march of ants toward a sugar bowl. Somebody here is having the most memorable evening of her life.

Say what you will about the cooking at the French cafés Keith McNally has founded—Balthazar, Lucky Strike, Odeon, Café Luxembourg, and now Pastis—the french fries are always just short of miraculous, and McNally has the restaurant-as-theater thing down cold.

There are a lot of reasons to dislike Pastis. It is as deeply inauthentic as its neighborhood, for one thing: a meat-market bistro in an area where the meat wholesalers are being driven out by restaurants and high-priced boutiques; a watering hole for the sort of bohemians who live in fifth-floor walk-ups that rent for $3,200 a month; a magnet for exactly the kind of people the neighborhood's gamier nightclubs sought to escape by moving to this obscure corner of the city.

The area was not without late-night bistro representation before Pastis: Le Gans, Markt, and not least Florent, where Roy Lichtenstein ate every day for the last several years of his life. Pastis's salad of beet, endive, Roquefort, and walnuts is a pale imitation of Florent's signature salad; the onion soup has almost no flavor under its thick mantle of oozing cheese. The *ratatouille* will remind you less of Nice than of a coffee-shop Denver omelet. Wines are meted out in tourist-trap carafes—thick-walled, false-bottomed bottles that hold less than half as much as a regular 750-milliliter bottle.

This time around, we know that McNally hired artists to tint his high tin ceilings the sort of nicotine yellow all but impossible in this age of smoking restrictions, to dirty the grout, to smear on fake water stains. We have now seen McNally's trick of bottle-laden shelves extending as far as the eye can see, the square water carafes, the diner china masquerading as rough café crockery. Sometimes, in fact, it even seems as if Pastis is secretly a British restaurant signaling the traditional English distaste for everything French, and it is true there are many Englishisms on the menu, from mustardy Welsh rarebit to a frightful brunch dish of baked beans on toast, a predilection for undercooked bacon and warm beer, and the tendency to serve fries with everything but salad. The fish-and-chips—thick, meaty slabs of cod fried to a superb, tempuralike crispness—are actually more refined than most of the French dishes.

But, almost in spite of itself, Pastis may be the most important restaurant to open this season: a grand, well-lit place and the focal point of one of the truly ancient areas of Manhattan. It sits at the apex of a broad, cobblestoned plaza (ringed by buildings so old they are no longer quite perpendicular to the ground) that was barely tangible as a public space before the restaurant appeared and gave it life. Open early and quite late, at least ostensibly democratic, Pastis takes reservations only for seatings between 6 and 7 P.M. Even if you disdain the place, you may find yourself dropping in a couple of times a week. At this point, I think I may be as familiar with the cooking here as I am with the cooking in my own home.

McNally's Balthazar is marvelous for so many reasons: the exquisitely designed lighting that makes even accountants seem as glamorous as Kate Moss, the sense that this is a real bistro that has just somehow been unearthed—like an old subway station suddenly restored to use after 70 years of being mothballed—instead of built up from scratch. The wine list is filled with French village oddities that are both uncannily appropriate with the food and relatively inexpensive. And the dense, rustic breads and delicate tarts and *galettes* from the bakery are first-rate. Balthazar is a large-scale fantasy of a grand Parisian brasserie.

.   .   .

Pastis, on the other hand, is a quite different place, a riff on the kind of working-class Parisian café where the cigarettes are as important as the cuisine and the *pastis* flows as freely as milky water, where truck drivers and piano movers stare glumly into glasses of coarse red wine before work and breakfasts consist of rude hunks of boiled beef, where American tourists stare blankly into tiled holes in the ground, and patrons consume *café au lait* quickly while standing at the bar. The kind of people who go to Balthazar would never be caught dead in those places (not to mention the rough Parisian neighborhoods where those places tend to be), but the meat district has at least a patina of raffishness, an odor of decline without, now, the actual danger.

Yet I find myself drawn to the restaurant for its perfect, crackle-crusted bread; for the *oeufs sur le plat* (a couple of fried eggs plopped down into what resembles a bowl made out of fried ham); for the regiments of grilled sardines; for the luscious leeks vinaigrette, so much better than the grease-soaked frisée *aux lardons*. Instead of the traditional pressed sandwich, the splendid *croque-monsieur* here is made with a big slice of country bread blanketed with good ham, drizzled with béchamel, and crowned with a broad swath of Gruyère cheese broiled into a shallow lake of goo.

One slushy afternoon I had a perfect meal of a carafe of Alsatian Pinot Blanc and a dozen plump Washington State oysters, refreshing as a jolt of raw ocean, followed by a simple trout amandine—firm, fleshy, sauced simply with lemon, butter, and almonds—and a bowl of rice pudding. Another perfect meal might involve a big chunk of beef braised into winy softness with glazed carrots or the Saturday special of prime rib with a milky potato gratin, a touch of home cooking designed for a clientele that hasn't eaten a meal at home in three weeks.

The Thursday special of venison stew in a little casserole, hiding under a thin cap of potatoes and swimming (swimming!) in about two inches of yellow, thyme-scented grease, is a little bit revolting but also compelling, the culinary equivalent of those parts in a horror movie that you have to watch through your fingers but end up watching anyway. Sundays there is cassoulet, big crocks of the stuff, properly creamy, intensely garlicked, thick with gelatinous pieces of skin and fat that give the mass an ineffable creaminess.

The restaurant, in fact, is at its best with fat, which its chefs—Riad Nasr and Lee Hanson—wield with the same glee with which the guy in the Munch mask wields the knife in *Scream*. Huge, soft slabs of fat pork belly practically melt into a bed of lentils; rich, rare hanger steaks ooze juice; chicken garlanded with stewed garlic cloves sinks into buttery mashed potatoes. The grilled dorade with olives and the sautéed skate with brown butter and capers are not bad precisely, but they are also indistinguishable from the three other orders of that fish you may have had in the past week. (When our backs were turned, apparently, skate replaced striped bass as the official fish of the New York City restaurant.)

There are many desserts at Pastis, all the usual French stuff: *riz au lait* and crème caramel; big, dry hunks of floating island and bowls of chocolate mousse. The dessert event to celebrate is the welcome return of crêpes Suzette—thin pancakes gently flavored with orange zest. A decadent Belle Époque dessert brought back for one more go.

Harper's Magazine

FINALIST, REVIEWS
AND CRITICISM

Stupor Mundi

The Glory of J. F. Powers

Interlacing elements of biography with sharp literary criticism, these essays bring their dead subjects back to life. Lewis Lapham appraises the work of Patrick O'Brian, combining personal anecdotes with vivid descriptions of several meetings with the naval scholar. Donna Tartt restores the reputation of lost writer J. F. Powers, who, in his day, was feted by the likes of Flannery O'Connor and Evelyn Waugh, and also won a National Book Award.

Lewis H. Lapham

Stupor Mundi

"Come, sir, cannot I prevail upon you to go to sea? A man-of-war is the very thing for a philosopher, above all in the Mediterranean: there are the birds, the fishes—I could promise you some monstrous strange fishes—the natural phenomena, the meteors, the chance of prize-money. For even Aristotle would have been moved by prize-money. . . ."

"A ship must be a most instructive theatre for an inquiring mind. . . ."

"Prodigiously instructive, I do assure you, Doctor."

Patrick O'Brian

Newly commissioned as a captain in the Royal Navy, a young Jack Aubrey presents his assurance to Stephen Maturin, a learned but unemployed physician, on the afternoon of April 2, 1800, over a plate of oysters in Port Mahon, Minorca. The two men sit at a table in the bow window of an inn with a handsome view of the eighteenth-century shipping in the harbor—square-rigged naval vessels, Algerian xebecs, miscellaneous snows, pinks, settees, trabacolos—and their conversation has come to the point of the doctor accepting the warrant of surgeon aboard H. M. S. *Sophie*, a fourteen-gun sloop bound for Sardinia and the north Italian coast.

So begins, in the early pages of *Master and Commander*, the long voyage that carries the captain and the doctor twice around the globe, through the smoke of the Napoleonic wars, in and out of the social and political scenery that was England in the reign of George III. Before Patrick O'Brian died last January, in Dublin at the age of eighty-five, he had extended the narrative into a series of twenty novels and furnished his readers with a course of prodigious instruction. I know of no other set of books in which I take such unqualified delight, and their popular success (more than 3 million copies sold, translations into nineteen languages, a Web site, a newsletter, a book of maps) I accept as proof that the rumors about the end of literacy have been much exaggerated. The television networks and the Internet undoubtedly have done a good deal of damage to the art of letters, but if O'Brian can be read with pleasure by so many people in both Charleston and Osaka, not so much damage that the hope of rescue has been entirely lost.

I came across O'Brian's writing in the summer of 1992, haphazardly on a Friday afternoon when I was on the way to Rhode Island for a weekend apt to require an informed remark about a yacht rounding Brenton Point on the long starboard tack for Martha's Vineyard and the Cape. A reviewer's copy of *H. M. S. Surprise* had arrived that day in the mail, the cover illustration showing the foremast and bowsprit of a twenty-eight-gun frigate in an Arab port, and I picked it up confident in the opinion that I was venturing into familiar waters. Long acquainted with the adventures of C. S. Forester's Horatio Hornblower—deck crews running out the guns and the drummers rousing up the starboard watch to the tune of "Heart of Oak"—I'd been fond of seaborne stories ever since as a child of seven I'd listened to my mother read aloud the whole of *Moby-Dick.*

The year was 1942, Admiral Halsey's Pacific fleet clearly in sight in San Francisco Bay, and I'd been attracted to the book by the Rockwell Kent drawings of Queequeg and the Whale. My father's family owned what had been a prosperous steamship company (forty cargo vessels in the intercoastal trade) before the Japanese attack on Pearl Harbor. The navy requisitioned all the ships on December 8, 1941, but we still had hopes that some of them would be returned. My mother thought Melville's prose too difficult and his story too abstract, but she agreed to read the book on condition that I could keep a firm hold of the narrative. Every evening at six o'clock I was obliged to tell her where she had left off the day before; only then would she begin the next sentence.

My attention wavered but didn't falter, and by the time I was fifteen I'd read the collected works of Joseph Conrad, written a dutiful high school synopsis of Admiral Mahan's naval strategy, studied the notations (strength and direction of the wind, number of days out of Boston, etc.) in the logbooks kept by many of my own ancestors on their passages through the Sunda Strait and around Cape Horn.

Thus pleased to think myself prepared to spot the difference between a seventy-four-gun ship of the line and a captain's gig, I opened O'Brian's book (in the train making its way east from New Haven) with a light heart and careless hand. Well before the train passed through Old Lyme I understood that my complacence was poorly judged, and somewhere north of Mystic I knew that I was in the company of a writer making sail for the distant shore of genius. In Newport that weekend I missed the dinner for the retired admiral, also the boat race and the golf tournament. Having discovered that *H. M. S. Surprise* was the third in a series of novels that O'Brian had been writing since 1969, I found in a bookstore on Thames Street the other fourteen volumes then in print, and over the next three days (amusing my children and annoying my wife) I sat motionless in a chair (also on sofas, at the kitchen table, under trees) reading my way west of Ushant and south from Tenerife.

Over the last eight years I've pressed O'Brian's novels on as many as a hundred prospective readers, always with the advice that they allow an interval of at least six months before proceeding from one voyage to the next. Otherwise the ships sail without their full complement of stored memory, and it's easy to mistake Java Head for Table Mountain, or confuse the talk aboard *Sur-*

prise—"general considerations upon fish, a wholesome meat, though disliked by fishermen; Dover sole is commended; porpoises, frogs, puffins rated as fish for religious purposes by Papists"—with the discussions in the gun room of *Agamemnon* or the *Nutmeg of Consolation*.

What is most remarkable about the books is their spaciousness of mind. O'Brian writes from the early-nineteenth-century premise that the world can be known and understood, or, if not understood, at least accurately perceived and lovingly examined, and he carries forward his long narrative in the same spirit of investigation that prompted Honoré de Balzac to write the *Comédie humaine* in fifty volumes, or J. J. Lalande, in 1801, to count and catalogue 47,390 stars. As much of the story takes place on land as it does at sea, the scenes of a London drawing room or debtor's prison as finely drawn as those of the wharf at Portsmouth or a single ship action in the Indian Ocean. The novels encompass the whole of a society as completely imagined as the England of Jane Austen. They present the portrait of an age afloat on the flood tide of the Enlightenment, all hands on deck keeping a sharp watch for monstrous strange fishes and the chance of prize money.

Maturin accepts Aubrey's invitation to sea the day after their chance meeting at a performance of Locatelli's C Major Quartet in the governor's house at Port Mahon. Both enthusiastic musicians—Maturin plays the cello, Aubrey the violin—they divert themselves on their long voyaging around the world with the *duettos* of Handel, Boccherini, and old Bach. The voices of the two instruments express their different qualities of character and temperament, Maturin's introspective melancholy opposed to Aubrey's ardent exuberance, and on the counterpoint between the two melodic lines, O'Brian constructs his long series of polyphonic variations on the theme of man's humanity to man.

The physician, Maturin, "a small, dark, white-faced creature in a rusty black coat," his wig unpowdered and his age indeterminate, is an intellectual in the finest sense of that much abused word—a naturalist as apt to come aboard ship with an imperfectly pre-served giant squid as with a wombat or a sloth; a surgeon but also a spy, fluent in the Spanish and the French; a man who can "whip your leg off in a moment, tell you the Latin name for anything that moves, . . . speaks languages like a walking Tower of Babel." His unbounded curiosity prompts him to extensive digressions on the use of trocars, ball-scoops, saws, and bone-rasps (the rough sur-gery on the orlop-deck no better than a butcher's shambles), to reflections on the society of Augustan England (its manners, lan-guage, opinions, terms of endearment, means of conveyance), general observations ("I have never yet known a man admit that he was either rich or asleep"), notes on the habits of the greater albatross and the lesser wax-moth.

Aubrey's is the more splendid figure, "a most gallant, deserving officer, a thorough-paced Tory," rejoicing in fox hunts and toasted cheese, a romantic creature, "eager in the article of battle," appren-ticed to the navy at the age of twelve, generous to a fault but apt to mix up his schoolboy proverbs ("Gather ye rose-pods while ye may"; "They have chosen their cake, and must lie on it"; "Here's a palm in Gilead"). Like Maturin a man who knows his trade, Aubrey approaches the world as a problem in navigation, and it is by means of his cheerfully repeated explanations ("in the unusu-ally distinct, didactic voice used at sea for landmen and on land for half-wits") that O'Brian acquaints the reader with the theory and practice of early-nineteenth-century seamanship—the distinc-tion between steering small and sailing large, the proper storing of the gunner's powder (mealed, corned, best-patent), the difference between the several kinds of cannon shot (bar, chain, case, grape, or plain round).

O'Brian sustains the counterpoint between the two voices

across seven oceans and a span of roughly twenty years, almost always to as fine effect as in their first conversation in the bow window at Port Mahon:

Aubrey—"What is Catalan?"

Maturin—"Why, the language of Catalonia—of the islands, of the whole of the Mediterranean coast down to Alicante. . . . Of Barcelona. Of Lerida. All the richest part of the peninsula."

Aubrey—"You astonish me. I had no notion of it. Another language, sir? But I dare say it is much the same thing—a *putain*, as they say in France?"

Maturin—"Oh, no, nothing of the kind—not like at all. A far finer language. More learned, more literary. Much nearer the Latin. And by the by, I believe the word is *patois*, sir, if you will allow me."

Aubrey—"*Patois*—just so. Yet I swear the other is a word: I learnt it somewhere."

Given longer space, I could multiply many times over the proofs of O'Brian's capacity for portraying women as well as men, for telling a love story with the same force and affection that he brings to his depiction of a rolling broadside fired into the rigging of a French privateer. Over the course of the novels he names upwards of 500 individuals, nearly all of them as memorably observed as Aubrey and Maturin. I could write a monograph about Diana Villiers, her impetuous spirit as changeable as the weather in the Gulf of Lions, and still I would lack occasion to mention Admiral Drury among his concubines and cassowaries in Penang, or the angry Mrs. Williams, "devoid of scruple, convinced of her divine rectitude," governing the affairs at Ashgrove Cottage with the iron hand of the Lord Protector. By the time I'd come to the last volume of the series (*Blue at the Mizzen*, published in November 1999, two months before the author's death), I could bring to mind at least thirty of his characters as easily as if I were listening to their voices in the hall.

To readers brought up in the modernist schools of literature, O'Brian's novels might seem insufficiently ambiguous, a trifle too Edwardian in their diction, books for boys belonging on the shelf with the tales told by Rudyard Kipling and Arthur Conan Doyle. All such criticism is not without a point. Having read other histories of Augustan England and the Napoleonic wars, I doubt that service in Admiral Lord Nelson's navy was quite so *all a-tanto* as O'Brian asks his readers to believe, and I suspect that few of the officers in the British Channel Fleet possessed Captain Aubrey's skill in handling a ship or a violin. But here we have an author who writes so well that I can overlook his offenses against the canon of contemporary literary taste. His gift for language and his love of words show up on every page, evident in his knowing what to show and when to tell, his control of grammar and play of wit.

I soon found myself reading the novels with both an atlas and a dictionary close at hand; occasionally I copied out one or another of O'Brian's paragraphs (for the pleasure of the rhythms as well as for the lesson in rhetoric), and sometimes I made short lists of definition—of terms specific to sailing ships (grumlin-futtocks, kevel, becket, Bentinck courses, crosscatharpings, etc.), also of words unknown that fell graciously on my ear:

chouse—to dupe or swindle
mammothrept—a pampered child
Stupor Mundi—the marvel of the world, object of awe or wonder

O'Brian as an author met the requirement indicated by the latter phrase, but during the first years of my acquaintance with his writing, I knew nothing about the man. Nor did I come across many people in New York literary society who were conversant with his books. Those few of his readers whom I chanced to meet almost invariably tended to favor yacht-club blazers and the reactionary forms of politics—subscribers to *The Weekly Standard* and *National Review*, opposed in principle to the insult of an income tax, standing four-square and full-rigged on the side of property (that sacred text), florid gentlemen, well fed and heavyset, who struck me as being the sort of "thorough-paced Tories" likely to think that "a hundred lashes at the gangway" was just the thing to teach the slackers on society's lower cable tier a lesson in civility. They formed the majority of the other people present when I first met O'Brian in April of 1995 aboard the frigate Rose, docked at the South Street Seaport in Manhattan. O'Brian's American publisher, W. W. Norton, had provided the ship—a frigate of the same design, era, and dimension as Aubrey's beloved *Surprise*—as the setting for a party to mark the publication of *The Commodore*. The quarterdeck was crowded with pillars of the investment community, shining with gold buttons and flushed with Mount Gay rum.

O'Brian I but briefly glimpsed. He was seated splendidly aft, at a table under the fine curve of the windows in the captain's great cabin. I made my own polite compliment, wishing him joy in his success, and from the few moments required by the formality I came away with the impression of a fierce intelligence, the face hawklike and the expression sardonically amused, not as tall a man as I had supposed, stooped and almost frail but as watchful and implacable as one of Maturin's wandering Antarctic birds.

Before I met O'Brian a second time, a year later at a small dinner in an uptown New York club, I had discovered a few facts about his life, work habits, place of residence, and sources of inspiration. Twice married, he had lived since 1949 with his second wife in a French fishing village on the Roussillon coast below Perpignan. He was a close friend of Picasso's and an enthusiastic naturalist blessed with extraordinarily keen eyesight, said to be capable of distinguishing, at a long distance, a rook from a carrion crow. Although his novels were filled with vivid descriptions of landscapes as remote as the Malabar coast and the Magellan Strait, he was not the kind of writer who traveled around the world with a pencil and a camera. He relied on his imagination and prodigious research, exploring volumes of old maps and early voyages, reading the *Naval Chronicle* and magazines popular in London in the years 1790–1820. Apparently he wrote with a pen, first with his left hand on the left-hand page in a bound notebook, then on the opposite page with his right hand.

The dinner at the Links Club, given by Michael M. Thomas, a columnist for *The New York Observer*, cleared up the difficulty about the character and political sympathies of O'Brian's readers. Only twelve people were present, among them the authors Robert Hughes and John Gregory Dunne (neither of whom qualified as mess-mates of the hard Republican right) as well as Starling Lawrence, the editor at Norton who had brought O'Brian's novels to the United States in 1990, and Richard Snow, the editor of *American Heritage* who had written, for the *New York Times*, the first and foremost of the welcoming reviews.

Table talk among New York literary people ordinarily resembles a competitive auction in a cotton pit, everybody loudly interrupting one another and bidding up the price of his own cleverness. Not, however, in the presence of O'Brian. Well aware of his gifts as a writer and thus acquainted with his capacity for irony (mortal irony, sir, lions ain't in it), we conducted ourselves in the manner of midshipmen seated at dinner with the admiral aboard *Boadicea* or *Orion*, careful to remember our spherical trigonometry and how the ships were placed at Trafalgar and the Nile. The table was burnished oak, the silver reassuringly heavy, and the conversation a match for the vintage port—general considerations upon literature, a wholesome art but disliked by critics; historical fiction commended; reasons why authors of genre novels seldom receive promotion to the rank of genius; approving references to the works of John Le Carré and Elmore Leonard; an anecdote of a churlish adjective once presented to Mr. Thomas by a reviewer in the *Washington Post.*

The evening ended as satisfactorily as one of Locatelli's quartets, on a sustained chord of fond agreement and mutual esteem. O'Brian was at work on another manuscript, the *Surprise* still somewhere in port or at sea, and we all knew that one of these days, if not next year then somewhere nearer the meridian of the millennium, Aubrey was bound to capture the prize of a rear admiral's blue flag. He did so in the last of the novels, which now can be read and reread not only as a completed work but also, and probably to their best advantage, while bearing in mind Maturin's observation that no arrival "can amount to the sum of voyages" and that a natural philosopher offered any decent choice in the matter would do better "to travel indefinitely."

Donna Tartt

The Glory of J. F. Powers

A writer's work is resurrected

Discussed in this essay:
Morte d'Urban (336 pages, $12.95), *Wheat that Springeth Green* (327 pages, $12.95), and *The Stories* (570 pages, $14.95) by J. F. Powers, New York Review of Books Press.

When the American writer J. F. Powers died in Minnesota last summer, at eighty-one, all of his books were out of print—including *Morte d'Urban*, the novel for which he won the National Book Award in 1963. This and his other works had received the highest praise only to sink into obscurity and neglect, buried in the murk of small-town libraries and secondhand bookshops. Of *Wheat that Springeth Green* (which was nominated for a National Book Award in 1988), the *New York Times* remarked that its excellence ought to shame the literary establishment into rushing Powers's early books back into print. But the literary establishment is not so easily shamed, and the books slumbered on.

I had not heard of Mr. Powers. I first learned of him last year when his obituary (and his wary, intelligent photograph) caught my attention. The notice of his death made a little too much of his religion (Catholicism) and his subject matter (the Church)—so much that I was under the brief impression that he had been

Father Powers. (In fact, he was married, with five children.) Praise for his work—a whole chorus of it—ranged from formidable orthodoxy (Evelyn Waugh, Flannery O'Connor, Thomas Merton) to writers who, one presumes, couldn't give a hoot about Catholic concerns: William Gass, Philip Roth, Gore Vidal. Yet Powers's Catholicism (and his status as a "Catholic writer") was so violently stressed by all commentators that it made me a bit suspicious. If he was as good as he was cracked up to be, how then did this greatest of living storytellers (as Frank O'Connor called him) die virtually unknown, with his works out of print?

I say "virtually," not "wholly." Denis Donoghue, in the introduction to a new edition of Powers's stories put out by the New York Review of Books Press (which also has reissued the novels), writes that the works of Powers are "guarded with jealousy by those who know of them. News of their quality is passed from one adept to another. . . ." One wonders if Powers enjoyed being such a well-kept secret among his admirers. After reading the books for myself in their new editions, all I can say is that I wish a few of these adepts had passed on the good news during Powers's life one-tenth so strenuously as they are crying it through the marketplace after his death. Powers's work is remarkable not for the author's much vaunted Catholicism, or for its "message" (it hasn't one), but for its style. Each sentence is a marvel: clear and polished, always surprising, with a comedic bite that might be characterized as a hybrid of E. B. White, Charles Portis, and the Kingsley Amis of *Lucky Jim*, peppered—sparingly, but enough to sting—with the horrors of Nathanael West. The resulting prose is pure American, as tough and nervy in its way as the prose of Raymond Chandler but tempered throughout with a gorgeous precision and acidity that one tends to associate with such high British stylists as Waugh and Maugham. Its particular flavor of hardball elegance seems to me quite original.

Catholic priests are a recurring subject in Powers's fiction; and doubtless the word "priest" repeated overmuch in jacket copy has over the years repelled many an otherwise sympathetic reader. To judge from the sugared blurbs on Powers's older editions, many an unwary seeker of piety and "uplift" has been attracted to Powers at the book-sale table, and one can only imagine the dismay of such hopefuls at his caustic portraits of the clergy: the haggard curates and ripe old glad-handing bishops; the preening monsignors, the angry assistants, the whiskey bottle hidden in the rectory bathroom. Powers's eye is ruthless, with something of a child's icy, microscopic freshness, and with fascination one senses behind his work the weight of a childhood spent in Catholic schools: long silent years, hands folded on the desk, observing the black robes at close range. Several of Powers's boyhood friends grew up to be priests, but although Powers was a man of principle (he spent thirteen months in prison rather than fight in World War II), he seems to have been sufficiently familiar with Church hierarchy—and his own reclusive nature—to know that orders were not for him. In his fiction he constantly reminds us that a priest is a public servant in the most exhausting sense of the word, at the constant mercy of any drunk, any bore, any bully or bigot or parish nut.

This refusal to romanticize the priesthood, or to dramatize the more philosophical aspects of the faith, sets Powers apart from the great convert novelists who—for most readers—have virtually defined the Catholic novel in the last century. Waugh's Sebastian Flyte and Lady Marchmain, rare confectionery that they are, cannot be said to typify the Catholic experience of their age and nation, certainly not ours. And Graham Greene's Manichee romances—in which a point of dogma can stop an impassioned lover as fast as a revolver—bear about as much relevance to actual Catholic practices as do the James Bond novels.

Such characters and conventions are notably absent from Powers's work, though Father Joe Hackett, the hero of *Wheat that Springeth Green*, is a distant relation of Greene's whiskey priest,

and, further, seems to have a rather bitter and tragicomic awareness of himself stranded on the weedy edges of that tradition, isolated in American surburbia. It's always hot at the rectory in
Inglenook; Father Joe is always irritated, always mopping the
sweat from his brow, moving through the rectory "like a fighter in
trouble," always looking at his watch and craving another drink.
And urbane Father Urban, the greatest of Powers's characters,
daydreams of himself as a celebrity cleric, confessor to the great,
but his adventures among the Minnesota rich fall comically short
of the aristocratic Brideshead vision of Catholicism. The world of
Father Urban and Father Hackett and Powers's other priests
(priests with names like Father "On" Wisconski and Father "Cat-
fish" Toohey) is a disheartening landscape of parking lots, low-rise
rectories, and convents of "frosty orange brick," of furnaces that
don't work, and Chinese and Canadian coins in the collection
plate; of hard drinking, hard-sell fund-raising, loneliness and
despair, and "ill-lit church basements with steam tables, echoes,
and mice."

.   .   .

For fiction that has been so persistently labeled "religious," religious fervor plays little part. Nor is there in Powers's work the
grappling with philosophical questions that we have come to
expect from Catholic novelists like Walker Percy. Powers's priests,
who reside solidly in the chipper consumerism of the 1950s and
'60s, walk more by sight than faith. It's an aesthetic stance that,
incidentally or not, reflects the "inculturation" directives of the
Church in the twentieth century. Liberal Jesuit theologians such as
Gustave Weigel and Walter J. Ong endeavored to reconcile the
conformism and materialism of middle-class Protestant values
with medieval theology, resulting—such was the hope—in climate control and air-conditioned comfort all around. (Said Ong:

"The charges urged against Catholicism in the United States—superficiality, mechanization, routine—are exactly the charges which are leveled against mass culture itself, and which are, we are beginning to see, themselves rather superficial charges.") Instead of distancing itself from worldly interests, the Church at mid-twentieth century was doing its best to assimilate with the dominant culture, and it moved very quickly from an oppressed immigrant minority to wealth and social prominence. The great American cities—Detroit and Baltimore, Boston and Philadelphia, Chicago and New York—were driven by Catholic political engines: ruled by Catholic bishops and mayors, shaken down by Catholic mob bosses, patrolled by Catholic beat cops. But it was perhaps Hollywood, more than anything else, that really brought Catholicism out from a cloud of Protestant suspicion into the American cultural mainstream. Films transformed priests, in the public mind, from suspicious foreigners in fancy dress to regular, golf-playing, down-to-earth guys. Those were the days of Bing Crosby and Spencer Tracy, when army chaplains in war movies invariably wore the Roman collar, when a fellow might run into Bishop Fulton J. Sheen smoking a cigar and laughing it up with Milton Berle down at the Friars Club.

Powers's work incorporates—sarcastically for the most part—this jaunty popular type. His Father Urban dreams of starring in his own television program; his Father Hackett (who thwarts a robbery in progress at the liquor store, where he is an embarrassingly regular customer) is disgusted when the loitering onlookers mistake him—Father Hackett—and his "partner" (a fellow priest) for "a couple of colorful TV-type troubleshooters." Powers was writing at a moment when these winning popular images of Catholicism were first beginning to abrade with age and turn sour or obsolete; when the flight from the cities to the suburbs was draining the lifeblood from the great urban centers of Catholicism; when the "mild confabulations of clerical hippies" (to quote a phrase of Thomas Merton's) had begun, with their sandals and their Volkswagens and their guitars, to infiltrate the fraternity of the black robes.

Powers's three books of stories (*Prince of Darkness*, 1947, *The Presence of Grace*, 1956, and *Look How the Fish Live*, 1975), which have been collected in one volume, cover this cultural period from beginning to end: from Bishop Sheen and the glory days of Cardinal Spellman's "Powerhouse" to the Vietnam War. To read the first story ("The Lord's Day") in this collection is to put down the book with the sense of having read as great a short story as any ever written, and I mean by anybody: by Cheever, Sherwood Anderson, Chekhov. What ease they have is in the style; there are no easy morals here, no edifying lessons, but their vigor and correctness make them delightful to read. And while they're terribly funny—laugh-out-loud funny, in spots—they're also complex and deeply serious. "The Devil Was the Joker" is a brilliant character study of an overly earnest young Catholic who accepts a job chauffeuring a sleazy itinerant salesman named Mac McMaster—purveyor of Catholic newspapers and nudie matchbooks—throughout the Great Plains. (McMaster, and several other characters in this story, will reappear later in Powers's novels.) "Prince of Darkness" is characterized by a lingering sense of evil—passive evil, born of sloth. Father Burner is a cynic who operates on the principle of "discord at any cost. He did not know why. It was a habit. Perhaps it had something to do with being overweight." In fact, he is so overweight that he suspects the tailor of skimping on the cloth for his pants because of the ecclesiastical discount. When he's driving around in his car, he escapes some of the claustrophobia of the confessional (several of Powers's priests are claustrophobic), but even when Father Burner is speeding down the highway in his large American automobile there's a persistent sense of being strangled, trapped:

Father Burner touched the lighter on the dashboard to his cigarette and plunged his hams deeper into the cushions. A cloud of smoke whirled about the little Saint Christopher garrotted from the ceiling. Father Burner tugged viciously at both knees, loosening the binding black cloth, easing the seat. . . .

A billboard inquired: "Pimples?"

Like many of the stories in this collection, "Prince of Darkness" ends with a jarring sense of discomfort, of narrative expectations reversed. Although we feel sorry for some of Powers's characters, we laugh at them too—at them, not with them. Like most Catholic humorists (O'Connor and Waugh, Alexander Pope)—Powers is ruthless; he doesn't flinch from a joke at the other fellow's expense.

Of the first two collections of short stories, Flannery O'Connor said: "Those that deal with the clergy are as good as any stories being written by anybody; those that don't are not so good." The preference may seem suspicious, but the author of "A Good Man Is Hard to Find" is scarcely a propagandist for the Church. No one had less patience for the fiction of "uplift": saintly freckle-faced orphans, bluebirds twittering around the golden head of St. Bernadette at prayer—"pious trash," she called it. What she would have admired in these stories was Powers's cold eye for detail, the walk-on characters realized perfectly in a gesture, the acid description of a pop culture that Powers loathed but whose every nuance he understood perfectly—"the bingo game going on under the Cross for the seamless garment of the Son of Man."

What pieties are to be found in Powers's work are in his stories about race. These must certainly have irritated Miss O'Connor, with her ear for dialogue, because alone among all Powers's characters his African Americans have a stagy quality. Empathy and indignation practically vibrate throughout an early story like "The Trouble," which deals with a lynch mob, but Powers does not carve the characters with his sharpest or even second sharpest knife; he's trying to show us a social evil, and as a result the story is clouded by an anxiety not present in his finer work.

This is to be somewhat overcritical; the level of craftsmanship in these stories is extremely high. And they're not all about Catholicism or social issues by any means. "The Poor Thing" is about a cheerful, controlling invalid and her paid companion. "Look How the Fish Live"—a charming story-title, like the title of a lost work by Seymour Glass—is about a baby dove fallen from the nest in a surburban back yard, and how its caretakers, the children, lose interest as their father's involvement increases. Powers is typically pessimistic about the possibilities of progress— human progress, social or political progress—but here he's disillusioned with nature too, the chirping stupidity of birth and death. "Any bird but the dove would try to do something. Somewhere in the neighborhood this baby dove's mother was posing on a branch like peace itself, with no thought of anything in her head."

Morte d'Urban—the novel that beat out John Updike, Vladimir Nabokov, and Katherine Anne Porter for the National Book Award—is the story of a mediocre (and fictional) religious order called the Clementines, and of Father Urban, who struggles— unsuccessfully, for the most part, against stubborn superiors—to bring it up to speed. Father Urban is a connoisseur of gloss and surface, and when his unfashionable little order ("generally referred to as the Rinky Dinks") is, due to Father Urban's efforts, donated a fashionable office at a "prestige address," near the lake in Chicago, Father Urban knows exactly how it should look in order to appeal to wealthy visitors: "He had wanted the handsome room facing the street to be a showplace—mellow prints, illuminated manuscripts, old maps, calf-bound volumes, Persian carpets, easy chairs, and so on—everything in keeping with the oak-paneled walls, the bow window, and the fireplace."

He had wanted the room to be a rendezvous where passers-by would always be welcome to drop in and chat, to peruse the latest in worth-while books and periodicals. Famous visitors to Chicago might be induced to show themselves there, and talks might be given too, not all on religious subjects and none on narrow, controversial lines. A surprising amount of good might be accomplished in that way, indirectly. . . . If converts were made in such surroundings, they would probably be of a type badly needed and generally neglected—the higher type.

But Father Boniface had said no to all this—the idea of such a nook was associated in his mind with Christian Science—and the room was furnished with junk trucked in from the Novitiate: claw-footed tables and chairs, inhumanly high and hard, and large, pious oils (copies of Renaissance masterpieces, executed by a now departed Clementine) in which everybody seemed to be going blind. The room could have been a nuns' parlor at the turn of the century.

Father Urban is a politician and a charmer, and he possesses many of the qualities that characterized America as a nation before the 1960s. He is convivial without intimacy, canny in business, and confident in society; he is optimistic in outlook, obedient but calculating with authority, chaste but censorious in his morality. In his energy and ambitions, in his manipulative winning ways, he reminds one of the characters of Sinclair Lewis and also of Gatsby, especially in his optimism and love of the world. He has a taste for Scotch whiskey and private railroad cars, for good dinners and fine cigars and fancy hotels, for convertibles and golf. He even has an eye for a pretty woman, which may seem a quaint touch to many in this day and age. Father Urban likes women, and they like him; and part of his struggle is to resist the temptations they present.

Father Urban's efforts for his dim, unattractive little order are tireless. From his exile, in a run-down and disconsolate Minnesota retreat, he woos a wealthy layman named Billy Cosgrove and a hateful old heiress named Mrs. Thwaite; he brings down the house in his address to the Great Plains Commercial Club at their annual Poinsettia Smorgasbord. Donations are made, promotions received, and soon—despite the efforts of dull Father Boniface to quash him—Father Urban is back on top:

> Father Urban wanted to set up a serious program—talks by himself and others (if others worth hearing could be found), classes in the papal encyclicals, the Great Catholic Books and so on—but there just wasn't the time for it, and perhaps more than time would've been lacking at St. Monica's for such a program.
>
> So Father Urban played it safe and engaged the people on their own ground. He gave card parties for "seniors." He put on barn or square dancing (as they preferred to call it) for "young marrieds." He tried a rock and roll dance for "teens"—once. No trouble, no, but he found he didn't care for it when he saw what it was like. . . . For Men's Club, he sent away for films of Notre Dame football games, and these were studied at smoker sessions. . . . The school nuns were not forgotten. He gave them the use of his (Phil's) car, permission to shop at supermarkets, and occasionally he threw the boss a ten-dollar bill—"Buy yourself some cigars, Sister." They all loved him.

The battle in *Morte d'Urban* is less the classic scenario of God and Mammon than God and Management. (One of the chapters is entitled "Second Only to Standard Oil," referring to the efficiency of the Church as a worldwide corporation.) Father Urban's benefactors force him to choose, finally, between what's good for business and what's right. Some critics—Saul Bellow is one—have

found the book spiritually dry, but what *Morte d'Urban* lacks is
not spirit. What it lacks is faith in American values—values of
progress and self-fulfillment, of individualism and "limitless hori-
zons"—values that are so pervasive in popular culture that they
are often mistaken for spirituality. Cause and effect, the trusty old
American engines, don't drive the plot of this book. Certainty
recedes, just as we are on the verge of grasping it; there is the pervasive sense of an overarching reality that we don't quite understand. Powers's flat, restrained sentences are like puzzle pieces that
we admire for their color and brilliance; only as they start to accu-
mulate do we begin to see the pattern. But not completely. In Powers's fiction the picture never comes wholly clear. There is only a
partial clarity—but it gives a sense of vastness and openness, like
a partially restored fresco.

.   .   .

Wheat that Springeth Green is Powers's darkest work. It picks
up, in a sense, where *Morte d'Urban* leaves off, with the cheap dishonest side of American enterprise. Its waspish humor, its sense of
the absurd, its distrust of the mob, and its open-mouthed horror
at the seediness and transience of American culture all remind one
of Nathanael West—and I wonder if it's a coincidence that Father
Joe Hackett, the hero of this book, has the same last name as Tod
Hackett, the disillusioned protagonist of *The Day of the Locust.*

We meet Joe Hackett before he is Father Hackett: while he is still
in the nursery. The first few pages of the novel convey with great
poise and artistry the befuddlement of early childhood, the hints
and jokes that fly over Joe's head when he tiptoes downstairs to
join the party, his confusion when the adults laugh at the wrong
time. He thinks he's entertaining the party by his clever remarks
("I eat cheese!") when actually the joke is on him; and this nagging

sense of trying very hard and not getting it quite right sets the tone for the rest of the book, through Joe's dissipated youth well into his lonely, cynical adulthood.

What leads Joe to the priesthood isn't clear. Certainly the priest's life is very different from the life of the fast-talking bachelor uncle that young Joe admires: a bootlegger who likes to brag about "heavy dates" and ride around in a Chrysler "honking at chicks." The reader can see that glib Uncle Bobby (who gets "a lot of fun out of life") isn't all he's cracked up to be; but still he's a more attractive figure than the priests at Joe's church: Father Day, with his face like a monkey, who disgraces himself by public drunkenness; Father William Stock (known, for his pulpit moneygrubbing, as "Dollar Bill"), who, at the church bazaar, leaps into action when a smelly old tramp tries to walk off with an ice cream cone:

> Father Stock said: "Five cents, Mister."
>
> The old man licked the cone. "Try and git it."
>
> Joe was astonished to see Father Stock lie across the counter and, like a swimmer doing the breaststroke, swat the cone to the ground, the ice cream, only one dip, coming out of the cone and settling in the grass.
>
> "No way to do," the old man said, squatting down—Joe saw he wasn't wearing socks—and was trying to scoop up the ice cream with the cone, but couldn't, and was going to use his fingers when Father Stock helped him to his feet and pointed him toward the rectory. The old man still had the cone and was chewing on it with his gums.

Joe—predictably—is not an innocent for long. After a blistering interval of teen sex (group sex, no less, described with a meticulous, poker-faced precision worthy of Voltaire), Joe gets the clap. In a masterful cut the story jumps forward from the office where

Joe is confessing his predicament to Father "Germany" Zahn, his high-school track coach, and all at once—without explanation— Joe is in seminary. At the "sem" Joe strives to be a contemplative, but this ambition earns him no friends; "contemplative," apparently, is a byword for "slacker" in clerical circles. His ordination (overseen by "Dollar Bill") is a disillusioning experience; out in the world, he struggles with decreasing success to maintain his ideals.

If the young Father Joe is always doing battle against himself, Father Joe in middle age just gives up. Pitfalls abound: poker at St. Isidore's ("a hard- drinking rectory"); local politics; crafty parishioners with hidden agendas. Father Hackett is a tough talker—a father knuckling under to the archbishop ("the Arch") is said to "take a dive"—and his life, too, begins to take on a tough bachelor loneliness that reminds one of Philip Marlowe: the bottle in the drawer alongside the shoe polish, the solitary meals. Too many drinks with his pal Father Lefty Beeman in the Little John Lounge of the Robin Hood Room, and Father Joe wakes up the next morning unable to recall whether or not he has (imprudently) committed the archdiocese's printing jobs to a sharpie named "Buzz" whom Father Lefty met in the men's room.

And so on. The loss of the mystical sensibility has robbed Father Joe of his capacity to make much sense of the world in which he lives: a purposeless round of fund-raising, infuriating politics ("Get those mothers out of the government," he exclaims at the television during the Chicago Democratic Convention), liquor-store runs, televised sports, and—of course—shopping malls, which are described with the fishy unsympathetic eye of an anthropologist. And some of the funniest passages in the book are about this contrast, about Father Joe's movement away from St. John of the Cross and the pious ideals of the "sem" to more worldly skills:

Once, after he'd walked in on some electricians and told them off for playing hell with his insulation and walked out, he'd been pleased to hear Steve, his janitor, respond to the question "What's wrong with that mother?" in kind, "Father, he don't take no shit."

There are things wrong with *Wheat that Springeth Green*. Some (not all) of the women characters are types, though this may be excused as a subtle means of characterizing Father Hackett's worldview. Some of the chapters stand admirably on their own as short stories. But—partly because of the exquisite artistry on a word-to-word level; partly, too, because these stories were written over the course of twenty-five years—the overall structure of this book isn't as strong as it could be.

What makes the novel extraordinary is its humor (bitter and clear, it never stops) and minute attention to language. There is not a misplaced comma, not a wrong word. Like many prose writers who have studied Latin, Powers sets up his sentences to explode at the end, so that there are marvelous little internal combustions going off like firecrackers all over the page. This book took Powers twenty-five years to write, and, although it's not long or complicated, it feels like it took him twenty-five years, every minute of that time, word by word, comma by comma, sentence by sentence, such is its clarity and polish. One shudders at what he must have gone through to write it; one wonders that he had the heart to stick it out; one despairs to think he never saw it reach the audience it deserved. And while the ending is a little abrupt, the book as a whole is free of complacency. Powers has not grown overly fond of the sound of his own voice, as many aging masters do. It's exhilarating to see an older writer still struggling so relentlessly with himself, taking the hard way, pushing himself as an artist right up to the end.

Powers didn't think of himself as a Catholic writer; he disliked the term, and one can see why, considering that it quite injustly confined him to a ghetto of special-interest fiction where he scarcely belongs. When interviewed by a nun for the *American Benedictine Review,* Powers was asked if he had any ideas about the special vocation of the Catholic fiction writer. He replied: "No, I'm afraid I don't, Sister, except that obviously he should not write junk." Later in the same interview, when questioned about the existentialist and pessimistic strains in his work, he replied, succinctly: "You can't be a winner, but you can go down like a winner." If Powers's work and indeed Powers himself can be summed up in one sentence, this is it. So many writers in America lose heart, lose nerve, self-destruct—but not Powers. Up in his lonely little corner of the North, he went down swinging.

Vanity Fair

FINALIST, REVIEWS
AND CRITICISM

Forever Young

As columnist James Wolcott ranges over the ever-expanding field of pop culture, he makes imaginative connections, punctures the self-serious, and always illuminates his subjects. Wolcott is fan and scourge, sociologist and anthropologist all rolled into one.

James Wolcott

Forever Young

On March 24, 1958, Elvis Presley was inducted into the U.S. Army, his hepcat pompadour and sideburns mowed down in a regulation G.I. haircut. Captured by news photographers under the direction of his manager Colonel Tom Parker, Elvis's turn in the barber's chair was a public ceremony: a symbolic shearing, not only of Elvis—who would return from the service a meek semblance of himself, a mama's boy without a mama (his distraught mother, Gladys, died while he was stationed at Fort Hood, soon to depart for Germany)—but of rock 'n' roll itself. Rock's Tarzan yell was about to be emasculated into a transistorized tweet. In Albert Goldman's biography of Elvis, Presley's removal from the scene was among the many losses rock 'n' roll took in the late 50s: Buddy Holly, Ritchie Valens, and the Big Bopper died in a plane crash; Little Richard, hounded by the tax man, scurried to Europe; Chuck Berry and Jerry Lee Lewis scandalized the nation by consorting with minors (Berry was busted for violating the Mann Act); Eddie Cochran was killed in a car accident that injured Gene Vincent; and radio host Alan Freed, apostle of the airwaves, was brought down on payola charges. With these deaths, skids, and partial eclipses, rock's chocolate-vanilla mix—its marriage of black rhythm and blues and white southern swagger—was melted down and bleached into sugar candy. With Freed dethroned, the reigning ambassador to youth became Dick Clark, whose *American Bandstand* showcased the latest crop of "teen twerps" (Goldman's term), wholesome role models who looked as if they had been squirted from the same cake-decorating gun. Unnaturally peppy, they were pop singers, not rock 'n' rollers, their very names sounding carbonated. Fabian. Frankie Avalon. Paul Anka. Bobby Darin. Bobby Rydell. Pat Boone. Connie Francis. Shelley Fabares. It was as if Elvis Presley had sired a litter of squealing albinos.

One name soon separated itself from this Brylcreem brigade. Born Walden Robert Cassotto, raised in a rough section of the Bronx, Bobby Darin (he picked the surname out of the phone book) came up through the showbiz ranks like a featherweight fighter. He played the Catskills at the age of 15, signed a recording contract at 20, and landed his first Top 40 single at 22 with "Splish Splash," a bathtub aria which he dashed off in 35 minutes and which sold more than 100,000 copies. Subsequent hits included "Dream Lover," "Beyond the Sea," and "If I Were a Carpenter" (the song which asks the baffling musical question "If I were a carpenter, and you were a lady / Would you marry me anyway, would you have my baby?"—what a hypothetical!). Darin's breakthrough number and signature tune was his revival-meeting rendition of "Mack the Knife" from *The Threepenny Opera*, recorded in 1959 despite the mushmouthed advice of Dick Clark, who told him it would alienate his bubblegum fans. Instead, its success made Darin a crossover sensation, broadening his appeal to adults who wouldn't have been caught dead watching Frankie Avalon leave a damp stain. Unlike the disposable items the music industry was manufacturing, the multitalented Darin was a throwback to durable, knock-'em-dead blue-ribbon hams such as Al Jolson, Eddie Cantor, Sammy Davis Jr., and Darin's hero, Frank Sinatra; he sang, did impressions, played instruments, ad-libbed, and danced like a Veg-O-Matic, slicing, dicing, and chopping, one of the few white men capable of executing the James Brown slide step without looking dorky. As brazen as Cassius Clay, Darin had the audacity to herald his own rising star and specify his timetable for success. In interviews, he vowed to be a star by 21, a legend by 25, and, failing that, an institution at 30. His Napoleonic plans to conquer the Copacabana irked reporters and fellow performers. *Time* magazine called him "an immodest boy with modest ability." *The Saturday Evening Post* published a profile called "Little Singer with a BIG EGO," which quoted Sammy Davis Jr. telling Darin, "Let me know when you stop being a legend, so we can start being friends again." Undaunted, Darin answered only to his own drumbeat. "Conceit is thinking you're great; egotism is knowing it," he said.

.   .   .

A great man needs a great lady, and Darin found his in Sandra Dee, a blonde starlet whose Hostess Twinkie success as Gidget and Tammy (*Tammy and the Doctor*, etc.) made her the teen queen of the 50s and early 60s. They met on the set of *Come September*, where Darin glued on to her and wouldn't let go. Before he married Dee in 1960, Darin informed the world that the great search was over: "I've finally found someone more important to me than myself." He must have believed that when two stars mate it's bowling night on Mount Olympus, an exalted thunder. Hubris and immaturity were about to exact an excess toll. The marriage revealed them both as emotional babies. Unworldly, isolated, her movie career defunct (the sexual revolution had stranded Gidget in her sandbox), Dee turned into an alcoholic with a clever mean streak. She would tell Darin his toupee was on crooked just before he went onstage, sending him scurrying back to the dressing room as his fanfare played. In turn, he would ruin her TV appearances by torpedoing her morale before the broadcasts. The tensions escalated beyond head games. Their only son, Dodd Darin, author (with Maxine Paetro) of the memoir *Dream Lovers: The Magnifi-*

cent Shattered Lives of Bobby Darin and Sandra Dee, recounts a fight in which Dad slapped Mom so hard she hit the wall and slumped to the floor, and, in a grand understatement, sadly concludes, "They were trying, but they weren't communicating very well." In 1966, Darin and Dee separated, and later divorced.

.　　.　　.

Darin mustered a modest comeback in the early 70s, headlining his own TV variety series and specials. Once a raucous phenomenon, he was now an accomplished pro, his rough edges smoothed to an acrylic finish. Given the lofty goals he had set for himself early in life, reestablishing himself as a snappy all-around entertainer didn't seem enough. Unlike his fellow former teen heartthrobs Elvis and Sinatra, Darin was unable to break through the twilight. When he died in 1973 at the age of 37, the obituary notices echoed the sad refrain of unfulfilled glory. He had piddled out before reaching the promised land. Each word of its brief obit carrying institutional weight, *Time* magazine seemed to have the final say: "A divorce and a new image gave him a boost, but he never achieved his outspoken ambition 'to become a legend.'"

Time has proven *Time* wrong. More than a quarter of a century after his death, Bobby Darin's legend has never been more alive. In 1990 he was inducted posthumously into the Rock and Roll Hall of Fame. In 1995, Rhino Records released a four-CD set, *As Long as I'm Singing: The Bobby Darin Collection*, whose 96 tracks span the full rainbow of his recording career, from up-tempo finger-snapping hits to folk-rock reveries, and inspired serious reconsiderations of his reputation. (Robert Hilburn, the pop-music critic of the *Los Angeles Times*, said the set disclosed Darin as perhaps "the most versatile, ambitious and misunderstood artist of his time.") In 1998, PBS broadcast a documentary called *Bobby Darin: Beyond the Song*, which contained vintage footage of Darin using cribnotes to sing the lyrics of "Rock Island Line" in his first TV appearance and doing a duet with Judy Garland. Earlier this year, a DVD and video of his last TV concert—*Bobby Darin: Mack Is Back!*—was sprung from the archives. On the horizon is the seemingly keen prospect of Kevin Spacey playing the lead in Darin's life story. (No one's going to tell Spacey his Velcro's on crooked without a fight!) The Bobby Darin revival isn't a memory-lane stroll, a golden-oldies bash. The all-out attack he launched as a performer hasn't dated, and we're more aware of the demons that drove him. In 1973 his death seemed a shame. Now, knowing what we know, it has the shape of tragedy.

.   .   .

Born in 1936, Darin was a hard-luck case of questionable origin. His father was said to be "Big Sam Curly" Cassotto, a penny-ante racketeer and acquaintance of Mob boss Frank Costello. Darin never knew his alleged father, who died in Sing Sing prison before he was born. His mother, Polly, was nearly 50 years old when Bobby was born, and her advanced age was used to explain the condition of an infant so frail that, according to *Dream Lovers*, "neighbors expected the scrawny thing to die in the cardboard box that served as his crib." His mother, his teenage sister, Nina, and her husband, Charlie Maffia, doted on this little bundle of woe, who had difficulty digesting food, suffered from eye troubles, broke his leg at the age of three, and was excruciatingly sensitive to pain. And those were just the warm-up blows. When he was eight, Bobby was struck with rheumatic fever, the first of a series of attacks which battered his heart muscle and exhausted his puny frame. He couldn't roughhouse with other kids, missed months of school, and recuperated for a year in an alpine sanatorium. Suffering a screaming bout of rheumatic fever when he was 13, he overheard the doctor tell his uncle Charlie that he wasn't going to live to see his 16th birthday. The doctor was wrong about the date, but the death sentence stood. Darin spent his entire life racing the calendar, knowing that at any moment his heart might collapse. As his son writes in *Dream Lovers*, "Bobby needed to become a legend by twenty-five because he expected to be dead by thirty."

With no time to spare, Darin couldn't brood in song the way Sinatra did, as if the night would never end, or croon a mellow tune with tonsils dipped in molasses, like Dean Martin or Perry Como (whose sedate cool Darin once blew by asking before they rehearsed a TV duet, "All right, babe, how will it be? Do you want to take the harmony or the melody?"). Darin's meter was running too fast for him to slow down, dim the lights, and quietly milk a ballad. As Will Friedwald writes in his idiosyncratic study *Jazz Singing*, "On slower tempos Darin is a big, friendly dog who wants to jump on your lap when you're trying to do something else." Darin recognized his need for speed, telling reporters, "I'm a saloon performer, a nightclub animal. The super-energizing source for me is the kind of performing which I want to be perfect." He sought to cram in as much as he could without manhandling the material. At his best he did a virtuoso job of taming animal spirits and making them jump through hoops. Audiences loved his live act, and critics discerned the craft in his vocal salesmanship. At his nightclub peak he had the unstoppable force of a James Cagney, with a smile equally disarming. The jazz critic and music historian Gene Lees wrote, "When [Darin] breaks in a new tune, he talks about working out the 'choreography' for it. And he does indeed move like a dancer. He has a loose-limbed agility that permits him to intermix shuffles, kicks, and countless eccentric steps the semantics of which probably died with vaudeville." Revived by Darin, these fancy moves were given a soul transfusion through the influence of black marvels such as Louis Armstrong, James Brown, and Sammy Davis Jr. "Rhythmically, Darin is the most successful of all fusionists," Friedwald wrote in *Jazz Singing*, "for early on he found the X that marked the spot where swing and R&B could meet." In his restless ambition, Darin would stray from that spot, and spend his last few years trying to reclaim it.

.   .   .

As a recording artist Darin never surpassed the hat trick of his jukebox classics "Dream Lover," "Mack the Knife," and "Beyond the Sea," released in 1959 and 1960. They are the songs with which he is still most identified. His follow-up singles found him putting his brassy stamp on old standards such as "Won't You Come Home, Bill Bailey," "Lazy River," and "You Must Have Been a Beautiful Baby." Riverboat music! In *Jazz Singing*, Friedwald says Darin "limited his importance to good music by deserting it so early." Perhaps, but I blame another culprit for his hamstring pull. I blame Hollywood, that hussy.

Like Elvis Presley, Darin wasn't satisfied being a chartbuster. He wanted to be a movie star. "The pictures are my first love," he told *Newsweek* in 1962. "I've attacked the movies with the same ferocity I did other things." After some horsing around, that is. On the set of his second film, *Come September*, he showed up late—"He was used to having the party start when he got there," his son writes in *Dream Lovers*—and played stupid pranks that hampered production. Ross Hunter, the producer of Dee's *Tammy Tell Me True* and *Tammy and the Doctor*, claims that Darin pursued Dee because she was a golden piece of Hollywood. "He did not want a wife to be a wife. He wanted a movie star, and he always had." Although Darin was a team player in the war drama *Hell Is for Heroes* (whose director, Don Siegel, called him "a fine actor, an underestimated actor"), earned an Oscar nomination for his performance in *Captain Newman, M.D.* with a harrowing flashback monologue that put to shame Gregory Peck's inane pandering in the title role, and tackled the role of a racist bigot in *Pressure Point*, he had more talent than taste or opportunity. He never became as egregious a moosehead on-screen as Elvis—who betrayed the sullen promise of his performance in Don Siegel's *Flaming Star* by coasting through a series of cheapo musicals, where he presided over Hawaiian luaus and invited an apathetic nation to "Do the clam"—but he made schnooky faces in comedies such as *If a Man Answers* and *That Funny Feeling*, dim-bulb efforts to turn him and Sandra Dee into the junior-division Rock Hudson–Doris Day. Like Elvis, Darin frittered away his musical capital by letting the movie studio distract him from the recording studio. Darin's most grievous film folly was *The Vendors*, which he wrote, directed, produced, scored, and funded with $350,000 of his own money. The tender saga of a druggie folksinger and the hooker who shares his personal space, *The Vendors*, filmed in 1969–70, sounds as if it belongs in the same spittoon of in-your-face cinéma vérité as Norman Mailer's *Maidstone* and the films of John Cassavetes (who directed Darin in *Too Late Blues*). We'll never know, because the film was such an unsalvageable dud—"I'm one of the few people who have seen *The Vendors*," Dodd Darin reports in *Dream Lovers*, "and it is bad"—that it couldn't nab a distributor. As they say in Hollywood, it died in the can. Although Darin shrugged off its failure, at this point in his life he couldn't afford to bury any more mistakes. He was already living in a trailer.

·   ·   ·

To explain how Bobby Darin, who once owned a Beverly Hills home complete with tennis court and pool, ended up living in a land-level submarine (that's what trailers are like), it's necessary to backtrack a bit. The year is 1968. Vietnam. Race riots. Campus revolts. Nixon's five-o'clock shadow looming across the White House lawn. Tweaking your bow tie and checking your cuff links backstage suddenly seems passé and absurd. The ghettos are burning, and you're out there doing a Sammy Cahn medley? The times call for direct involvement. A natural ally of the downtrodden, having faced so much poverty and adversity in his childhood, Darin began to campaign as a liberal activist and became a familiar of the Kennedy clan. (A year earlier he had donated his time to a telethon sponsored by Ethel Kennedy, where he became buddies with the Washington journalist Barbara Howar.)

One night in New Jersey, where Darin was playing a club date, his sister Nina said she needed to have a talk with him. Are you going to continue pursuing politics? she asks. Yes, he says. Well, then, there's something you should know: I'm not your sister, I'm your mother. The woman Bobby had been told all his life was his mother, Polly, was actually his grandmother. For reasons too obscure and byzantine to unravel, Nina felt she had to keep her maternity secret all those years. According to his son's reconstruction of the event, Darin's response to this bombshell was "My whole life has been a lie." A man who prided himself on knowing the score, he had been the dupe of deception. And a major piece of the puzzle remained missing—Nina refused to reveal the name of his real father.

.　　.　　.

A mystery father, a surprise mother: it was a one-two soap-opera punch that would have made anyone wig. But instead of taking up permanent fetal position on a therapist's couch, Darin, reckoning that private lies and political lies were symptoms of the same social sickness, redoubled his efforts on behalf of change, supporting Robert Kennedy's presidential bid. The cruelest blow to Darin's personal faith was delivered when Bobby Kennedy was assassinated in Los Angeles in the summer of 1968. Kennedy's murder stunned Darin perhaps even more than the news about his real mom—because Nina's confession opened a hole in the past, while Kennedy's death tore a hole in the future. A year later, Darin chucked it all and moved to Big Sur.

Darin said that Big Sur was his Walden Pond, noting that his first name was Walden, after all. I wonder if he hadn't another model in mind. After Bob Dylan cracked up his motorcycle in 1966, he did a J. D. Salinger vanishing act into the sheltering woods, an asylum that cloaked him in another layer of mystique and inspired lurid speculation ("He's become a complete vegetable," I remember hearing in high school). While Dylan was removed from the scene, psychedelia fanned its peacock feathers. When word came that Dylan was recording a new album, fans and commentators wondered how it would fare against the splendor of the Beatles' *Sgt. Pepper*, with its modernist-graveyard cover art and montage-collage song cycle (building to the resonating death chord of "A Day in the Life"), or the multitudinous rumble of Jefferson Airplane's *After Bathing at Baxter's*. Dylan brilliantly deflected the challenge by releasing *John Wesley Harding*, a parchment scroll of mythopoeia that seemed to drift earthward out of a gray sky. The album's spare, anonymous, nowhere sound gave the allegorical lyrics a stark platform.

In Big Sur, Darin devised a similar simplicity to confront chaos. He recorded message songs with a twang, trading in his sharp threads for folk-rock denim. To blend further into Bob Dylan, he shortened his stage name to Bob Darin. What made the mind-meld incompatible was that Darin intended to dip into the protest bag Dylan had abandoned on the side of the road of *Highway 61 Revisited*. The righteous sneer with which Dylan baited Mr. Jones in "Ballad of a Thin Man" didn't sit comfortably on Darin's lips. Unlike Dylan, who was off fishing the cosmic stream, Darin still sought to entertain, enlighten, and persuade. Booked for two weeks at the Sahara Hotel's Congo Room in 1969, he tried to prepare his fans for culture shock by having a cutout of himself in his new down-home duds stationed at the entrance, but his act, a precursor to *MTV Unplugged*, couldn't have been unveiled in a worse venue. In a neon oasis devoted to high-rolling hedonism, Darin was trying to conduct a musical teach-in. He even shrugged off pleas to sing "Mack the Knife." That was the old him. The new him was harvesting a different groove. His former manager Steve Blauner recalls in *Dream Lovers*, "There he was, with the jeans, with four pieces behind him. It was the smallest band in the history of Vegas. And this was not a lounge. This was the main room. And Bobby was brilliant." Didn't matter. Expecting the old ring-a-ding-ding, the audience voted with their feet, fleeing to the waiting arms of the slot machines.

Darin wasn't stupid or stubborn. He adjusted his act and wardrobe in subsequent bookings, trying to forge ahead while satisfying his fans' expectations. Two videos recorded in the 70s, *The Darin Invasion* and *Mack Is Back!*, document him shifting between the demands of being both showman and troubadour as if balancing on a pair of skis. *The Darin Invasion*, a 1970 television special shot in Toronto, opens with a rousing "Your Love Keeps Lifting Me Higher," the arrangement building roof after roof for him to raise. The bombast of the show's big numbers, a hybrid of Vegas horn attack and countercultural chorus (his backup singers are a multiculti mix of white hippie chicks and soul mamas), yields to a mellowing-out as a young Linda Ronstadt, with her sweetie-pie face and Elsie-the-cow eyelashes, croons, "For a Long, Long Time," and Darin takes his leave with "If I Were a Carpenter" and his own socially conscious ditty, "Simple Song of Freedom." *Mack Is Back!*, an NBC special taped nine months before Darin's death, is even more of a straddle. Looking dapper in his tux and patent-leather shoes, without an ounce of fat on his lean frame or a speck of rust in his delivery, Darin obliges with his old favorites only to subvert them or toss them aside. "Beyond the Sea" drains off into a long coda (". . . ta-ta, H_2O"), the band patiently vamping as Darin kids his way through various impressions and snatches of other songs. Despite the title *Mack Is Back!*, "Mack the Knife" wasn't performed as part of the concert, but was lip-synched separately and tacked on at the end like a nervous afterthought. Darin's musical dexterity in *Mack Is Back!* sends up caution flags, too. As if to prove he can handle every idiom like a hot pair of dice, Darin wastes his snap on material that doesn't do anything for him, such as Johnny Rivers's "Midnight Special" and the syrup drip of "Help Me Make It Through the Night." Trying on so many different musical hats, he neglected the great lesson Sinatra taught, which is: If you can't make a song distinctively yours, lose it; otherwise, you're just carrying someone else's luggage. Darin may have felt he needed to pave the comeback trail with cover versions to win acceptance from a (slowpoke) mainstream audience which is happiest hearing something it has heard before. Like the Kennedys, he was a pragmatic idealist—a shrewd dreamer.

.   .   .

It was during the taping of the Toronto special that Darin's heart, always delicate, began to jackhammer on him. He was so battered with heart murmurs and fibrillations—his heart beating up to 160 times a minute, about twice the normal rate—that he crumpled backstage, unable to stand. He underwent an advance procedure called cardioversion, which involved the use of anticoagulants and a synchronized defibrillator (which, as his son explains, "essentially stops the heart, then shocks it into the proper rhythm"). Darin did a two-week run at the Desert Inn in Las Vegas, where after his last show they had an ambulance waiting ready to rush him into open-heart surgery. After the successful operation, he mended for six weeks and went back on the road, playing a return engagement at the Desert Inn. His career was on an upswing. He headlined an NBC summer variety series in 1972 that was picked up for the fall and did a rave stint at the Copa. Maybe he would break through the twilight after all. "Just when things couldn't be any better," Dodd Darin writes in *Dream Lovers*, "my dad made a tragic mistake. He went to the dentist to have his teeth cleaned. Heart patients are supposed to take antibiotics when having dental work done, as a preventive against bacteria invading the bloodstream.... For reasons known only to my father, he didn't take the antibiotics. And he went off his anticoagulants as well."

Was it reckless confidence or an unconscious desire to let go? It defies logic that a chess buff like Darin—who was such a devout convert that he set up tournaments and tried to solve chess problems on his variety show!—could be that sloppy and heedless. Whatever the explanation, Darin gambled with his health and lost. Months later he was diagnosed with septicemia—blood poisoning caused by a bacterial infection the antibiotics would have prevented. He also developed blood clots on the brain as a result of abandoning the anticoagulants. The last year of his life was a tailspin of fear, anguish, hospital visits, and mental dissociation. Darin, who possessed a politician's memory (he could work a room and tick off every person's name afterward), began repeating himself, resisting treatment, forgetting dates, and jabberwocking, a mortifying dénouement for a man who had always maintained tight control. On December 20, 1973, Darin died of heart failure following surgery. His survivors behaved like hapless bystanders. There was no funeral service, no viewing (his remains were donated to the U.C.L.A. Medical Center), no proper mourning. The actor Jackie Cooper and his wife invited some of Darin's friends over to their house, where the guests got loaded and watched a tape of Darin's final NBC show. His ex-wife Sandra Dee, their son, Dodd, and Darin's sister Vee spent Christmas together, sharing a meal of Kentucky Fried Chicken. It doesn't get much grimmer than that.

.   .   .

Posterity has more than compensated for this sad sayonara. Bobby Darin's abbreviated life has gained the flashing glory of

Romantic myth, his lobby photo joining that gallery of young idols from Keats, Shelley, Byron, and Wilfred Owen to Buddy Holly, James Dean, Janis Joplin, and Kurt Cobain who were snuffed out before reaching full altitude. The sight of Darin cutting loose in documentary footage is a constant amazement. We respond not only to what he was and might have become, but also to what he represented. He was an entertainer when entertainment meant putting oneself on the firing line, doing battle with drunks, hecklers, jealous boyfriends, and crooked club owners. Today entertainers keep themselves under a protective seal, and performers barely perform. Once a stand-up comic gets a sitcom or movie deal, it's too déclassé for him or her to work clubs again. Who needs the aggravation, that battery of sweaty, backslapping hands? Rock stars can become equally pristine. Once they move into the mansion, years may go by before they re-emerge with a new tour or album (which is usually overproduced down to the finest nose-hair quiver). The most glittering divas—Barbra Streisand, Diana Ross—only caress the mike when they're embarked on yet another farewell tour, while cabaret stars such as Karen Akers and Andrea Marcovicci are relegated to boutique niches. The impact of a big-scale live show, the smack of talent in the flesh, the excited word of mouth that drew audiences to see Dean Martin and Jerry Lewis when they started, or Bette Midler at the baths, all seem quaint in an age of Internet feeds and Napster downloading. Catching a live act means occupying "meatspace," and too many of us are busy evolving into cyberspace ghosts, haunting our favorite sites. Because the body is disengaged in cyberspace, a floating phantom limb, adrenaline has nowhere to travel, excitement nowhere to resound. Bobby Darin's body and soul remind us, with a jolt, of everything we're missing, of our longing to dispense with intermediaries and be intimately, passionately, metabolically wowed.

Which makes me skeptical about the prospect of a Bobby Darin biopic. An original is always tough to duplicate. For every passable impersonation of a music sensation (Gary Busey in *The Buddy Holly Story*), there's a fumbled ball (Forest Whitaker as Charlie Parker in *Bird*), or a blatant travesty (Dennis Quaid's duck-assed Jerry Lee Lewis in *Great Balls of Fire*). Perhaps the most seamless depiction of a pop presence was Tim McIntire's Alan Freed in *American Hot Wax*, where McIntire, tugboating from D.J. booth to recording studio with entourage in tow, seemed as natural and nocturnal as the moon. Since Freed wasn't a musical performer, McIntire wasn't required to compete with his subject under the spotlight. For an actor to do Bobby Darin, however, he'd have to be able to dazzle as a singer-dancer-musician-actor-jokester. Kevin Spacey has the charisma and laser focus, and is a brilliant impressionist, but he's older now than Darin was when he died, and he doesn't have Darin's transforming smile. (Spacey's smile is a small click-device.) And who could play Sandra Dee? It would be hard to resist presenting her perplexed, virginal pout and wind-resistant bouffants as kitsch artifacts. Producers would probably want to twirl Britney Spears into cotton candy for the part. To return these dream lovers to their 60s dollhouse would be a retro undertaking, and Bobby Darin isn't retro, he's right-now. The jubilant ring of his voice busts through the past, providing a clear, direct link between him and the listener, undiminished by time or fashion. Because Darin knew he would die young, he lived his whole life in the present tense. That, on record, disc, and tape, is where he still prevails. Death was just another door he slammed behind him.

Permissions

2001 National Magazine Award Winners

General Excellence

1973	Business Week
1981	ARTnews
	Audubon
	Business Week
	Glamour
1982	Camera Arts
	Newsweek
	Rocky Mountain Magazine
	Science81
1983	Harper's Magazine
	Life
	Louisiana Life
	Science82
1984	The American Lawyer
	House & Garden
	National Geographic
	Outside
1985	American Health
	American Heritage
	Manhattan, inc.
	Time
1986	Discover
	Money
	New England Monthly
	3–2–1- Contact
1987	Common Cause
	Elle
	New England Monthly
	People Weekly
1988	Fortune
	Hippocrates
	Parents
	The Sciences
1989	American Heritage
	Sports Illustrated
	The Sciences
	Vanity Fair
1990	Metropolitan Home
	7 Days
	Sports Illustrated
	Texas Monthly
1991	Condé Nast Traveler
	Glamour
	Interview
	The New Republic

1992	Mirabella
	National Geographic
	The New Republic
	Texas Monthly
1993	American Photo
	The Atlantic Monthly
	Lingua Franca
	Newsweek
1994	Business Week
	Health
	Print
	Wired
1995	Entertainment Weekly
	I.D. Magazine
	Men's Journal
	The New Yorker
1996	Business Week
	Civilization
	Outside
	The Sciences
1997	I.D. Magazine
	Outside
	Vanity Fair
	Wired
1998	DoubleTake
	Outside
	Preservation
	Rolling Stone
1999	Condé Nast Traveler
	Fast Company
	I.D. Magazine
	Vanity Fair
2000	National Geographic
	Nest
	The New Yorker
	Saveur
2001	The American Scholar
	Mother Jones
	The New Yorker
	Teen People

Personal Service

1986	Farm Journal
1987	Consumer Reports
1988	Money

1989	Good Housekeeping		1985	Texas Monthly
1990	Consumer Reports		1986	Rolling Stone
1991	New York		1987	Life
1992	Creative Classroom		1988	The Washingtonian and
1993	Good Housekeeping			Baltimore Magazine
1994	Fortune		1989	The New Yorker
1995	SmartMoney		1990	The New Yorker
1996	SmartMoney		1991	The New Yorker
1997	Glamour		1992	The New Republic
1998	Men's Journal		1993	IEEE Spectrum
1999	Good Housekeeping		1994	The New Yorker
2000	PC Computing		1995	The Atlantic Monthly
2001	National Geographic Adventure		1996	The New Yorker
			1997	Outside
			1998	Rolling Stone
			1999	Newsweek
			2000	Vanity Fair
			2001	Esquire

Special Interests

1986	Popular Mechanics
1987	Sports Afield
1988	Condé Nast Traveler
1989	Condé Nast Traveler
1990	Art & Antiques
1991	New York
1992	Sports Afield
1993	Philadelphia
1994	Outside
1995	GQ
1996	Saveur
1997	Smithsonian
1998	Entertainment Weekly
1999	PC Computing
2000	I.D. Magazine
2001	The New Yorker

Feature Writing

1988	The Atlantic
1989	Esquire
1990	The Washingtonian
1991	U.S. News & World Report
1992	Sports Illustrated
1993	The New Yorker
1994	Harper's Magazine
1995	GQ
1996	GQ
1997	Sports Illustrated
1998	Harper's Magazine
1999	The American Scholar
2000	Sports Illustrated
2001	Rolling Stone

Reporting

1970	The New Yorker
1971	The Atlantic Monthly
1972	The Atlantic Monthly
1973	New York
1974	The New Yorker
1975	The New Yorker
1976	Audubon
1977	Audubon
1978	The New Yorker
1979	Texas Monthly
1980	Mother Jones
1981	National Journal
1982	The Washingtonian
1983	Institutional Investor
1984	Vanity Fair

Public Interest

1970	Life
1971	The Nation
1972	Philadelphia
1974	Scientific American
1975	Consumer Reports
1976	Business Week
1977	Philadelphia
1978	Mother Jones
1979	New West
1980	Texas Monthly
1981	Reader's Digest
1982	The Atlantic

1983	Foreign Affairs
1984	The New Yorker
1985	The Washingtonian
1986	Science85
1987	Money
1988	The Atlantic
1989	California
1990	Southern Exposure
1991	Family Circle
1992	Glamour
1993	The Family Therapy Networker
1994	Philadelphia
1995	The New Republic
1996	Texas Monthly
1997	Fortune
1998	The Atlantic Monthly
1999	Time
2000	The New Yorker
2001	Time

Design

1980	Geo
1981	Attenzione
1982	Nautical Quarterly
1983	New York
1984	House & Garden
1985	Forbes
1986	Time
1987	Elle
1988	Life
1989	Rolling Stone
1990	Esquire
1991	Condé Nast Traveler
1992	Vanity Fair
1993	Harper's Bazaar
1994	Allure
1995	Martha Stewart Living
1996	Wired
1997	I.D.
1998	Entertainment Weekly
1999	ESPN The Magazine
2000	Fast Company
2001	nest

Photography

1985	Life
1986	Vogue
1987	National Geographic

1988	Rolling Stone
1989	National Geographic
1990	Texas Monthly
1991	National Geographic
1992	National Geographic
1993	Harper's Bazaar
1994	Martha Stewart Living
1995	Rolling Stone
1996	Saveur
1997	National Geographic
1998	W
1999	Martha Stewart Living
2000	Vanity Fair
2001	National Geographic

Fiction

1978	The New Yorker
1979	The Atlantic Monthly
1980	Antaeus
1981	The North American Review
1982	The New Yorker
1983	The North American Review
1984	Seventeen
1985	Playboy
1986	The Georgia Review
1987	Esquire
1988	The Atlantic
1989	The New Yorker
1990	The New Yorker
1991	Esquire
1992	Story
1993	The New Yorker
1994	Harper's Magazine
1995	Story
1996	Harper's Magazine
1997	The New Yorker
1998	The New Yorker
1999	Harper's Magazine
2000	The New Yorker
2001	Zoetrope: All-Story

Profiles

2000	Sports Illustrated
2001	The New Yorker

Essays

2000	The Sciences
2001	The New Yorker

Reviews and Criticism

2000	Esquire
2001	The New Yorker

General Excellence Online

1997	Money
1998	The Sporting News Online
1999	Cigar Aficionado
2000	Business Week Online
2001	U.S. News Online

Best Interactive Design

2001	SmartMoney.com

Essays & Criticism

1978	Esquire
1979	Life
1980	Natural History
1981	Time
1982	The Atlantic
1983	The American Lawyer
1984	The New Republic
1985	Boston Magazine
1986	The Sciences
1987	Outside
1988	Harper's Magazine
1989	Harper's Magazine
1990	Vanity Fair
1991	The Sciences
1992	The Nation
1993	The American Lawyer
1994	Harper's Magazine
1995	Harper's Magazine
1996	The New Yorker
1997	The New Yorker
1998	The New Yorker
1999	The Atlantic Monthly

Single-Topic Issue

1979	Progressive Architecture
1980	Scientific American
1981	Business Week
1982	Newsweek
1983	IEEE Spectrum
1984	Esquire
1985	American Heritage
1986	IEEE Spectrum
1987	Bulletin of the Atomic Scientists
1988	Life
1989	Hippocrates
1990	National Geographic
1991	The American Lawyer
1992	Business Week
1993	Newsweek
1994	Health
1995	Discover
1996	Bon Appétit
1997	Scientific American
1998	The Sciences
1999	The Oxford American

Single Award

1966	Look
1967	Life
1968	Newsweek
1969	American Machinist

Specialized Journalism

1970	Philadelphia
1971	Rolling Stone
1972	Architectural Record
1973	Psychology Today
1974	Texas Monthly
1975	Medical Economics
1976	United Mine Workers Journal
1977	Architectural Record
1978	Scientific American
1979	National Journal
1980	IEEE Spectrum

Visual Excellence

1970	Look
1971	Vogue
1972	Esquire
1973	Horizon
1974	Newsweek
1975	Country Journal
	National Lampoon
1976	Horticulture
1977	Rolling Stone
1978	Architectural Digest
1979	Audubon

Service To The Individual

1974	Sports Illustrated
1975	Esquire
1976	Modern Medicine
1977	Harper's Magazine
1978	Newsweek
1979	The American Journal of Nursing
1980	Saturday Review
1982	Philadelphia
1983	Sunset
1984	New York
1985	The Washingtonian

Fiction & Belles Lettres

1970	Redbook
1971	Esquire
1972	Mademoiselle
1973	The Atlantic Monthly
1974	The New Yorker
1975	Redbook
1976	Essence
1977	Mother Jones

Special Award

1976	Time
1989	Robert E. Kenyon, Jr.

2001 National Magazine Award Finalists

NOTE: All nominated issues are dated 2000 unless otherwise specified. The editor whose name appears in connection with finalists for 2001 held that position, or was listed on the masthead, at the time the issue was published in 2000. In some cases, another editor is now in that position.

General Excellence

to honor a magazine for its performance in achieving its editorial objectives.

Under 100,000 circulation

The American Scholar: Anne Fadiman, editor, for Spring, Summer, Autumn issues.

DoubleTake: Robert Coles, editor, for Winter, Summer, Fall, issues.

Harvard Medical Alumni Bulletin: William Ira Bennett, editor-in-chief, for Winter, Spring, Summer issues.

nest: Joseph Holtzman, editor-in-chief and art director, for Spring, Summer, Fall issues.

Transition: Kwame Anthony Appiah and Henry Louis Gates, Jr., editors; Michael Colin Vazquez, executive editor, for Winter, Spring, Fall issues.

100,000 to 400,000 circulation

Harper's Magazine: Lewis H. Lapham, editor, for January, June, November issues.

Mother Jones: Roger Cohn, editor-in-chief, for May/June, September/October, November/December issues.

Nylon Magazine: Marvin Scott Jarrett, editor-in-chief, for October, November, December issues.

Saveur: Dorothy Kalins, editor-in-chief, for April, May/June, September/October.

Texas Monthly: Gregory Curtis, editor, for April issue; Evan Smith, editor, for October, December issues.

400,000 to 1,000,000 circulation

Fortune: John Huey, managing editor, for March 6, May 29, November 13 issues.

Gourmet: Ruth Reichl, editor-in-chief, for September, October, November issues.

Jane Magazine: Jane Pratt, editor-in-chief, for March, May, August issues.

Men's Journal: Mark Bryant, editor, for April, June, December issues.

The New Yorker: David Remnick, editor, for January 31, February 21 & 28, October 30 issues.

Over 1,000,000 circulation

Health: Barbara Paulsen, editor-in-chief, for September, October, November/December issues.

Rolling Stone: Jann S. Wenner, editor and publisher; Robert Love, managing editor, for April 13, May 25, November 9 issues.

Sports Illustrated: Bill Colson, managing editor, for June 26, October 2, December 18 issues.

Teen People: Christina Ferrari, managing editor, for March, June/July, August issues.

Vanity Fair: Graydon Carter, editor, for October, November, December issues.

Personal Service

for articles that clearly and compellingly help readers take action to improve the quality of their lives.

Esquire: David Granger, editor-in-chief, for *This Man Survived Breast Cancer*, by Ted Allen, June.

Money Magazine: Robert Safian, managing editor, for *The Ultimate Guide to Retirement*, July.

National Geographic Adventure: John Rasmus, editor-in-chief, for *The Rules of Adventure*, by Laurence Gonzales, January/February.

Newsweek: Richard M. Smith, editor-in-chief; Mark Whitaker, editor, for *Your Child: Birth to Three*, Fall/Winter.

The New Yorker: David Remnick, editor, for three articles by Jerome Groopman, *Second Opinion*, January 24; *The Prostate Paradox*, May 29; *Hurting All Over*, November 13.

Special Interests

for articles that foster the enjoyment of leisuretime interests through clear and instructive writing and infographics.

Esquire: David Granger, editor-in-chief, for *How to Be a Better Man*, November.

The New Yorker: David Remnick, editor, for *The Sports Issue*, August 21 & 28.

The Oxford American: Marc Smirnoff, editor, for its Fourth Annual Double Issue on Southern Music, July/August.

The Paris Review: George Plimpton, editor, for *The Poetry Issue*, Spring.

Texas Monthly: Gregory Curtis, editor, for *A Celebration of Texas Music*, May.

Reporting

for articles that give a definitive account of, or uncover new information about, an event, a situation or a problem of contemporary interest and importance.

Esquire: David Granger, editor-in-chief, for *The Perfect Fire*, by Sean Flynn, July.

The New Yorker: David Remnick, editor, for *Overwhelming Force*, by Seymour M. Hersh, May 22.

Rolling Stone: Jann S. Wenner, editor and publisher; Robert Love, managing editor, for *In the Jungle*, by Rian Malan, May 25.

The Texas Observer: Louis Dubose and Michael King, editors, for *Color of Justice*, by Nate Blakeslee, June 23.

Wired Magazine: Katrina Heron, editor-in-chief, for *The Truth, the Whole Truth, and Nothing but the Truth*, by John Heilemann, November.

Feature Writing

for an article that treats its subject with imagination, originality and stylish writing.

Esquire: David Granger, editor-in-chief, for *My Favorite Teacher*, by Robert Kurson, March.

Esquire: David Granger, editor-in-chief, for *The Long Fall of One-Eleven Heavy*, by Michael Paterniti, July.

National Geographic Adventure: John Rasmus, editor-in-chief, for *The Endless Hunt*, by Gretel Ehrlich, September/October.

The New Yorker: David Remnick, editor, for *A Cold Case*, by Philip Gourevitch, February 14.

Rolling Stone: Jann S. Wenner, editor and publisher; Robert Love, managing editor, for *The Weasel, Twelve Monkeys and the Shrub*, by David Foster Wallace, April 13.

Profiles

for an article that presents an original and illuminating portrait of a person, whether famous or obscure.

The Atlantic Monthly: Michael Kelly, editor, for *The Million-Dollar Nose*, by William Langewiesche, December.

GQ: Art Cooper, editor-in-chief, for *The Ghost*, by Elizabeth Gilbert, December.

The New Yorker: David Remnick, editor, for *Delta Nights*, by Bill Buford, June 5.

The New Yorker: David Remnick, editor, for *The Pitchman*, by Malcolm Gladwell, October 30.

Rolling Stone: Jann S. Wenner, editor and publisher; Robert Love, managing editor, for *The Prince of Darkness*, by Erik Hedegaard, July 6–20.

Public Interest

for outstanding examples of analytical or expository journalism that bring exceptional clarity, interpretation and insight to their subject, and have the potential to influence national or local public policy.

The Atlantic Monthly: Michael Kelly, editor, for *Health Care: A Bolt of Civic Hope*, by Matthew Miller, October.

The New Yorker: David Remnick, editor, for two articles by Nicholas Lemann, *The Redemption*, January 31; *Gore Without a Script*, July 31.

Technology Review: John Benditt, editor-in-chief, for *The Great Gene Grab*, by Antonio Regalado; *The Case for Gene Patents*, by William A. Haseltine; *Toward Sharing the Genome*, by Seth Shulman, September/October.

Texas Monthly: Evan Smith, editor, for *They Haven't Got a Prayer*, by Pamela Colloff, November.

Time: Walter Isaacson, managing editor, for three articles by Donald L. Barlett and James B. Steele, *Big Money & Politics: How the Little Guy Gets Crunched*, February 7; *Soaked by Congress*, May 15; *Throwing the Game*, September 25.

Design

to honor a magazine for excellent and innovative visual presentation that enhances the magazine's mission.

Entertainment Weekly: James W. Seymore Jr., managing editor; Geraldine Hessler, design director, for June 30/July 7, October 27, December 22/29 issues.

Esquire: David Granger, editor-in-chief; John Korpics, design director, for February, March, July issues.

Martha Stewart Living: Martha Stewart, editorial director; Gael Towey, EVP/creative director; Stephen Drucker, editor-in-chief; Eric Pike, creative director; Barbara de Wilde, design director, for October, November, December issues.

nest: Joseph Holtzman, editor-in-chief and art director, for Spring, Summer, Fall issues.

W: Patrick McCarthy, chairman and editorial director; Edward Leida, executive vice president/design director; Kirby Rodriguez, art director, for February, March, April issues.

Photography

for a magazine's excellent use of photography as a part of its editorial presentation.

Esquire: David Granger, editor-in-chief; John Korpics, design director, for July, September, December issues.

Martha Stewart Living: Martha Stewart, editorial director; Gael Towey, EVP/creative director; Stephen Drucker, editor-in-chief; Eric Pike, creative director; Barbara de Wilde, design director; Craig Paull, managing editor/photography; Mary Dail, senior photography editor, for October, November, December issues.

National Geographic: William L. Allen, editor; W. Allan Royce, senior editor, illustrations; Kent J. Kobersteen, senior editor, photography, for January, February, November issues.

nest: Joseph Holtzman, editor-in-chief and art director, for Spring, Summer, Fall issues.

Vibe: Emil Wilbekin, editor-in-chief; George Pitts, director of photography, for June/July, September, December issues.

W: Patrick McCarthy, chairman and editorial director; Dennis Freedman, vice chairman/creative director; Edward Leida, executive vice president/design director, for February, March, May issues.

2001 National Magazine Award Finalists

Fiction

to honor a magazine for its publication of excellent fiction.

The Atlantic Monthly: William Whitworth, editor, for *Tyrants*, by Marshall N. Klimasewiski, January; Michael Kelly, editor, for *I Am the Grass*, by Daly Walker, June; *Family Christmas*, by Roxana Robinson, December.

Esquire: David Granger, editor-in-chief, for *Lobster Night*, by Russell Banks, March; *July '69*, by Tim O'Brien, July; *The Deep Sleep*, by Aleksandar Hemon, November.

GQ: Art Cooper, editor-in-chief, for *Cow-Cow*, by Russell Banks, April; *The Black Woman in the Chinese Hat*, by Walter Mosley, August; *Sharing*, by John Edgar Wideman, December.

The New Yorker: David Remnick, editor, for *Nettles*, by Alice Munro, February 21 & 28; *Revival Road*, by Louise Erdrich, April 17; *The Smoker*, by David Schickler, June 19 & 26.

Zoetrope: All-Story: Adrienne Brodeur, editor-in-chief, for *Fialta*, by Rebecca Lee, Spring; *Fair Warning*, by Robert Olen Butler, Summer; *The Cavemen in the Hedges*, by Stacey Richter, Fall.

Essays

this category is designed to include a wide variety of nonfictional points of view, including personal reflection, political and/or social commentary, editorial opinion and humor.

The American Scholar: Anne Fadiman, editor, for *Mail*, by Anne Fadiman, Winter.

The American Scholar: Anne Fadiman, editor, for *Narrow Ruled*, by Nicholson Baker, Autumn.

Harper's Magazine: Lewis H. Lapham, editor, for *In the Land of the Rococo Marxists*, by Tom Wolfe, June.

The New Yorker: David Remnick, editor, for *Like a King*, by Adam Gopnik, January 31.

Outside: Hal Espen, editor, for *Skating Home Backward*, by Bill Vaughn, January.

Reviews And Criticism

for short reviews and longer critical pieces that analyze and comment upon specific works of art, performances, movies, broadcasts, products, and the like.

Gourmet: Ruth Reichl, editor-in-chief, for three restaurant reviews by Jonathan Gold, *Luxury Triumphant*, January; *Paris on the Hudson*, April; *Magnificent Obsession*, November.

Harper's Magazine: Lewis H. Lapham, editor, for *Stupor Mundi*, by Lewis H. Lapham, April; *A Life in the Maze*, by Guy Davenport, June; *The Glory of J.F. Powers*, by Donna Tartt, July.

The New Yorker: David Remnick, editor, for three pieces by Anthony Lane, *The Maria Problem*, February 14; *The Eye of the Land*, March 13; *The Light Side of the Moon*, April 10.

Sports Illustrated: Bill Colson, managing editor, for three pieces by Steve Rushin, *Let There Be Light*, September 25; *Blessings in Disguise*, October 2; *The Mock Olympics*, October 9.

Vanity Fair: Graydon Carter, editor, for three pieces by James Wolcott, *Lovers Come Back*, April; *How to Succeed in Business Without Really Breathing*, June; *Forever Young*, November.

General Excellence Online

to honor an Internet site that most effectively serves its intended audience and reflects an outstanding level of interactivity, journalistic integrity and service.

Business Week Online: Bob Arnold, editor-in-chief

The Chronicle of Higher Education: Phil Semas, editor, new media

Hint Fashion Magazine: Lee Carter, editor-in-chief

U.S. News Online: Chris Sturm, editor

Wine Spectator Online: Marvin R. Shanken, editor & publisher

Best Interactive Design

to honor an Internet site that meets the criteria for General Excellence Online, but that also makes exceptional use of the digital medium.

The Atlantic Online: Wen Stephenson, editorial director

Business Week Online: Bob Arnold, editor-in-chief

CQ.com On Congress: Dave Rapp, executive editor

Nerve.com: Susan Dominus, editor-in-chief

SmartMoney.com: Marc Frons, editor and chief technology officer